TAOISM

Taoism: The Enduring Tradition offers fresh perspectives on a religious and cultural tradition which has unfolded since the fifth century as a form of integration into the unseen realities of life. Exploring Taoist voices in sacred texts and current scholarship, and showing how Taoism differs from, and overlaps with, other Chinese traditions such as Confucianism and Zen Buddhism, it examines Taoism's ancient classical roots, contemporary heritage, and role in Chinese daily life.

From Taoism's spiritual philosophy to its practical perspectives on life and death, self-cultivation, morality, society, leadership, and gender, Russell Kirkland brings to life the Taoist vision as expressed by followers through the centuries. Through attention to Taoism's key elements and examples from the lives of Taoist men and women, he reveals the real contexts of the *Tao te ching* and *Chuang-tzu*, and of Taoist understandings of life which still reverberate in modern practices such as *feng-shui* and *t'ai-chi ch'üan*. His guide to this long misrepresented tradition presents a new paradigm for understanding Taoism in the twenty-first century.

Russell Kirkland is Associate Professor of Religion and Asian Studies at the University of Georgia. He is a member of the executive board of the Society for the Study of Chinese Religions, and of the board of directors of the US Taoist Association. He has been writing on Taoism for over twenty years.

TAOISM

The enduring tradition

Russell Kirkland

Foreword by Norman J. Girardot

NEW YORK AND LONDON

First published 2004 in the USA and Canada
by Routledge
29 West 35th Street, New York, NY 10001

Simultaneously published in the UK
by Routledge
11 New Fetter Lane, London EC4P 4EE

Routledge is an imprint of the Taylor & Francis Group

Typeset in Sabon by
BOOK NOW Ltd
Printed and bound in Great Britain by
Biddles Ltd, King's Lynn

Library of Congress Cataloging in Publication Data
A catalog record has been requested

British Library Cataloguing in Publication Data
A catalogue record for this book is available from the British Library

ISBN 0-415-26321-2 (hbk)
ISBN 0-415-26322-0 (pbk)

CONTENTS

FOREWORD

> We do not see its form,
> We do not hear its sound,
> Yet we can perceive an order to its accomplishments.
> We call it "the Way" [Tao].
>
> *Nei-yeh/Inward Training*, trans. Harold D. Roth

Russell Kirkland has written an important introductory book for Wayfarers who are curious about, and are seriously seeking out, the spiritual path known ambiguously and recalcitrantly in the West as Taoism. As one of the forgotten early Taoist texts, the *Inward Training*, says: we – Chinese and others – call it the Way or the Tao. The problem is that we have not really seen its form; and we have not heard its sound. Or perhaps more accurately we have encountered a cacophony of strange forms and sounds, many of which often have little affinity with the Tao of Chinese history or with its extravagant efflorescence throughout the world today. To be sure, we in the West have perceived an "order," or orders, of dichotomous meaning associated with the Taoist tradition – most frequently described as a contrast between the philosophical purity of some early "classical" texts and the absurd religious practices of the later sectarian traditions.

It has been known for some time that the received opinion about Taoism in the West was in need of drastic revision. But fantasies about Chinese tradition die a slow and lingering death and, in fact, are always subject to surprising moments of zombie-like reanimation in sometimes silly and frightening ways (witness, for example, the spawn of the "Tao of Pooh" and its ilk such as the "Tao of Steve" and, most improbably, the "Tao of Elvis"). Even after a quarter-century of revolutionary scholarship, it may still be said that the actual "accomplishments" of the Tao, along with its sinuous path throughout Chinese and world history, are only very recently coming into general awareness in both scholarly and popular circles.[1]

There is good and bad news connected with these developments. The bad news for many is simply that the compelling and beguiling simplicity of the old "order" of understanding Taoism in relation to the philosophical purity and romantic mystery of a few ancient texts has now been absorbed into a vast, and at times bewildering, labyrinth of texts, ideas, and practices. No longer is it possible to invoke a few pious platitudes of poorly translated verse by the Old Boy, Laotzu, or an elusively pithy parable from the *Chuang-tzu*, and feel confident that one is dealing with the "essential" or "original" meaning of the tradition. Nor is it possible blithely to assign students a copy of Steven Mitchell's "version" of the *Tao te ching* so that they might meditate on the Zennish heart of Taoism. Even the blessed butterfly dream of effortless non-action (*wu-wei*) which so enraptured generations of Western commentators from Oscar Wilde to Timothy Leary has largely evaporated – like the *ch'i*-mist of a Chinese landscape painting – into the intertextual caverns and ritual practices of Taoist history.

I could go on with a litany of now outdated and misleading assumptions about Taoism, but more positively I am happy to report that for the first time it is possible to encounter actual Taoist "accomplishments" in time and space that are not hopelessly overwhelmed by willful and wistful Orientalist fabulation. This good news is dramatically manifest in Russell Kirkland's discussion of the "enduring tradition" of Taoism. This book can, therefore, be considered among the very first sinologically informed and popularly accessible products of the pioneering labors by Taoist and comparative scholars during the past twenty or thirty years. Kirkland's little book, along with just one or two other recent works, shows us that Taoist studies have finally come of age. What he has given us is not just another technical monograph for a small community of specialists; rather he has produced a kind of "first take" synthetic interpretation of the history and meaning of Taoism that forces us to see the overall tradition in fresh and unexpected ways.

Kirkland has, indeed, given us a new framework for understanding the Taoist tradition – an iconoclastic perspective that often boldly challenges many stereotypical conceptions favored by both popular enthusiasts and sinological scholars. Another especially appealing aspect of this work is Kirkland's acerbic sensibility and his ability to write comprehensibly and inquisitively. In the best sense of a teacher who is in command of his subject and knows that real understanding, like the Tao itself, is ever changing, he invites his readers to confront and to interrogate the complexities of the tradition. Nothing is taken for granted and, as curious Wayfarers, we are clearly asked to respond argumentatively and critically. This book is, then, not just a significant groundbreaking introduction to the Taoist tradition. It is also a kind of revelatory evocation of the spirit of the tradition – a multifarious tradition (or "omnidoxy," as Kirkland suggestively describes it) that calls all of us to be forever students of a Way that "endures" through constant transformation. There are no final or definitive conclusions to be drawn; only more questions to ask.

As a new and stimulating overview of the Taoist tradition, this book is particularly helpful for clarifying some of the dense confusions of Taoist history for a general audience. Striking examples of Kirkland's innovative approach are also seen in such matters as his treatment of the role of women in Taoism; his dismissal of the simplistic notion that the ideal of the *hsien* (often misleadingly identified as a reclusive "immortal") is the central goal or meaning of the Taoist religion; and his rejection of the notion that the later Taoist sectarian religious movements were mostly derivative of Buddhism. The major interpretive contribution of this work is, however, to be found in his persuasive discussion of the religious "goal" of the "cultivated life" in Taoism (stressing bodily, mental, and spiritual practices of personal transformation) which was predominantly accomplished within a social framework.

There are other revelations and virtues to be found in this book. But I must leave it to the reader to make these discoveries. This is, after all, part of the real serendipitous and educative joy of Kirkland's treatise – you never know what you will find along the way.

Norman J. Girardot
University Distinguished Professor
Religion Studies Department
Lehigh University

PREFACE

Scholars argue with each other. They often do so on quite reasonable terms, as for instance when a British historian might argue that Churchill was the most important leader of the twentieth century while an American might argue that Roosevelt truly was. Either thesis could viably be argued, provided that we first accept a certain set of criteria for determining the characteristics that constitute "importance." Of course, scholars will generally, and not always consciously, identify the criteria of "importance" on the basis of what their *own* tradition values, and on their personal response to that tradition. In so doing, they often dismiss or ignore any criteria that rest upon assumptions that they do not share, do not wish to share, or do not wish to be seen to share. In other words, scholarly interpretations are themselves products of a specific temporal and cultural matrix.

What I write here is both an expression of, and a response to, current conditions in "the field" – specifically, in how educated Westerners think and write about Taoism in the early twenty-first century. I shall present an interpretation of Taoism which is, admittedly, a product of one mind's response to those conditions. When I present contrary arguments, I shall attempt to provide a good reason for accepting my own positions. When those who hold contrary positions read my arguments, they may, quite properly, draw attention to data that I have unduly neglected, to alternative lines of reasoning, etc. As they do so, I shall learn from those responses, and shall revise my understanding of Taoism in ways that cannot presently be predicted. In sum, what I say about Taoism in this book is as sound and constructive as I can make it, given the data available and the state of the discourse at this particular moment in history.

If it seems that such matters should go without saying, I believe that reporting them explicitly may be prudent because of the nature of some of my arguments. That is, I shall argue here (1) that scholarly positions, including my own, are ultimately no more than cultural/intellectual constructs, even if they be carefully devised and reasonably justified; and (2) that critical thought about *how we understand Taoism* has barely begun. This book is thus intended to be a contribution to that hermeneutical endeavor, as well as a presentation of Taoism "itself." The hermeneutical task involves not only a critical (re-)examination of "the data" pertaining to Taoism, but also a critical (re-)examination of *the discourse pertaining to Taoism*. Hence, readers who seek an analysis of Taoism that simply confirms what they already believe may find in what follows much to shock them. Of course, that shock is intentional. And the precise nature and direction of such shocks will vary according to the reader's background and propensities. Newcomers may be less shocked than readers who believe that they already "know" the nature of Taoism and its place within Chinese civilization. That is because my efforts to frame Taoism within an appropriate framework of thought and discourse will quite loudly address the contours of the interpretive frameworks that we have inherited from the scholars of the twentieth century, and their forebears in earlier times.

I shall assume that all aspects of all twentieth-century discourse about Taoism are fitting targets for critical analysis. And I shall, to the best of my knowledge and ability, seek to preserve only such elements of that discourse as seem – under my early twenty-first-century gaze – to allow us to perceive the data of Taoism without undue discourse-bound distortion. At the same time, I shall argue for new identifications of "the data of Taoism" themselves. I shall argue, for instance, that in our selection of pertinent data we should become intensely aware of the selections that have been made over the centuries by those who *self-identified as participants in the tradition itself*. It may not be clear, at this point in history, exactly what criteria were used by Taoists of every stripe, in every period, when they thought about what was, or was not, "Taoist." But the research of specialists of the late twentieth century has begun to reveal at least some of the criteria employed by Taoists of some stripes in some periods. And that research has begun to allow us to see some of the *diversity* within the tradition, some of the transitions and reidentifications that took place over time, and some of the *continuities* that resulted as Taoists over many generations chose to identify the elements of their own Taoism in ways that coincided with the choices made by other Taoists at other times.

My goal in writing this book is not to demonstrate that I have better arguments about, say, the "importance" of Ko Hung or Wang Che than other specialists living today. Indeed, such might not at all be the case. And certainly there are scholars whose specialized knowledge of specific phases or subtraditions of Taoism far exceeds my own. For those specialists, what I present here represents merely certain interpretive possibilities, based upon certain readings of certain data. Other specialists will, I hope, constructively advance such debates by articulating *other* interpretive possibilities, based upon an increasingly sound and thoughtful reading of an increasingly large and well-known body of data.

Ultimately, it is not the interpretations of such specialists that I hope to change. Rather, I wish to reshape what is thought and said about Taoism among those who are not specialists. Most specifically, I wish to use the findings of the best specialists at the turn of the millennium to shock educated readers, at all levels, into seeing Taoism as something quite *different* from what they have usually been told that it is. In so doing, I shall sometimes argue that such readers have frequently, in effect, been lied to. The accused liars here are *not* my fellow specialists – other scholars in "Taoist studies" who might, for instance, assign Tu Kuang-t'ing a somewhat different place in Taoist history than I do. Rather, I refer to those who have purported to explain Chinese history and culture, and the place of Taoism within that history and culture, without even knowing, for instance, who Tu Kuang-t'ing *was*, what he wrote, when he wrote it, why he wrote it, and for whom he wrote it. In other words, I am writing here, on one level, to show that what many twentieth-century writers said about Taoism was, on several fundamental levels, simply false.

I intend to show that the place of Taoism in the history of Chinese civilization can be reasonably said to have been explained *only* when such explanations carefully utilize the pertinent historical data to show a reasonable person the precise sense in which, for instance, Tu Kuang-t'ing should be recognized as having been as important a historiographer as the *non*-Taoist historiographers who received the exclusive attention and respect of twentieth-century historians and sinologists. At the opening of this millennium, those who write about Chinese *history* have simply never had anything at all to say about the significance of Tu Kuang-t'ing's historiographical products. That is because those who write about Chinese history have generally never heard of Tu Kuang-t'ing and, if asked to explain such ignorance, would simply dismiss the question: they would presume that, if Tu Kuang-t'ing was really of any significance in discussing Chinese historiography, they would have learned his name from their teachers, would have found summaries of his writings in their textbooks, and would have supervised generations of students in trying to understand Tu's place in the study of Chinese history and the activities of Taoists within that history. The problem with that presumption is that it assumes that those before them were well informed and unbiased. And, as the millennium opens, it is now quite simple to use the data of Taoism to show that what "sinology" has usually told us about Taoism has never truly been based on much real knowledge of the pertinent facts. What I intend to do in this book is to show intelligent readers what some of those pertinent facts are, and to render thoughtful and viable conclusions as to what those facts truly teach us. Over time, scholars – myself and others alike – will adduce additional facts and construct better conclusions than those offered here.

Why discourse about "Taoism" needs radical reconstruction

The main reason why I contend that we need a radical reconstruction of what we say about Taoism is that, to the end of the twentieth century, even leading scholars in the field often perpetuated a set of notions that *predetermined* the pertinent discourse, and did so for reasons that were not inherent to the data themselves. For instance, that discourse was often predicated upon the seldom-examined assumption that this "Taoist" datum and that "Taoist" datum (e.g., living liturgies and ancient texts) have nothing at all to do with each other, and that it is thus impossible to identify them as elements of a common "whole." But the issues involved in recognizing the *continuities within "Taoism"* are mostly issues that have not yet been fully and thoughtfully addressed. When we look very closely at the historical data of a given culture or tradition, we always see elements of continuity along with elements of discontinuity. The "China" of Confucius's time and the "China" of today are clearly not "the same." And yet, within the "China" of today there is a certain *range* of elements that *also* existed within the "China" of the classical period. The fact that today's China is quite different from the context in which Confucius lived does not lead us logically to a conclusion that "there is no continuity at all" between the two. Yet even today, some scholars, and many in the general public, keep on insisting that "there is no continuity at all" between *this* Taoist datum and *that* Taoist datum. In other words, in our discourse, the fact that there have been different Taoist voices, and that those voices have changed over time, has often been exaggerated, in order to uphold conclusions about Taoism that are themselves cultural constructs. And the interpretive errors of such scholars cannot entirely be attributed to "Orientalism" in Western minds, for among the loudest voices in that chorus were not only China's best-known *intellectuals* – some of whom, such as Fung Yu-lan and Wing-tsit Chan, converted Western scholars to their position – but also by the political establishment of China throughout the second half of the century.

Some might say that it is too strong to argue that such interpreters were guilty of "errors": they were "only products of their day and age," and we cannot blame them if their beliefs about Taoism did not conform to the facts as we know them today. Indeed, by such standards, all that I write here would assuredly qualify as "erroneous" from the perspective of future generations. One must indeed forgive interpreters who have no way to appreciate the significance of pertinent facts that are unknown, and unknowable, within their day and age. For instance, during the height of the Cultural Revolution, scholars outside China sometimes reached the false conclusion that Taoism in China was virtually extinct.[1] Today, we know that Taoists suffered terribly during that period, and that their tradition was hard-pressed, but that it survived. Based on all the facts that were available to scholars outside China in the 1970s, their conclusion that Taoism was virtually dead in mainland China was incorrect, but *not culpably* so: the conclusion was a very reasonable one, based upon the data that the interpreters were able to ascertain.

But does the same hold true in regard to scholars of that period who contended, for instance, that "Taoism never really existed in China during the Ming dynasty"? In the latter half of the twentieth century there were scholars who made just such contentions. Consequently, novices and non-specialists felt justified in believing such things as well. But the difference between contentions of this nature and the previous example is that, even in the day and age when such scholars were spreading such ideas, there *were* materials available that demonstrated the vitality of Taoist teachings and practices during Ming times. The twentieth-century scholars who contended that "there was no real Taoism in Ming times" simply *ignored* the surviving writings of Ming-dynasty Taoists, and pertinent sources *about* those Taoists. Moreover, the scholars who ignored those sources did so *not* on the basis of a judgment formed from careful, critical examination of such materials. Rather, the very idea of *looking at* such materials was often dismissed as simply preposterous.

Let us compare this situation with that of biblical scholars in the days before, and after, the discovery of such non-transmitted texts as we now have from Nag Hammadi. Scholars who wrote before that time cannot reasonably be called to task for having been unable to include *The Gospel of Thomas* in their reasoning about the nature of gospel traditions. And one may simply disagree with the arguments of someone who has read such non-canonical gospels and concluded that we have nothing to learn from them. But it is another thing for such a scholar to assume the insignificance of extant texts without bothering to read any of them. For a Christian theologian to decide, on the basis of his or her articles of faith, that one ought not include non-canonical gospels in his or her ruminations on Christian origins would be understandable. But for a scholar who claims to be "objective" to do so would be wholly unjustified. While even the best scholar will at times make mistakes, and will sometimes fail to understand the true implications of his or her material, any responsible scholar will allow his or her position to be based upon a fair reading of all the pertinent facts that are knowable.

It is true that good scholars often differ in what they regard to be a fair reading of the facts. So other specialists today may fairly conclude, for instance, that my own views about the relative importance of, say, Ming-dynasty "Inner Alchemy" are different from what the pertinent data truly imply. Discussing such interpretive differences is healthy and appropriate, for doing so helps us all reach a better understanding of the issues. It would be a very different matter, however, for someone to argue that my views on Ming Taoism are wrong because "there were simply no Taoists in Ming China." Though few know it, the fact is that we have hundreds of writings from people of that period who (a) regarded themselves as Taoists; (b) thought about many of the same things that many earlier Taoists did; (c) tried to bring their lives into a proper state, on terms that were often continuous with those embraced by earlier Taoists; and (d) are acknowledged as part of the Taoist tradition by the living representatives of that tradition today. It is at these levels that I shall attempt here to explicate the facts of Taoism as it evolved over the ages.

Another vital way of perceiving, and gaining insight into, such historical and cultural continuities is to scrutinize the specific differences between a tradition that shows certain elements – albeit shifting over time, as all things do – and *other* traditions that do not share those elements. Again, in the past, scholars, and the public who believed them, often reached false conclusions about Taoism by making misleading contrasts – contrasts often designed, for instance, to prove that Taoists did not have the wisdom or sophistication of Confucians, or Buddhists (or, at least, had not done so for many centuries). Taoism, it has thus been argued, is not even worthy of discussion when we are debating ethical values, for Taoism does not display the ethical values that we find in Confucianism, or in humanism, or in Christianity, or in whatever value-system in which we have been taught to perceive such things. Conversely, some have just as simplistically insisted that Confucians were typically staid, superficial, and repressive, and never valued the individual the way the Taoists supposedly did.

Today, one can demonstrate that all such arguments are deficient. One can now demonstrate, to some extent at least, that the differences between Confucianism and Taoism are differences that are noteworthy, but subtly nuanced. As I shall demonstrate in what follows, it is quite clear that most Confucians and most Taoists would generally agree that a good person should engage in *self-cultivation*. It is also clear that some Taoists would disagree with each other over the details of what self-cultivation means. But then again, it is quite clear that Confucians would disagree with each other on the same issue, as well. Most educated people know today, for instance, that Mencius's program of self-cultivation assumed a need for the good man to embrace and extend "what is natural" within himself, and that Hsün-tzu (Xunzi), a century later, argued adamantly to the contrary: for Hsün-tzu, a good man must rigorously suppress "what is natural" within himself (which is inherently selfish, hence immoral), and must learn instead to acculturate himself to the wholesome values that society has passed down from the days of the ancient sage-kings. Meanwhile, in later centuries, other Confucians argued that real self-cultivation means integrating oneself with the original structures and forces of the universe itself – an argument that seems more in line with what Buddhists and Taoists generally say than with anything ever said by Confucius, or Mencius, or Hsün-tzu. Yet, all found justification for their views in the traditions that were generally accepted as "Confucian" traditions.

In fact, some scholars today say that it is the fact that a given thinker sought justification for his views in one particular cultural source, rather than another, that is the best indicator of that thinker's true cultural identity. Thus, any thinker in Chinese history who cited, for instance, the *Chung-yung* (*Zhongyong*) to justify his ideas is someone whose values can legitimately be interpreted as a representative of Confucian traditions. Yet in Chinese culture, especially after the Yüan period, there were many writers who cited, with equal aplomb, from "Confucian" texts, *and* from "Buddhist" texts, *and* from "Taoist" texts, all in the same passage. Moreover, such writers often frequently asserted that all such texts were "really saying the same thing," albeit in different terms, and that consequently "the 'Three Teachings' are truly one." Should we dismiss such writers, as though they are confused about what it actually means, for instance, to be "a Confucian," or "a Taoist"? Anyone who reads such materials soon becomes aware that their authors were certainly not confused. Yet, modern readers often find it difficult to recognize value in the ideas of anyone who fails to uphold our inherited categories.

In general, it is fair to say that, with certain important exceptions of course, twentieth-century scholars were so intent upon maintaining the integrity of such categories as "Confucianism" and "Taoism" that they would often look away from all the data – historical, textual, or sociological – that seemed to threaten their accepted beliefs about the category. If, therefore, a scholar found, for instance, teachings about meditation from the brush of someone who otherwise argued Confucian positions, on the basis of Confucian precedents, the scholar would simply dismiss the very existence of such a figure: a "Confucian" who taught or practiced *meditation* was, by definition – by our, modern definition – not really a Confucian, so what he did or said did not warrant even being considered in any examination of what "Confucians" do and say. Of course, by that reasoning, the fact that the person in question simply had his *own* definition of "what Confucianism is about" – perhaps one that was shared by *others*, centuries earlier or centuries later – is simply irrelevant. In other words, scholars writing about Confucians have taught us to believe that a Confucian who understood himself to be Confucian in different terms from those found in certain *modern* preachments was not really a Confucian at all, even if others in his own day and age had shared his belief that he was quite certainly "a Confucian."

These issues are very pertinent to understanding Taoism, because, until nearly the end of the twentieth century, virtually everyone who wrote or spoke about Taoism – including scholars, Asian and Western alike – maintained, sometimes with irrational vehemence, a definition of "Taoism" that excluded *virtually all* of the Taoist thinkers of the last two thousand years, along with virtually all of the practitioners of Taoism over that period. Of course, that fiercely defended interpretation of Taoism also defined away every trace of all the *women* who had practiced and preserved Taoist traditions over that two thousand years. And that interpretation was never presented to any *living* Taoists for their consideration or debate. One imagines the amusing ramifications of someone who decided to "define Christianity" strictly on the basis of the canonical gospels (or even, for that matter, all the gospels), denying to "Christianity" anything that was ever done or said by Paul, or the Nicene council, or Augustine, or Luther, or in fact any living Christian of our own, or any previous, age. Yet, even at the opening of the twenty-first century, there are very few depictions of Taoism that simply present, fully and fairly, all of the aspects of Taoist belief and practice that were produced over the centuries by the people of China. What follows is simply a beginning – a new interpretive analysis of key themes and patterns in the history of Taoism, designed to facilitate new insights into what *Taoists* of all periods understood "Taoism" to be.

ACKNOWLEDGMENTS

The understanding of Taoism expressed in this book is of course indebted to many people. Some were my teachers, among whom Judith Berling deserves special mention. Others were the scholars whose works and ideas have informed and stimulated my thought about Taoism over the years. Sadly, their ranks have been depleted by the untimely loss of Edward Schafer, Anna Seidel, Michel Strickmann, Isabelle Robinet, and, most recently, Evgeny Tortchinov.

In some ways the most important contributors to this project have been my students, not only at the University of Georgia, but also in my earlier years at Oberlin, Stanford, and Macalester: my efforts to use the fruits of recent scholarship to help students of the last fifteen years past some of the confusion about "what Taoism is" that frustrated students of my own generation were often key in forcing me to rethink my own interpretive paradigms. It was not until 1998 that I began to imagine that it might be possible to produce a new introduction to Taoism. I am indebted to Mark Csikszentmihalyi for emboldening me to carry out such a project, and to Norman Girardot for his wise counsel and steadfast encouragement.

Chapter 1 contains material that originally appeared in "Explaining Daoism: Realities, Cultural Constructs, and Emerging Perspectives," in Livia Kohn, ed., *Daoism Handbook* (Leiden: Brill, 2000). Reprinted by permission of Brill.

Elements of Chapter 2 first appeared in "Varieties of 'Taoism' in Ancient China: A Preliminary Comparison of Themes in the *Nei yeh* and Other 'Taoist Classics'," *Taoist Resources* 7.2 (1997), 73–86. Reprinted by permission of Stephen Bokenkamp. Other elements of Chapter 2 first appeared in "The Book of the Way (*Daode Jing*)," in

Ian McGreal, ed., *Great Literature of the Eastern World* (New York: HarperCollins, 1996), 24–9. Reprinted by permission of Ian McGreal.

Elements of Chapter 3 first appeared in "Tung Chung-shu," in Ian McGreal, ed., *Great Thinkers of the Eastern World* (New York: HarperCollins, 1995), 67–70. Reprinted by permission of Ian McGreal.

Some of the material on Yeh Fa-shan in Chapter 4 originally appeared in "Tales of Thaumaturgy: T'ang Accounts of the Wonder-Worker Yeh Fa-shan," *Monumenta Serica* 40 (1992), 47–86, copyright Monumenta Serica Institute. Reprinted by permission of Monumenta Serica Institute. Some of the material on women in Taoism in Chapter 4 first appeared in my entry "Taoism," in *Encyclopedia of Women and World Religion* (New York: Macmillan, 1999), 2: 959–64. Copyright the Gale Group 1999. Reprinted by permission of the Gale Group. Chapter 4 also contains material that first appeared in my entry "Taoism," in *The Encyclopedia of Bioethics*, 2nd edn (New York: Macmillan, 1995), 5: 2463–9. Copyright the Gale Group 1995. Reprinted by permission of the Gale Group. Other material in Chapter 4 first appeared in my entry "Taoism," in J. J. Chambliss, ed., *Philosophy of Education: An Encyclopedia* (New York and London: Garland, 1996). Reproduced by permission of Garland Publishing/Taylor & Francis Books, Inc.

Several chapters contain material that originally appeared in "Person and Culture in the Taoist Tradition," *Journal of Chinese Religions* 20 (1992), 77–90; and other material that originally appeared in "The Historical Contours of Taoism in China: Thoughts on Issues of Classification and Terminology," *Journal of Chinese Religions* 25 (1997), 57–82. Reprinted by permission of Stephen Bokenkamp.

1

UNDERSTANDING TAOISM

Realities, constructs, and hermeneutical challenges

The Chinese public today, like most in the outside world, generally know little about the Taoist tradition, though some are curious about whether it might have something to contribute to their lives. Meanwhile, many Westerners still imperialistically assume that the primary reason for them to study the religions of other cultures is to identify elements that can be appropriated into their own lives, or even new religious identities that can be assumed at will by "any of us."[1] A proper understanding of Taoism requires one to recognize *all* such motivations, to ensure that they do not interfere with one's interpretive efforts, for instance by causing one to discount elements of Taoism that do not suit one's own taste or reinforce the biases of one's own age or culture.

The efflorescence of Taoist studies among scholars of the late twentieth century gave rise to a new set of interpretive perspectives, which consciously repudiated the Orientalist assumptions that had theretofore been the dominant interpretive paradigm. Those new scholarly perspectives generally insisted (1) that we must recognize the *Chinese-ness* of Taoism; (2) that we must privilege the factual *data* of Taoism itself, in social, historical, and textual terms; and (3) that we must acknowledge the importance of the living forms of Taoism that survive among Chinese communities today.

As the twenty-first century opens, the educated public needs to be made very aware of aspects of Taoist history, thought, and practice that have heretofore been ignored or misinterpreted.[2] And scholars of Taoism need to do more to show the public how such heretofore unappreciated realities expand and correct our understanding of what "Taoism" is.

For one thing, most scholars who have seriously studied Taoism, both in Asia and in the West, have finally abandoned the simplistic dichotomy of *tao-chia* and *tao-chiao* – "philosophical Taoism" and "religious Taoism." A few have begun offering new models for understanding the continuities among the ideas and practices presented in the data of Taoist texts of various periods. In the early 1990s some scholars, myself included, suggested that we try to understand Taoism in terms of a heuristic contrast between two soteriological models: "mystical" models – seen both in *Chuang-tzu* and certain later traditions – and "liturgical" models that developed in other later traditions. More recently, Livia Kohn suggested that, "within the Daoist tradition . . . one can distinguish three types of organization and practice: literati, communal, and self-cultivation."

> Literati Daoists are members of the educated elite who focus on Daoist ideas as expressed by the ancient thinkers. . . . They use these concepts to create meaning in their world and hope to exert some influence on the political and social situation of their time, contributing to greater universal harmony, known as the state of Great Peace (*taiping*) [*t'ai-p'ing*]. . . . Communal Daoists . . . are found in many different positions and come from all levels of society. They are members of organized Daoist groups [who] have priestly hierarchies, formal initiations, regular rituals, and prayers to the gods. . . . The third group of Daoists focus on self-cultivation. . . . They, too, come from all walks of life, but rather than communal rites, their main concern is the attainment of personal health, longevity, peace of mind, and spiritual immortality.[3]

Today, none of those interpretive models seems sufficiently nuanced to ensure a full and accurate understanding of all the diverse but interrelated forms of Taoism that evolved over the long history of China. But every time thoughtful scholars test out such models, we seem to move closer toward a more subtle, and more useful, perception of how to understand Taoism. It should be noted in this connection, however, that Taoists have never made *any* distinctions of such kinds, and it is such very facts that challenge our hermeutical imagination.

In addition, today's best specialists are still only beginning to appreciate some of the basic realities of Taoism in terms of *social and political history*, not to mention in terms of the realities of *gender*. The present book is, in part, intended to stimulate further awareness that our concept of "what Taoism is" needs to assimilate it on those terms as well.

It should also be noted that many of today's specialists in all lands still privilege the Taoist traditions that evolved during the Han to T'ang dynasties, i.e., from about 200 to 600 CE. While all such traditions are important, there remains an unfortunate tendency for scholars to say "Taoists believe X," when in fact such "X belief" may have been true only in a certain generation, in a certain region, or even in a single individual's mind. For instance, a historical study of the Taoist priesthood might adduce a single Taoist text, explicate its contents, and reify them as "Taoist tradition." Far too seldom have scholars asked the degree to which *the social realities of Taoists* truly correspond to the data that we find in such texts. To reify the contents of any such text, or group of texts, as "Taoism" can warp our perspective just as deeply as scholars of bygone days did when they reified the contents of *Lao-tzu* or *Chuang-tzu* as "Taoism."

Only at the very end of the twentieth century did scholars of Taoism even really begin to give consideration to the distinct Taoist subtraditions that emerged in China during the past millennium – an era that nearly all twentieth-century minds regarded as the heyday of "Neo-Confucianism." Even the expert contributors to the *Daoism Handbook* – a wide-ranging state-of-the-field reference work published in the year 2000 – often caution that their findings, particularly regarding the Sung and later dynasties, should be read as an "interim report" rather than a definitive analysis.[4] And the editors of a collection of expert articles on the Ch'üan-chen (Quanzhen) tradition published in 2002 note: "Few comprehensive surveys of Quanzhen Taoism exist, and most of those are unpublished dissertations."[5] Such "modern" forms of Taoism deserve much greater attention, for a variety of reasons:

1 they survived, more or less intact, into the twentieth century, which is not true of such well-studied Six-Dynasties subtraditions as Shang-ch'ing or Ling-pao;

2 they have often featured prominent roles for women practitioners and even women leaders;
3 they maintained the ancient Taoist practices of *self-cultivation*, thereby revealing vital continuities between "classical Taoism" and the Taoism practiced from the T'ang period to today;
4 they compare favorably with other Chinese and non-Chinese traditions in terms of both religious *thought* and *models of personal practice*, which was not true of most pre-T'ang subtraditions.

Also, today's specialists often ignore a helpful heuristic distinction that modern Taoists often make between "Northern Taoism" (i.e., traditions like Ch'üan-chen) and "Southern Taoism" (i.e., Cheng-i). "Northern Taoism" displays more of the charactistics listed above than does "Southern Taoism," and as members of the educated public become more aware of "Northern Taoism," they may develop the same intense interest and respect that they showed toward other major traditions, such as Buddhism, throughout the twentieth century.

Perhaps the most important new emphasis that we should give to our presentations of Taoism today should be upon those historical and living realities of Taoism, which belie the misconceptions that dominated the twentieth century. For instance, the misconception that "religious Taoism" was the province of the "illiterate masses" – not of "the educated elite" – can be corrected simply by directing attention to the hundreds of Taoist texts preserved in the *Tao-tsang* and elsewhere, only a few of which have yet been translated into Western languages.[6] Similarly, giving due attention to the models of *personal practice* articulated by Chinese intellectuals such as Ssu-ma Ch'eng-chen easily disproves the misconception that Taoism "degenerated into superstition" after classical times. Above all, the many versions of *Nei-tan* ("Inner Alchemy") theory and practice – a fundamental element of Taoism for the last thousand years – demonstrate the absurdity of the lingering "anti-Catholic" charge that later Taoism was "ritualistic nonsense" that ignored the spiritual needs and aspirations of individual practitioners. Increasing sophistication in ritual theory can help us understand and explain the depth and richness of all forms of Taoist ritual, past and present. Not only do we now know that the training and practice of

Cheng-i liturgists were grounded in Taoist models of self-perfection that we see in such "mystical" models as Inner Alchemy. But even today's "Northern Taoism" values ritual action as an element of the Taoist life.

Further attention is due to the rich diversity of Taoist conceptions of the religious life. Virtually no one today knows, for instance, that T'ang-dynasty Taoists wrote extensively about "Tao-nature" (*tao-hsing*) – a concept of "the true reality of all things, including ourselves," which parallels the concept of "Buddha-nature" that many know from Ch'an (Zen) and other East Asian forms of Buddhism. Nor do most know that much of Ch'üan-chen thought actually parallels, and interacted historically with, that of Ch'an Buddhism, and with many elements of late imperial Confucian thought and practice.[7] To explain that, for hundreds of years, Taoist practice was often taught in terms of "cultivating the heart/mind (*hsin*)" or of "integrating our inherent nature (*hsing*) with our destined lives (*ming*)" will correct and greatly expand the very narrow and misleading depictions of "Taoist thought" and "Taoist practice" that characterized most twentieth-century presentations.

It is also important to draw attention to the historical facts that demonstrate that Taoism was not, as has often been taught, a tradition practiced by people who stood outside the normal social order and attacked it, whether philosophically or politically. At no point in Chinese history were the majority of Taoists actually hermits, misfits, members of rebel movements, or critics of conventional values – all common stereotypes that still flourished even among some specialists of the late twentieth century. During most periods, Taoists came from all segments of society – including the educated "upper-classes"; supported – and often helped legitimize – the imperial government; and were often well known and well respected by other members of China's social and cultural "elite."

Finally, the public needs to know much more about the living realities of Taoism in China today. Today's Taoists still maintain many elements of premodern Taoism, including personal self-cultivation, a monastic life for men and women alike, and a rich panoply of traditional practices. It should be noted that the liturgical traditions of Taoism survive not only in the "Southern Taoism" of Taiwan and the southeast coast, but also in temples throughout mainland China, even at those identified as Ch'üan-chen. But it should also be noted that, by the end of the twentieth century, decades of Communist rule and secularistic trends may have left Taoist practice marginalized in new ways. Among the general public, practices that had become loosely associated with Taoism – such as *t'ai-chi ch'üan* (*taiji juan*) and *ch'i-kung* (*qigong*) – remained popular, but often without the practitioners knowing their full historical background or religious implications (though, in some circles, T'ang texts such as the *T'ien-yin-tzu* (*Tianyinzi*) continue to inform such practices).[8] And in temples and monasteries, Taoist clerics continued to keep a relatively low profile, and sometimes taught outsiders a quite modernized understanding of Taoist meditative and ritual traditions.[9] As China's economy and society evolves away from the Communist restrictions of the third quarter of the twentieth century, observers should remain alert to possible redomestication of elements of Taoism among the expanding middle class in China, especially reformulations of the more intellectualized traditions of "literati Taoism."

What "Taoism" is: fact, tradition, and self-identification

Through the twentieth century, general discussions of Taoism usually came from, or pandered to, an audience that felt entitled to gratify itself by defining "Taoism" in terms that made "us" feel good about ourselves. For the general public in the West, Taoism was often to be defined as something "for us," specifically, a set of ideas and values that (a) complement and/or correct our own cultural/religious heritage, yet (b) do not require us to learn anything that we do not already believe, or to do anything that we would find difficult or unpleasant to do. For scholars, meanwhile, Taoism was to be defined in terms of the arguments already going on among Chinese intellectuals of the late imperial and modern age, with such adaptation as was needed to integrate them with the arguments that were already going on among non-Chinese intellectuals. To the best of my knowledge, no one has ever suggested that we ought to define Taoism, in the first instance, by asking *Taoists* to guide us in learning to understand what Taoism is.

There have been some legitimate, or at least unavoidable, reasons for past interpreters' refusal to take Taoists as their conversation partners. Those reasons involve certain stubborn realities of history, geography, politics, and language, not to mention the subtler hermeneutical problems – i.e., problems of understanding what we are told because we are different from the people telling it to us. All those problems still exist at the dawn of the twenty-first century. Consequently, this very book is still, in certain regards, a colonialistic product. That is, it is written by an outsider – someone who is not a Taoist, was not raised in a society where Taoists flourished, was not educated in a culture informed by Taoist values, and has never been taught to understand Taoism by living Taoists. Yet it is conceivable that this book may make some contribution to the decolonialization of our understanding of Taoism, by approaching some of the basic issues in a new way.

To a great extent, all that someone like me can do, at the present juncture in history, is to argue for the development of an interpretive playing-field that may be suitable for us – i.e., all modern people, in the West and in Asia alike – to learn to see "how Taoism is played" by Taoists and how it has been played by Taoists of earlier ages. When challenged to answer the question "Who is 'a Taoist'?", I shall say that the correct answer must begin by determining how *Taoists* of past and present have answered that question. In deciding what we should acknowledge to be "Taoism," therefore, we do *not* get to choose an outcome that will result in the satisfaction of any of *our own* needs or desires. Instead, we have to recognize and acknowledge what the *Taoists* have understood to be Taoism, whether or not we happen to enjoy, or find benefit to ourselves in, their self-understanding.[10]

In twentieth-century terms, this approach is a methodological oddity, for throughout that century most explainers (even the most elite postmodernists) presumed that they – not the people whom they were explaining – were ideally or even exclusively qualified to decide the terms of their explanatory process.[11] My own approach begins from the premise that I am not in an ideal position to explain Taoism. Yet, my own position is the only one that I have to work from, and I presume that intellectual honesty, awareness of my own historical moment, respect for those whom I am "explaining," and careful avoidance of past interpretive errors should yield a useful, if not definitive, window on the subject. Here I offer a new architectonic model, one designed to provide structural support for an understanding of Taoism that is honest and accurate – i.e., a non-colonialized understanding – while providing little support for older, more insidiously colonialistic models.

The data-set of "Taoism": a taxonomic approach

Our preliminary task is to identify a reasonable set of criteria for determining the range of data that represent "what Taoists say Taoism is," and for weighing those criteria in the balance with other criteria that might otherwise seem reasonable and appropriate. It is not my contention that we must *conclude* our interpretive efforts by understanding Taoism as the Taoists do, for at times an outsider sees given realities more clearly than someone who has a vested interest in perceiving him/herself (or in being perceived by others) as having a special and important relationship to those realities. For instance, in Taiwan today, one can easily find a given person who will, with sincerity and self-assurance, tell observers that "Taoism is basically to be defined in terms of the texts and practices that are in my possession." But in Boston or Birmingham, one can likewise find persons who will tell us that Christianity is basically to be defined in terms of how that person and his or her community understand and practice. Yet, we know that there is significant diversity in how Christians understand their own tradition, despite the fact that certain central elements are nominally "agreed upon." And we know that over the centuries even those "central elements" of Christianity have been deeply debated among members of the Christian community. To privilege as "central" to Taoism the positions of certain specific groups or individuals would be improperly to disenfranchise other Taoist groups and individuals. And to privilege the positions common in certain specific periods would be improperly to disenfranchise the Taoists of other periods. It shall be my position that we may not, at the outset, legitimately identify any particular Taoist data as normative, but must make a concerted attempt to take fully into account *all* the data pertaining to *all* the Taoists of every period, past and present.

My approach here is different from that of most scholars who were trained in the twentieth century. My criteria for deciding who we should regard as representatives of "Taoism" are fairly new. I begin with a taxonomic analysis that (1) casts its net as broadly and inclusively as the facts today seem to allow, and (2) neither endorses nor denies the inherent validity or value of any particular element of any particular phase or tradition of Taoism. We may not, I contend, legitimately privilege ancient Taoists over medieval or modern Taoists, or vice versa. We may not legitimately privilege the experiences of expressions of male Taoists over females, or vice versa. We may not legitimately privilege intellectualized expressions of Taoism over those that are "just lived" – a common bias among scholars who study *any* tradition. And we may not legitimately privilege the Taoists of one particular region over those of another, even if we know much about one region and little about another. In sum, we may not legitimately privilege any particular *form* of Taoism as intrinsically *normative* for proper identification of the category. There are certainly Taoists today who may wish us to believe that their particular form should be accepted as normative, just as there are Hindus and Christians who do so. But I shall argue that no Taoists' claim to have a normative understanding of Taoism may legitimately be accepted. Rather, I shall argue that *all* such claims must be *evaluated*, not only in terms of *each other*, but also in terms of *all* the claims of *all* of the Taoists of the past.

This definitional reasoning – and its consequences – will shock many of those who are satisfied that they already know what Taoism is, for what this reasoning reveals is often deeply at odds with what was commonly believed about Taoism by most twentieth-century minds. It will also shock those who would argue that "Taoism" is merely a construct, and that, since the validity of all constructs is contestable, it is theoretcially impossible for anyone ever to present an understanding of "Taoism" that is anything but arbitrary. I will argue that that position – common among "post-modern" theorists of "continental" sensibilities – need not be taken seriously. Such issues will need to be addressed more fully in other settings. Suffice it here to say that the pronouncements of all "postmodern" theorists are themselves a product of a particular time and place, and are themselves therefore unreliable guides for anyone attempting to determine how we can determine what is true. The doctrines of that particular school of relativism – though quite popular among members of an intellectual elite in the present day – may no more be logically privileged than any other doctrines accepted by anyone of past or present. One such doctrine – accepted by many as a cardinal tenet of faith – is that we can never actually identify a "fact." But that doctrine is demonstrably false: most facts are arguable, but some pertinent arguments can easily be shown to be much better than others, and some arguments can be shown to be utterly absurd. Whatever emerges from a process of rational analysis and debate regarding the facts, their pertinence, and their significance may never quite be "objective truth," but it is certainly far from arbitrary, and will certainly help the better-informed better to inform the less-well informed about the subject under discussion.

There are indeed quite *a lot of facts* in regard to Taoism, *most* of which remain generally unknown to most people who discuss Taoism. The discovery of facts is a historical process. Today, scholars know many more facts about Taoism than did scholars of the early twentieth century. And scholars of the future will know yet more, by means of which they will be able to correct and refine whatever statements about Taoism we make today. That having been said, it is legitimate to discuss what we know about Taoism today, and to demonstrate that certain things that were said about Taoism in past ages can be shown to have been false. For instance, among the general public at the turn of the millennium, it was quite common to hear that "Taoism is basically about *wu-wei*." There can be little legitimate dispute about such a contention, because the number of actual facts that are at variance with such a statement are so overwhelmingly superabundant that no reasonable person – once made aware of those facts – would ever again seriously consider entertaining it. What scholars can do is discover more and more of the facts of Taoism, and to make more and more of them part of the twenty-first-century discourse about Taoism. Only in the last generation or two have scholars who specialize in the study of Taoism made serious progress in identifying many of those facts. Yet, a sound and reasonable understanding of Taoism must be based upon such facts, and a non-colonialistic understanding must begin with *what the Taoists of China, in every age, have said and practiced*.

Transcending invalid reifications of "tradition"

Late in the last century, the theorist Bernard Faure "examined the constitution of Chan/Zen as an epistemological object," attempting "to unsettle the object (Chan/Zen) by the use of alternative methods, while avoiding to dissolve this object into mere ideological discourse." My approach to Taoism is on the same level. But Faure also argued that "Chan is not primarily a concrete social reality, but a complex and elusive epistemological object that never existed as a given outside representations, but was always in the making, through the classificatory decisions of people who saw themselves as members of the tradition."[12] Yet, if such shifting and disparate "classificatory decisions" can be taken as constitutive of the "epistemological object" that we call Chan/Zen, then it seems to follow that the life-actions of the centuries of men and women who made those decisions can properly be regarded as a "social reality."

And while those people's decisions may not have been "concrete," there is certainly a concreteness to some of the *results* of those decisions. For instance, some very "concrete" individuals built and rebuilt the White Cloud Abbey in Beijing, from the time of the T'ang emperor Hsüan-tsung in the eighth century down to the present day. Such concrete individuals engaged in pertinent "classificatory decisions," as did those who staffed the abbey over the centuries, those who came there to engage in practices of self-cultivation, and those who articulated the code of personal conduct expected of all who engaged in such practices there. And another quite concrete *result* of those people's decisions was a massive collection of writings left behind by people of earlier ages who had likewise engaged, sometimes quite consciously, in such "classificatory decisions" – the *Tao-tsang*, a collection of writings by and about "Taoists" who had lived, and had made their own "classificatory decisions" about being "Taoist," in every age of imperial and pre-imperial China. The *Tao-tsang*, the White Cloud Abbey, and even the Lung-men subtradition, whose leadership has been housed in that abbey for centuries, can certainly be regarded as quite concrete "facts" of Taoism.[13]

But what such facts show about Taoism is that it was not "a tradition" whose leaders ever even sought to articulate any "orthodoxy," nor one that sought to impose any particular set of ideas about "what Taoism is" upon its practitioners. Therefore, to acknowledge that there was, and is, historically and socially such a "tradition" as Taoism does not, as Faure seems to have feared, tacitly reify such "orthodox" positions, nor does it tacitly import such positions into the thought-processes of today's careful interpreters. So I contend that we should acknowledge and seek to understand "Lung-men Taoism" as a social and historical reality, while recognizing the data of history and society as tools to help us put into proper perspective any traditional claims by or about Lung-men Taoists. I shall also recognize that Lung-men Taoism has, on various levels, important continuities with other subtraditions of Taoism, though not necessarily on terms that any of its historical representatives may have recognized.

"Self-identification": the value of the Tao-tsang *for identifying "the facts of Taoism"*

Are there, or have there ever been, ideas or practices that "were generally agreed upon" by all, or even most, Taoists? The data with which I am familiar today leads me to say no. It is important to remember that – if we accept, for instance, the *Tao-tsang* as representative of "Taoism" – Taoists did not generally regard themselves as followers of a single religious community that shared a single set of teachings, or practices. Unlike Buddhism, Confucianism, or Christianity, Taoism did not begin from the efforts of a community to practice the teachings of a great leader.[14] And since there were no "original teachings" of any such "original community," Taoists through history never felt obliged to hew their beliefs and practices to any putative original "standard." The diversity of Taoist beliefs and practices cannot reasonably be explained in terms of orthodoxy versus non-orthodoxy, of orthopraxy versus non-orthopraxy.

Nor would it be correct to reify traditional terminology and identify "Taoists" as those who "believed in Tao." By that token, the facts would make *Confucius* a key early Taoist, and would *not* include many of the centuries of men and women who understood themselves to be Taoist, were understood to be Taoist by their contemporaries, and were understood to be Taoist by those of later ages who self-identified as Taoists. It is true that in many Chinese temples, as in late imperial art, one often sees a depiction of Confucius alongside a depiction of a Taoist figure such as Lord Lao. But the decisions of such artists and temple-arrangers do not seem to be explainable primarily as decisions by a self-identifying Taoist to portray Confucius as "Taoist." The message of such phenomena lies on different social and cultural levels.

The primary fact that I shall use here to determine the proper criteria for identifying "Taoist phenomena" is that there have been people for centuries who self-identified as Taoists, and were generally recognized as "Taoist" by others around them. "Taoism" must be identified, in the first instance, in terms of that historical heritage.[15] If, therefore, someone says that clouds found in Chinese landscape paintings represent "Taoist values," we can test such statements against the pertinent social and historical data from all periods. While we may eventually revise and refine such approaches in many ways, it is quite defensible for us to take the position today that we can identify "the self-identifying Taoists" *as the people whose ideas, values, practices and institutions are expressed in the writings that have been included in the vast, amorphous collection called the Tao-tsang, its predecessors and later continuations.*[16]

The people involved in the production of the extant *Tao-tsang* were, quite indisputably, leading participants in the Ming-dynasty community of self-identifying Taoists. And their work was also recognized as "definitionally significant" by the ambient society, for the emperor of China in the Cheng-t'ung era – like various emperors in earlier centuries – ordered *Taoist leaders* to collect all the writings of their tradition, past and present. In 1445, as at the completion of such earlier compilation processes, both "the Taoists" of that era and the imperial government agreed that the result consisted of *all* the extant written materials, from every preceding age, that should be regarded as a worthy element of the Taoist tradition. The "definitiveness" of this particular set of "classificatory decisions" lies in the fact that they were accepted by two distinct groups of people: first, the period's Taoist leaders, as so regarded by themselves and, at the very least, by the imperial government, if not also by most members of the living communities who practiced various forms of Taoism in Ming times; and, second, the government authorities, who recognized Taoism as important – in cultural and political terms alike – and wished it to endure, or at least wished to be perceived as rulers who wished it to endure.

To study the data of Taoism, one must study all that is revealed, intentionally and unintentionally, by the centuries of material preserved in the *Tao-tsang* and related collections. That material has very diverse origins, and thus reveals many distinguishable "Taoist" messages. Some of that material can now be identified, more or less clearly, as the patrimony of certain identifiable historical groups. Some of them did not survive more than a generation or two, others survived for centuries, and several survive today. There is also material in the *Tao-tsang* from some groups whose historical realities we can now show to have been deliberately *contrived* to give an *impression* of a group that had "survived for centuries," when in reality no such "survival" is demonstrable on any objective analysis of the known facts. By means of available historical data, we can today establish, to some degree, the historicality of certain "traditions," and draw into question the historicality of others.

We must also bear in mind that when we examine a given text we often cannot know how many people believed or practiced what that text suggests. We cannot even know how many people took a given text seriously as a representation of Taoism. It is conceivable that at times the collectors of anthologies such as the *Tao-tsang* may have made some of their decisions with some degree of reluctance, as when the Hebrews and Christians decided to include *Ecclesiastes* in their canons. So to accept the *Tao-tsang* as a general collection of "the texts of Taoism" does not necessarily entail any recognition that any given text within it was, in practice, truly embraced by centuries of Taoists as a valid representation of their own values, beliefs, or practices. The preponderance of historical data, and sociological data from our own times, makes clear that some of the texts in the *Tao-tsang* – such as the classical *Mo-tzu* (HY1168) and *Han-fei-tzu* (HY1169) – were seldom, if ever, regarded by Taoists as texts whose teachings "we, as Taoists, should follow." We may thus ultimately conclude that some of what is found in the *Tao-tsang* is not particularly pertinent for determining "what Taoism is," just as we may conclude that certain texts that did not survive in the *Tao-tsang* are indeed quite relevant. After all, over the centuries, wars and fires often destroyed the libraries where precious Taoist manuscripts were housed. Some such texts survived elsewhere, in collections that were not generally regarded as "Taoist," or buried away at sites such as Tun-huang. Thus, we may find good reason to acknowledge as "Taoist" materials such as the *Pen-chi ching*, the *Nei-yeh*, or the writings of various Taoist literati of T'ang and later times. Yet, to accept the *Tao-tsang* as reasonably representative of the voices of centuries of Taoists, however diverse, seems to be a quite valid way of establishing the boundaries of what Taoists considered Taoist, and of assessing the contents of their tradition.

Beyond those boundaries, our historical sources sometimes recognize as "an important Taoist" someone regarding whom it is, at best, unclear that he or she ever participated in any of the activities of his or her Taoist contemporaries, or that he or she ever imagined that anyone would ever identify her or him as a Taoist. One such example was the T'ang-dynasty thaumaturge Yeh Fa-shan (631–720).[17] Yet, Taoist tradition did in time certainly embrace Yeh as an ideal exemplar of some of its most cherished values, as seen by the texts in the *Tao-tsang* which so represent him. Then again, there are those such as Lin Chao-en (1517–1598) who have sometimes been called "syncretists," because their lives and thought clearly included elements of Buddhism and Confucianism as well as Taoism. There are doubtless many comparable cases of men and women who may perhaps be worth including in our discussion of "Taoism," even though we may not always be able to show that the individual self-identified as "a Taoist."

My contention here is *not* that "Taoism" is, or ever was, a monolithic social or historical entity: the evidence makes clear that Taoism never had the coherence that we see in "the Christian Church" over the centuries, much less that organization's social, political, or economic power. Nor is it my contention that "Taoism" is now fully known, and must be explained in a single, specific way. Rather, my contention is that Taoism is *well enough* known for us to sort out *certain* explanations that are clearly *correct*; others that are *not entirely certain* but are supported by *most* readings of the pertinent data; and a variety of explanations that we can now clearly demonstrate to be *unsupported* by the pertinent data.

For instance, through the twentieth century it was common to read that Taoism after *Lao-tzu* and *Chuang-tzu* had no intellectual content and is best understood in terms of "popular religion." Scholarship of the last quarter of that century began to show that such beliefs are clearly incorrect. Likewise, through the twentieth century it was common to read that Taoism was "escapist," that Taoists had no real regard for the realities of social life, no interest in government, and no moral teachings. Such contentions, of course, were almost always made by people who had never made any attempt to read, much less carefully study, the material preserved in the *Tao-tsang* and related collections. Likewise, through the twentieth century it was common to read that Taoism was historically "marginal" to the Chinese "mainstream," for that mainstream was essentially "Confucian." But that belief was grounded in the contentions of Confucians, and reflects the biases of modern interpreters.

It is now possible to offer sound, if not quite fully definitive, explanations of what Taoism was to various practitioners from age to age, provided that we set aside the preconceptions that plagued past generations, and look objectively at the data of Taoism, as defined primarily in terms of the materials found in the *Tao-tsang* and related materials. And we may emend and expand what we learn from those materials by means of fieldwork in Chinese societies, analysis of pertinent works of art and material culture, and examination of pertinent documents that were preserved at places such as Tun-huang, in the Buddhist canon, in "eclectic" collections such as the *Lü-shih ch'un-chiu* and *Kuan-tzu*, in inscription texts, in local histories, in "standard histories" and other imperial collections, such as the *T'ai-p'ing kuang-chi*, and even in literary works, such as *ch'uan-ch'i* tales, novels, and plays.

The historical Taoist "community"

The first socio-cultural group whose participants consciously identified themselves as "Taoist" – and began conceiving the first comprehensive collection of Taoist texts – appeared in what some would call "early medieval China," during the fifth century CE. That group consisted specifically of people whose sense of Taoist identity was stimulated by the fact that Buddhism had gained acceptance and political favor throughout the land, which was, at that time, politically divided, with one imperial regime in the north and another in the south. There were many then, in the north and south alike, who had no wish to identify themselves with Buddhism. Data pertaining to the lives, and decisions, of "the common people" in that period is scant: most of our textual data clearly originated among the aristocracy. And what that data reveals is that members of the aristocracy who respected and cherished *indigenous* religious traditions – what they regarded as "our" religious heritage – began trying to *organize* those traditions – institutionally, textually, and even conceptually – so that "our religion" could better compete with Buddhism.

Those efforts, which were moderately successful, constituted the *creation* of what *the Taoists* called "Taoism" – *Tao-chiao.* "Taoism" was thus not – as has often been wrongly claimed – a development among those in China who rejected Confucianism. The facts of history generally show that Taoists actually had *no problem at all* with Confucians or their values. In fact, Taoists and Confucians were generally partners and allies, up to the time of the Mongol conquest. Even beyond that point, they continued to influence each other's ideas and practices, and in late imperial times many Confucians and Taoists were quite happy to acknowledge the value of both as elements of "the Three Teachings."

The only Confucians who ever really claimed to be resisting an antagonistic Taoist tradition were members of a very narrow community consisting of followers of the twelfth-century ideologue Chu Hsi (1130–1200).[18] Chu claimed to inherit a "transmission of the Way" (*tao-t'ung*) that originated with Confucius and Mencius then jumped over a millennium to the eleventh-century teacher Ch'eng I, then of course to Chu himself. The ideologues of the "Ch'eng/Chu school" essentially gained political control of the mechanisms for expression of ideas in late imperial China, and, from their hostility toward all other religious, intellectual, and cultural systems – including Confucians outside their own school – modern minds throughout the world gained the false impression that Taoism should be understood in relationship to Confucianism. The facts clearly show that Taoists never understood *themselves* on any such terms.

If there was anything that Taoists of imperial times really feared, it was not Confucianism, or even Buddhism. Rather, Taoists of several periods feared – often with good reason – that the rulers of their day could be misled into imagining that the activities of Taoists were somehow continuous with disreputable "cults." Thus conceived, "cults" (whatever their actual social or cultural dynamics) had little appeal to rulers or to aristocrats – a segment of society that increasingly included Taoists as well as Confucians. In fact, when the Taoists of the fifth century first tried to put together a collection of their sacred writings – a collection that could compete with that of the Buddhists both in scope and in diversity – they conceived that collection as consisting primarily, indeed perhaps exclusively, of those writings that interested *aristocrats* of that day. As first designed, the corpus of the *Tao-chiao* gave *no place* to such ancient works as the *Lao-tzu* and *Chuang-tzu*: those writings were *not*, at that time, writings that Taoists considered foundational for their tradition or important for defining their identity.

More tellingly, these Taoists' first corpus – their first great effort to tell the ruler and the people of China "this is who we are, and this is what we value" – specifically *excluded* writings by, and about, the "Heavenly Masters" of the late Han period – an organization that had long struggled to differentiate itself from the disreputable "cults" with which it was sometimes apparently confused. That exclusion is ironic, for some of the medieval aristocrats' traditions were in some ways tied back to the earlier "Heavenly Masters" movement, and some "Heavenly Masters" traditions were maintained, albeit in new forms, throughout medieval China, across all social levels. But the problem for the creators of the aristocratic *Tao-chiao* was that, by the time Buddhism had begun posing a threat to those of Taoist sensibilities, the "Heavenly Masters" movement – which had not originally emerged from the "upper classes" – had become marginalized, not in terms of the Chinese social order, but within "Taoism" itself: new "revelations" among fourth-century aristocrats – the Shang-ch'ing and Ling-pao revelations, in particular – now gave "respectability" to aristocrats who were trying to construct *a comprehensive non-Buddhist religious tradition* of their own. Among those "aristocratic Taoists" of the fifth century, the traditions and practices of the earlier "Heavenly Masters" appear to have been, at best, a profound embarrassment, certainly *not* something to be featured in any public exposition of "what we, as Taoists, do and value." Only a century later was the original three-section Taoist "canon" expanded with four "supplements," including one for "Heavenly Masters" materials, as well as other texts that interested the aristocratic target audience, such as the *Lao-tzu* and *Chuang-tzu*.[19]

Taoism *qua* Taoism thus developed within a specific historical setting, within a specific social setting, for specific and easily explainable reasons. Once such realities are understood, it is quite easy to see the silliness of many of the inherited misconceptions in modern minds about "what Taoism is." For instance, most modern minds inevitably link "the origins of Taoism" with the "person" who was long believed to have produced the *Lao-tzu*. We shall see that there is no sense in which such beliefs have any historical validity, though the ideas and images in the *Lao-tzu* were certainly appropriated by many later Taoists, and the figure of "Lao-tzu" – a creation of early Han historians, as I shall show – was appropriated for its legitimatory value by emperors of many periods, and by some Taoists as well.

We shall also see that modern minds are quite mistaken when they imagine that "early Taoism" consisted of a "school of thought" – to be understood in terms of a set of ideas found (or imagined to be found) in the *Lao-tzu* and the *Chuang-tzu* – an unrelated text of quite dissimilar provenance. I shall lay out what we can now say about those texts on the basis of actual fact, and about the historical context from which they sprang. It will quickly become apparent that back in "classical times" – before "the first Ch'in emperor" unified "the middle kingdoms" and all neighboring states in 221 BCE – there was actually no "school of Taoism" on any intellectual terms, and certainly *no group of people* who considered themselves "Taoists" or wished to be understood as "Taoists" by others. That is not to say that there were no people in that age whose understanding of life, and whose way of living life, can now be seen to have been, in certain important ways, *continuous* with those of the Taoists of imperial China. But scholars have still only begun to sort through some of those continuities. And until they give full respect to the many varieties of "Taoism" that came and went over the course of later centuries, they will remain unable to say much about the continuities and discontinuities among the various phases and segments of the tradition.

2

THE CLASSICAL LEGACY

Taoism and "the hundred schools"

To understand the earliest threads of what would later become Taoism requires an accurate assessment of certain kinds of data pertaining to "classical times" – the period that ended when Ch'in shih huang-ti extinguished the nation of Ch'u and began homogenizing the cultures and institutions of earlier days. Such an accurate assessment requires undoing centuries of reifications of supposed "schools of thought" – most of which sprang from the imagination of post-Ch'in minds – and even of some supposed "thinkers," including the fictitious "Lao-tzu" and the doubtful "Chuang-tzu." As the millennium opens, it remains unclear just what the pertinent data may be, and how they should be understood. But we can certainly dispel some of the most serious misconceptions.

Anyone who has read even the most cursory presentation of Chinese civilization has learned about "the hundred schools" (*pai-chia*), which were – supposedly – important cultural and intellectual forces in "classical China." In the twenty-first century, we now know enough to be able to show – without fear of contradication – that no such "schools" ever existed. Even "Confucianism" is an umbrella label used to cover certain historical people and teachings that were – when carefully analyzed – quite distinguishable from each other, and not always fully distinguishable from other historical people and teachings that have never heretofore been considered "Confucian." One case in point, to which we shall often have occasion to refer, is the fact that the idea that a person should literally "cultivate" an invisible life-force called *ch'i* ("vital energy") – a prominent element of several important strands of Taoism, from classical times to the present – is very prominent in the teaching of the "Confucian" thinker Mencius. Yet, twentieth-century minds were taught that no such ideals or practices were ever embraced by "Confucians." And those minds were taught that "the Confucians" and "the Taoists" were two actual *groups* of people, whose beliefs and values were quintessentially antithetical to each other. In those ways, also, they were taught falsely.

Such categories as "Confucian" and "Taoist" originated not in the lives, or even in the minds, of any of the real people who lived, wrote, or taught disciples back in the days before Ch'in. Rather, those categories originated after the Ch'in dynasty had been replaced by the rulers of the Han dynasty (206 BCE–CE 221). Apparently the various Han taxonomists – which included the composer of the final chapter in our current *Chuang-tzu* (chapter 33) – made up their categories the way that a person today might sit down and invent the contents of a category such as "the smartest politicians of the twentieth century," or "the best football players alive today." Such "groups" have no social, political, economic, or historical reality. Readers of the closing chapter of today's *Chuang-tzu* – now believed to date from the second century BCE – will generally not even recognize its groupings of bygone thinkers, its characterizations of their ideas, or its assessment of their value. That is because its composer had perspectives about bygone thinkers that differed from those which guided the characterizations and groupings concocted by men such as Ssu-ma T'an or Liu Hsiang – the historians and librarians at the Han court whose categorizations were accepted as "standard" by most, though not all, later governments. Yet, in actual social or historical terms, both of those groupings were merely the result of decisions by the writer himself, grouping past thinkers into this "school" or that "way" based on his own personal tastes and inclinations. If we are to understand the actual teachings found in our surviving texts from ancient China, it is imperative that we unlearn "the schools" of "classical thought" that remained standard in virtually all twentieth-century presentations.

"Classical Taoism" never existed, *either* as a social entity *or* as a set of coherent ideas or values. Even well-known texts – such as the *Tao te ching* – can be imagined to have "coherence" only if one does violence to the facts of what is written within them. And all such texts have come down to us in forms that took shape only in Han times, or, in the case of the *Chuang-tzu*, the third or fourth century CE. So an accurate reconstruction of "classical Taoist ideas" is simply not possible, for there was never really any such thing.

That having been said, there are now some data that help us identify and dispel certain specific misconceptions. Perhaps the most important is that many of the most famous "classical Taoist ideas" – such as "wu-wei" – were actually epiphenomenal, not "basic Taoist ideas." In fact, there were never any coherent *ideas* that were actually shared by those in classical times whose contributions were embraced and preserved by later Taoists. What later Taoists inherited from "classical" times was actually an *assortment* of *cherished behaviors and practices*, and a richly varied *matrix of interpretive frameworks* within which to think about those practices.

Some Taoist interpretive frameworks were stimulated by elements of the values and practices of other traditions that were also evolving across the Chinese landscape:

1 the Mohist organization;
2 several divergent Confucian schools ("schools" in an actual social sense);
3 several "Legalist" theorists, who were part of no school or organization at all; and
4 the murky groups who produced the ideas of *yin* and *yang* and the "Five Forces" (*wu-hsing*).

All of those traditions originated quite independently from anything that has ever been commonly regarded as "Taoist," e.g., "Lao-tzu" and "Chuang-tzu." And yet, over the course of time, all of those currents would eventually mingle their waters, in ways that scholars have not yet fully sorted out. Nonetheless, the continuities and discontinuities among the ideals and values found in all those traditions are important for understanding the roots of "Taoism."

"Mohism" and its relation to Taoism

"Mohism" was the only classical Chinese value-system that was ever embodied in a cohesive social organization. Its reputed founder was an otherwise historically unknown figure named Mo Ti (Mo Di, *ca.* 470–400 BCE; later known as Mo-tzu/Mozi, which was also the title of the collection of writings and sayings attributed to him).[1] Mo, like K'ung Ch'iu, was apparently from the northern state of Lu, part of the Chou confederacy. But, unlike K'ung, Mo despised the Chou aristocracy. Perhaps because his own social background was plebian, he rejected Confucius' assumption that the ills of the age could be reversed by restoring the social virtues that Confucius believed the nobility ideally possessed.

It can also be said that most of the contributors to "classical Taoist texts" saw no inherent "nobility" in the Chou aristocracy. But whereas they looked *beyond* human society, Mo-tzu felt compelled to correct society's ills by training his followers to become missionary activists, who would work to recruit a communal society dedicated to carrying out Mo's socio-cultural goals, by suasion if possible, by armed action if necessary. In one sense, Mo was an idealist: like Confucius – and, indeed, contributors to later layers of the *Tao te ching* – he believed that society should be led by the wise and the virtuous. But his definitions of wisdom and virtue revealed a much more practical mentality, and an intense dedication to achieving a dynamic society in which people worked to save each other from harm and deprivation.

Mo understood virtue purely in terms of *doing good*, not in terms of *being good*: the Mohist's goal was simply to stimulate the desired social activity. Such goals, and methods, contrast sharply with those of other value-systems of classical times. The Confucians also sought a well-ordered society, but insisted that such a society would result only from the individual's dedication to moral self-cultivation, which Confucians (except for Hsün-tzu) understood as an elevation of the human spirit. But for the Mohists, the ultimate goal was merely to ensure that all people are sheltered, well fed and unharmed. Mo-tzu may have hailed his ideal as "impartial solicitude" (*chien-ai*, usually mistranslated as "universal love"). But his ideal world was not one in which people felt any real affection for each other or tried to provide each other with emotional support. The prima facie egalitarianism that moderns have often imagined to lie within Mo's teachings is belied both by his endorsement of an inexorable socio-political hierarchy, and by the authoritarian structure of his own communal organization. Within that organization, members were expected to abandon their homes and families, forswear all other personal attachments, and renounce all political allegiances. Moreover, all were expected to submit to their leader's directives with unswerving obedience.

Modern interpreters congenial to "religion" often misidentified Mo-tzu as a significant "religious teacher." In reality, history offers up few examples of a thinker whose attitude toward religion was more cynical. The Mohist "missionaries" were exhorted to employ theological arguments simply to manipulate people's behavior. The individual was never to reflect independently upon right and wrong, or upon Heaven and its relationship to humanity: it was axiomatic that Heaven's will could never be other than what Mo himself taught. Mo's "Heaven" was not a caring or forgiving God, nor one who "loved" people in the sense that it wished them to be happy or spiritually ennobled: it played only the role of disciplinarian, analogous more to a police officer than to a loving parent who facilitates a child's growth toward responsible independence – an unthinkable goal in light of Mo's misanthropic assessment of human nature. Nor could people attain any real communion with Mo's "Heaven" through meditation, or prayer, or ritual activity, or any elevation of the human soul.

To most in the "Middle Kingdoms," the Mohist view of life seemed sterile and uninspiring, for Mo envisioned a world in which life ultimately has little meaning beyond physical survival. That fact, coupled with Mohism's ideological rigidity and disregard for what some called "natural human feelings," led to the extinction of the Mohist movement by the end of the classical period.

Still, Mohist influence was significant. "Legalists" inherited the Mohists' authoritarian principles. The Confucians – especially Mencius – gained definition and intensity from reacting *against* Mohist ideals. And Mo's work influenced Taoism in several ways. On a broad level, the Mohists' universalistic social vision may have helped inspire similar tendencies in Taoism – from the inclusive teachings of the *T'ai-p'ing ching*, through the universalistic soteriology of the Ling-pao revelations, to the comprehensive universal order envisioned by such later rulers as Sung T'ai-tsung, and on to the altruistic ideals of later Taoist traditions. All of those elements will be discussed more fully below.

And, though such matters have not yet been researched, the

hierarchical structure of Mo's communal organization may have been one forerunner of the earliest "Taoist" religious movement – the T'ien-shih movement of the second century. The vehicle of transmission from pre-Han Mohism to the late Han "Heavenly Masters" may well have been the Han-dynasty collection called the *T'ai-p'ing ching*. As one specialist has said, "In it we read, just as in the *Hsün-tzu* and in the *Ch'un-ch'iu fan lu* [attributed to the early Han Confucian theorist Tung Chung-shu], that in order to have *t'ai-p'ing* [Great Peace] each creature should be in his place and the rulers should keep in accord with the will of Heaven (*t'ien-hsin*)."[2] Yet, to the end of the twentieth century, scholars well versed in the "classical texts" hardly ever read the *T'ai-p'ing ching*. So while a few could bring themselves to speak of the *T'ai-p'ing ching* as showing "naive echoes" of Mohist values, the philological and historical research necessary to determine the actual connections has yet to be conducted.

Even more shocking to traditional sinological sensibilities is the fact that later Taoists decided to accept the *Mo-tzu* as one of their "canonical" scriptures, and to accept Mo Ti himself as one of the earliest practitioners of "alchemy." The text of the *Mo-tzu* itself was actually included in the *Tao-tsang* (HY 1168). And even more unexpectedly, the Shang-ch'ing "Perfected Ones" who revealed the *Chen-kao* ("Declarations of the Perfected"; HY 1010) vouchsafed that Mo Ti was among those "who declared their end was nigh when they had taken the Gold Elixir (*chin-tan*)."[3] And in the closely related *Hou-sheng chi* ("Annals of the Sage Who is to Come"; HY 442) – also sent down by the Shang-ch'ing "Perfected Ones" – Mo Ti is listed along with Chang Tao-ling and others as one of the "seven perfected and eight elders" of whom the sage promises, "I shall delegate certain ones to descend and give instruction to those who are so destined and who devoutly maintain their zealous study to achieve immortality."[4]

Naturally, it seems odd to modern readers to think of the starkly utilitarian writer Mo Ti as a heavenly being who descends to earth to save deserving "Taoists," much less as an imbiber of "the Golden Elixir." But other, equally unpromising figures would eventually find their way into the ranks of "the immortals," such as the imperial librarian Ho Chih-chang.[5] Naturally, what is at work on one level is that Taoists eventually placed a *retroactive claim* on all the great names of bygone days, just as Mo-tzu, and the Confucians, had retroactively claimed various legendary "sage-kings" as proponents of their own values. Yet, more research must be done to understand why the *Mo-tzu* was included in the *Tao-tsang*.

"Legalism" and its relation to Taoism

If, on the basis of the taxonomies of traditional sinology, it seems odd to find the *Mo-tzu* preserved among the "sacred writ" of later Taoists, it might seem even odder that the *Tao-tsang* also contains the writings of the most infamous thinker of the "Legalist school" – the *Han-fei-tzu* (HY 1169), by Han Fei (d. 233 BCE). Is its inclusion by Taoists as a Taoist text to be explained only by the fact that the T'ien-shih movement's "prohibition of 'excessive cults'" was prefigured by Han Fei's denunciation of ritual abuses?[6] Or is it owing to the fact that the *Huai-nan-tzu* (HY 1176) – perhaps not coincidentally catalogued very near the *Han-fei-tzu* – quotes approvingly not only from the writings of Han Fei himself, but also from those of "Legalists" such as the official Shen Pu-hai (d. 337 BCE), and even from "The Book of Lord Shang" composed by the Ch'in official Shang Yang ("Lord Shang"; d. 338 BCE)?[7]

What all those writings shared was a concern with statecraft and a disinterest in Chou ideals. Unlike Shang Yang, however, Shen Pu-hai was concerned not with state control of its subjects, or even with "law," but rather with internal operations of the state. He worked out new organizational methods and procedures (*fa*) for enhancing effective statecraft.[8] Also, however, Shen Pu-hai employed certain terms more familiar to most people from "classical Taoist" texts, including both *tao* and *wu-wei*. Shen used *tao* as a general term for "methods" of procedure, and *wu-wei* as an exhortation that the ruler should keep his hands off the workings of the government. The fact that those terms would eventually be elevated to "key ideas" by the redactors of the *Tao te ching* shows that the latter hoped to appeal to those who knew Shen's teachings, i.e., to those in government service.

Meanwhile, the thought of the final "Legalist" thinker, Han Fei, is pertinent because his argument for the cosmological transcendence of the ruler was adapted from ideas that have traditionally been labelled "Taoist." Han did not, of course, imagine himself to be "borrowing" from another "school," or even to be "blending" or "syncretizing" alien idea-sets. Many other texts from late classical and early Han times – some discovered only toward the end of the twentieth century – also show a cosmological conceptualization of government, in terms that sometimes resonate with those of texts commonly classified as "Taoist" or "Legalist."[9]

Han Fei is also noteworthy here for another reason. Two chapters of his text explicate sections of the *Tao te ching*: chapter 20, *Chieh-Lao* ("Explaining Lao"), and chapter 21, *Yü-Lao* ("Illustrating Lao"). Notably, those chapters provide the first true historical reference to the text of the *Lao-tzu*. But it is also highly significant that both of them – just like the Kuo-tien (Guodian) bamboo slips discovered in the 1990s – lack any reference to any passage found in sections 68–81 of our received text of the *Tao te ching*. That fact demonstrates that, by about 240 BCE, something corresponding very closely to the Kuo-tien "Lao-tzu" – *rather* than to the received edition, or to either of the Ma-wang-tui silk texts – was circulating among at least some of the intellectuals working in government in the northern land of Han, and possibly in some of the other "middle kingdoms."

The shorter *Yü-Lao* chapter appears to have little additional relevance for understanding "Taoist origins."[10] The *Chieh-Lao* is quite another matter. Though both writings are framed as commentaries on *Lao-tzu*, they are utterly different from each other in form as well as in content. Nowhere in the *Chieh-Lao* does one find Legalist positions at all. Moreover, though the *Chieh-Lao* deals mostly with ethical issues, it also contains passages on the biospiritual practices that the *Nei-yeh* recommends. For instance, it says, "Therefore the Sage saves his essence (*ching*) and spirit (*shen*), and esteems resting in quietness," and, "If the Sage treasures his spirit (*shen*), then his essence (*ching*) will flourish." Elsewhere it says, "He who is moderate (*se*) saves his essence and spirit, and safeguards (*se*) his wisdom and knowledge. Hence it is said (in *Tao te ching* 59), 'In ruling the people and serving Heaven, there is nothing like moderation.'"[11] An even closer parallel to the *Nei-yeh*'s teachings appears in the following passage:

> One who knows how to obey Heaven keeps his sense-organs empty. If one thinks and ponders in repose, one's old

> "virtue" (*te*) will not leave. If one keeps one's sense-organs empty, a harmonious vital-energy (*ho-ch'i*) will come in every day. . . . Indeed, one who can make the old "virtue" not leave and the harmonious vital-energy come in every day is a person who returns early. Hence the saying (in *Tao te ching* 59), "to return early may be called 'accumulating abundant virtue'."[12]

Moreover, at certain points, the composer of the *Chieh-Lao* shows a keen appreciation of Confucian values, and he never attacks them, as do passages of the *Chuang-tzu* and the "full-text" version of *Lao-tzu*. All these facts demonstrate not only that the *Chieh-Lao* is closely linked to the *Nei-yeh*, but also that it is more in harmony with elements of the earlier Guodian *Lao-tzu* than with the later "full-text" editions. The full significance of these facts for our understanding of "Taoist origins" remains to be determined.

Peering into the unseen to discern the subtle structures and currents of the world: the I ching, yin *and* yang, *and the "five forces"*

Another possible source for some of the ideas and values which we now consider elements of "Taoism" held no favor among twentieth-century sinologues. That is that there were people in pre-Ch'in China whose understanding of life was tied to their ability to peer into the unseen. Their job was to explain, on a professional basis, life's unfolding events on the basis of the patterns and processes that they perceived underlying and informing those events. Such people were active in the "middle kingdoms" long before any of the Confucians, Mohists, or Legalists. They were the official diviners, who had served both kings and feudatories since the early days of Chou rule and were heirs to an office that had been central to the imperium of the preceding Shang kingdom, more than three and a half millennia ago. Their legacy to later ages was the *I ching* (*Book of Change*).[13]

One of the *I ching*'s early commentaries, the *Shuo-kua*, states that the *I ching* was devised long ago by ancient sages: those exceptional people observed the processes operating in the world and discovered underlying principles by which one can understand why certain activities lead to success and others lead to failure. According to that explanation, those principles are unvarying, because they are inherent within the nature of things; meanwhile, everything else in the world changes constantly. Whoever originally composed it, the *I ching* was essentially a textual oracle: it allowed people to peer into the processes that operate in the ever-changing world, and to determine how to bring our activities into alignment with those processes. Such concerns would remain vital for all later Taoists – from *Lao-tzu* to living liturgists – and were never of prime concern for non-Taoists.

According to some traditional Chinese interpretations, the *I ching* was a prime inspiration for "Taoism." According to twentieth-century sinologists, Taoism never owed anything significant to ancient diviners' perspectives or methods. To them, it originated either among misfits who dissented from Confucian values, or from "shamans" – supposedly plebians with no education, no social status, and no system of thought or moral values. In other words, those "shamans" are imagined to have been no more than "witch doctors" – "ritualists" who indulged the superstitious masses and had no part in the so-called great tradition that Confucians supposedly upheld. But the court diviners of pre-Ch'in times – the people whose understanding of life was handed down in the *I ching* – have never been considered "shamans." Diviners were skilled technicians working at the highest level of the socio-political order. They did not dance; they did not heal; they did not do what they did on behalf of "the masses." The idea that members of "the upper classes" – respected then, respectable now – could have been instrumental in the creation of a value-system that was other than Confucian remained unthinkable for most of the twentieth century.[14] But the diviners' legacy – the *I ching* – was clearly a foundation on which elements of the Taoist worldview would perennially evolve.

It should come as little surprise that the *I ching* itself has been preserved within the *Tao-tsang*, along with numerous commentaries by Taoists, and non-Taoists, over the centuries.[15] More importantly, however, the *I ching*'s underlying principle – that, to navigate the world of the seen, the discerning person draws upon the ancient sages' understanding of the unseen – became a fundamental building block for the compiler of the germinal text of "cosmological alchemy," the *Chou-i Ts'an-t'ung ch'i*, and eventually an integral element of the thought-system called "Inner Alchemy" – the core of late imperial Taoism. *I ching* symbology provided useful tools for Taoists, as well as non-Taoists, who wished to explain life's subtle forces and unseen processes. But even the Guodian *Tao te ching* – one of the very earliest texts of "classical Taoism" – was already teaching men of political standing that they should seek to perceive, and follow, subtle patterns and processes – an "unseen order" that connects the future with the past and the present, and allows a perceptive and humble person to engage in a process that would lead inevitably to success by drawing on lessons learned by wise and foolish people of past and present.

Elsewhere, perhaps in the far northeast, other minds were evolving another explanatory system, which the Han taxonomists would later label "the *yin–yang* school."[16] Often, the concepts of *yin* and *yang* are said to be fundamental to "the Chinese view of the world," or to have constituted a basic element of "Taoism." Both those views are highly inaccurate. The concepts of *yin* and *yang* actually evolved within a distinct tradition. No one knows any historical details about the people who first formulated such ideas: we know no names of any ancient teachers of *yin* and *yang*, nor do we have any ancient texts that set forth their ideas. It is conceivable that such ideas developed among students of the *I ching*, but such would be merely a conjecture. All that we know is that all those ideas emerged independently of any of the individuals or communities that produced the "classical Taoist" texts, and that they had little real influence on those texts.

At some point, the "*yin–yang* school" blended with proponents of another set of ideas, which interpreted life's processes in terms of five distinct aspects of reality, rather than two. Those aspects of reality were called the "five forces" *(wu hsing)*.[17] That explanatory system was traditionally associated with the name of a thinker named Tsou Yen, but his writings were lost in ancient times, and there is no way to form a reliable judgment about his thought. The "school" itself – if there ever really was such a thing – had died out by Ch'in times, but its ideas endured, and became very influential during the Han period.[18]

During the first century of the Han, the thinkers who contributed to the "classical Taoist" work called the *Huai-nan-tzu* began to integrate such ideas into the Taoist worldview – just as Tung Chung-shu (*ca.* 195–115 BCE) and later Han Confucians integrated *yin–yang* thought, and later "five forces" thought, into the Confucian worldview. But the Taoist traditions of "cosmological alchemy" found in texts such as the *Chou-i Ts'an-t'ung ch'i* often focused more on the even-numbered ideas found in the *I ching* and its "wings," or with odd-numbered ideas *other* than the "five forces." And, in any event, those who defined and participated in the Taoist tradition were generally less interested in identifying numerable aspects of the cosmos than with the *practices*, and developmental *processes*, by which a person may *elevate* or *perfect* himself. Hence, as we shall see, models such as the "ninefold-refined elixir" – common to Ming thinkers like Lin Chao-en (1517–1598) and to "Inner Alchemy" texts such as the *Hsing-ming kuei-chih* ["Balanced Instructions about Inner Nature and Life-Realities"] – were simply a "shorthand" for a nine-step process by which a practitioner refines his/her mind/heart (*hsin*), thereby returning to the primordial purity of "the Tao mind/heart" (*tao-hsin*).

"Confucianism" and its relation to Taoism

The realities involved in the creation and perpetuation of the various cultural constructs that go by the name of "Confucianism" cannot be fully addressed here.[19] Setting aside common oversimplifications, we can say that "Confucianism" is a useful label for a series of loosely interrelated cultural systems, of which some, but not all, were eventually exported to neighboring lands. One of them – two millennia old and still living – is a *liturgical* tradition in which Confucius is venerated as a divine being. At temples at Ch'ü-fu, and throughout China and the Chinese diaspora, priests pray and sing hymns to that divine being, who "existed before the sun and the moon." Of course, the Confucian intellectuals of the nineteenth and twentieth centuries were aware that Western intellectuals of that period would have no truck with such practices, so they taught Westerners that "Confucianism" was really just a humanistic value-system based upon the teachings of K'ung Ch'iu (Kong Qiu, 551–479 BCE), later known by some in China as K'ung-tzu (Kongzi). Thus stripped of its religious elements – priests, temples, prayers, hymns, and all other revoltingly "Catholic" phenomena – the sanitized construct of "Confucianism" offered to post-Enlightenment

Westerners (and back to all later twentieth-century Chinese) was, as Max Weber assured us, not "a religion" at all, but merely a set of ethical and political teachings.

It is quite valid to identify many elements of Confucianism as "humanistic." But Confucian ideals were originally grounded in a belief that a man can fulfill the role of "the gentleman" (*chün-tzu*) and aid in restoring society's proper order by fulfilling the designs of *T'ien*. Since Westerners – and the Confucians who sought their approval – were threatened by the fact that Confucius and his followers based their prime values upon a belief in "God" – clearly the optimal translation of the term – the orthodox translation of *T'ien* became "Heaven," and to translate it otherwise remains sinological heresy even today. It is also sinological heresy to refute the Confucian denial that, for many hundreds of years, Confucian self-cultivation also included meditational practices that were in no important way different from those of the Ch'an (Zen) Buddhists from whom they had been learned.[20]

When we set aside, to the best of our ability, all such biased perspectives about "Confucianism," what can we say about its relationship to the origins of Taoism?

First, we can, indeed must, dismiss the simplistic trope that "Taoism arose as a reaction against Confucianism." In reality, the contributors to the texts of "classical Taoism" shared *much* with their Confucian contemporaries. All of them, even those who produced the *Nei-yeh*, insisted that it is not only possible, but indeed morally necessary, for individuals to *develop or transform themselves* in ways that most people do not, thereby enhancing both their own well-being *and* the well-being of others around them. In addition, both Confucians and "Taoists" took for granted that the world should have a human ruler, and that he should rule by, and promote, the proper ideals. Chuang Chou may have considered government irrelevant, but he did not demand its abolition. Where Confucians and "Taoists" parted ways is that the former viewed the world primarily in terms of inherited socio-political principles, while the latter looked more to people's continuities with invisible dimensions of reality with which most Confucians concerned themselves less directly.

Twentieth-century interpreters often mistakenly claimed that such differences simply resulted from a Taoist concern with something called "Tao," which Confucians did not recognize or value. But, in actuality, Confucius taught his followers to follow the correct and noble *tao*. And he also advocated that rulers should practice *wu-wei*, just like the *Tao te ching* and such "Legalists" as Shen Pu-hai.

What most distinguished "classical Taoists" from others in early China was their interest in non-personalized spiritual realities, and in the transformative power of the person who has properly cultivated them. The Confucians' primary goal was to transform society by cultivating moral virtues and persuading rulers to do likewise. "Classical Taoists" were more focused on biospiritual cultivation, and sometimes suggested that such cultivation would transform the world. The newly discovered Guodian manuscripts of the *Tao te ching* have little further socio-political program. The fact that they lack the received text's condemnation of Confucian ideas demonstrates the error of the notion that Taoism arose as a reaction against Confucianism.

What the *Tao te ching* and *Chuang-tzu* share is not disinterest in society or the political order per se, but doubt that collective individual/societal effort, without reference to life's deeper realities, can effect desirable change.[21] It was not that the producers of such texts distrusted "human nature," as Mo-tzu and Hsün-tzu did. Rather, they insisted that we should rely upon *natural* realities, the subtle salutary forces that humans did not create and cannot control. Thus, the *Nei-yeh* advocated the cultivation of *ch'i* ("life-energy"), *ching* ("vital essence"), and *shen* ("spirit"); the *Chuang-tzu* advocated reverting to a "heavenly mechanism" (*t'ien-chi*) that is independent of psycho-cultural constructs; and the *Tao te ching* advocated abandonment of self-concern and a return to the motherly force that is the life-matrix of all things. All three suggest that a properly cultivated person can exert a subtle transformative power, acting as a conduit for the natural salutary forces that should guide and empower peoples' lives.[22]

The "useless words" of Chuang Chou

According to modern understandings of Chinese tradition, the text known as the *Chuang-tzu* was the production of a "Taoist" thinker of ancient China named Chuang Chou. In reality, it was nothing of the sort. The *Chuang-tzu* known to us today was the production of a thinker of the third century CE named Kuo Hsiang. Though Kuo was long called merely a "commentator," he was in reality much more: he was the actual *creator* of the 33-chapter text of *Chuang-tzu*, which all readers since Kuo's day – Chinese and non-Chinese – have read. Every analysis of what appears in the text of *Chuang-tzu* is really an analysis of Kuo's work.

Regarding the identity of the original person named Chuang, there is no reliable historical data at all. At the end of the twentieth century, virtually all scholars continued to accept the idea that there was a "historical" Chuang, who lived at about the same time as Mencius. Whether scholars at the end of this century will still accept that notion is quite another thing. The primary "historical data" on which all scholars – modern and premodern, Chinese and non-Chinese – based their attempts to identify "the historical Chuang-tzu" are *all* quite suspect. There are, of course, stories *inside* our text of the *Chuang-tzu* in which a character named "Chuang Chou" appears. Some scholars still mistake those stories for autobiographical confessions – reliable reports from the hand of "the man himself." In reality, however, there is no good reason to put any faith at all in the historical authenticity of any of those stories, any more than one can trust them as authentic records of the words of Confucius or "Lao-tzu." There is simply no way to know who first penned any of those stories. There is no evidence that any of them actually reflects any historical reality. And it is quite conceivable – indeed, altogether likely – that *every* such story was quite simply a work of creative fiction.

Regarding external data for "the historical Chuang," there is virtually none, and none that is demonstrably reliable. *No* historical evidence regarding *any* such person is found in any record of a historical nature before the *Shih chi* of Ssu-ma Ch'ien. And what Ssu-ma provides as "biographical data" regarding "Chuang" is even sparser that what he gives regarding "Lao," and just as dubious.[23] Moreover, nowhere in the text of the *Chuang-tzu* itself do we find the narrator – who is often quite casual and intimate in his "confessions" – mentioning any datum that can be connected in *any* way to *anything* in Ssu-ma's little report. It follows that, if one accepts Ssu-ma's identification of "Chuang Chou," one does so simply on the basis of blind faith.

By the end of the twentieth century, Chinese scholars such as Liu Xiaogan and Western scholars such as Angus Graham had identified different strands or layers within the *Chuang-tzu*, though their ideas about such strands were somewhat different.[24] It is true that scholarly analysis of such products can result in conclusions that are more accurate than traditional ideas, just as scholarly analysis of Confucian *Analects* or the Christian gospel materials have done. But even the results of such analysis can provide only a "better" or "more likely" perspective on what Jesus, or Chuang Chou, may truly have said. And, at best, such analysis leaves us with a partial and imprecise notion of what the person in question may have wished others to believe, much less what he himself may have believed. Can we ultimately determine the true contents of the mind of the historical Jesus, K'ung Ch'iu, or Chuang Chou? Certainly not, and today's readers should be cautious about any representations of such men's ideas, for all such representations rest on certain assumptions, which may or may not be correct, and are frequently disputed by other scholars.

With those facts in mind, what should people today think about the teachings and values that have traditionally been seen in the 33-chapter text known as *Chuang-tzu*? Regarding the text itself, a sound conclusion by a critical scholar of today may well be that it is, as Ssu-ma Ch'ien said long ago, a sparkling work of free-flowing prose that effectively ridicules some of the ideas of other thinkers and some of the values of other "schools" of the day. It is intriguing that the final chapter of our modern text of *Chuang-tzu* – "The World" (*T'ien-hsia*) – consists mostly of characterizations of various "thinkers," including "Chuang Chou" himself. In terms nearly identical to some of what Ssu-ma says, the unknown author of *T'ien-hsia* says that Chuang's "writings are a string of queer beads and baubles," full of "brash and bombastic language [and] unbound and unbordered phrases."[25] But, unlike Ssu-ma, the *T'ien-hsia* author makes no suggestion that Chuang wrote what he wrote "in order to satirize the followers of Confucius and illumine the positions of "Lao-tzu." Indeed, Ssu-ma's contention to that effect is clearly false, if we accept Graham's conclusions about the various strands and layers of the text. If his analyses are correct – and most of them are fairly plausible – then in the earliest layer of the *Chuang-tzu* we find little that can reasonably be interpreted as being based upon anything found in our *Tao te ching*. And, indeed, current scholarly dating of the *Tao te ching* would make it something that "Chuang Chou" could never have seen if he indeed passed away before the end of the fourth century BCE.

In addition, the contents of the *Chuang-tzu* are in certain key ways *utterly* at odds with the contents of both the *Nei-yeh* and the *Tao te ching*. Unlike those works, the *Chuang-tzu* gives no instructions for engaging in biospiritual practices. (Indeed, if there is an incisive thinker from the period of King Hui of Liang and King Hsüan of Ch'i who *does* show some evidence of having learned something from such traditions, it is not the composer of the *Chuang-tzu*, but rather the Confucian thinker Mencius!) Many other common themes and interests found in our modern *Tao te ching* are also quite alien to the *Chuang-tzu*. For instance, the *Chuang-tzu* does not teach that the reader should "not do and nothing will be undone" – a theme oft repeated in the *Tao te ching*. Also, it does not urge us to believe in, and trust our lives to, a beneficent guiding force inherent to life, and it nowhere suggests any "motherly" principle at work in the world. It likewise shows no trace of the *Tao te ching*'s frequent suggestions that one should practice "feminine" behaviors, both to secure one's own benefit and to allow the world to be as it should. Nor does the *Chuang-tzu* in any way agree with a primary thesis of the *Tao te ching*: that the world will be rectified if the ruler will only practice self-restraint, engage in "feminine" behaviors, and draw upon unseen spiritual forces by means of biospiritual cultivation. If, therefore, "Chuang Chou" was, as Ssu-ma Ch'ien claimed, writing in order to "illumine" what we find in the writings attributed to "Lao-tzu," then he did an abysmally poor job of it! Since, as Ssu-ma himself agrees, "Chuang Chou" was brilliant and adept at exposition, it follows that the person who wrote what we find in the *Chuang-tzu* was certainly *not* trying to explain or build upon anything that we find in the *Tao te ching*.

So if we simply explain the teachings of the *Chuang-tzu* in terms of what we read in the *Chuang-tzu* itself – and *not* as an expression of a supposed "school of thought" that artificially, and illogically, conflates "Lao" and "Chuang" into one big fuzzy thing – then the *Chuang-tzu* can be seen as a repository of a specific range of ideas and interests, which do not even overlap in most ways with the specific range of ideas and interests that we see in the *Tao te ching*.

Does that mean that these "queer beads and baubles" have no coherent message? Not at all. In fact, when we set aside the false notion that we ought to read the *Chuang-tzu* in *terms of* other texts such as the *Tao te ching*, the thrust of the *Chuang-tzu* as we actually have it is not hard to apprehend. To wit, the world in which we truly live is in fact quite distinguishable from the world in which everyone agrees that we live. The latter – when carefully examined – can easily be shown to consist of what modern/postmodern minds would call "cultural constructs." There is no clear way to determine whether any such construct truly does, or does not, correspond to the characteristics of life itself. Hence, the reader should "steer by the torch of doubt," rather than assume that one can rely upon rational thought to lead one safely to a sound conclusion and a happy life. If one attempts to live one's life according to one's socially derived "common sense," or upon some notion derived from logical analysis, one will often find that what one actually experiences is a surprise. Life is never fully predictable, and if we simply enjoy the surprises that occur, and adjust our lives to what shows up, then our life can be pleasant to the day that we leave it. Of course, living on such terms means that one cannot fit one's life into any plan or pattern, and in that sense one who is living sensibly becomes "useless." Nonetheless, such "uselessness" is not in itself a bad thing: it is only "bad" in the view of those who assume that a wise person reasons himself to truth, or makes the world a better place by means of concerted social or political actions. People who make such assumptions are not contemptible, merely laughable. The wiser alternative is to live one's life as "a real person" (*chen-jen*) – one who simply abides in the processes that are so of themselves (*tzu-jan*) rather than trying to manage and control life's events. Such a person is, in fact, in accord with a reality that is boundless and unending. Consequently, such a person cannot be understood by those who live their lives according to socially based constructs, and will thus be called wild or useless. Nonetheless, one should let go of one's typical human approaches to life, and live "in the boundless," without regard for what society and its clever people think or do.

However, the *Chuang-tzu* does *not* present those ideas as a program for *self-development*. It gives no specific directions as to how one might go about *attaining* the ideal state that it describes. And it does not suggest that experiencing a revolutionized perception of reality can *solve* any of "the thousand natural shocks that flesh is heir to."

The *Chuang-tzu* greatly appealed to alienated Westerners of the late twentieth century. Their culture had, in the first half of the century, been bereft of most of its certainties. Rationalism had become suspect; "society" had become – especially in the post-war era – "oppressive"; and "spontaneity" was, of course, always a lot easier and a lot more fun than sober efforts to be rational and responsible. Meanwhile, the *Chuang-tzu* has always appealed to Chinese readers, from Han times onwards, as a lively work of provocative literature. Yet, most of the Chinese people of the Han dynasty – and indeed, in all the dynasties that followed – did *not* live within a culture that had been bereft of all of its certainties. To such readers, rationalism had *not* become suspect, society had *not* become "oppressive," and life's most important experiences could *not* simply be reduced to "cultural constructs." Most – even those who found the *Chuang-tzu* a delightful read – continued to be beset by those "thousand natural shocks": their father would get ill or get angry; their mother would die unexpectedly; they would suddenly find themselves pregnant or needing to support someone who was pregnant; and the government would demand its tax payments. *Chuang-tzu* tells the reader "to live in the boundless," but not what to do when the rent is due, or when the children are hungry, or when the taxman comes. Is a hungry baby to be told to "steer by the torch of doubt" and to "be useless"? Is a baby who falls into a well to be left to fall to its death? Is a neighbor who is being attacked to be left to the mercy of her attacker?

To be sure, none of those are issues to the writers of the *Chuang-tzu*. To those writers, one should accept death with equanimity. Yet, all the text's passages to that effect present a scenario in which the death in question has *already occurred*: *never* do they tell a tale of how "the real person" responds to a death that has not yet occurred, but will soon happen unless one intervenes. To the writers of what we have as the *Chuang-tzu*, one does not really have to *solve* any such problems: we simply have to see life as it truly is, and allow life's grand pageant to unfold. And that is a beautiful ideal by which to live . . . though, if one has children who consequently die of neglect, family members will be aggrieved, neighbors will be outraged, and the authorities will indict one for homicide. For these reasons, the ethical implications of *Chuang-tzu* have been much debated, by centuries of Chinese critics, as well as by recent Westerners.[26]

For centuries of Chinese people, the *Chuang-tzu* can be said simply to have raised interest in going places to which it provided no help in getting them. It was like a travel brochure for a splendid beach resort, though the beach to which it inspired one to visit was one to which it gave no directions at all. If it is theoretically possible to find no road that can lead there, no ship that can sail there, and no plane that can fly there, then one must logically seek elsewhere than in such a travel brochure for a way to achieve such a goal.

For centuries of Taoists, it was *not* to the *Chuang-tzu* that they looked for a means to achieve the goals of the Taoist life. Many looked instead to other classical texts, texts that offered *practices* by which one might, at least theoretically, achieve the ideal characteristics of "the true person." Others, unable to believe that they could achieve such goals by reading what they found in ancient texts, soon found themselves receiving all kinds of *new* teachings about such matters in all kinds of new texts, and in the lives and deeds of living men and women of their own day and age. Over the ages, many such people – especially the most learned – continued to look back into the delightful text of the *Chuang-tzu* and to find there terms and images that helped them understand and express elements of what they could now see to be a viable and worthwhile spiritual life. And, in the fourth century CE, one group of such people suddenly found themselves receiving spontaneously produced new writings, writings channeled down to mortals from some of the "real people" (*chen-jen*) that Chuang Chou had urged his readers to become. In such ways, generations of China's Taoists found indirect ways to make use of ideas that, in the words of Ssu-ma Ch'ien, "great people could not make into useful things."

Cultivating life's subtle forces: the *Nei-yeh*

Through the end of the twentieth century, the *Chuang-tzu* and *Tao te ching* were universally renowned as the primary texts of "classical Taoism." Their continuities with later Taoist traditions formed the subject of debate. Only at the very end of the century did a few scholars begin to enrich that debate by consideration of another ancient text, about which few in the twentieth century – even among scholars of Chinese thought or religion, in Asia or in the West – knew very much at all. It is entitled the *Nei-yeh* ["Inner Cultivation"], and its continuities with later elements of Taoism are far more easily discerned than is the case with the *Chuang-tzu* or even the *Tao te ching*.

The *Nei-yeh* is an extremely brief text, of a mere 1,600 characters – i.e., about a third the length of the succinct *Tao te ching*.[27] Like the *Tao te ching*, it is written in verse, though its line lengths and rhyme patterns are irregular. There is no information regarding its compiler's identity, and, like the *Tao te ching*, it contains no references whatsoever to any specific person, place, or historical event. In other words, the *Tao te ching* actually has far more in common with the *Nei-yeh* than either has in common with the *Chuang-tzu*. And, in fact, there are reasons to believe that the *Nei-yeh* may have profoundly affected both the form and the contents of the *Tao te ching*, with which we today are so familiar.

The few scholars who have studied the *Nei-yeh* to date have presented different scenarios to explain how it came to be. Most have argued that it emerged from the northern land of Ch'i, specifically from the Chi-hsia academy established by its fourth-century rulers (discussed at more length in the following section). Others, meanwhile, have cited linguistic evidence that suggest that the *Nei-yeh*, like the *Tao te ching*, had roots in the southerly land of Ch'u.[28] Some scholars have combined the data and argued that the *Nei-yeh* was produced by people from Ch'u who had travelled north to Ch'i.[29] In either case, scholars generally agree that it came into being during the period 350–300 BCE. That is, it was presumably compiled by a contemporary of Chuang Chou, and apparently predates the *Tao te ching* as we know it.[30]

The *Nei-yeh* fell out of general circulation sometime before the middle of the second century BCE, when it was incorporated into a larger collection known as the *Kuan-tzu*.[31] When bibliographers of the Han period began sorting out the various texts and traditions of their past, they classified them into whatever categories they saw fit. There was *never*, for instance, consultation with "Taoist leaders" as to whether "*tao-chia*" was an appropriate category, or whether the materials allocated to that category were indeed correct, or whether pertinent materials were being misclassified. The contents of the *Kuan-tzu* were not reducible to any common category, such as

"Confucian" or "Taoist" or "Legalist."[32] So it was categorized as "eclectic" or "miscellaneous," along with collections such as the *Lü-shih ch'un-chiu* ["The 'Springs and Autumns' of Master Lü"] of *ca.* 240 BCE, which also contain a great deal of material related to what we find in the so-called Taoist classics.[33] Such "miscellaneous" works were essentially stigmatized as unimportant throughout later history. They were assigned the lowest possible value as "classical works," and were seldom plumbed by Chinese scholars or philosophers until the twentieth century. Even today their significance has barely begun to be explored.

Yet, the influence of some of the ideas found in such collections on Chinese thought was profound and extensive, though such facts have seldom hitherto been noticed. For example, it is in the *Lü-shih ch'un-chiu* that we find our first discussion of the relationship between a person's *hsing* ("inner nature") and his/her *ming* ("life-realities").[34] Those ideas remained key elements of *Taoist models of self-cultivation* down to the writings of Wang Che and the practices of later practitioners of Ch'üan-chen Taoism to the present day. *Hsing* and *ming* are also key elements of many Taoist models in the "Inner Alchemy" tradition, as seen for instance in the late imperial *Hsing-ming kuei-chih* ["Balanced Instructions about Inner Nature and Life-Realities"].

Other important elements of those very same Taoist models go back not to the *Lü-shih ch'un-chiu* but rather to sections of the *Kuan-tzu*, most notably to the *Nei-yeh*. It is in the *Nei-yeh*, for instance, that one first encounters comprehensible references to the personal cultivation of such forces as *ch'i* ("life-energy"), *ching* ("vital essence"), and *shen* ("spirit" or "spiritual consciousness"). The cultivation of those forces became common teachings in writings of the mid-third century BCE, from the *Lü-shih ch'un-ch'iu* to Han Fei's chapter *Chieh-Lao* ["Explaining 'Lao-tzu'"].[35] And they became central themes not only in later Taoist self-cultivation traditions, but also in the living traditions of "traditional Chinese medicine."[36]

Those who write and teach about "early Chinese thought" – following centuries of Confucian interpretations – have generally fetishized "canonical classics" such as the *Tao te ching*, and have never even read the *Nei-yeh* or the *Lü-shih ch'un-ch'iu*. Most of them have little idea that so many common themes of later Taoism have roots that can be seen only if we examine the contents of texts that the Han bibliographers decided not to list as "*tao-chia*." Overall, scholars around the world have yet to give any real attention to such continuities, or to explore their significance for our understanding of Taoism and its place in Chinese culture overall.[37]

Nor have scholars yet to give any real attention to the fact that the *Nei-yeh* may also have influenced *Confucian* models of self-cultivation, by way of Mencius and later writers who liked his ideas. The *Nei-yeh*, for instance, exhorts the reader to engage in a "cultivation of the mind/heart" (*hsiu-hsin*; see *Nei-yeh* V.13 and VI.5) – arguably the central thesis of Mencius himself, as well as of centuries of "Neo-Confucians."[38] Moreover, the *Nei-yeh* describes that practice of cultivation in terms that not only force us to think of such general teachings of Mencius, but even provide a meaningful context for understanding his otherwise unexplained (and, to Confucians and twentieth-century scholars, unexplainable) comment that one should cultivate a "flood-like *ch'i*" (*hao-jan chih ch'i*: see *Mencius* 2A.2).[39] Standing somewhat outside the Confucian mainstream was the British sinologist Arthur Waley, who observed in 1934 that "the passages in which Mencius deals . . . with the use of man's 'well-spring' of natal breath are unintelligible unless we relate them to the much fuller exposition of the same theories in *Kuan Tzu*," specifically in *Kuan-tzu* chapter 49, the *Nei-yeh*.[40] Mencius's own term "flood-like *ch'i*" appears in *Nei-yeh* XV.4, where its meaning and significance are much easier to perceive.[41] The significance of the *Nei-yeh* for our understanding of Confucianism – as well as for our understanding of traditional Chinese medicine – must await future analysis. But I will touch upon its significance for our understanding of later Taoist traditions throughout later chapters.

Here I will concentrate on explaining the contents of the *Nei-yeh* and on identifying thematic differences between it, the *Chuang-tzu*, and the *Tao te ching*. The primary difference between the *Nei-yeh* and the *Tao te ching* is signalled by the former's title: *nei* means "inside," and, in ancient times, *yeh* meant in one sense "cultivation *or* production (as of a crop)" and in another sense "what one studies." The text itself is thus simply labelled "Inner Cultivation" or "Inner Development." Its contents provide advice and unsystematic instructions for applying oneself to developing what is inside oneself. Specifically, it teaches one how, and why, to practice certain forms of what I term "biospiritual cultivation." In fact, unlike the *Chuang-tzu* – which raises epistemological issues – or the *Tao te ching* – which raises moral and political issues – the *Nei-yeh* is concerned with biospiritual cultivation and little else. Yet, it, too, is about "Tao": as the *Nei-yeh* says, "What gives life to all things and brings them to perfection is called 'Tao'."

The teachings of the *Nei-yeh* seem to begin with the assumption of a powerful ambient reality called *ch'i*, "life-energy." *Ch'i* is present both within all things and all around them. Within each being, *ch'i* is centered in the "vital essence," *ching*, which Harold Roth well describes as "the source of the vital energy in human beings [and] the basis of our health, vitality, and psychological well-being."[42] Yet all these energies or essences are somehow fundamental to our living world, as well as to each living being. The opening lines of the *Nei-yeh* read:

> The vital essence (*ching*) of all things –
> This is what makes life come into being:
> Below, it generates the five grains,
> Above, it brings about the constellated stars.
> When it flows in the interstices of Heaven and Earth,
> It is called "spiritual beings";
> When it is stored up inside [a person's] chest,
> It is called "sageliness."[43]

The message of these lines is quite different from that of the coyly cryptic opening lines of our modern *Tao te ching*. There, and in certain other oft-cited passages, one encounters what appear to be cosmogonic ideas couched in ontological abstractions.[44] The *Nei-yeh*, however, contains no such passages. It posits no eternal reality that is ontologically prior to, or separate from, the present world – no "noumenon" to contrast with the "phenomena" of life as we know it.[45] In fact, it displays no cosmological theories at all. Rather, its opening lines ask readers to accept the existence – and the *vital* importance – of an unseen life-force that operates *within* the world – a generative force that is spiritual in nature, but can be localized either within separate spiritual beings or within the torso of someone who successfully collects and stores it.

Such teachings challenge the modern imagination, and have even led some highly trained scholars to seek "explanations" from highly alien cultures. Some, finding no way to comprehend such teachings within their own realm of discourse, interpret them in sexual terms. (One wonders how "sexual" forces can be localized within a sage's *chest.*) Others have misconstrued the *Nei-yeh*'s teachings about cultivating *ch'i* and *tao* as a sublimation of "shamanic" practices.[46] (One wonders whether we should also look to "shamanism" for our understanding of Mencius's program of "recovering the stayed mind/heart"!) Others have been so intent to pry our interpretation of such texts out of the dessicated stereotypes foisted upon us by generations of secular rationalists (in China and the West alike) that they have tried to force both the *Tao te ching* and the *Nei-yeh* into a "perennialist" model.[47]

Reading the *Nei-yeh*'s opening lines as they were written – rather than forcing them to fit patterns that one thinks one sees within the ideas or practices of other ages or other cultures – shows us the world in terms that we have simply not encountered in other ages or cultures. But they are comprehensible nonetheless, particularly if we read them in light of the self-cultivation practices expressed and observed by centuries of later Taoists. As will become clear, those later practices were understood and expressed in a variety of terms, including some that were pegged back to ideas seen in the *Tao te ching* and *Chuang-tzu*; others that were grounded in ideas first found in "eclectic" texts such as the *Lü-shih ch'un-ch'iu*; still others couched in terms extracted from the *I ching* or even from alchemical texts. As we shall see in later chapters, many later Taoists engaged in self-cultivation practices clearly based on the teachings of the *Nei-yeh* – where, for instance, the term *tao* refers not to some abstract transcendent, but rather to a transient reality that one needs to attract and retain in order to live and flourish. And yet, in terms that are not comparable to those of any other religious tradition with which I am familiar, those realities, while quite clearly impersonal, are the energies that underlie all living things – including humans, cereals, stars and ghostly spirits. The idea that all such living things are subtly interconnected, that they have their own lives yet are filled with the same subtle life-force, is an idea that we might call *holistic*. And the holistic worldview evidenced in the *Nei-yeh* reverberates through most forms of Taoism over the centuries, from the messily comprehensive worldview of the *T'ai-p'ing ching* to the neatly intellectualized "Inner Alchemy" practices of late imperial times. Here is perhaps the most profound and abiding legacy of the *Nei-yeh*.

Nonetheless, we must resist the temptation to conflate different ideas and practices, which were articulated by different minds, in different ages, in response to different social and historical conditions, as well as in response to individual proclivities. In the *Nei-yeh*, for instance, the nature of life's wonderful forces and energies remains vague. One key term there is "spirit" or "spiritual consciousness" (*shen*). In this context, "spirit" is largely a matter of true perception and comprehension of reality: it is the basis for all higher forms of awareness. According to the *Nei-yeh*, the practitioner must align his/her biospiritual nexus with the unseen forces of life in order to attract "spirit" and take it into his/her quietened "heart/mind" (*hsin*).

Within the *Nei-yeh*, one's ability to succeed in this endeavor is expressed in terms of *te*, a term generally rendered as "virtue." Twentieth-century minds often reified *te* into a "key concept" of "philosophical Taoism," often in neatly systematized terms that corresponded to little that actually appears in any given passage of any given text. In the *Nei-yeh*, the meaning of the word *te* hardly resembles any of the twentieth-century descriptions of what it supposedly means in the more familiar texts, although it does retain the generic Chinese meaning of "the inner moral power of an individual," and even the old Shang-period connotation of "a proper disposition toward the unseen forces."[48] But here, *te* is clearly *not* a force that is intrinsic to specific individuals or species, as many twentieth-century representations would have us believe. Rather, like "spirit," *te* is something that the practitioner *acquires* when all elements of his/her body/heart/mind are completely peaceful and properly aligned. This precise set of ideas appears neither in the *Chuang-tzu* nor in any edition of the *Tao te ching*.

From the *Nei-yeh*, however, we can discern the full meaning of the age-old Chinese comment that the word *te* ("inner power *or* virtue") must be understood in terms of the homophone *te* – the common verb for "getting" or "acquiring," in both classical and modern Chinese.[49] In the *Nei-yeh*, *te* may be termed "the acquisitional agency," for it is not just *what* we attract and receive, but *that whereby* we attract and receive the higher forces of life – *tao*, *ch'i*, and *shen*. What is more, the *Nei-yeh* – unlike the more familiar "Lao-Chuang" texts – states that one's *te* is something that one must *work on*, each and every day. The practitioner must work to *build up* his/her *te* by practicing diligent self-control over all thought, emotion, and action.

One who succeeds at these practices can become a *sheng-jen*, a "sage." That concept may well have influenced the *Tao te ching*, where the same term is used for the fully accomplished practitioner. (There, however, the nature of the accomplishment is described in somewhat different terms, as I explain in the following section.) The term "sage" is also the *Chuang-tzu*'s most common term for the human ideal, though no research has yet illuminated the development of that term in different layers of the text. In the *Nei-yeh*, the "sage" is described as "full of spirit" and "complete in heart/mind and in body" – terms reminiscent of sundry references to various ideal figures in the *Chuang-tzu*.

Yet, the *Nei-yeh's* ideal can be understood somewhat more precisely, in terms of the text's advice about how the individual should manage his/her *hsin*, the "heart/mind."[50] The "heart/mind" is the ruling agency within an individual's biospiritual nexus, i.e., in the entire personal complex of body/mind/heart/spirit.[51] The *Nei-yeh's* principal teaching is that a person should work constantly to ensure that his/her "heart/mind" is balanced and tranquil – without excessive cogitation or emotion. If one maintains a tranquil "heart/mind," one will become a receptor of life's healthful energies, and will be able to retain them and live a long life. Otherwise, they will depart, and one's health – and very life – will become threatened.[52]

To this point, however, I have said little about the term "Tao" in regard to the *Nei-yeh*. The term *tao* in fact appears in the *Nei-yeh* twenty times – more often than such terms as *ch'i* (seventeen references), *ching* (twelve references), or *shen* (seven references). Only the term *hsin*, "heart/mind," appears more often (twenty-five references). And yet, the sense in which the term "Tao" is used in the *Nei-yeh* does not coincide with the way it is used in the more familiar texts, much less with common twentieth-century misconceptions.

In the *Nei-yeh*, the term *tao* is actually quite vague. It is sometimes used, rather indiscriminately, to refer to the healthful energies that the practitioner is working to cultivate. For instance, one passage reads as follows:

> Now *Tao* is what fills one's form, yet people cannot secure it.
> Its going forth cannot be recalled;
> Its return cannot be retained.
> Silent! None hears its sound.
> Sudden! Yet it rests in the mind.
> Obscure! None sees its form.
> Surging! It comes to life along with me.
> None sees its form, none hears its sound,
> Yet there is a sequence to its completion.
> Call it "Way."[53]

One also encounters a line in the *Nei-yeh* that is virtually identical to certain passages in the *Tao te ching*: "What gives life to all things and brings them to perfection is called *tao*." But otherwise, the *Nei-yeh* generally uses the term *tao* as an equivalent for its other terms for the spiritual realities that the practitioner should attract and retain by tranquillizing the heart/mind.

It is clear that the *Nei-yeh* has an identifiable focus, articulated in terms comprehensible to a careful reader. But, if we are intellectually honest, it is also clear that its teachings are quite distinguishable from what we are used to seeing in the more familiar texts of "classical Taoism" – the *Lao-tzu* and *Chuang-tzu*. For instance, while terms such as *te* and *tao* appear frequently in all three texts, they appear in each text – and in various passages of each text – in *different senses*. Neither term is thus a clearly defined "basic concept" of some unified system that runs through all such works.

Second, it should be noticed that the portrait of the Taoist life in the *Nei-yeh* is in some ways quite dissimilar from what we encounter in the *Tao te ching* and *Chuang-tzu*. For instance, the key to life in the *Nei-yeh* is the practitioner's diligent effort to attract and retain the spiritual forces called *ch'i*, *shen*, and *tao*. While each of those terms does occur here and there in the *Tao te ching* and the *Chuang-tzu*, nowhere there do we find the specific teachings that are basic to the *Nei-yeh*.[54] In particular, it is hard to think of passages from either of the more familiar texts that suggest that the thing called *tao* is a force that can come into, or go out of, a person. Nor do those texts say, as does the *Nei-yeh*, that one must engage in specific practices to "attract" *tao* or to keep it from "departing."[55] In the more familiar texts, the term *tao* generally seems to suggest a universal reality from which one can never be ontologically separated.[56]

An additional point is of particular importance for sorting out the relationship of "classical Taoism" with the "Taoism" of later imperial times: the practices commended in the *Nei-yeh* are much more clearly *physiological* in nature than most twentieth-century readers were taught to think of "Taoist" practice. Indeed, one of the reasons that some of the teachings of the *Tao te ching* became so readily domesticated in Western culture is that the public enjoyed the mistaken belief that its teachings involved *no* definable practices at all.

According to those facile misreadings, the Taoist life is essentially stative: it never involves specific *practices* (certainly not any practices that carry historical or cultural "baggage"), and it certainly never involves any actual *effort*. But one *must* note that the *Nei-yeh* nowhere presents the Taoist life in terms of "practicing *wu-wei*." In the *Nei-yeh*, the Taoist life can *never* be a stative life of "just being" or of "being spontaneous." Rather, it is a very active life of specific practices, which must be carefully learned and properly performed if one is ever to bring such elusive forces as *tao* into one's being. In this context – as indeed in the context of virtually all later forms of Taoism – the Taoist life involves personal responsibility, dedication to a life of constant self-discipline, and conscientious daily practice. Moreover, it involves the purification and proper ordering of one's *body* as well as one's "heart/mind." It would be quite excessive to say that the *Nei-yeh* teaches a "Taoist yoga," but it clearly does assume that the spiritual life involves practices that also have physical components. But those components, like moderation in eating, pertain to how a person should govern his or her everyday life, not to activities that are disconnected from one's regular, everyday life.

Neither the *Tao te ching* nor the *Chuang-tzu* are so clearly focused upon biospiritual practices or upon any particular model of self-cultivation. While they do contain passages that allude to such practices, their compilers had many *other* teachings that they were trying to convey, teachings generally absent from the *Nei-yeh*.

For instance, as Allyn Rickett observed long ago, the concepts of *yin* and *yang* are seen nowhere in the *Nei-yeh*.[57] Other differences between the *Nei-yeh* and the more familiar texts seem not to have been remarked upon heretofore. For instance, there are few teachings in the *Nei-yeh* involving issues of government. Though modern conceptions commonly associate Taoism with the life of the individual rather than with social or political concerns, such was never really the case, as we shall see in later chapters. The *Nei-yeh*, however, displays little interest in political or social issues.[58]

In addition, the *Nei-yeh* differs from both the *Tao te ching* and the *Chuang-tzu* in that it never critiques or ridicules Confucian beliefs or practices. Once again, twentieth-century misconceptions held that Taoism arose primarily as a reaction against Confucianism. But there is nothing whatever in the *Nei-yeh* that criticizes Confucian teachings, any more than there is in the bamboo-slip *Tao te ching* found at Guodian.

The fact that common twentieth-century understandings of the interplay of elements of "Taoism" and "Confucianism" were wholly inadequate is clearly demonstrated by the unmistakable continuities between the teachings of the *Nei-yeh* and certain elements of the teachings of the "Confucian" known as Mencius.[59] Those continuities are not limited to the key idea that personal cultivation involves the development of "a flood-like *ch'i.*" One may also note that both Mencius and the *Nei-yeh* assume that

1 one is born with a heart/mind that is inherently as it should be;
2 our heart/mind became confused as our thoughts and passions intensified; and
3 by returning our heart/mind to its original qualities, we allow a natural harmony to take the place of unnatural confusion.

When one reads in the *Nei-yeh* that "the mind's inner reality is benefited by rest and quiet," one cannot but think of Mencius's comments about Ox Mountain in *Meng-tzu* 6A8.[60] Either Mencius had personal connections with the community in which the *Nei-yeh* evolved, or he encountered a proponent of it at the Chi-hsia academy in Ch'i, where both the *Nei-yeh* and the *Tao te ching* apparently reached their final form. Certainly, the common elements are too pervasive, and too basic to Mencius's thought, to be explained away as later interpolations.

The main element of Mencius's teachings that is *missing* from the *Nei-yeh* is the Confucian emphasis upon saving society by reviving the principles of proper moral/social behavior known as *li*. Those were ideas common to both Mencius and Hsün-tzu, but were denounced in the Han and post-Han versions of the *Tao te ching*. The *Nei-yeh*, however, is written from a point of view of people who have no interest at all in that debate. Its reader is simply taught to align him/herself with the natural forces at work in the world, because doing so is necessary for his/her own well-being. There is little trace of a belief that one is responsible for changing society, though those who held such beliefs are neither faulted nor mocked.

Another theme conspicuously absent from the *Nei-yeh* is the idea – deemed "primitivist" by some scholars – that the ideal society is a small-scale community without much technology or socio-political institutions.[61] Those ideas are most familiar to modern readers from the penultimate chapter of the *Tao te ching*, though there are also other examples in the *Chuang-tzu*. Yet it would seem that a person could follow the teachings of the *Nei-yeh* within any social setting at all, and there is no reason to conclude that the text's compilers ever deemed any social context to be preferable to any other. Thus, the Rousseau-esque idea that Taoism consists primarily of a rejection of "civilization" is baseless.[62]

Nor does the *Nei-yeh* ever explain life in terms of "change." There is no trace of a notion that there is an unchanging cosmic force beyond the world of change. For a certainty, the term "Tao" never carries such connotations here. Nor is there any poetic imagery of a sage person who blissfully drifts along with life's ongoing processes. Such ideas – imagined by many in the twentieth century to have been the very core of "Taoism" – may be present in parts of the *Chuang-tzu*, but there is nothing like them in the *Nei-yeh*, any more than in the *Tao te ching*.

The *Nei-yeh* also gives the lie to yet other misconceptions of Taoism, including some held by thoughtful philosophers. One such misconception is that "Taoist" teachings are deeply iconoclastic, antinomian, even revolutionary. According to that view, the basic thrust of "Taoism" is to jolt the individual into a realization that he/she should reject traditional beliefs and values, and should condemn them as the artificial constructs of an oppressive society. This misinterpretation of Taoism was not simply the conceit of 1960s hippies straining to find in other cultures some justification for their condemnation of "the establishment." Generations of Westerners misread the *Tao te ching*, and parts of the *Chuang-tzu*, as a post-Enlightenment gospel of individual freedom, freedom from the uncomfortable aspects of "society" in general, and of Western culture in particular.[63] The *Nei-yeh*, however, does not critique "conventional society" and urge us to reject it. Nor does it critique language. Nor does it urge us to beware socially inculcated valuations. Those concerns of twentieth-century minds groping their way from "modern" perspectives toward "postmodern" perspectives were certainly foreshadowed by some thoughts of some contributors to the *Chuang-tzu*. But they were certainly not concerns that were *typical* of the people of classical China whose values and practices were continuous with later Taoist values and practices. As we shall see, if there was a classical cornerstone of "Taoism," it was not the "useless words" of Chuang Chou, but rather the cultivation of life's subtle forces suggested by the *Nei-yeh*.

There are yet more distinctive features to the teachings of the *Nei-yeh*. For instance, unlike the *Tao te ching*, the *Nei-yeh* has nothing at all to say about issues of gender. There are several passages in the *Tao te ching* that commend a "feminine" attitude or behavior. But though the compilers of the *Nei-yeh* indeed teach that there are attitudes and behaviors that we should embrace or forego, there is no gender imagery associated with any of them. Nor is "Tao" ever characterized in maternal terms, as it often is in the *Tao te ching*.

Another distinctive feature of the *Nei-yeh* is that it lacks the idea that *T'ien* (commonly translated "Heaven") is a benign guiding force in life. The Confucians and Mohists both shared that idea, in various formulations. Most scholars have presumed such ideas to be a reflection of a more broadly held belief, which "Chinese society" displayed as far back as the second millennium BCE. In the twentieth century, such ideas were generally not associated with Taoism, for "Taoists" were presumed to believe, instead, in an impersonal reality called "Tao" that transcends all other realities, including "Heaven." But such was not the case, even within the classical texts. Several chapters of the *Tao te ching* speak of "the Way of Heaven" (*T'ien-tao* or *T'ien-chih-tao*), a beneficent force that seems to have will as well as agency.[64] But there is little trace of any such ideas in the *Nei-yeh*.[65]

Finally, we should address the issue of morality. Is the *Nei-yeh* concerned solely with "internal" matters, as its title suggests? Is the practitioner of its teachings ever to give any thought to anyone other than him- or herself? This is a key question for correcting twentieth-century misconceptions, because virtually all modern interpreters, Chinese and Western alike, loudly accused "Taoists" of being essentially "egotistical." But such accusations are quite baseless. Even the *Tao te ching*, for instance, enjoins the reader to practice "goodness" (*shan*), which involves extending oneself toward others impartially, so as to "benefit" them. In the *Tao te ching*, the Taoist life is one in which one achieves self-fulfillment *as* one is selflessly benefiting others.[66] Yet, one can find little evidence of such ideals in the *Nei-yeh*. There are a few passages on the basis of which one might be able to construct an argument that the *Nei-yeh*'s reader is to think of providing benefits to others, but none that seems to express such ideals in a clear or unmistakable fashion.[67]

In sum, it is clear that the *Nei-yeh* is quite distinct in content from either the *Tao te ching* or the *Chuang-tzu*, despite those texts' many similarities. The *Nei-yeh*, we should recall, appears to have been earlier than the *Tao te ching*, and could even be described as "the earliest Taoist teachings." As we shall see in the following section, the *Tao te ching* shows clear evidence that at least its final redactors were deeply concerned with the social and political issues that were the prime concern of other "schools," particularly the Mohists and Confucians. The *Tao te ching* may have developed in part from the same general tradition that produced the *Nei-yeh*, just as Mencius clearly did. But the people who wrote the later layers of the *Tao te ching* were, like Mencius, interested in the issues of how we should live in regard to human society, and they were interested in those issues as much as, if not more than, they were interested in "inner cultivation." Further attention to the differences among the concerns seen in all such texts will provide greater insight into the divergent communities that produced those materials, the historical flux of changing ideas, and the diverse origins of Taoist values and practices.

From "the elders" of Ch'u to the Chi-hsia academy: the *Tao te ching*

The text that we know as the *Lao-tzu* or *Tao te ching* is the best-known work of Chinese civilization, and likely the best-known of any non-Western culture. It is known throughout the world, for it has been translated into every major language on earth, as well as many minor ones. There are over a hundred versions in English alone (many of those by people who have never learned to read Chinese). In fact, the *Tao te ching* has been translated more often into more languages than any other work in history except the Bible. But, like the Bible, its *meaning* is contested, not only *within* a traditional "faith-community," but also *between* that community and an *alien* "faith-community" – a late imperial denomination of Confucianism – *and between* all those *traditional Chinese* communities and the interwoven communities of modern scholars, and dilettantes, in all lands.

The *Tao te ching* has often wrongly been imagined to have emerged from the mind of an ancient philosopher named "Lao-tzu." As the twenty-first century opened, the finding of most scholarly research was that the *Tao te ching* – like the Bible – was the product of a complex compositional process that spanned generations. And, as in the case of the Bible, the unravelling of that process is an unfinished scholarly project that has been aided somewhat by recent archaeological discoveries.[68]

Our three "editions" of the Tao te ching

The text known as the *Tao te ching* has existed in some form since at least the early third century BCE. However, our familiar "received text" – on which all translations and all expositions up to the 1980s was based – is much later indeed. Like our received text of the *Chuang-tzu*, it dates back only to the early centuries of the Common Era. Just as our *Chuang-tzu* was actually fashioned by Kuo Hsiang, our *Tao te ching* was finalized only when a young intellectual named Wang Pi (226–249) wrote a commentary to it. And there is reason to believe that the text that Wang Pi was reading when he wrote his commentary was not at all the same text that has come down to us over the ages as "the Wang Pi text of the *Tao te ching*." In other words, even what we know as "Wang Pi's text" cannot be accepted as Wang Pi's text.[69]

Until the late twentieth century, scholars could only conjecture about the true history of the *Tao te ching* in the period before Wang Pi. That state of affairs changed radically with two archaeological finds in the latter part of the twentieth century. In the mid-1970s, Chinese archaeologists discovered two separate versions of the text – written in ink on silk – in a tomb in the locality of Ma-wang-tui (Mawangdui) near the city of Ch'ang-sha, in what is now Hunan province. In the "late Warring States era" (i.e., the fourth to third centuries BCE), that locality was not within any of the "middle kingdoms," but rather within the old non-Chou nation of Ch'u. Yet the silk manuscripts from Ma-wang-tui can be shown to date from two specific reign periods in the early Han dynasty – i.e., to about 200 BCE and about 170 BCE.[70] For that reason, even the discovery of the Ma-wang-tui manuscripts did not provide incontrovertible evidence that the *Tao te ching* really pre-dated the Han dynasty. And it did not really do much to tell us who had created the text in the first place, much less why, or what it meant for the evolution of Taoism.

That situation changed only in the 1990s, with the discovery of a set of engraved bamboo slips which correspond to various sections of what we call the *Tao te ching*. In 1993, Chinese archaeologists hastily – and without due care – excavated several "Warring States period" tombs in a village called Kuo-tien (Guodian) in Hupei (Hubei) province, near the ancient capital of Ch'u itself.[71] The first scholars to examine the tomb and its contents concluded – on the basis of reasoning that does not fully withstand analysis – that one of the Guodian tombs was that of the tutor of the crown prince of the state of Ch'u, and that it dates quite precisely to 300 BCE, give or take a few years. Floating inside the tomb were some eight hundred bamboo slips inscribed in the ancient Ch'u script (i.e., the indigenous script of Ch'u before the Ch'in-dynasty standardization of the writing-systems of all the lands of its new "empire" late in the third century CE). Scholars who examined those bamboo slips found seventy-one containing lines that correspond to passages of our *Tao te ching*.

The original order of the materials within the *Tao te ching* seems to remain indeterminable. In the Ma-wang-tui manuscripts, what appears in our more familiar edition of Wang Pi as chapters 38 to 81 is placed at the beginning, before what we have always hitherto known as chapters 1 to 37. And it is quite clear that none of the inscribers of the bamboo slips was following anything that corresponded either to our Wang Pi arrangement or to our Ma-wang-tui arrangment.[72]

No one has attempted to argue that what is now called "the Guodian *Laozi*" is "the original" *Tao te ching*. It does take us back in time a hundred years further than the Ma-wang-tui versions do, but not to "the beginning." Chinese and Western scholars have deliberated and debated about the meaning of the find.[73]

No matter which of the three "editions" one is reading, the *Tao te ching* is, at first glance, a jumble of unrelated sayings. Even before the discoveries at Ma-wang-tui and Guodian, some scholars explained the text as having originated as separate elements of an oral tradition, and that the unknown person(s) who collected them simply imposed no structure upon the resulting anthology. Others, however, believed that no one would have been likely to have composed so formless a text, and concluded that it must in fact once have possessed a coherent structure, which was somehow subsequently lost. A few scholars speculated that the text once became deranged when strings binding the ancient bamboo strips came undone, but such imaginings do not withstand critical analysis. A number of twentieth-century scholars, Chinese and Western alike, have taken the peculiar liberty of reorganizing the text itself.[74] Such rearrangements are often little more than an arbitrary imposition of the interpreter's own perspective onto the text, and they may destroy subtle vestiges of meaningful order already present within it.

"Lao-tzu"

Until the twentieth century, the *Tao te ching* was almost universally accepted as the creation of an ancient wise man known as Lao-tzu (whence the other name by which the text is commonly known). In the twentieth century, that attribution became subjected to increasing criticism, by Asian and Western scholars alike. The traditional attribution rests ultimately upon the reports of the historian Ssu-ma Ch'ien (Sima Qian) in his *Shih-chi (Shiji)*, composed *ca.* 100 BCE.[75] By ancient standards, Ssu-ma was a conscientious historian. And, in many regards, his annals are quite trustworthy. But when he attempted to sketch the lives of the great thinkers that the people of his own day imagined to have lived in the classical era of the past, he ran across a problem: there were little or no trustworthy data in his day regarding the identity of many of them. That dearth of information included the supposed "author" of the *Tao te ching*, as well as that of the *Chuang-tzu*. So Ssu-ma provided several conflicting stories about the identity of "Lao-tzu," admitting ultimately that he had no real way to decide which of them, if any, was correct.[76] In later times, uncritical writers – in China and other lands – simply took the first of Ssu-ma's stories to be correct, and ignored all the others, as well as the issues raised by their presence.[77]

The most recent scholarship suggests that someone of the third century BCE concocted that story in an effort to lend it the lustre of a respectable name.[78] Yet, the mistaken belief that the *Tao te ching* was written by a wise man named "Lao-tzu" endured into the twenty-first century. Readers today, however, should bear firmly in mind that such notions rank alongside such traditional attributions as Moses' composition of the Pentateuch, Solomon's composition of the book of *Proverbs*, or John's composition of the fourth canonical Christian gospel. In other words, in all such traditions – as in later Taoism, as well – many people could not deal with the fact that they had a great text unless they could satisfy themselves that it was the product of a single great man.

The origins of the Tao te ching*: the elders of Ch'u*

Most efforts to explain the *Tao te ching* pass over its literary form and the internal and external data related to its provenance. Generations of interpreters have felt free to ignore such issues and dive straight into the text's supposed "teachings," with perhaps a little guidance from traditional expositors. But such approaches to the text are unproductive and misleading, from several perspectives. Only by understanding how the *Tao te ching* evolved, and the specific concerns and strategies of its final redactor, can one truly understand its contents.

I will begin by exploring the ideational and textual "pre-history" of the *Tao te ching*, using internal and external data to reconstruct key junctures in the text's long process of development. I believe that the contours of that process can be reasonably, if incompletely, deduced by combining analysis of the work's form and contents with a knowledge both of contemporary texts and figures and of the social and intellectual history of the ambient culture.[79]

The contents of "the *Tao te ching*" changed over time, as new hands added material of their own to it, and likely discarded parts that did not suit their purposes. We certainly know that the *Chuang-tzu* evolved in such a way, though no archaeological discoveries have produced any older versions of that text.[80] In the case of the *Tao te ching*, the discovery of the Ma-wang-tui and Guodian texts both complicate and facilitate our efforts to understand its nature and significance: they help answer certain types of questions, but give little assistance in answering others. We also see in them at least *five* separate redactions of what appears to have been a given body of material – two from Ma-wang-tui and three from Guodian. The logical deduction is that that body of material was continually being edited and re-edited, at least from the beginning of the third century BCE into the early Han period. Today's readers are unaccustomed to thinking about the materials that they read on such terms: both in China and in the West, it is all too readily assumed that by perusing the *Analects* as we have it today we can learn what Confucius believed, and by studying the *Tao te ching* as we have it today we can learn what "Lao-tzu" believed. Both assumptions are demonstrably false, in just the same way that it is false to assume that by reading the Christian gospels one can gain a full or accurate understanding of what Jesus taught, or that by reading the Buddhist *nikayas* one can gain a full or accurate understanding of what Gautama taught.[81] All of those texts actually arose within a "faith-community" of sorts, and were written and shaped to suit the needs and tastes of its members – not to transmit to later generations a full or accurate picture of the words or deeds of the community's nominal founder.[82]

Yet the evidence is now quite clear that the "community" in which the *Tao te ching* arose was in one highly important way quite unlike the early Christian community or the early Confucian community. Unlike either of those communities, the one which produced the material that evolved into our *Tao te ching* quite clearly had *no nominal founder*. Nowhere in the Guodian slips, or even in the later Ma-wang-tui silk texts, do we find the characters *lao-tzu*. Nor is there *any* indication there – or in the received text, for that matter – that the contents represent the teachings of some single person. In other words, the internal evidence no more supports the idea that "Lao-tzu" produced these words than internal evidence supports the idea that "John" wrote the fourth canonical Christian gospel.

There are many *later* Taoist texts – of which the best known may now be the *Hsi-sheng ching* ("Scripture of [Lao-tzu's] Western Ascension") – in which *each section* opens quite clearly with the phrase "Lao-tzu says" (*lao-tzu yüeh*).[83] Readers of other classical texts, such as the *Analects* of Confucius, find the same "quotation" form wherever the redactors wish readers to believe that some great person's words are being presented. But in *no* extant version of the *Tao te ching* does any such phrase appear. The simplest and most reasonable conclusion is that none of the people who took part in shaping and redacting this text – either in pre-Han or in Han times – understood, or wished readers to understand, its teachings as having originated as the teachings of any single person, much less as one to which the community traced its origins.

In these regards, the *Tao te ching*, like the *Nei-yeh*, has little in common with the *Analects* or the *Mo-tzu*, much less with the Christian gospels or the Buddhist *nikaya*. Instead, like the *Nei-yeh*, it can better be compared to works of "wisdom literature" such as the biblical book of *Proverbs*. In other words, it did not originate as a community's depiction of one person's thoughts, but rather as the collective wisdom of the community itself. Like *Proverbs*, its primary purpose is to provide the reader with profound – and reliably useful – advice about how to live, based on the lessons learned by members of previous generations.

Twentieth-century scholars, like their Confucian predecessors, usually misread the *Tao te ching* as having originated within the socio-political debates of "the hundred schools" of the "middle kingdoms." Even today, many scholars continue to read the *Tao te ching* as the work of members of the same social/intellectual elite that produced many of the leading spokesmen for Confucian ideas, Legalist ideas, or the other "schools of thought" mentioned above. It is quite true that the *Tao te ching* – in the form that would eventually be transmitted through Chinese history – does give admonitions and advice for rulers. And, as in the *Mo-tzu*, some of those passages dispute, and even ridicule, Confucian assumptions and values. So many twentieth-century scholars interpreted the *Tao te ching*, like the *Mo-tzu*, as the product of "alienated idealists" who were trying to critique existing social and political conditions from a set of assumptions different from those of the Confucians, and to argue that a polity based upon correct assumptions would promote not only the general welfare but also the ruler's own security.

Clearly, such socio-political positions are present in *the received text* of the *Tao te ching*. But there are two key reasons to believe that such positions were likely not present in the *original* body of material. One is that the Guodian texts show *no* signs of anti-Confucianism, and few signs that the reader is to reject the ideas of *any* of "the hundred schools."[84] And the extant texts of both the *Nei-yeh* and the *Chuang-tzu* demonstrate that at least *some* of the people in "classical China" who produced and transmitted texts expressing ideas about how to live life did so for reasons that had *nothing* to do with giving advice to rulers, *or* with refuting other "schools of thought." The *Chuang-tzu* displays some of the latter, but none of the former, while the *Nei-y*eh displays neither. In other words, to read the *Tao te ching* as having originated from intellectual battles among "the hundred schools" is not an interpretation that emerges logically from the form or contents of the text itself.

More importantly, both the form and the contents of the *Tao te ching* – whichever edition one examines – have *far* more in common with those of the *Nei-yeh* than with those of the *Chuang-tzu*, or with the primary works of such socio-political programs as those of the Mohists or Confucians. It is for that reason that we should look to the *Nei-yeh*, not to any of those other materials, in trying to understand how the *Tao te ching* may have evolved, and what its teachings may have been at the various stages of its evolution.[85]

As the compilers and transmitters of the *Nei-yeh* and *Chuang-tzu* evidently realized, the problem of devising effective governmental policies and procedures really has very little to do with *life* as most people experience it and need to understand it. What all three texts – the *Tao te ching*, *Nei-yeh*, and *Chuang-tzu* – share is the idea that one can live one's life wisely only if one learns how to live in accord with life's unseen forces and subtle processes, *not* on the basis of society's more prosaic concerns. And it is here, of course, that all three can be understood as forerunners of, and sources for, later Taoism.

Though the *Nei-yeh* and *Chuang-tzu* mostly ignore socio-political concerns, all extant versions of the *Tao te ching* suggest that learning how to live in that way can conduce to wise and effective government. If we read the *Tao te ching* as though it represented the ideas of one person or group at one single time, its ideas about government certainly conflict with each other, as do its ideas about wise behavior in general. The most famous of them involve the term *wu-wei*, whose varied meanings are often quite difficult to reconcile. Many twentieth-century writers mistakenly believed that *wu-wei* simply denoted a condition of "naturalness" or "spontaneity." A careful reading of the *Tao te ching* reveals that the text actually does *not* promote such qualities.[86] Indeed, the "full-text" *Tao te ching* (i.e., the Wang Pi and Ma-wang-tui editions) provides many conflicting counsels for rulers and even war-leaders, though no "natural" person ever "spontaneously" engineered a government or engaged in armed combat.[87]

An honest analysis reveals that in the full-text *Tao te ching* the term *wu-wei* constitutes part of an intricate complex of ideals and images. It includes analogies to the natural qualities of water, as well as to idealized "feminine" behaviors, such as those of a selfless mother. Yet, the full-text *Tao te ching* also makes clear that "the idea of *wu-wei*" encompasses shrewd tactics – among them "feminine wiles" – which one may utilize to achieve success in a range of human activities, including both statecraft and war. While one or two chapters do exhort the reader to *wei wu-wei* (i.e., to "act without acting"), others acknowledge that "acting" (*wei*) is fully justified on certain terms, and one chapter even praises the "advantages" (*i*) of practicing *wu-wei*.[88] Despite twentieth-century notions about Taoist "spontaneity," the teaching that one should behave properly because doing so leads to "benefits" (*li*) is actually quite common in the *Tao te ching*.[89] Indeed, much of it is written to make it quite clear that its lessons are primarily pragmatic suggestions for achieving personal success: one can achieve such success while simultanously enhancing others' welfare, provided that one practices self-restraint.

Some might find it odd that the *Tao te ching* simultaneously works to persuade readers to trust themselves to certain subtle processes at work in the world, rather than foolishly believe that they can control life's events through their personal choices and actions. If one *really* were to *wei wu-wei*, would one not just live one's own life according to those natural processes, foregoing all individual goals, much less the social and political issues that obsess "leaders" and "experts"? Such ironies actually help explain the *Tao te ching*'s complex textual history. Originally a collection of recommendations for living in accord with life's subtle processes, it was later transformed into a socio-political tract comparable to the teachings of the Confucians and Mohists.[90]

The best explanation for these facts seems to be as follows. At some point before 300 BCE there was a community in the southerly land of Ch'u that passed down an oral tradition of homespun wisdom. Originally, it consisted of real-life advice, such as parents and other elders, in any culture, typically provide to young people as they grow: "behave in a wise and healthy manner, and you will have a long and comfortable life, free from conflict or unexpected suffering." Here we can see why neither Ssu-ma Ch'ien, nor anyone else in third- to second-century China, could identify the "wise man" whom they imagined the term *lao-tzu* to designate. Far from representing a personal name, the term *lao* here simply had its usual, everyday meaning of "aged." It was originally *not* a title for some wise "Master Lao" – whose historical identity we must labor to ferret out – but rather a generic reference to "the old ones," the *elders* from whom anyone, in any culture, receives one's earliest and most important lessons.

By the late fourth century BCE, someone had committed those lessons to writing, though *not* in a *single* codified version. Various literate members of the community (or even members of various communities) wrote down what seemed to them to be the wise lessons to remember. In time, such people acquired and discussed each other's lesson-books, and added – and removed – interesting elements that appeared in some of the *others'* texts. In other words, there was no single "original text" of the *Tao te ching*, any more than there was some single *person* whose "thought" it expounds.

Just as the earliest Christian communities had no single body of verbal material that they transmitted as "the teachings of Jesus" – but rather a variety of verbal traditions that actually circulated within different communities – so the traditions that "the elders" had taught in Ch'u had diverse "starting points" and a fluid evolutionary process. In the minds of those who transmitted such texts, there was no idea of "*the* text," as something whose form or contents was fixed, much less inviolate: no one was "changing" a preformulated text or "altering" some earlier person's "philosophy."

Scholars today still presume that the *Chuang-tzu* originated in one man's personal jottings, which later hands emended and supplemented. It remains to be seen whether such assumptions will continue to be accepted. But even before the discovery of the Guodian slips, scholars had begun to show that the *Lao-tzu* was the result of a comparable process. In this case, at least, it was not a *single* evolving tradition, but rather the result of various minds' thoughts and teachings, which evolved over time, and eventually flowed together, like streams flowing into a river.

One of those streams clearly flowed through a specific and most remarkable valley – where people had compiled a quite *different* set of teachings. Its geographic location remains unidentified: some scholars place it in the northern land of Ch'i, while others note linguistic data suggesting that it may have been somewhere in Ch'u.[91] In any event, this was a locale whose people collected teachings about cultivating invisible forces of life, such as *ch'i*, "life-energy." Far from practical advice to help young people achieve a successful personal life, these were teachings of a very different order, designed to encourage certain *specific practices*. Though its ideas about "practice" were fairly consistent, the lesson-books that *this* community produced also included a variety of vague ideas about the unseen forces with which such practices were designed to help a person align his/her own life-force. This, of course, was the community that produced the *Nei-yeh*, one which clearly took no interest whatever in matters such as government or war. Nor did it offer advice for getting one's own way by astute non-assertiveness – as the *Tao te ching* does – or other such "practical" behaviors. The community that produced the *Nei-yeh* articulated *no* concept of *wu-wei* – either as a practical behavior or as an exhortation to refrain from behavior.

Yet in another nearby valley, *another* distinctive rivulet entered the stream. This was a voice found in no other materials that have come down to us from "classical China." Someone fond of labels might well call it "the maternalist" voice, for it found great value in the relationship between a mother and her child, and urged a view of life that combined *earlier* values with images based upon such a relationship. In addition, this voice produced poignant lines that are couched in the first person. In form, at least, they confess intimate introspective reflections upon the speaker's own life-experience, and offer those personal experiences as lessons for others. The ideas that this party added to the material were totally *apolitical*, and were quite the *opposite* of pragmatism. For instance, one passage from this voice appears in chapter 20 of the received text:

> The multitudes are joyous,
> as though feasting after the great sacrifice of oxen,
> or as though climbing a terrace in springtime;
> I alone am unstirring, ah, giving no indication (of what I might do),
> like an infant who has not yet begun acting like a child.
> Listless, ah,
> as though having nowhere to go back to.
> The multitudes all have more than enough; I alone seem to be lacking.
> Alas, my heart/mind is that of a fool, ah, so muddled!
> Ordinary people are so bright and clear; I alone am benighted.
> Ordinary people are so painstaking; I alone am stupefied.
> Bestirred, ah, like the ocean, windblown, ah, as though having no place to come to rest.
> The multitudes all have something to do, but I alone am obtuse and uncouth.
> I alone differ from others, but I value taking nourishment from mother.[92]

Here, only an overactive imagination could find signs of political advice, or of cosmological theory, or of biospiritual practices.[93]

It would thus appear that, by this time – shortly after the Guodian versions were written down – there were people who contemplated the world's workings to the point of perceiving a *subtle force* that seemed best *symbolized* by maternal imagery. This force is expressed in terms quite different from any of the subtle forces named in the *Nei-yeh*: it is not said to have been elusive or transient, nor does one have to work to attract it. Yet, these passages would eventually end up applying the term *tao* to that force. In any event, this voice clearly imagined a universal, non-transient force – *to* which we owe our existence, and *from* which we can never truly be separated. Moreover, it added the idea that one can link oneself back to that force by means of meditative introspection. Both ideas, of course, endured throughout later Taoism.

Yet, this particular model of "meditation" is highly distinct from what one finds in the *Nei-yeh*: the practice suggested by the *Nei-yeh* is couched in terms of self-control, self-cleansing, and the attraction of energies that are ambient yet transient. Here, however, one turns *away* from what is "outside" oneself. Here, one "closes the gates" on what is outside "oneself." This quasi-romantic voice is not cynical, or critical, of "others" or "the world." But it does place a negative value upon them, in terms that suggest jadedness, disillusionment, and a sense of having learned to perceive something of greater importance within "oneself."

The composers of these passages – perhaps originally distinct texts – may have been expressing the findings of their own life-experience. These passages have little organic connection with any other part of the text's "stream," and have a distinctive style – a confessional, almost lyrical tone. They do not seem to have been written by someone who is concerned with teaching lessons about how to develop strategies for achieving success, on *any* terms.

But, whatever its provenance, this material, too, was ultimately integrated into what we now know as the *Tao te ching*. By integrating this literary tradition with elements from the other, earlier traditions, a redactor eventually produced a new and quite striking "lesson for life": we should learn to perceive the unseen reality which is the source of our life and our sustenance (much like a cosmic mother); by focusing upon that reality, we can better return to the behaviors that are "natural" for us – i.e., living a quiet life of humble beneficence, giving selflessly to others, as a mother does.

But before explaining the later stages of the text's evolution, I should note that the specifics of this "lesson" seem *not* to have held much interest for later *Taoists*. Though the "maternalist vision" may have originated partly as an effort to express the contents of certain "meditative experiences," its preferred imagery seldom reappears in later Taoism. We should also note here that twentieth-century interpreters sometimes read some such passages and mistakenly concluded that "Taoism has feminist values." In reality, when these life-lessons are examined carefully, they have nothing in common with the primary values or goals of modern feminism. Another common mistake has been to imagine that women in later

China were attracted to Taoism because of the existence of such lessons in the *Tao te ching*. Here again, such beliefs are baseless. These lessons were never aimed specifically at women, and later Taoist women never attributed any particular importance to them. In Chapter 4 below, we will look at women's involvement in later Taoism.

The creation of "Taoist" ideas: the Chi-hsia academy

For modern attempts to understand the intellectual traditions of early China, the most important, though least well-known, locality in all the "middle kingdoms" was a building near the western gate of the city of Lin-tzu, capital of the northern nation of Ch'i.[94] It was in the shadow of that gate – the "Chi gate" – that the kings of Ch'i in the fourth century BCE constructed what we today would likely term a conference center. Toward the end of the century, the Ch'i king named Hsüan (r. 320–301) summoned thinking men from every corner of the known world, endowed them with sinecure positions, housed them, fed them, and charged them to think, talk, debate, and write about life.

At that "think-tank" beneath (*hsia*) the Chi gate – hence called the "Chi-hsia academy" – sixty years of the best minds of "the middle kingdoms" and neighboring lands would gather to discuss important things and express profound thoughts. Among the seventy-six such men housed at Chi-hsia in the late fourth century were the most famous minds of that era, including such Confucians as Mencius and Hsün-tzu; the *yin–yang* theorist Tsou Yen; and an array of thinkers who "studied the methods (*shu*) of Huang-Lao, *tao* and *te*."[95] Among the members of the last category was a man from Ch'u named Huan Yüan, of whom we know only that he authored a work in two sections.[96]

To the best of my knowledge, no one anywhere has ever suggested that Huan Yüan's two-section work on subjects such as "*tao* and *te*" may have been what we now call the *Tao te ching*. To the best of my knowledge, no one has ever suggested that Huan Yüan had any connection at all – direct or indirect – with what we now call the *Tao te ching*. But if, today, we were law-enforcement agents seeking a crime suspect who clearly fit the proper profile, who was clearly in the right place at the right time, and had both motive and opportunity to have perpetrated this particular "crime," we would have little difficulty persuading a judge or grand jury that Huan Yüan *could* indeed have been the *Tao te ching*'s final redactor.

Such being the case, why has no one ever suspected this particular man of having been at least an accomplice in the creation of the *Tao te ching*? My answer is that Ssu-ma Ch'ien produced a chapter on the identity of the shadowy "Lao-tzu," thereby leading investigators in sundry other directions, directions that clearly do not, in reality, fit the actual facts of this case.[97] Whatever the reason for Ssu-ma's absurdly incoherent "biography" of "Lao-tzu," it is certainly the case that, for over a century, no one had had any idea of the actual source of the writings that had, by the mid-third century, come to be known by that "name." It is true that we are also at nearly as great a loss to identify "the man" who supposedly penned "the inner chapters" of the text called *Chuang-tzu*. But at least the *Chuang-tzu* does feature a *character* by that name, as one of its spokespersons for its ideas. But in regard to "the *Lao-tzu*," there are no such data: no character of "Lao-tzu" appears anywhere in the text, and no reference to any such "name" appears anywhere in the Guodian texts, or in the early Han Ma-wang-tui manuscripts.

To conclude, I suggest the following scenario to explain the origins of what we now call the *Tao te ching*. Various traditions of oral wisdom had circulated for some decades in Ch'u, where they were committed to writing by various different hands, recirculated, re-edited, and rewritten. Some of the parties involved – conceivably themselves visitors to the early Chi-hsia academy in Ch'i – learned of the cultivational practices suggested in the text called the *Nei-yeh*, and added new material of a related nature. Others – archaeologists claim that it was the tutor to the crown prince of Ch'u – gathered three such texts and refocused them on practical tasks that might befall a future ruler; those texts were buried in the tomb at Guodian. Later, someone else – hardly imaginable as a Chi-hsia participant – added an introspective "maternal voice" to the growing body of "the elders' wisdom," while others – quite *likely* at Chi-hsia – continued to add new socio-political messages, and even applications for real or aspiring warmongers and executioners.

Eventually, some redactor brought all those materials together, added new flourishes of his own, and produced something very like "the full text" that we know today. The rulers of Ch'u maintained their strong interest in such wisdom as lessons for effective rulers, even during the early days of the Han empire. So even after "the full text" was touched up (e.g., with the removal of certain tabooed characters) at the early Han court, the text was still honored enough in Ch'u for it to be inscribed on silk for burial with an eminence at Ma-wang-tui. But no one there entitled that text "Lao-tzu," presumably because there had been no such name associated with any of the earlier oral or written materials within Ch'u.

Meanwhile, it is quite likely that members of the Chi-hsia "academy" also had a hand in shaping the final form of the *Nei-yeh*.[98] Chinese scholars of the mid-twentieth century often accepted the notion that Chi-hsia intellectuals "authored" the *Nei-yeh*. More recent scholars found philological evidence to believe that it was really composed at Chi-hsia by a person who had travelled there from Ch'u.[99] It is indeed conceivable that Chi-hsia intellectuals edited *both* the "*Lao-tzu*" and the *Nei-yeh*, possibly deleting some elements and adding some others (e.g., where the model person is given the specifically Confucian denomination *chün-tzu*, "gentleman"). But, wherever the two texts originated, the Guodian finds show that elements of the Ch'u "ruling class" regarded the *Lao-tzu* material to be ideal for use in determining effective government principles. It was thus not much of a stretch for Chi-hsia scholars of "*tao* and *te*," such as perhaps Huan Yüan, to mold that material into something that could be offered to rulers as a handbook of such principles. The *Nei-yeh*, on the other hand, was no more useful to rulers than the *Chuang-tzu* was. So it was not until the Han king Liu An convened his later "Taoist think-tank" at Huai-nan that the *Nei-yeh*'s model for biospiritual cultivation was integrated into a program designed to guide and inform wise rulers.

What Taoists inherited from classical texts

The question "What effect did the *Nei-yeh*, *Chuang-tzu*, and *Tao te ching* have upon later Taoism?" has two simple answers that are wrong and a variety of nuanced answers that have great validity, though for a variety of important reasons.

The first wrong answer is the one given by the enemies of Taoism – the Confucians of late imperial and modern China – and by Western sinologues before the 1970s, who learned virtually everything they knew about Taoism, and Chinese civilization as a whole, from those enemies. Naturally, their answer was that all of later Taoism – with all its supposedly Catholic, even "superstitious," elements – is wholly and utterly alien to all that is found in the *Chuang-tzu* and the *Tao te ching*. The *Nei-yeh*, meanwhile, is not part of that story at all.

The second wrong answer seems to follow from the findings of a few specialists at the end of the twentieth century. That answer is that the *Tao te ching* and *Chuang-tzu* should be seen as the *foundation* on which much of later Taoism was built. In that view, those two texts continued to play a central role in later Taoist thought and practice. In this case, as well, the *Nei-yeh* – and the references to biospiritual cultivation found in the *Chieh-Lao*, the *Lü-shih ch'un-ch'iu*, etc. – is a quite marginal part of that story. The fact that precisely such practices of personal cultivation reappear in centuries of later Taoist material, throughout imperial and modern times, has not yet received much attention.[100]

My nuanced answers to the question of how the *Nei-yeh*, *Chuang-tzu*, and *Tao te ching* affected later Taoism are as follows:

1 All three of those texts actually played a *marginal* role in the lives and thoughts of *most* later Taoists, with a variety of important *exceptions*, many of which remain little known even among scholars.
2 Many later Taoists, of all periods, looked back to the *Lao-tzu* and *Chuang-tzu* for *concepts and models* that could *help* them *practice* Taoism. Others did not, but continued to *honor* those texts.
3 Few later Taoists read *or* honored the *Nei-yeh* – as *a text* – yet its *ideas* and *practices* did become abiding elements of Taoist practice from age to age, as well as of Chinese traditional medicine, and even the cosmological theories usually termed "Neo-Confucian."

Common to *all three* of those elements of Chinese tradition – Taoism, Chinese medicine, and Neo-Confucian philosophy – is the idea that our world consists of *ch'i* ("vital energy"), and that our own lives cannot be properly understood without reference to that fact. Within Taoism, more specifically, the *Nei-yeh*'s model of biospiritual cultivation was passed down in such disparate Han-dynasty collections as the *Huai-nan-tzu* and the *T'ai-p'ing ching*. It continued to find expression in later centuries, from Ssu-ma Ch'eng-chen's *Fu-ch'i ching-i lun* of the eighth century to modern versions of "Inner Alchemy," such as those found, for instance, in the *Chin-hsien cheng-lun* ["The Testimony to Golden Transcendence," dated 1799) and in the writings of Li Hsi-yüeh (fl. 1796–1850).[101] In later chapters, I shall do what is possible, on the basis of the data that are now known to us, to show that both scholars and the public need to become much more aware of those continuities within Taoism. It is largely on the basis of *that* heritage – *not* on the basis of Lao-tzu and Chuang-tzu, *nor* on the basis of Chang Tao-ling and his alleged successors – that it is possible to speak meaningfully, and precisely, about Taoism as "an enduring tradition."

Regarding the *Tao te ching* and the *Chuang-tzu*, what is important to bear in mind is that later Taoists did, nearly always, honor such texts.[102] But, for the most part, *Taoists* throughout history modelled their lives on the teachings found in the *Tao te ching* and the *Chuang-tzu* to about the same extent that Christians, from the time of Jesus's crucifixion to the present day, have modelled their lives on the teachings contained in Jesus's parables. Over the centuries, Taoists developed *many* different models of how to live the Taoist life, and precious few of them were based, for instance, on realizing the emptiness of cultural constructs such as "beauty" or on living with a mirror-like mind – characteristic teachings of *Chuang-tzu* – much less on behaving like water or returning to "the Mother" – common teachings in the received *Tao te ching*.

Nonetheless, Taoists through history frequently did turn back to the *Tao te ching* and *Chuang-tzu* for elements that could be picked out of their peculiar, long-outdated context and integrated into a useful and effective new religious model. Hence the "perfect person" (*chen-jen*) which the *Chuang-tzu* presented as an idealized spiritual exemplar became, in turn, the term for the Celestial Master's disciples in the *T'ai-p'ing ching*: beneficent heavenly teachers of the Shang-ch'ing revelations – who taught, not incidentally, a visualizational exchange of *ch'i* ("vital energy") between the practitioner and the heavenly teacher – and ultimately a standard honorific for any accomplished Taoist, from T'ang times through the living traditions of "Northern Taoism." Continuities of this kind, which are important for a nuanced understanding of "what Taoism is," also remain unappreciated by most today.

Where it is *easiest* to see the influence of "the classical legacy" is on the Taoist traditions that were centered upon *practices of spiritual transformation* by means of some model of personal "cultivation and refinement." Where it is *hardest* to see its influence is on such traditions as the late Han "Heavenly Masters" (*T'ien-shih*), which survive, at least vestigially, in "the liturgical structure of local communities."[103] It is true that, even there, the *Tao te ching* continued to play an important role, for even the *Hsiang-erh* – presumably a central *T'ien-shih* text composed by Chang Lu himself – presents itself as the teachings of someone who was "thinking along" with the implications of each line of the *Tao te ching*.

The effective dividing line seems to have been at the level of *personal practice*. In the Taoist traditions that were generally focused on personal cultivation, such as those called "Inner Alchemy," the ideas found in the *Tao te ching* always continued to find clear expression. For that matter, even the liturgical models of modern Cheng-i traditions require personal cultivation by the man who will conduct liturgical ceremonies on behalf of the community. The Cheng-i priest is quite certainly an example of "Taoist self-cultivation," along lines that still resonate, to some extent, with the ideals and practices of the *Chuang-tzu*, *Lao-tzu*, and *Nei-yeh*. But since that priest is "embodying the Tao" on behalf of others, who themselves are *not* engaging in any such practices, it seems fair to say that the Cheng-i *priest's* life may still be informed by such texts' ideals, but that the lives of *his audience* are rather difficult to interpret on those terms.

Another strand of continuity – which itself requires much more nuanced understanding – concerns "Lord Lao": both the figure of "Lao-tzu" and the earliest text associated with "him" were imbued with profound import by Taoists throughout later history, down to the present day. To begin with, it should not be forgotten that the "divinization" of "Lao-tzu" *pre-dated* the *entire* "Taoist religion," even if one identifies its founder as Chang Tao-ling rather than a fifth-century aristocrat such as Lu Hsiu-ching. Contrary to what modern audiences around the world were led to believe by their Confucian guides to Chinese civilization, "Lord Lao" was *not* the creation of members of China's "peasant masses," nor of people trying to compete with Buddhism. In reality, "Lord Lao" – the transcendent being whose blessings we mortals appreciate – originated as the focus of formal sacrifices at the Han imperial court, and as an element of imperial legitimation. As we shall see in Chapter 4 below, for century after century "Lord Lao" was *first* and *always* a figure of fundamental *political* importance for China's *rulers*. Such facts also give the lie to the hackneyed misconception that China's rulers were typically surrounded and guided by "Confucians," except perhaps for a few gullible fools.[104] In a sense, one could even say that Taoists actually *borrowed* "Lord Lao" from the Chinese *imperial state*. The inverse, however, cannot historically have been the case. We may also note in passing that no one has yet found that the figure of "Chuang-tzu" was ever viewed in any such light in China, either by Taoists or by dynasts.[105] Centuries of Taoists *did* draw upon elements of the *text* that went by that name, but Chuang "himself" never played a major role in later Taoism.

What, then, of the role of the text called the *Tao te ching* within later Taoism? A comparison should help us understand this issue in a properly nuanced manner. The *specifics* of "the four noble truths" meant little to many Buddhists over the last two millennia, just as the *specifics* of Jesus's parables meant little to many Christians over the last two millennia. In just such a sense, the specific *teachings* ascribed to "Lao-tzu" himself often meant *little* to many Taoists of the last two millennia. To the people in all those categories, "Lao-tzu"/"the Buddha"/"Christ" was truly important *not* primarily for the *words* that he is thought to have spoken – however much we should honor those words – but rather for the fact that he showed us the essential truth of life, and ushered us from an unsatisfactory into a truly sublime way of living. In other words, the founder's actual words were merely one integral element of the truth that he made the possibility of "salvation" known to us, pointed us in the necessary direction, and offered what help he *could* provide for those who wish to embrace that truth and experience that "salvation."

To *non*-Taoists – in Asia and in the modern West – the *Tao te ching* was basically a record of one ancient thinker's wise suggestions, and may help an individual reader decide how to understand and live his own life. That hermeneutic premise may resonate with philosophers' readings of Aristotle, or with modern secularists' readings of *all* cultures' sacred works of "wisdom." But it does *not* resonate with *Taoists'* readings of the *Tao te ching*.

Centuries of data – unknown to virtually anyone, in Asia or the West, until the turn of the millennium – show that *Taoists* frequently read the *Tao te ching* as a *scripture*, which was bequeathed to mortals like us by a transcendent being, who existed long before the historical "life" of some man who supposedly lived at some point in Chou times.[106] To many Taoists, the *Tao te ching* was sacred *not* for what it *says*, but rather for what it *is* – a textualized cosmic reality, which gives its possessor immense power and responsibilities, as well as – even at times instead of – wisdom or insight.[107] For some Taoists, learning and reciting the words of the text enabled one to (re)assimilate his/her personal reality with the deeper, unseen realities of the cosmos, in accord with the model demonstrated by "Lao-tzu" himself. In those settings, Lao-tzu "is the image and the model of the entire universe," and through meditation and/or ritual the practitioner can *become* "Lao-tzu."[108]

From the perspective of other Taoists down through history, the *Tao te ching* represented "the final intellectual result of practical efforts to achieve longevity, . . . a theoretical treatise referring to these practices and alluding to them in a coded form."[109] For centuries of such practitioners, the *Tao te ching* served as a testament to the validity and efficacy of their own religious practices. This was *especially* so for those whose goal in life was not "longevity" – a greatly exaggerated "Taoist" goal – but rather a spiritual transcendence of the mortal condition. Both for centuries of "aristocratic Taoists" and "gentry Taoists," and for followers of Ch'üan-chen Taoism – perhaps the primary form of Taoism in China over the last eight hundred years – *spiritual transcendence of the mortal condition*, not "longevity," was the actual religious goal. And, for them, the *Tao te ching* served splendidly as an ancient yet living testimony to their understanding of life and their efforts to achieve the Taoist goal.

Yet, we must also beware overestimating this scripture's importance in Taoist life. To Taoists of most periods, the *Tao te ching* was indeed an honored scripture, but it would be misleading to imagine it as a "basic scripture" comparable to the Christians' Bible or the Muslims' Qur'an. It may have been an esteemed revelation, but it was virtually never understood as a final or definitive revelation. For that reason, its scriptural value may be more properly compared to that of the principal scriptures of Mahāyāna Buddhism: except for Nichiren Buddhists' exclusive devotion to the *Lotus Sutra*, Mahāyāna Buddhists treasured and learned from an immense array of authoritative texts, all of which were viewed as complementary components of a comprehensive revelatory corpus. Likewise, Taoists of all periods acknowledged and valued the *Tao te ching* as part of a similar corpus, one that included not only the *Nan-hua ching* (known to non-Taoists as *Chuang-tzu*), but also a throng of other scriptural texts revealed by or through "Lord Lao" and other transcendent beings.

"Taoists" were not a monolithic group, nor people who held to a given set of "essential beliefs." Rather, they were the people in different ages who contributed their ideas, values, and practices to a diverse and ever-evolving cultural tradition. Yet, to say that it was "diverse and ever-changing" is not to say that we cannot or should not recognize specific continuities and specific contrasts among the various movements and teachings that Taoists generally embraced as part of their heritage. The chapters that follow seek to identify those movements and teachings – as specific historical, social, and textual realities – and to sort through their continuities and discontinuities, as best we can do so on the basis of present knowledge.

3

THE COURSE OF THE TAOIST TRADITION

Throughout the twentieth century, the history of Taoism remained poorly known. Today few people, even scholars, have a good understanding of the whole sweep of Taoist history, and few presentations of Taoism have successfully shown its changes and continuities from one period to the next. Even today's scholarship still sheds very limited light on many elements of Taoist history that are quite noteworthy or might someday be found to be noteworthy. And there remain historical arguments that are pegged to broader interpretive disputes about whether given data are or are not important, or even relevant, for understanding "Taoism."[1]

Explaining the beginings of Taoism, for instance, is like explaining the beginings of Judaism: in each case, one could peg it to several different figures or groups, based on different ideas about the precise contents of the category itself. Avram, for instance, never had a *bris* or observed Passover; Moses never went to temple or had a *bar mitzvah*; and neither believed that our lives would be better if what we are doing today could be done "next year in Jerusalem." So one could easily argue that "being Jewish" began long after those figures lived, sometime when a *definable group* of people *self-consciously* carried out a certain array of definably Jewish practices, with an implicit or explicit agreement that such practices set all such practitioners apart from others, who had other traditions and practices.

Along those lines, we may determine the beginings of Taoism only after we have identified a *definable group of people* who self-consciously went through a certain array of definably Taoist practices. As we have seen, the twentieth-century notion that "Taoism" emerged from a set of ideas supposedly found in the *Lao-tzu* and

Chuang-tzu does not rest upon any social or historical facts. Nor does it make much sense in terms of what *Taoists* of past and present have often said about their origins. For instance, in the year 1335 a Taoist historian of noble descent, compiling accounts of great Taoists of bygone days, duly pondered what the Han historian Ssu-ma Ch'ien said about "the Taoist school," but concluded that, "in actuality, the starting point of 'the Taoist school' is the well-worn grooves of the grand Perfected Ones, [that is] in the pattern of establishing a teaching to restore the world."[2] Of course, all such explanations must be examined critically, with reference both to divergent Taoist explanations and to all the pertinent historical facts. But at least we should be *familiar* with them, and familiar enough with all the pertinent facts to be able to make a sound case regarding their validity. Instead, most twentieth-century writers about Taoism simply ignored the fact that Taoist historians such as the one just cited ever existed, and dismissed all such *Taoist* explanations of how Taoism began as irrelevant.

It is also important to remember that most twentieth-century audiences learned about Taoism not by interacting personally with living Taoists and hearing them explain their heritage, but rather just by reading expositions by intellectuals, people whose expertise and self-esteem rest on their ability to articulate and analyze ideas, more than on their ability to understand people's lives. Taoists, on the other hand, have not, as a rule, been interested in figuring out how to articulate or defend specific propositions about life. So the effort to understand "Taoism" by identifying and analyzing its "basic ideas" has always led, and will always lead, to inaccurate conclusions. The more meaningful approach is to ask not what a Taoist *thinks*, but rather what a Taoist *does*. And from that perspective, it seems that Taoists throughout history have generally been people who agreed that they should *refine and transform themselves to attain full integration with life's deepest realities*.

We now know that there were some people in "classical China" who had some such inclinations. And, by the fourth century BCE, some of them anonymously wrote about such practices, presumably to encourage others to engage in them. Nonetheless, there were actually no "Taoists" per se in pre-Ch'in/Han China, for nowhere in the "middle kingdoms" was there *a self-conscious group* of "Taoists" who *talked together* about what their practices should be and why. As we shall see, it was not until about 500 CE that certain people began to become "Taoists" in a coherent social sense.

In early Han times, as we have seen, historians and bibliographers did try to bring order to the plethora of writings from earlier times. It was only then that a label, *tao-chia* (literally, "the house of Tao"), came to be applied, retroactively, to such surviving writings as those catalogers saw fit to group together. Of course, the people who had originally produced those texts never heard of each other, and would have been surprised to learn that anyone considered them members of a common "school."

Taoism *per se* did not develop until medieval times, when people who wished not to count themselves as Buddhist decided to identify all the indigenous writings about how we can attain full integration with life's deepest realities. Those people, such as Lu Hsiu-ching, were members of the higher classes of Chinese society, and were obviously highly educated. Yet, to judge from the extreme diversity of the writings that they regarded as their patrimony, they did not cling to any particular set of ideas about life. Nor did they give primacy to such materials as the *Lao-tzu* or *Chuang-tzu*. They did include such texts in their collections, but ranged them among lots of other texts from all earlier ages, and all of those writings seem to have been seen in comparable terms. Many Taoists did find interesting and inspiring thoughts in texts such as *Lao-tzu* and *Chuang-tzu*, but those texts' greatest value seems to have been that they could be used to show how ancient and noble the new "tradition" – the *Tao-chiao* – actually was.

In what follows, I will outline how that tradition evolved, on the basis of what is now known from scholarly analysis of Taoist and non-Taoist sources.[3]

Wellsprings: the Han dynasty

By the end of the twentieth century, many scholars of Taoist studies around the world had found that many elements of what would later become Taoism could reasonably be traced to a variety of social, political, and religious currents of Han times. For instance, as noted above, it was the Han imperial government that deified "Lao-tzu." Eventually, as that government weakened, new religious movements emerged, which claimed a special authority by virtue of having received a mandate from that "Lord Lao." Toward the end of the last century, many specialists had come to accept those movements as "the beginnings of Taoism." Yet, those movements, and their professed belief to be following in the path of Lord Lao, cannot be understood without also understanding certain other intellectual and religious developments of Han times. Those developments were – like the deification of Lord Lao – centered squarely at the imperial court, among political elites who were all, in their own ways, trying to shape the conceptual framework within which the government operated.

One such development involved a fairly well-known textual collection, the *Huai-nan-tzu*. The *Huai-nan-tzu* was a composite work produced in 139 BCE at the court of Liu An, the Han king (or "prince") of Huai-nan. Liu gathered a number of scholars interested in ideas and practices that had emerged in late classical times and the early imperial period, including the practices of personal cultivation outlined in the *Nei-yeh*, as well as ideas about the origins and nature of life's processes. But, unlike those who produced most classical texts, even those at the Chi-hsia academy in Ch'i, the contributors to the *Huai-nan-tzu* were part of a common intellectual enterprise that was a reflection of recent political and cultural events.

Han thinkers did not, for the most part, regard themselves as continuing the work of any of the supposed "hundred schools." During the first century of Han times – roughly the second century BCE – such retrospective categories had not yet been concocted: there was, quite simply, no "Taoism" or "Confucianism." It is quite true that we can retroactively align some thinkers of that period rather closely with others whom we can similarly identify as "Confucian" or "Taoist," but the thinkers themselves seldom did so. Their concerns were not so much to defend specific classical ideas as to achieve a coherent system of thought that would provide a rational explanation of the entirety of human experience – history, government, religion, thought, and all other aspects of life.

The existence of such a system, which might be able to render the world orderly and comprehensible, was profoundly important to the thinkers of early Han times, because their world had been dominated by disorder for as long as anyone alive could remember. The Ch'in regime had been incredibly successful in certain practical regards. But it had operated on the principles of "Legalists" such as

Shang Yang, who had placed state power above all other concerns. Consequently, the Ch'in regime was particularly resented by later idealistic intellectuals, for good reason: the Ch'in regime had regarded such men as a threat, put many of them to death, and collected and burned all written works that contained ideas that were at odds with the state's purposes.[4]

After the wreckage of the Ch'in dynasty had been cleared, thinking people wanted to understand – and to explain in clear and comprehensible terms – what had happened in their world, and *why*. Much of the thought of the Han period was therefore based upon a search for principles that could explain *why* things happen the way they do. To a certain extent, the Han search for causes paralleled the development of the natural sciences in Europe. Both represented a search for "objective" principles underlying life's events. And both believed that those principles could be discovered and understood through rational human thought. But in Han China, the primary effort was to identify basic principles that explained not only the events of the natural world, but also the events of human history.

The rise of the ruthless Ch'in regime – which had deliberately eradicated the political and intellectual traditions of the lands that had competed against it – seemed to disprove the comfortable arguments of Confucians and the *Tao te ching* alike. Those arguments had also emerged from the minds of men who had lived in times of socio-political turmoil. Yet those men had felt quite certain that a secure and orderly government could and would exist when the ruler followed their ideals – humanistic ideals in Confucian terms, and holistic ideals in terms of the *Lao-tzu*. The triumph of Ch'in totalitarianism, however, suggested that idealistic values did not truly make a land peaceful or secure. Yet, the collapse of the Ch'in after less than a generation offered a very different historical lesson: it suggested that there is justice in the world's events after all, and that the *Lao-tzu* was thus indeed correct when it insisted (in chapter 29 of the received text) that "all under heaven" is "a spiritual entity," in which anything too extreme is soon destroyed. That fact is one reason that in the first decades of the Han period rulers looked to the *Lao-tzu* for life's explanations. By their time, the text that we call the *Tao te ching* had evolved into its "modern" form, including passages insisting that brute power violates the natural order and always ends in failure.

The thinkers of the early Han did not question the value of the imperial system that the Ch'in had created, nor did they question the necessity of having a ruler. Their problem was (a) that rulers had continually been overthrown by other rulers, and (b) that all of the classical thinkers had offered different explanations of those facts, and different ideas about a form of government that could be both successful and morally sound. Indeed, everyone except the Legalists and the Mohists (who had virtually died out) agreed that *moral principles were essential to effective government*. But the fact that the ruthless Ch'in dynasty had managed to conquer all the other ancient states – including those with high-minded rulers – seemed to prove that idealism alone was not a sound basis for state or society. So Han thinkers were anxious to find a solid foundation for their political ideals, one that was grounded not just in lofty abstract concepts, but rather in "objective reality."

One such thinker was Tung Chung-shu (*ca.* 195–115 BCE).[5] Tung can very easily be aligned with "the Confucians" (despite the fact that Chu Hsi, and the late imperial orthodoxy based on his writings, never recognized Tung as a "real Confucian"). When the Han emperor Wu-ti came to the throne in 141 BCE, Tung offered his explanations of life in three undatable memorials.[6] The earlier Mohists and Confucians had all vaguely agreed that "Heaven" (*T'ien*) had instituted the world, and that it played a significant role in human life, as well as in the world's ongoing processes. But for all of those thinkers, a few basic principles had sufficed in this connection, primarily as justification of other principles that each of them considered more pressing. Tung Chung-shu, however, professed to discover fundamental principles for a complete explanation of life within a historical chronicle from the old state of Lu known as the *Ch'un-ch'iu* ("The Spring and Autumn Annals," generally considered the work of Confucius himself). What Tung discovered in the *Ch'un-ch'iu* was that Heaven is at work in worldly events, mandating certain outcomes in the course of human affairs. He argued that the activity of "Heaven and Earth" is fulfilled by humanity's civilizing activity: humanity completes or perfects all things by maintaining proper patterns of action, though those patterns are not the product of human invention, but rather Heaven's own design. Tung elaborated with ideas drawn from natural philosophers such as Tsou Yen, who had explained the world in terms of *yin* and *yang* and the "Five Forces" (*wu hsing*). To Tung, the world must be understood not as a field of self-contained natural processes and human deeds, but rather as a field in which Heaven acts. And he argued – no doubt to Han Wu-ti's satisfaction – that kingship was a key to such matters: the king ensures that his rule is successful by *aligning his actions with the natural processes that Heaven has instituted*. Yet, history shows that each of the earlier dynasties had reconfigured certain of its predecessor's patterns, to demonstrate that Heaven's mandate had been transferred to a new ruling house. From that fact, Tung concluded that Heaven had actually established not a single invariable pattern, but rather a revolving sequence of patterns. Accordingly, each ruler must be wary of possible deviations from Heaven's constantly shifting pattern, as intimated by irregular natural events – a belief attested in an edict of early Han times. Here, Tung integrates political principles with the idea of a dynamically correlative cosmos, in which actions on the level of humanity, whether proper or improper, stimulate responses on other levels. The effects of such beliefs on the various movements and thinkers of later Taoism were profound.

Analysis shows that Tung's throught drew not only on classical Confucians such as Mencius and Hsün-tzu but also on thinkers such as Tsou Yen and Mo-tzu, as well as on contemporary *I-ching* interpreters and even the just completed *Huai-nan-tzu*. Yet, Tung shows little trace of the thought of "Taoist" texts such as *Lao-tzu*. The explanation for that fact could not be more clear: the emperor Wu had recently executed his own kisman, Liu An, for daring to construct a theoretical model that was grounded on ideas found in the *Tao te ching* and *Nei-yeh*. Tung clearly took pains to ensure that the emperor Wu would not associate Tung's theory of life with any such ideas, and that he would find his own imperial authority duly glorified.

Yet, within a century or so, Tung's vision of a harmonious union of cosmos and polity would inspire other Han officials to produce new and different kinds of texts – "revealed" texts in which Heaven warns that it might soon withdraw its mandate from the Han. These ideas would, in subsequent centuries, inspire not only rebel political movements that eventually toppled the Han, but also new religious movements, some of which eventually flowed into the Taoist tradition.

The most important stimulus to the new religious movements of late Han times was a textual tradition that began at the Han court at the end of the first century BCE. Its exact origins are not, and, because the surviving sources are from a later period, may never be clear. Some scholars have related the new texts to the activities of sundry individuals who would later come to be classed as "masters of expansiveness," *fang-shih* – specialists regarding knowledge and activities that lay beyond the pale of ordinary civilian or technical officials.[7] Such individuals became influential courtiers by offering rulers such as Han Wu-ti colorful new methods for aggrandizing himself. But, within a few generations, what became more important were new texts that claimed to tell rulers what was now happening in the world, on the basis of *subtle unseen realities*. Here, of course, is another of the wellsprings of later Taoist "revelations."

One of the first such texts was presented to the throne in 166 CE by a group of "scholars" (*ju* – a term usually understood as suggesting the values of mundane "Confucians," as distinguished from all loftier figures as well as from *fang-shih*). But that long-lost text – "The Book in Blue for Grand Tranquillity" (*T'ai-p'ing ch'ing-ling shu*) – appears to have been anything but mundane. It apparently suggested, along lines that might have made good sense to Tung Chung-shu, that "Heaven" was inclined to institute a new political era: it offered the Han ruler the opportunity to enact such a transformation; otherwise, a new dispensation would occur.[8]

The surviving vestiges of that text appear in the rather messy remains of a very diverse work that scholars in both Asia and the West generally ignored until the 1970s. It is known as the *T'ai-p'ing ching* ["Scripture of Grand Tranquillity"]. According to the *T'ai-p'ing ching*, ancient rulers had maintained an "air (*ch'i*) of Grand Tranquillity (*t'ai-p'ing*)" by virtue of practicing *wu-wei* ("non-action") – the behavioral ideal of trusting to the world's natural order that the *Tao te ching* had recommended. (Here, at the outset, it is quite easy to see the fallacy of twentieth-century notions that the "philosophy" of the noble *Tao te ching* had no real effect on the "superstitions" of later Taoists.) The *T'ai-p'ing ching* says that later rulers meddled with the world, thereby causing "Grand Tranquillity" to be disrupted. Now, therefore, one must look to oneself. The text goes on to provide specific directions for personal holistic reintegration with life's unseen dimensions, including moral injunctions, instructions for meditation, and recommendations for enhancing one's personal health and longevity through hygienic practices (such as breath control), medicine, acupuncture, and even music therapy. It could thus easily be argued that the *T'ai-p'ing ching* was the prime fountainhead for most later Taoist practices, as well as a key link in the historical continuum that ran from the *Tao te ching* and *Nei-yeh* through much of later Taoism.

The *T'ai-p'ing ching*'s focus was upon providing people with practical advice for reintegrating with the natural order: it explained that we must now take *personal* responsibility for that reintegration because of our recent rulers' failure. The *T'ai-p'ing ching* also disproves the twentieth-century misconception that the degraded Taoists of imperial times, unlike the classical Taoist "philosophers," pursued "immortality": the *T'ai-p'ing ching* commends a wide array of personal practices, but does not maintain that those practices would result in "immortality" of any sort. In retrospect, it is also notable that some of the text's teachings are depicted as instructions which a "Heavenly Master" (*T'ien-shih*) imparted to a group of "perfected" (*chen*) disciples, while other teachings appear as teachings of a "Heavenly Lord" (*T'ien-chün*).

In late Han times, the *T'ai-p'ing ching* helped inspire several new social movements. One attributed its founding to an obscure healer named Chang Tao-ling, whose very historical existence remains uncertain.[9] According to later texts, Chang experienced a revelation from "Lord Lao" (*Lao-chün*) in the year 144 CE, which resulted in a covenant (*meng-wei*) between Chang and his heavenly lord. One element of that covenant was that Chang now possessed a divine mandate to replace the obsolescent Han government and establish a new social order in its place. According to the later texts, Chang claimed the mantle of "Heavenly Master," and he, and his heirs, oversaw a religious organization in which male and female "libationers" (*chi-chiu*) healed the sick by performing expiatory rituals. That organization, now often called T'ien-shih ("Heavenly Master" or "Celestial Master") Taoism, was based on the idea that a healthy society depended upon the moral, physical, and spiritual health of all its members.

In the entire history of Taoism, the early "Heavenly Masters" organization was the *only* Taoist tradition that was ever truly based among "the masses." (Contrary to twentieth-century misconceptions, most later Taoist traditions were founded and maintained by aristocrats, or by members of the later well-to-do "gentry" class.) The early Heavenly Masters organization apparently ignored participants' social status. Its leaders, including Chang himself, were evidently commoners, and its power structure was open to both men and women, and to Chinese and non-Chinese alike, with no perceptible discrimination.[10] Yet its leadership was hereditary, and remained in the hands of members of the Chang clan for uncounted generations.

The T'ien-shih "libationers" were organized hierarchically, with women apparently arrayed in ranks parallel to those of men. Though historical facts are exiguous, such "libationers" presumably supervised their followers' religious lives, and taught them how to obtain relief from illness, and absolution from inherited sins (*ch'eng-fu*), by means of confession and good works. The libationers also conducted liturgical ceremonies, in the form of official petitions to various unseen powers, who were imagined as government officials within the higher dimensions. All followers received graded "registers" (*lu*) that were associated with specific spiritual forces. And they were all required to renounce the worship of any and all unapproved spirits. The religious activities of those outside the organization were consequently stigmatized as "licentious cults." We can also say that the followers of "the Heavenly Masters" did not conceive of themselves as opposed to Confucians, and that their moral code included both standard "peasant values" and principles that were common to Confucian tradition.

Other than claiming authority from Chang Tao-ling's covenant with Lord Lao, the early T'ien-shih claimed no relationship to any of those whom we think of as major figures of "classical Taoism." Yet that is not to say that the T'ien-shih movement did not know and make use of texts such as the *Lao-tzu*. One of their most important texts was actually a commentary to the *Lao-tzu*, called *Hsiang-erh* ["Thinking Along"].[11] The *Hsiang-erh* provides teachings that may have been addressed not just to the masses, but also to aristocrats. It integrates the *T'ai-p'ing ching*'s general worldview with ideas of biospiritual cultivation inherited from the *Nei-yeh*, and tags all such thoughts to specific passages of the *Tao te ching*. For instance, it teaches that humanity lost its accord with "Tao" through improper behaviors, which resulted in the harmful loss of "life-energy" (*ch'i*) and "vital essence" (*ching*). By returning to healthy behaviors, such as self-restraint and moral correctness, one will reverse that loss, and Tao will stay rather than depart.

As the twentieth century closed, however, only a handful of specialists had begun to ponder what the *Hsiang-erh* teaches us about the evolution of Taoism, especially about the impact of the *Nei-yeh*'s teachings on later Taoists, who were heretofore imagined to be unable and unwilling to read such "philosophical" texts or to consider engaging in such practices. Neither Asian nor Western scholars have yet noticed, or debated the significance of, the fact that the specific concepts articulated in the *Nei-yeh* reappear both in the *Huai-nan-tzu* – the product of the land's greatest thinkers at a ruler's court – and in the *Hsiang-erh* – the product of a leader of the most populist Taoist movement in all of history. In other words, the common notion that there was a "religious Taoism" that was unrelated to "philosophical Taoism" is simply untenable.

Related texts in the *Tao-tsang* preserve thirty-six moral precepts said to have been part of the original *Hsiang-erh*. Nine consist of "prescriptive precepts" pegged squarely to the *Tao te ching* (e.g., "practice clarity and stillness" and "practice desirelessness"). The others consist of "proscriptive precepts." Some of those go back to the *Tao te ching* (e.g., "do not delight in arms") or the *Nei-yeh* (e.g., "do not waste your vital essence and life-energy"), and others preserve the wider social framework of the *T'ai-p'ing ching* (e.g., "do not pray or sacrifice to spirits and gods").[12]

Regrettably, neither the *Hsiang-erh* nor other T'ien-shih texts of the second to sixth centuries were preserved intact. It is thus not possible to get an accurate and fully textured understanding of the nuances of what the participants in those traditions thought and did. One thing that is clear, however, is that women were represented as having played active roles in the tradition, not only as faithful members of the laity but also by fulfilling sacerdotal functions. We shall return to such matters in Chapter 4.

Southerly currents

In the fourth century CE, north China was invaded by peoples from the northern border regions, and the leaders of the Celestial Master movement fled south, to the region known as Chiang-nan, "South of the (Yangtze) River." There they found a rich indigenous religious culture, parts of which centered upon the pursuit of personal perfection through ritual activity. Unlike the Celestial Master tradition, the indigenous traditions of Chiang-nan apparently took little interest in ideals of a healthy society: their focus was almost exclusively upon the individual.

"The Old Traditions of Chiang-nan" included writings that were concerned with methods of invoking spirits and ritual use of talismans, such as the *San-huang wen* ["Text of the Three Sovereigns"] and *Wu-fu hsü* ["Explanations of the Five Talismans"].[13] But they also included writings about "alchemy" (*wai-tan*), presenting it as a pursuit of personal perfection through a transformative process that involved the preparation of efficacious artificial substances. Those substances were known collectively as *tan*, a term generally translated as "elixirs." A set of three scriptures lay out the practices of this tradition, which was known as the T'ai-ch'ing ("Great Clarity") tradition.[14] Those texts present a process that begins with a transmission of the necessary knowledge from master to disciple. It then requires the establishment of a sacred ritual area, the selection of an auspicious time, the compounding of the "elixir" itself, an offering to the deities, and finally the ingestion of the *tan*. Successful completion of the process was said to elevate the practitioner to a heavenly sphere called T'ai-ch'ing ("Great Clarity"). This process, which required secrecy, was studied and written about by a number of Chiang-nan aristocrats, though we do not know how many people, of what social background, may actually have engaged in such practices.

Our primary source for much of our knowledge of all such traditions of that day is a famous work called the *Pao-p'u-tzu* ["(The Writings of) the Master who Embraces Simplicity"], written by Ko Hung (283–343). Ko was an aristocrat as well as a government official, and much of his *Pao-p'u-tzu* – the so-called Outer Chapters (*wai-p'ien*) – expresses the interests and values of the *ju*

"Confucians" of his time.[15] Yet, he also claimed to have inherited a variety of special ritual methods, which went back through several distinct lineages. His intention was to demonstrate not only that such methods could elevate a person to a deathless state, but also that such a pursuit of immortality was a fitting goal for upstanding gentlemen (i.e., for Confucians and fellow aristocrats).

It is clear that Ko did not identify himself with the teachings found in classical Taoist texts, and he had no use for the T'ien-shih Taoists. So it might be said that he is best characterized as a maverick Confucian who sought to integrate various traditions about spiritual practices into the elite culture of his society. Nonetheless, he did have a significant impact on later Taoist traditions, and later Taoists claimed him as a significant figure within their heritage. However, twentieth-century writers, Chinese and Western, often mistakenly cited Ko Hung as a principal representative of "religious Taoism." In so doing, they misrepresented the realities of Taoism in imperial times.

The fourth century CE was a period of rich interaction among all those diverse traditions, and there were two new developments, both of which occurred as the result of revelations from celestial beings. The first, known as the Shang-ch'ing ("Supreme Clarity") revelation, was received from angelic beings called "Perfected Ones" (*chen-jen*), who dwell in distant heavens of "Supreme Clarity." The Perfected Ones revealed methods by which the diligent practitioner could ascend to their heavens, particularly visualizational meditation.[16] One model for such visualization was a marriage between the practitioner and one of the various female Perfected Ones.[17]

But Shang-ch'ing Taoism also subsumed the older southern pursuit of personal perfection by means of alchemy. Though often misunderstood as a typical element of religious Taoism, alchemy actually had its own distinctive premises, and was a current that many Taoists found difficult to honor as highly as their own, more spiritualized practices. Yet, it was embraced by certain Shang-ch'ing Taoists as a practice believed to elevate the aspirant's spiritual state for eventual ascent to the heavens.[18] What the alchemical tradition shared with Taoism was a vital concern with *self-perfection* based on an assumption that the individual's being is not comprised, as Western minds imagine, of incommensurable realities such as "matter" and "spirit," but is rather a unified whole. For exceptional aspirants, alchemy provided secret knowledge that permitted control of the forces of the cosmos, which also inhere within the constitution of the individual. To outsiders, the whole undertaking was often misunderstood as merely a pursuit of physical longevity. But within Taoism, alchemy was actually *a method of moral and spiritual self-refinement*: through proper knowledge and action, one could pare away the grosser elements of one's being and eventually ascend to a higher plane of existence.

One such system that emerged from south China was a tradition of symbolic alchemy based on the *Chou-i ts'an-t'ung ch'i* ["Tally for Threefold Integration in terms of the *I ching*"].[19] From Han times on, the validity and value of the *I ching* (also known as the *Chou-i*) were generally accepted by Taoists and Confucians alike, though few ever regarded it as central to their lives or their practice. One major exception involved centuries of Taoists who grounded their ideas about practice on the *Chou-i ts'an-t'ung ch'i*, an undatable text of late antiquity attributed to a legendary figure named Wei Po-yang. Since the *I ching* allows us to peer into the processes that operate in the changing world, and to discover how to bring our activities into alignment with those processes, it is easy to see how some Taoist minds would turn to it. Whatever the origin of the *Chou-i ts'an-t'ung ch'i*, Taoists came to regard such texts as divine revelations which, when supplemented with proper oral instruction, provided the secret keys that allowed a practitioner to manipulate cosmic forces in such a way as to achieve a transcendent state by becoming assimilated to eternal realities, beyond the world of change. That process could be understood either as an external (*wai*) material process of compounding an ingestible "elixir," or as an inner (*nei*) process of spiritual transformation or refinement.

In this context, however, "alchemy" was not the product of a sequence of ritual actions – as in the T'ai-ch'ing tradition – but rather the result of a systematic study and application of the cosmological principles that certain intellectuals perceived within the *I ching*. Yet within most Taoist traditions, alchemy seems to have remained, for the most part, primarily of theoretical interest. Unless a given set of ideas could be used for religious *practice* – that is, embodied in one's actual life, whether in a ritual process or in a form of meditation – Taoists of all ages tended to acknowledge such ideas' validity, but to turn to other, more practical principles as the basis for their lives.

In addition to acknowledging the ideas of alchemy, the Shang-ch'ing revelations included elements that we would regard as messianic and millenarian.[20] The Perfected Ones revealed that the chaotic world of fourth-century China was actually in the process of being purged by demonic forces. The revelation instructed the heedful to perfect themselves, among all other reasons, in anticipation of the descent of a "savior," a being known as "the Sage of the Latter Days" (*hou-sheng*, sometimes rendered "the Sage Who is to Come"). The Perfected Ones promised that the coming sage would establish a new world order for the righteous remnant who had properly prepared themselves, the "seed people" (*chung-min*). In the millenarian soteriology of the Shang-ch'ing revelation, one thus sees a synthesis of the southern concern with individual spiritual perfection and the northern concern with religious rectification of the socio-political order.

The Shang-ch'ing revelations were immediately followed by a quite different set of revelations, known by the term Ling-pao ("Numinous Treasure"). "Ling-pao Taoism" was distinguished by its incorporation of certain elements from Mahāyāna Buddhism, and by a conspicuous emphasis upon the importance of the entire human community. Ling-pao scriptures, such as the *Tu-jen ching*, "Scripture for the Salvation of Humanity," told of a great cosmic deity – a personification of the Tao simply called Yüan-shih T'ien-tsun, "The Heavenly Venerable One of the Primordial Beginning."[21] Anxious to save humanity, that deity sends an emissary to reveal the *Tu-jen ching*, which is itself an emanation of the Tao. The practitioner was instructed to recite the text, thereby reactualizing its primordial recitation by the deity and participating directly in its salvific efficacy. Though materials like the *Tu-jen ching* had significant influence upon later generations of Taoists, the entire Ling-pao corpus remained unknown, even to most specialists, until nearly the end of the twentieth century.[22]

Later, in the fifth century, the Ling-pao tradition was refocused by Lu Hsiu-ching (406–477), an aristocratic scholar who was instrumental in the effort to give shape and clarity to the traditions of all of "Taoism." In several important senses, it was really Lu Hsiu-ching who *founded* Taoism, for it was he who first gained *community acceptance* for a *common canon of texts*, which established the boundaries, and contents, of "the teachings of the Tao" (*Tao-chiao*).[23] Lu also reconfigured the ritual activities of the tradition, and formulated a new set of liturgies, which continue to influence Taoist practice to the present day.[24] One central liturgy is the *chiao*, a lengthy sequence of rituals that renew the local community by reintegrating it with the heavenly order. Other liturgies, called *chai*, had diverse aims. One was designed to prevent disease by expiating moral transgressions through communal confession. Another labored for the salvation of deceased ancestors. A third was intended to forestall natural disasters and reintegrate the socio-political order with the cosmos. Through such liturgies, Taoism incorporated ritual frameworks derived from all segments of society, from the imperial court to the local village, and unified them through the activity of priests (*tao-shih*), some of whom were women.

Northerly currents

Meanwhile, other Taoist traditions were evolving in the northern parts of China. After the migration of the "Celestial Masters" in the early fourth century, efforts to continue their tradition ensued in the north. The foremost figure in those efforts was K'ou Ch'ien-chih (365–448), the brother of a provincial general in the region of the capital city, Ch'ang-an. His ideal of restoring the T'ien-shih community in the north reportedly met with heavenly response, for in 415 he received a revelation from Lord Lao, consisting of "the Precepts of the New Code" for the Taoist community. A later divine dispensation bestowed upon him the title of "Heavenly Master." In 424, he found a Confucian ally at the court, and together they validated the third emperor of the "Northern Wei" dynasty (a leader of a newly sinicized people called the Toba) as "the Perfected Ruler of Grand Tranquillity." The Toba-Wei adopted Taoism as a state religion, and most of the Toba emperors underwent ceremonial induction in Taoist holy orders.[25] Meanwhile, T'ien-shih institutions were established throughout the countryside, in accordance with K'ou's "New Code." After K'ou's death, however, state patronage ceased, and other traditions came to the fore.

Taoist masters from centers in the north continued to initiate various rulers into holy orders through the sixth century.[26] Foremost among those centers was one based at the abbey called Lou-kuan, not far from the capital. Since the abbey had been established near where "Lao-tzu" was said to have "departed to the West," many Lou-kuan texts feature teachings by and about "Lord Lao," understood as a divine being who descends to earth from age to age in order to reveal salvific teachings.[27] One such set of teachings is found in the *Hsi-sheng ching* ("Scripture of Western Ascension").[28] In it, one finds little trace of any element of T'ien-shih traditions, any more than one finds much that resembles the more famous Taoist traditions of fourth-century Chiang-nan. Yet, like most of the latter, it is clearly centered upon practices of self-cultivation, and the idea that it is a revelation from a heavenly being seems to function as little more than a "marketing device" to attract readers' attention.

Scholars of Taoist studies have often ignored texts, such as the *Hsi-sheng ching*, which do not fit neatly into any of their interpretive models regarding what Taoists of this "Six Dynasties" period believed and practiced. Yet, the overall contours of the *Hsi-sheng ching*'s teachings are in harmony not only with those of the *Nei-yeh* and *Tao te ching*, but also with those of such later Taoists as Ssu-ma Ch'eng-chen (eighth century), Wang Che (twelfth century), and Liu I-ming (eighteenth century). By their time, however, it no longer seemed necessary or useful to couch their traditions' primary teachings in revelatory terms.

Though texts such as the *Hsi-sheng ching* show the influence of certain Buddhist ideas, Buddhists of the Six Dynasties period were not pleased, and some composed texts intended to discredit many elements of Taoism.[29] Until the late seventh century, a variety of rulers in China, and in Tibet as well, compelled representatives of the two traditions to engage in staged debates. But the individuals who represented Taoism in those imperial debates were certainly doing so not because they were antagonistic toward Buddhism, or even because they regarded Taoism as true and Buddhism as false, but rather because they were enjoined by the emperor to present such arguments. For example, the Taoist Ts'ai Huang, who participated in a debate in 638, wrote, "I have studied the principles in the *Vimalakīrti* [a Mahāyāna sutra] and the [Mādhyamika] Three Treatises to the point at which their essential instructions flow spontaneously from me . . . Although the texts of the Taoists differ from those of the Buddhists, the tenets are essentially the same."[30] Most later Taoists shared those sentiments, especially aristocrats and members of the later "gentry" class.

Other northern Taoists of the Six Dynasties period occupied themselves compiling a variety of texts, including catalogs and "Taoist encyclopedias" such as the *Wu-shang pi-yao* ["Secret Essentials of the Most High"].[31] Most scholars of Chinese studies have paid little attention to the scores of scholarly and scientific works that Taoists of imperial times produced. Misled by modern Confucian ideologues, who projected a false image of "the Dark Ages" back on to the centuries between the Han and the Sung, few twentieth-century scholars ever bothered to examine the surviving works produced by Taoist scholars of that age. Fearful of how radically their understanding of China's history and culture would be undermined by looking at such data – much less by pondering the quantity of such data that has *not survived* – many scholars today continue to embrace the false belief that Chinese "scholarship," like Chinese "thought," was the exclusive province of "the Confucians."[32] In reality, Taoists were often the leaders in both the theoretical and the practical dimensions of the physical and biological sciences, and Chinese pharmacology and medicine evolved largely because of efforts of medieval Taoists intent upon "cultivating life."[33]

Nor should it be imagined that such works were produced by fringe thinkers at the outer margins of Taoism. Rather, such matters were quite central to the lives, and the writings, of the leading Taoists of the late Six Dynasties period and much of the T'ang, including Sun Ssu-miao (fl. 673), a cultured physician credited with numerous Taoist texts on the physiological aspects of "nourishing life," some of which are still used today in the training of Chinese physicians.[34] Related texts were associated with the name of Sun's most famous contemporary, Ssu-ma Ch'eng-chen, better known for his role as advisor to emperors, and for his writings on the meditative practices that had always been central to the Taoist spiritual life.[35] Admiring emperors sought to bolster their legitimacy by associating with Taoist masters such as Ssu-ma, and by having them perform liturgies for the sake of state and society. During the T'ang dynasty, cultural leaders in every field associated freely and intimately with such masters, and were deeply influenced by Taoist religious, artistic, and literary traditions.[36]

The high-water mark: the T'ang dynasty

By T'ang times (618–907 CE), when the north and the south were reunited, a common sense of *Taoist identity* had come into existence. That common identity remained quite generalized, and to modern minds – particularly those of Westerners accustomed to think of religious identity on Judaeo-Christian terms – the "Taoism" of T'ang times might still be difficult to recognize as constituting a common tradition. But it was, for by the opening of the seventh century the Taoists of north China – whom K'ou Ch'ien-chih had labored to unify – and the Taoists of south China – whom Lu Hsiu-ching had worked to unify – were all now subjects of a common ruler. Soon, their regional differences quickly submerged themselves into a common "ecumenical" tradition. Their prime motivation for forging a strong and lasting union was the political challenge. Aristocratic Taoist leaders of previous generations – K'ou Ch'ien-chih, Lu Hsiu-ching, T'ao Hung-ching – had all achieved imperial support, as would Taoist leaders for centuries thereafter, as we will see in Chapter 4 below. But through the seventh century, there remained a rivalry: Buddhists also sought imperial patronage, and their social and economic power eclipsed that of the Taoists. Hence, Taoist leaders worked to be seen by rulers not just as eminent individuals, but as representatives of a cultural tradition as worthy of respect, and support, just as Buddhism was.

Taoist leaders called that common tradition *Tao-chiao* ("the Teaching of the Tao"), a newly constructed category intended to strike rulers as comparable to, and therefore competitive with, "the Teaching of the Buddha" (*Fo-chiao*) and "the Teaching of the Confucian Scholars" (*Ju-chiao*). The foundation upon which such leaders constructed this new mega-tradition appears to have been the collection of sacred writings that Lu Hsiu-ching had first conceived in the fifth century. Since it had evolved in the south, it is not surprising that the first real collection of the writings of Tao-chiao – often called *San-tung* ("The Three Arcana") – consisted primarily of the texts of Ling-pao, Shang-ch'ing, and the old traditions of Chiang-nan. Later, four supplementary sections were added, incorporating texts pertaining to the *Tao te ching*, the *T'ai-p'ing ching*, the T'ai-ch'ing alchemical tradition, and the Heavenly Masters. This synthesis was certainly not based upon the T'ien-shih organization that Chang Tao-ling had established, though some scholars of the late twentieth century believed otherwise. Not only was the first Taoist "canon" clearly *not* the product of the T'ien-shih tradition, it was in fact the creation of people who implicitly *distinguished themselves* from that old tradition. If, as even some late twentieth-century scholars maintained, we should define "Taoism" in terms of the people who produced the *Tao-tsang* (the modern name for the complete corpus of Taoist texts), we find that the *central* social and religious components of the tradition were actually the traditions of southern aristocrats, such as Lu Hsiu-ching and the founders of the Shang-ch'ing and Ling-pao traditions.[37]

It was the Ling-pao religious synthesis that provided the real foundation for the enduring success of Taoism through imperial times.[38] It was not that Taoists made a sectarian decision to promote themselves as proponents of one narrow religious model to the exclusion of others.[39] Rather, Taoist leaders found the Ling-pao framework to be one that was resilient enough to hold up the entire umbrella called "the Teaching of the Tao." On some levels, the Ling-pao revelations had been a novel vision of Tao and of how we assimilate ourselves to it. But, on other levels, they had been a conscious creation of a "non-Buddhist" version of Mahāyāna Buddhism, a deliberate effort to appropriate elements of Buddhism that had proven, or might yet prove, appealing to *all classes* of Chinese society. From his roots in that Ling-pao tradition, Lu Hsiu-ching had expanded "the Teaching of the Tao" so successfully that it soon became a social and cultural bridge: it blended compatible Buddhist concepts and values with more traditional Taoist beliefs and practices in such an open and fluid way that members of any level of society could participate in a comprehensive religious system.

Eventually, the leadership of the tradition was assumed by masters recognized as participants in the Shang-ch'ing tradition, such as T'ao Hung-ching (456–536). T'ang leaders such as Ssu-ma Ch'eng-chen (646–735) apparently traced their authority back to T'ao – not to earlier T'ien-shih figures such as Chang Tao-ling. The reasons are not difficult to discern. Like T'ao and Lu Hsiu-ching before him, and contemporaries like Sun Ssu-miao – a Taoist scholar of medicine and meditation – Ssu-ma and his principal associates were aristocrats. They were all learned men of social standing and political relevance, qualities that had seldom been prominent among

T'ien-shih Taoists. And in fact, by Ssu-ma's day, T'ien-shih traditions endured only in vestigial form. There was certainly no coherent organization led by hereditary leaders of the Chang clan.

The reasons for the death of T'ien-shih Taoism are clear. First, it offered little to satisfy the probing minds of intellectuals, like most other Taoist traditions did. Second, T'ien-shih Taoism had won relatively few aristocratic followers: by the sixth and seventh centuries, members of the social elite had many other Taoist options – T'ai-ch'ing, Shang-ch'ing, Ling-pao, etc. – all of which had emerged from the upper classes and appealed to their needs and interests. Third, T'ien-shih Taoism could not easily be turned into a legitimatory system for the rulers of a unified empire such as the T'ang. The T'ang emperors were indeed interested in forming an effective legitimatory alliance with Taoists, and quasi-Taoists, of all stripes. But Chang Tao-ling's revelation had included a mandate for him to replace the existing rulers, and for his religious organization to supplant the existing political order. The rulers of reunified China certainly had little reason to associate themselves with any Taoists who imagined themselves as an alternative to their imperium, especially when other Taoist groups were willing to legitimize the rulers on other terms.

What the T'ang rulers accepted as their framework for religious legitimation was therefore the more ecumenical "Tao-chiao" that had come into being in the fifth and sixth centuries. It was a much more promising legitimatory system, for, unlike the now-archaic T'ien-shih model, the ecumenical "Tao-chiao"

1 was led by respectable aristocrats and learned scholars;
2 integrated many elements of respected classical texts (*Lao-tzu*, *Chuang-tzu*, etc.); and
3 offered a wide range of symbolic and ceremonial possibilities for emperors who wished to be perceived as having great spiritual importance.

So, from the late seventh century through the end of the "Northern Sung" dynasty in the early twelfth, Taoism generally maintained a warm relationship with the imperial government, as well as with the social and cultural elite. It would be wrong, however, to imagine that the T'ang emperors simply "became Taoists." Though happy to make use of Taoism, they were also alert to the potential for any religious organization – whether Buddhist or Taoist – to become a political or economic threat, and even Taoism's most enthusiastic imperial patrons were also careful to maintain regulatory control of such organizations.

Nonetheless, trying to control "the Taoist religious organization" was like trying to control the birds of the air, for the people who tended to gravitate toward Taoist traditions were generally people who were not terribly interested in "organization." Consequently, the Taoists of T'ang times came in all varieties, from poets to physicians, from liturgists to hermits, from philosophers to wonder-workers. Prominent leaders such as Ssu-ma Ch'eng-chen wrote new texts on personal refinement, explaining the path of spiritual transcendence (*shen-hsien*) in terms comprehensible to most educated people. And others, whose identities remain obscure, composed noteworthy works such as the *Tao-chiao i-shu* ("Pivotal Meaning of the Taoist Teaching") and the *Pen-chi ching* ("Scripture of the Genesis Point"). Though few scholars of Chinese thought or religion have ever heard of these works, both of them teach that all things contain a pure "Tao-nature" (*Tao-hsing*). That teaching was presumably inspired by the Mahāyāna Buddhist concept of "Buddha-nature," which is known to most Westerners as a key of "Zen." But that idea did not gain widespread acceptance among Taoists, who by this era had an extremely rich array of other religious models of their own from which to choose. What did develop in T'ang times were new traditions of personal refinement such as "Inner Alchemy" (*nei-tan*) and systems for developing and expressing spiritual power through ritual action along lines that both borrowed from, and deeply influenced, the "tantric" traditions that soon stretched from Kashmir to Kyōtō.[40]

Yet, untold numbers of T'ang Taoists simply lived lives of quiet piety, sometimes among the priests and priestesses (*tao-shih*) who maintained monastic centers in different regions of the land.[41] Emperors continued to solicit the leaders of such communities – such as Ssu-ma's successor Li Han-kuang (683–769) – to appear at the imperial court and perform special rituals of personal transmission, as well as the now standard liturgies (the *chiao* and *chai*) that integrated polity and society with the deeper forces of the cosmos. However, even Li himself chafed at such demands, preferring to live on his own terms, among like-minded peers at a mountain monastery.[42]

The T'ang was also a time when women Taoists, of whom I will say more in Chapter 4 below, seem to have flourished. Some of them became quite well known in their day, for example "Refined Mistress" Chiao Ching-chen, a disciple of Ssu-ma himself. Others had their lives commemorated in the writings of male aristocrats, who were clearly admirers of their religious activities and achievements. One such woman was Huang Ling-wei (*ca.* 640–721), who won acclaim after rediscovering a lost shrine to one of the legendary Shang-ch'ing "Perfected Ones," Lady Wei.[43] Another, Pien Tung-hsüan (*ca.* 628–712), reportedly earned ascent to a heavenly realm partly through the compassion that she showed toward creatures in need, such as hungry birds.[44] And later, a major new tradition, Ch'ing-wei ("Clarified Tenuity") Taoism, traced its origins back to a young woman of late T'ang times, Tsu Shu (fl. 889–904), as will be explained further below.

Among the many eminent Taoists of T'ang times, perhaps the most important from our perspective today was the great writer Tu Kuang-t'ing (850–933).[45] Tu was a court official, whose responsibilities included that of tutor to the heir apparent of one of the T'ang successor states. One such ruler dubbed him "the Heavenly Master who Transmits Truth" (*ch'uan-chen t'ien-shih*). In one sense, that title is highly misleading, for Tu had no real connection to the "Heavenly Masters" of pre-T'ang times. But, in another way, the title was quite accurate, for besides writing poetry and influential short stories, Tu composed expositions of Taoist classics and scriptures, instructions for performing liturgies, and numerous historical and biographical collections, by which all later ages could learn about the Taoist tradition that had flourished up to the tenth century. Tu's comprehensive works ranged from the *Li-tai ch'ung-tao chi* ["Records of Reverence for Taoism over the Ages"] – a history of how rulers over the centuries had honored and patronized the religion – to the *Yung-ch'eng chi-hsien lu* ["Records of the Assembled Transcendents of the Walled City"] – an anthology of biographies of praiseworthy Taoist women throughout time. Only at the very end of the twentieth century did a few scholars begin studying Tu's works, and hardly any of those works have been fully translated, so no one yet knows how our understanding of Taoism will be affected once we have a full awareness of all the "Truth" that Tu transmitted.

The damming of the Tao?

After the T'ang dynasty, historical changes in Chinese society as a whole led to changes for Taoism. As I will show, Taoism did survive all the shifts and twists of late imperial times. But those changes did have two major effects. First, Taoists themselves modifed many of the *terms* on which they expressed and practiced their religion, in ways that even today's specialists have often not yet taken fully into account. Second, from around the thirteenth century down to our own, Taoism lost some of the social, cultural, and political prominence that it had held during T'ang times. Under political and ideological pressure, certain elements of Taoism eventually became marginalized and constricted, the more so as the centuries passed. It was because of those events that Taoism had to evolve in new ways if it was to survive. And it was because of the incredible richness of the tradition at the end of T'ang times that Taoists in later eras had plentiful resources upon which to draw in their ongoing repackaging and remarketing of Taoist ideas and practices.

One major factor shaping the evolution of post-T'ang Taoism was a change in the tone of rulers' relationship to China's cultural and religious traditions. That change was related in part to the fact that several of the late imperial regimes were headed by non-Chinese, who had come to power against the wishes of the indigenous Chinese. Their need to enact effective control of a subject population led to socio-political dynamics rather distinct from what had typically been the case in T'ang times. The T'ang rulers themselves had both Turkic and Chinese ancestors, but their dynasty was not in any sense a "conquest," and they never felt threatened by their subjects. Their efforts to control religion and society were not much different from the way things had been in Han times and the Six Dynasties. But, by the eighteenth century, Manchu rulers had enacted fairly stringent measures of social control over the lives of their Chinese subjects. Those developments were to have significant effects upon Taoism, and the ways in which it changed cannot be understood unless one first understands the changing circumstances to which they were responses.

These new social and political dynamics can be traced to events that were already underway in the early tenth century, when Tu Kuang-t'ing was busy recording and preserving his tradition's earlier heritage. During those years, a small part of north China was annexed into a new nation called Liao, which was ruled by a non-Chinese people called the Khitan (the ultimate source of the old name "Cathay"). That state, however, was extinguished in 1125 by another people, the Jurchen, whose original home had been in what we now call Manchuria. As soon as the Jurchen had absorbed the Khitan-ruled areas, they quickly pressed onward, and conquered the entire northern half of China. The rulers of the existing Chinese dynasty, called Sung, were thus forced to flee south. They re-established their government there, but in a much weakened condition. Then, in 1279, the entire land of China was conquered by the Mongols, whose Yüan dynasty was the first in history to rule China from Beijing, the capital of the earlier Khitan state.[46]

To the end of the "Northern Sung" (i.e., the early twelfth century), Taoism was still an honored component of Chinese society and culture, even at the highest levels. As I will show more fully in Chapter 4, the Sung emperor Hui-tsung (r. 1100–1125) supported, and participated in, Taoism as enthusiastically as any earlier ruler had ever done. But, after 1126, emperors in both the north and the south faced pressing competitive challenges, and imperial sponsorship of Taoism was never again quite so strong as it had been before that key turning point. Taoist history in this period, and all later periods, remains quite poorly known, even among specialists. But it seems fair to say that, by late Sung times, the sense of identity that Taoists such as Ssu-ma Ch'eng-chen and Tu Kuang-t'ing may have shared seems to have faded.

The institutions familiar to medieval Taoists generally did survive. For instance, some of the abbeys where *tao-shih* had practiced together for centuries did continue to operate. But unlike the stronger, more confident rulers of earlier times – who encouraged and patronized strong Taoist leaders – the weaker rulers of "Southern Sung" times could not afford to do so. And the alien rulers of the Yüan period set precedents that would be followed by all later regimes (down to the twentieth century) by taking steps to shackle Taoism's leadership. The Mongols, and their successors in the Ming (1368–1644) and Ch'ing (1644–1911) dynasties, often tried to exercise control of Taoism by "recognizing" one specific group as the "official" leaders of Taoism, without regard for what the Taoists of the day actually believed or practiced. As we shall see, such acts certainly did not end Taoists' freedom of practice. But they did somewhat disrupt pre-existing currents, and gave Taoists good reason to reconfigure all traditions that jaundiced rulers might not welcome. In sum, the flow of the Taoist stream was, in a certain sense, dammed. Yet, all that that fact ultimately meant was that Taoism now had to find new channels or redefine older ones.

After the twelfth century, some Taoists created new vernacular traditions by accommodating non-Taoist religious movements, which enjoyed an independent social constituency. Others established new monastic traditions, most notably the one called Ch'üan-chen ("the Integration of Perfection"), with which most Taoists today identify themselves. And both within those new traditions, and among some literati who stood apart from them, Taoists were working to repackage many of their ancient ideals and practices for the new "gentry" class that had replaced the old aristocracy. In so doing, they accommodated themselves to certain Confucian traditions, and in turn contributed new elements – from cosmological theories to meditative practices – to the "Confucianism" of late imperial times. In those ways, Taoism was constantly being reimagined and reformulated to suit the needs of people in a constantly changing society. In so doing, it also spread more fully into all segments of that society, from the ceremonies of local village life to the intellectualized practices of the literati.

Scholars of Taoist studies have still barely begun to familiarize themselves with late imperial Taoism. In large measure, that is because of the intellectual residue of the Confucian ideology that late imperial regimes created and propagated in their effort to control the actions of their subjects. Under the Mongol and Manchu regimes, members of the "Han" Chinese elite – i.e., the high-born, the educated, and the politically active – were frequently under government suspicion and scrutiny, and their public activities were affected accordingly. The intelligentsia in those times succumbed to real or perceived political pressure, and aspiring young men developed their careers circumspectly, along lines that seemed to them politically safe and economically secure. Under those conditions, the more "prudent" course was simply to "cultivate sagehood" in private – as Chu Hsi's "Neo-Confucian" teachings suggested – rather than to participate in a tradition focused upon public liturgical activities, particularly if members of the lower classes were also involved in such activities. The Mongols, and later the Manchus, were wary of possible uprisings among their Chinese subjects, and kept an increasingly close eye upon collective activities among them. Even among the native Chinese rulers of the Ming dynasty, social control was a prime concern, for a very practical reason: isolated individuals can present little political danger, but people who gather in groups pose a potential threat. Hence, in those times, any Chinese man with prospects for socio-economic advancement would have seen the personal benefit of standing clear of highly visible religious activities.

After the Mongol conquest, the Taoist liturgical traditions were still evolving dynamically, but along new social trajectories. Those who stepped forward to participate as leaders of liturgical traditions were generally not members of the aristocracy – like the Taoist leaders of earlier centuries – or even members of the gentry. Rather, they were increasingly men who already had limited prospects for political or economic advancement. Those who did have realistic hopes for a career in government had little motivation to participate in liturgical activities. Because of the realities involved in "the civil service system," the further a man travelled down the road of government service, the less his life was grounded in the realities of his natural family, his local community, or even his own native dialect: those studying in hopes of attaining public office were compelled to endless hours of solitary mental activity, often under the tutelage of a mentor who represented both socio-political achievement and moral wisdom. These facts swayed such men toward either a Confucian religious model or one of the comparable Taoist models of self-cultivation, such as "Inner Alchemy."

Here we see the context for the emergence both of "Neo-Confucianism" and of new Taoist movements of the twelfth to fourteenth centuries. A generation ago, some specialists – myself included – followed the Japanese scholar Kubo Noritada in evocatively, if rather misleadingly, dubbing those movements "the Taoist Reformation." Thus conceptualized, the new Taoist movements of "the conquest period" rejected the social focus of the liturgical tradition in favor of a "return" to an ideal of individual purification, an ideal swathed in the rhetoric of classical Taoism but actualized in terms of the individualized meditative practices of Six Dynasties Taoist aristocrats. Here, such scholars saw a "parting of the Way" *within* what was long called "religious Taoism": from the conquest period onward, and *only* from that period, the "mystical" traditions of Taoism seemed to become distanced from the *liturgical* traditions that had theretofore been the more honored segment of the religion. From that perspective, it seemed that, from that period on, those who were religiously inclined began to fall into two camps: (1) a cultural elite who practiced an individualized, "mystical" pursuit of self-perfection, and (2) a far less elite component, composed of people who cherished Taoist ideals but faced the very practical necessity of making a living. The second group became the main participants in the modern liturgical tradition called Cheng-i. For them, the religious life became – by necessity – a profession, and their activities became – by necessity – a public service, performed, as always, for the benefit of all, but now underwritten by members of the local community.

Yet, it is at this point that we come up against the hermeneutical barriers posed by the modern prejudice against liturgical Taoism, a prejudice that, demonstrably, never existed in medieval or early modern China. Chinese historical and biographical materials reveal that, down through the Sung period, the literati elite – from politicians to poets – were frequently well acquainted with Taoist matters that most today would tend to consider quite "religious." And in those days, the leaders of the Taoist liturgical tradition had enjoyed the trust, and the respect, of both the Chinese government and the scholar-officials who made it run. But twentieth-century sinology held firmly that, from Sung times on, "religious Taoism" was stigmatized as "politically incorrect." The "Neo-Confucians" of Southern Sung times – such as Chu Hsi – are well known for their mania for "orthodoxy." Thinkers of his school actually competed to see who could be more "Confucian" than the next person, and branded one another as heretics – even sometimes as "closet Buddhists." Many intellectuals in that period felt a need to justify themselves ideologically, and to protect themselves politically, by professing their own ideological probity. And one ignoble but highly effective method of achieving those ends is to cast aspersions upon others: if we can paint some other party in unflattering colors, and succeed in having such a caricature accepted by society at large, that party's stock falls and our own stock rises. In the historical and literary sources of late imperial times, leaders of the Taoist liturgical tradition were increasingly represented as outcasts from the Chinese mainstream. As seen in those sources, the leaders of Chinese society became, with each passing generation, ever more alienated from the liturgical dimensions of the Taoist heritage.

In the last few years, questions have emerged concerning that perspective on how Taoism really changed during the second millennium. At present, it does still seem true that in late imperial China each generation arose in ever greater ignorance of the rich and noble heritage of liturgical Taoism and of its prominent place in earlier Chinese society and culture. And it does seem that each generation of the "Neo-Confucian" elite did become more antagonistic to Taoism as a social reality, finding an ideological exemption only for certain carefully sanitized remnants of the classical heritage, such as *Lao-tzu* and *Chuang-tzu*. Yet, the historical evidence now seems to demonstrate that, even in late imperial China, Taoists always continued to practice most of their inherited traditions, though with modifications that few scholars have yet begun to study.

Old currents, new channels

If we return to the metaphor of Taoism as a river formed by the confluence of different streams, we can now see factual evidence that the river did not cease flowing after the T'ang period. Down to the present day, older Taoist currents have continued to flow on, even as more new streams emerged to feed into the tradition and subtly shift its currents. Yet, until virtually the year 2000, even leading scholars of Taoism often acted as though little of any significance occurred in Taoism during late imperial times.[47] They usually gave a summary of "Inner Alchemy," usually as though it was a generalized system, not a diverse and evolving set of interacting traditions. Then they would jump to "Taoism today," generally doing little more than summarizing the practices of Cheng-i priests of Taiwan.

In reality, the later history of Taoism is just as rich, diverse, and nuanced as its earlier phases. But the later phases of Taoism were seldom studied by scholars of the twentieth century, so the continuities between "modern" forms of Taoism and those of ancient and medieval times have just begun to receive attention.[48]

Rather than treat late imperial Taoism as the inevitable evolution of the institutions known to scholars of, say, the 1970s, I shall attempt to present the realities of late imperial times in light of the facts concerning Taoist traditions of earlier times. What thus becomes apparent is that the later history of Taoism was neither a wholesale divergence from the primary currents of earlier Taoism nor a homogenization in which old and new currents were solidified into a systematized whole. Rather, the estuary of late imperial Taoism remained a complex and evolving array of ideals and practices which maintained old currents while assimilating new ones. Along the way, those currents reinforced many quite ancient channels, though often with waters that had entered the course from some of its lower tributaries.

Certain of those lower tributaries share certain common characteristics. For instance, a variety of *new ritual traditions* got their start before the "conquest period," i.e., before 1126. Most of those new traditions made little use of "Inner Alchemy," or even of earlier traditions of meditative self-cultivation. Nor did they make much effort to integrate Confucian, or Neo-Confucian, ideas or practices. They did include literati participants, both government officials and members of the gentry more broadly. But since conditions often made it difficult for these movements to receive support from the state itself, they tended to turn instead to the broader community, and survived by providing efficacious practices helpful to the community, especially in terms of healing.

The oldest of the ritual traditions that emerged after T'ang times seems to have been a complex of ritual traditions called Ch'ing-wei ("Clarified Tenuity") Taoism, which remains quite poorly known. Its origins were traced back to a young woman, Tsu Shu, who reportedly flourished around the year 900. Ch'ing-wei "thunder rites" (*lei-fa*) reportedly enabled a priest to internalize the spiritual power of thunder, which in turn enabled union with Tao. With that power, a priest could also help others by performing healings.

In the thirteenth century, disciples of an official named Huang Shun-shen reworked Ch'ing-wei traditions as part of a comprehensive ritual system that also included elements of the earlier Shang-ch'ing and Ling-pao traditions, along with Tantric Buddhist forms. A century later, the syncretist Chao I-chen edited the surviving Ch'ing-wei texts, and apparently incorporated them into a comprehensive ritual collection called the *Tao-fa hui-yüan* ["Assembled Origins of Taoist Ritual-Methods"], the largest single work in today's Taoist canon.[49] Thereafter, Ch'ing-wei had no separate existence, and modern scholars have seldom included it in their conceptualizations of "Taoism." Future attempts to understand and explain Taoism need to take fully into account the Ch'ing-wei religious model and its place within the broader range of Taoist beliefs and practices.

The same is true of another tradition of ritual healing, called T'ien-hsin ("Heart of Heaven"). This tradition was based upon scriptures discovered in the late tenth century by a retired official, Jao Tung-t'ien, who devised "a ritual system for literati in both local and national society."[50] When the Sung emperor Hui-tsung summoned Taoists to the capital in 1114 to compile a comprehensive canon, the T'ien-hsin material was presented to the court. Its scriptures teach priests how to heal illness by drawing down spiritual power associated with the stars. Though hardly mentioned by most scholars, T'ien-hsin ideas influenced several important Chinese novels of late imperial times, and T'ien-hsin traditions are still practiced among some people of Chinese descent in Thailand.

A third new ritual tradition arose at the court of Sung Hui-tsung himself, where an official named Lin Ling-su revived, and redirected, the Ling-pao revelations of the fourth century. This new liturgical tradition was called Shen-hsiao ("Divine Empyrean").[51] It began when Lin expanded the Ling-pao *Tu-jen ching* with new materials of a distinctly political nature. Through those acts, Lin could offer the emperor Hui-tsung authentic Taoist "revelations" that were centuries old, yet represented him as a divine ruler. Indeed, as Lin presented the Ling-pao revelations, it was Hui-tsung himself who embodied the salvific power of Tao. Instead of having the individual practitioner enact his or her own "salvation" (*tu*) by reciting the primordial words of "The Heavenly Venerable One of the Primordial Beginning" – as the original *Tu-jen ching* had done – the revised Shen-hsiao model presented the emperor as providing salvation to all beings through sponsoring liturgical re-enactments. For centuries, Shen-hsiao traditions survived as a combination of "salvation through (personal) refinement" (*lien-tu*) and therapeutic rituals. In modern China, Cheng-i leaders did give the "Shen-hsiao" title to some priests, but generally suggested that those priests' knowledge and power were of a lower order than those of Cheng-i priests. Certain twentieth-century scholars misled readers by perpetuating Cheng-i priests' slanderous attacks on the entire Shen-hsiao tradition.[52]

Another new movement that first emerged in the reign of Sung Hui-tsung was called "the Great Ritual-Methods of Youthful Incipience" (*T'ung-ch'u ta-fa*). "T'ung-ch'u Taoism" was reportedly founded by a son of rice merchants, Yang Hsi-chen (1101–1124), who claimed to have received revelations during a year that he spent in a cave. Some T'ung-ch'u rituals show continuity with the Shang-ch'ing tradition. Others were apparently borrowed from the Shen-hsiao system and other Sung ritual traditions.[53] The T'ung-ch'u movement had no separate existence after the thirteenth century, but some of its texts were preserved in the *Tao-fa hui-yüan*, one of a number of important Taoist anthologies produced during the fourteenth century.[54] Yet, none of those texts have yet been translated or even well studied, and the significance of the T'ung-ch'u system for our understanding of Taoism remains to be determined.

Of all the new Taoist traditions of Sung times, the only one that managed to survive intact down to the present was called Cheng-i ("Orthodox Unity"). Writings of the tenth century, including some by Tu Kuang-t'ing, mention Taoists of the Chang clan who lived at "Dragon and Tiger Mountain" (Lung-hu shan) in south China. Those men professed to be direct descendants of Chang Tao-ling, and they claimed that the ordinations which they gave to men of their own day continued a priesthood that had survived all those centuries under their unbroken hereditary leadership. Such claims were apparently accepted by a succession of rulers, though it is not clear that the populace as a whole, or even Taoist practitioners in other regions, accepted those claims as true, or even as particularly significant. What can be said with certainty is that Taoists of T'ang times had at no point believed that their actions, decisions, or practices needed to take into account the fellows at Lung-hu shan who claimed descent from Chang Tao-ling. In other words, the evidence of T'ang times shows that the Lung-hu shan Taoists were not widely regarded as having any particular significance, much less as having any claim to special authority or legitimacy. Yet, because of later historical events, many twentieth-century scholars continued to perpetuate the idea that the Lung-hu shan Taoists represented a real continuation of Chang Tao-ling's organization.[55]

The "Heavenly Masters" of Lung-hu shan were "recognized" by Sung emperors down to Hui-tsung, though such emperors also recognized leaders of other "surviving traditions," such as a Shang-ch'ing priesthood centered at another mountain center called Mao-shan. Neither at Mao-shan nor at Lung-hu shan is there clear historical evidence of a vital ongoing organization that had endured through the Six Dynasties and T'ang periods. In fact, there were periods when no one seems to have actually been maintaining either of those centers, at least on any institutional terms. Then, a century or two later, someone would arise who decided to revive the "tradition" of bygone days, and to claim historical continuity with its now semi-legendary representatives.

In that fashion, "lineages" of Taoist "patriarchs" were *retroactively* created in Sung times, just as among Ch'an Buddhists of that era: Ch'an Buddhists of the eleventh century concocted a fictitious "lineage" that they projected back onto their own history, claiming for themselves a direct historical link to great "patriarchs," going back to an early Chinese Buddhist known as Bodhidharma, and from him back to one of the Buddha's immediate disciples. The now famous story of "the flower sermon," still adduced to validate that "lineage," was itself a creation of Sung China, and the supposed "patriarchs" of Ch'an's early days, such as Hsin-hsing, never knew or imagined that they were links in any such "lineage."[56]

Those facts are important for understanding the history and "essential facts" of Taoism, because exactly the same thing was happening, at exactly the same time, among Sung Taoists: Lin Ling-su, among others, claimed to be a living representative of the Ling-pao tradition of early medieval times. And a fictitious Shang-ch'ing "lineage" was concocted which remade such T'ang ecumenical leaders as Ssu-ma Ch'eng-chen and Li Han-kuang into "patriarchs" (*tsung-shih*) of an exclusive Shang-ch'ing lineage that allegedly continued, unbroken, over the generations.[57] Such claims of historical lineage were hardly ever disputed, unless there was some political conflict. Yet, the evidence suggests that such was the case not because everyone accepted such claims as true, but rather because they had not yet attained the importance that they would retrospectively acquire.[58]

Later Sung and Yüan emperors continued to "recognize" leaders of a *variety* of Taoist traditions. The Mongol conqueror named Chingghis or Jenghiz (known to most Westerners as Genghis Khan) was a patron of the Ch'üan-chen tradition, which had emerged under his Jurchen predecessors, as we shall see below. Chingghis even summoned a prominent Ch'üan-chen leader, Ch'iu Ch'ang-ch'un, to his court. But when his successor, Qubilai (known to Westerners as Kubilai Khan), extended his control over south China – thereby becoming the first "foreign" ruler ever to rule the entirety of China – he decided to consolidate his control over the Taoists in the south by establishing what has sometimes been imagined as "a religious monopoly": Qubilai extended "exclusive authority" to the Cheng-i priests of Mount Lung-hu, and denied the validity of any ordination identified as that of any other Taoist tradition. When the Mongols were overthrown, the rulers of the ensuing Ming dynasty not only continued that "recognition" of the Cheng-i priests of Mount Lung-hu, but even intermarried with them.[59] They also entrusted a Cheng-i leader to recompile the Taoist "canon," and in 1444 or 1445 the *Cheng-t'ung Tao-tsang* – our main surviving collection of Taoist texts – was printed under imperial auspices, as several earlier collections had been.[60] But, by the mid-eighteenth century, the Manchu rulers of the subsequent Ch'ing dynasty lost interest in the Cheng-i priesthood, and, though Cheng-i priests continued to practice, their "authority" in modern times was actually negligible.

The characteristics of all these "new ritual movements" – Ch'ing-wei, T'ien-hsin, Shen-hsiao, T'ung-ch'u, and Cheng-i – can easily be distinguished from those of several *other* new Taoist traditions that had emerged in north China under the "conquest regimes" of the Jurchen and Mongols. The northern movements generally de-emphasized the liturgical traditions of earlier times, stressing instead the personal attainment of "spiritual transcendence" (*shen-hsien*) through moral and spiritual cultivation, either individually or in a monastic setting. They also tended to attract followers from *all* levels of society – including many literati – by offering models of self-cultivation that a "gentleman" could practice alone in seclusion, and by incorporating compatible elements of Confucian and Buddhist thought and practice. And just as the various new ritual traditions of Sung times were eventually amalgamated together under the auspices of only one – Cheng-i – the various new self-cultivation traditions that arose in north China under the conquest regimes were all eventually identified as part of one – Ch'üan-chen.

Two of the new northern movements founded in the twelfth century left behind few writings, and therefore remain almost completely unknown.[61] One, called T'ai-i ("Supreme Union") Taoism, was founded by an obscure figure named Hsiao Pao-chen (d. 1166). Of T'ai-i teachings and practices we know very little, though sources report that its leaders valued social virtues such as filial piety (*hsiao*) and loyalty (*chung*) – ideals which would resurface in the later Ching-ming Taoist tradition – as well as personal values such as yielding (*jo*) and maternal loving-kindness (*tz'u*) – which were clearly derived from the *Tao te ching*.[62] The other such movement, founded by an equally obscure man named Liu Te-jen (1122–1180), was called Chen-ta ("Perfected Greatness") or Ta-tao ("Great Way") Taoism. Of its values and practices we know virtually nothing, though anecdotal reports intimate that Liu was an ascetic agriculturalist who stressed humility.[63] Chen-ta Taoism received patronage from the Jurchen government, and T'ai-i Taoism was even popular with Khubilai Khan. But during the Ming dynasty both were absorbed into the Ching-ming tradition (to be discussed below) and were eventually reinterpreted as elements of the Ch'üan-chen tradition, which also had its roots in twelfth-century north China.

The term *ch'üan-chen* is usually translated as "Complete Perfection," but some now believe that it should instead be interpreted to mean "Integrating Perfection" – suggesting perhaps that the successful practitioner merges into "Reality" (*chen*).[64] The Ch'üan-chen tradition originated among the followers of Wang Che, otherwise known as Wang Ch'ung-yang (1113–1170), a scholar from a well-to-do gentry family. Wang is credited with several collections of didactic poetry and several texts on living the Taoist life, of which the best known is called *Ch'ung-yang li-chiao shih-wu lun* ["Fifteen Articles by Wang Ch'ung-yang for Establishing the

Teachings"].[65] The "Fifteen Articles" teach that "spiritural immortality" (*shen-hsien*) can be attained within this life by entering seclusion, cultivating one's internal spiritual realities (*hsing*), and harmonizing them with the realities of one's external life (*ming*). Wang's seven famous disciples included a woman, Sun Pu-erh (1119–1182). She is known to have couched some of her teachings in the form of poetry, though only a few examples survive. Much later, during the Ch'ing dynasty, a variety of texts appeared under her name, teaching "Inner Alchemy" for women, along such traditional models as "refining the spirit" (*lien-shen*).[66] Though little is known of women's practices in the early days of the tradition, Ch'üan-chen Taoism did attract many women practitioners, and women remain active in Ch'üan-chen life to the present day. Another of Wang's followers was a man named Ch'iu Ch'u-chi (1148–1227, also known as Ch'iu Ch'ang-ch'un), who attracted the attention of several rulers, including the Mongol general Chinggis.[67] Another sign of the movement's great success is that the largest collection of Taoist writings ever produced – the *Hsüan-tu pao-tsang*, a forerunner of today's smaller *Tao-tsang* – was compiled by Ch'üan-chen leaders and engraved in 1244.[68]

In time, the Ch'üan-chen tradition adopted a monastic setting, building upon earlier Taoist models as well as upon Wang Che's own teachings.[69] Ch'üan-chen practice centered upon self-cultivation, though it did not demand that followers cling to any single model. Some Ch'üan-chen teachings came to be couched in terms of the older Taoist model of spiritual refinement through meditation known as "Inner Alchemy." Others shared models that had been introduced by Buddhism, such as seated meditation that might ideally result in an "awakening" experience. And yet other Ch'üan-chen models featured ideas and practices shared with Confucians of that period, who had also found value in such Buddhist models.[70]

Ch'üan-chen Taoism endures today, centered at the White Cloud Abbey (*Po-yün kuan*) in Beijing. Or, at least, such is the understanding of China's people and government, as well as of the Taoists who have practiced at the White Cloud Abbey for the last three hundred years. As we shall see, however, the actual history of those Taoists cannot be so simply explained.

Life in the tideways

Though ethnically Chinese, the Ming emperors were not the secure and confident rulers that the native Chinese rulers of the T'ang and Northern Sung dynasties had been. The old aristocracy, generally a bulwark of the imperial state, was now gone altogether. The "gentry" class, which had emerged to replace it, was never so closely tied to the state. And the entire populace, especially in the north, had spent many generations under governments that were, by traditional Chinese standards, heavy-handed. By Ming times, the fiduciary bonds between state and subjects that had characterized most earlier periods had largely dissipated. Ming rulers, following Yüan precedents, imposed on their subjects a "unifying" social order, of which Taoism was a part.

To promote social harmony, and their own dominance, Ming rulers codified the notion that "the Three Teachings (Confucianism, Buddhism, and Taoism) are one," a notion that went back to much earlier roots. Yet, in 1374, the Ming founder (a) praised Cheng-i Taoists for their supposed focus on local mores, and (b) disparaged both Ch'an Buddhists and Ch'üan-chen Taoists for "devoting themselves to the cultivation of the person and the improvement of the individual endowment." In other words, in this "new world order," individuals who cultivated themselves – as Taoists, as indeed most Buddhists and Confucians, had done for many centuries – were now denounced by the state as subversive of established social patterns. This was no longer the China of T'ang Hsüan-tsung or Sung Hui-tsung, who never met a Taoist they did not like. Under these conditions, both Taoists and Buddhists realized the need to explain and practice their traditions in ways that the political authorities would find acceptable.

An important – though still little-known – example of how Taoists adapted to the environment of Ming China was a tradition known as Ching-ming ("Pure Illumination"). The social and religious changes that this tradition underwent over the centuries is itself a remarkable case-study in how Taoism evolved. Already in late T'ang times, Tu Kuang-t'ing had mentioned a local tradition in the southeast, called the Chung-hsiao tao ("Way of Loyalty and Filiality," two Confucian virtues), also called Ching-ming. The origins of that tradition went back to a figure hundreds of years earlier: Hsü Sun, an official of the Six Dynasties period, had become the focus of a popular cult on the basis of a reputation for having rescued people from disasters by means of ritual powers. Here we see echoes of the values and ideals of several of the new currents that entered Taoism in the late T'ang and conquest dynasties. At first glance, some might imagine those echoes as indications that Taoists were now engaged in wholesale adoption of altogether alien religious ideas, e.g., Tantric ideas presumably introduced from India or Tibet. There were indeed contacts in T'ang times between Taoists and Tantric masters, as we shall see more fully in Chapter 5 below. But talismanic rituals which altered one's surroundings had been a stream of Taoism from the days of "the old traditions of Chiang-nan" in the third century. Moreover, the ideal of altruistic heroism by a "Taoist master," who wielded powers developed and/or sustained through ritual and/or self-cultivation, did have roots in T'ang times, as seen in the case of the wonder-worker Yeh Fa-shan.[71] Indeed, though twentieth-century eyes never noticed, "saving others" was an element of Taoist ethos going back to the *Tao te ching* itself.[72]

By the opening years of the Southern Sung, however, the focus of the Chung-hsiao "cult" had been radically redirected. Its leader, Ho Chen-kung, received a revelation in 1131 from Hsü Sun himself. Hsü reportedly conveyed to Ho not only talismanic rituals, but also instructions on self-cultivation and a set of ethical teachings appropriate to the period. In all those elements, we see currents that had long been found somewhere in the Taoist stream. The same dynamic appears a century later, in the person of a Taoist leader named Po Yü-ch'an (Pai Yü-ch'an). Though identified as a Shen-hsiao master, he is remembered by Taoists as a champion of both "thunder rites" and "Inner Alchemy." And Po helped the Ching-ming tradition survive by promoting it along with other local traditions.[73]

A few generations later, Ching-ming Taoism was once again reformulated, this time by a writer named Liu Yü (1257–1308). Liu reiterated the mutual necessity of ideals and practices which modern minds tend to regard as incommensurable: ritual, cultivation of the heart/mind, and moral self-cultivation. In order to still the heart/mind – as Taoists had advocated since the *Nei-yeh* – Liu said that a person must first establish a moral foundation consisting of such virtues as loyalty and filiality. One might remember those virtues as elements of the value-system of Hsiao Pao-chen, the twelfth-century founder of the T'ai-i movement. It is not clear what role, if any, stilling the heart/mind may have played in Hsiao's teachings. But Liu Yü also revived the earlier Ching-ming emphasis on mastering ritual, saying that ritual practice helped engender the moral virtues needed for successful cultivation of the heart/mind.

It would be mistaken to surmise that the Ching-ming system was "more Confucian than Taoist," as twentieth-century perspectives might lead one to imagine. Nor can it be reduced to a "syncretism," which merely forced Confucianism and Taoism into some artificial combination. Rather, the Ching-ming system was another example of the key dynamics of Taoist religious models throughout history: fluidity, adaptability, and transformationality. To "be Taoist" did not require that one conform oneself to a single specific religious model that went back to some earlier leader or scripture. Rather, it just meant finding those elements of the immensely diverse Taoist heritage that could most richly fulfill one's own personal religious needs, in one's own historical conditions, one's own social conditions, one's own cultural conditions.

By providing a multi-part religious model that could satisfy diverse needs and interests, the Ching-ming movement not only survived and flourished in challenging times, but drew strength and vitality both from its local base in the southeast and from literati in other regions.[74] All the while, it managed to satisfy imperial demands that religious groups uphold wholesome values among the general public. Yet, this story of Taoism's success during Ming times was never part of the picture of Taoism in twentieth-century minds.

The same can be said for the story of Taoism's success in the last imperial dynasty – the Ch'ing (1644–1911). To the end of the twentieth-century, it remained impossible to find any substantial account of Taoist thought or practice during Ch'ing times. Sinologists and historians – themselves conditioned to believe that Confucianism dominated Chinese civilization and society right up to the time that Westernization occurred – led the public to believe that there was no longer any Taoism to speak of in late imperial China. Only at the opening of the present century did a few specialists begin demonstrating that Taoism was indeed an enduring feature of Chinese society and culture, even during Ch'ing times.

When the Manchus – a non-Chinese people descended from the

Jurchen – extinguished the Ming dynasty and took control of China in 1644, they maintained the Ming policy of strict government control of religion. But the Manchu rulers' interest in becoming "Chinese rulers" was in tension with their increasing feeling that, to maintain control, they had to suppress their much more numerous Chinese subjects. To demonstrate resistance to their foreign masters, many Chinese literati actually identified themselves as Ch'üan-chen Taoists, and Taoism thus regained a measure of the prestige that it had enjoyed in earlier times. This fact, however, was totally suppressed in virtually all twentieth-century accounts of Chinese history and culture.

The next great phase of Taoist history can now be explained in terms of the emergence of the Lung-men ("Dragon Gate") tradition. Like the Ching-ming traditions which it in fact absorbed, Lung-men Taoism was carefully crafted to pass government muster, while preserving not only inherited Taoist institutions but also Taoist self-cultivation practices. It originated in southeastern China near the end of the Ming period, among disciples of a Taoist scholar named Wu Shou-yang (1552–1641).[75] Like Po Yü-ch'an in earlier days, Wu appears in Taoist sources as a master of "Inner Alchemy" as well as of "thunder rites." And, since he lived in the age when the Ching-ming model of Taoism still prevailed, it should come as little surprise that Wu's "Forthright Discourse on the Authentic Principles of Heavenly Transcendence" (*T'ien-hsien cheng-li chih-lun*; dated 1639) explains "the Way of Immortality" (*hsien-tao*) in the age-old terms of cultivating one's spirit (*shen*) and vital-energy (*ch'i*).[76] Yet, Wu's historical importance rests not so much in his preservation of those ancient elements of Taoist tradition as in his claim to have received "Dragon-Gate" credentials in a revelation from the early Ch'üan-chen leader Ch'iu Ch'u-chi. His disciples handed down those credentials, along with his teachings on self-cultivation.

In 1628, a Lung-men master named Chao Fu-yang reportedly transmitted those credentials to a young Taoist named Wang Ch'ang-yüeh. Chao predicted that Wang would soon establish the "Dragon-Gate" tradition at the White Cloud Abbey in Beijing, which had long been accepted as the prime repository of the traditions of the early Ch'üan-chen master Ch'iu Ch'u-chi. In 1656, Wang did in fact bring the living tradition of Dragon-Gate Taoism to the White Cloud Abbey. By so doing, he forged a firm link between the religious model based on Wu Shou-yang's teachings and the earlier Ch'üan-chen movement. He also established a form of Taoism that would flourish into modern times, by providing "Inner Alchemy" practices with a workable institutional basis. Because the Ch'üan-chen movement had always welcomed women, both as leaders and as lay participants, the re-establishment of the Lung-men movement at the centuries-old center of Ch'üan-chen secured a framework within which both men and women could practice Taoist self-cultivation on terms that could succeed within the society of Ch'ing times.

The vitality of traditional self-cultivation practices during Ming and Ch'ing times has been documented in the works of a few modern scholars. But so tendentious was the "mainstream" of twentieth-century Chinese studies, in both China and the West, that virtually no references to such practices can be found at all in most depictions of thought or religion in late imperial China. Nearly unknown, for instance, is the *Hsing-ming kuei-chih* of 1615, which explains how one can reunify oneself with the primordial Tao by stilling one's heart/mind and harmonizing one's "inner nature" (*hsing*) with the realities of one's personal life (*ming*). In later generations, literati such as Liu I-ming (1734–1821) further simplified "Inner Alchemy," making it more accessible, and more attractive, to the public by removing more and more of the esoteric symbolism that had characterized medieval *nei-tan* texts.

In those ways, as by maintaining Taoist monastic traditions at abbeys in Beijing and throughout China, the literati Taoists of Ch'ing times were not only continuing the work of centuries of Ching-ming leaders. They were also continuing the efforts of T'ang leaders such as Ssu-ma Ch'eng-chen and Wu Yün, who had labored to package Taoist teachings and practices in a form that would appeal to emperors, aristocrats, and officials.

Though such efforts maintained Taoism through late imperial times, the extension of Taoist ideas among the literate gentry was also stimulated by the spread of printing and by increases in literacy among both men and women.[77] Novels such as the *Feng-shen yen-i* ["The Creation of the Gods"], *Tung-yu chi* ["Journey to the East"], and *Hsi-yu chi* ["The Journey to the West"] introduced the ideas of "Inner Alchemy" to thousands of readers who otherwise had no direct involvement with Taoist traditions.[78] As a result, such Taoist teachings became a part of Chinese popular culture, on a variety of levels. For example, instructions for a meditative manipulation of internal forces to achieve spiritual rebirth appear in a Lung-men text composed around 1800, the *T'ai-i chin-hua tsung-chih* ["Comprehensive Instructions on the Golden Flower of the Grand Unity"], which Carl Jung helped make famous in the West in a 1929 translation. And instructions on "Inner Alchemy" for women appear in dozens of texts, beginning around 1743.[79] Those materials show a popularization of Taoism that was rooted in centuries of Taoist efforts to make their traditions more comprehensible, and more interesting, for a lay public. They also eventuated in various appropriations by non-Taoists. For instance, Taoist inspiration was claimed by many twentieth-century martial-arts teachers, as well as by various purveyors of teachings about what some like to imagine as "sexual yoga."[80]

In modern times, Taoism neither died nor was dissipated into the broader fabric of Chinese culture. Even after the fall of the Ch'ing empire, Taoists continued to maintain their own traditions and practices, both at abbeys throughout China and in other settings. A fascinating report concerning life in the White Cloud Abbey during a wartime visit by a Japanese scholar was subsequently translated into English.[81] Later attacks on such religious centers, under the Communist government of the 1960s and 1970s, would chill, but not kill, the assiduous efforts of pious men and women to carry on the Lung-men traditions of monastic practice based on the earlier Ch'üan-chen institutions.[82] Visitors to China today will still find thousands of Taoists practicing age-old traditions at many storied abbeys such as Mao-shan and at many smaller hermitages.[83]

4

THE SOCIO-POLITICAL MATRIX OF TAOISM

As the third millennium opens, it remains very difficult to give an accurate, thorough, and nuanced explanation of the social dynamics of Taoism over the ages. Part of the problem is that an indeterminable amount of pertinent data remains unstudied. Another is that some of our questions may be questions for which the available data may, by their very nature, be largely if not wholly inadequate. For instance, if we were to ask how the understanding and practice of Taoist women differed from that of Taoist men in the fifth century, or in the fifteenth, it is quite possible that we simply do not have, and may never have, a sufficient range of pertinent data to formulate even a sound answer to such questions, much less a definitive one.

The same problems plague our efforts to learn the *social identity* of the participants in the many different Taoist traditions that came and went over the centuries. Some scholars of the present generation have been doing excellent fieldwork among Taoists of various descriptions in some regions of China.[1] But, for various reasons, Taoist practitioners and communities in other regions have not yet received the same attention. In all such cases, it remains at least *theoretically* possible to gain at least partial answers to our questions about *living* Taoists' social identities. If, for instance, we decide to seek to learn about the educational level of the women who have taken up residence in Ch'üan-chen temples in China today, or about whether their personal practices differ from those of their male counterparts, pertinent information is potentially available: we simply need properly trained researchers to make proper contacts with such Taoists, ask the proper questions, make the proper observations and analysis, and deliver the data to us in a proper fashion.

Such would not be the case, however, if we were seeking to learn how the educational level, or self-cultivation practices, of Taoist women may have changed over the centuries. The answers to questions of *that* nature require a careful analysis of *textual* data, along with certain other kinds of data that have all too often been neglected, such as the data of material culture. Much can be learned about aspects of Taoism by ongoing study of pertinent works of art in all media, of the architecture and ritual uses of space at temples and monastic centers, and even of Taoist musical traditions.[2]

Specialists of the early twenty-first century are in a position to *begin* to provide meaningful insights into *certain* issues regarding the social realities of *some* Taoists over the centuries. Some of those issues, of course, begin with our own modern values and prejudices: they involve the massive discrepancies between what our current data show and what earlier generations *believed* about Taoism. The disinformation spread by late imperial and modern Confucians resulted not just from an understandable failure by non-Taoists to comprehend Taoists on their own terms, but often from a determined campaign to undermine respect for Taoists as honorable members of society. Because Western scholars often accepted that disinformation at face value, it is now imperative that we re-examine all our inherited assumptions in light of the full range of pertinent data.

For example, even today, scholars of Chinese thought quite frequently probe a *single text*, or even one certain *idea* found in such a text, and simply reify the party who expressed it as "the Taoists." Our literature on Chinese civilization and "world religions" is full of such specious abstractions masquerading as references to actual elements of Chinese civilization: "Taoists," for instance, are often said to be the people in China who characteristically love "nature." Even Isabelle Robinet, a highly expert specialist of the late twentieth century, wrote: "The Taoist world is above all the world of nature rather than that of society. . . . Often hermits in distant mountains, they are the ones who taught the Chinese to appreciate landscapes with the feelings that we recognize as Chinese."[3] But when we seek actual *data* to confirm or clarify such statements, we are quickly at a loss, for they are hardly ever based upon actual analysis of specific, pertinent information. When, for instance, one asks questions such as "How important was 'the world of nature' to the late-T'ang chronicler Tu Kuang-t'ing, compared to Chang Po-tuan, the eleventh-century author of the 'Folios on Awakening to Reality' (*Wu-chen p'ien*)," it becomes patent that generalizations such as "the Taoist world is above all the world of nature rather than that of society" are quite meaningless. Such statements are *not* accurate summaries of the data of Taoism, but merely evocative *cultural constructs*, which originated either in outsiders' uninformed images concerning Taoists or in reifications of one idea from one mind, in one locality, in one period, as representative of "Taoism" overall. When one examines the actual lives of actual people in Taoist history, as noted for instance in the preceding chapter (or, for that matter, in Robinet's own presentations), one is hard pressed to find many actual "hermits in distant mountains."[4] And even if one could, it seems difficult to justify hailing such "hermits" as the *truest* exemplars of "the Taoist world," *instead* of the much more numerous Taoist men and women who were quite happy participating in "society." Judged fairly, the data of Taoism show that its practitioners have had diverse backgrounds, interests, and activities, and thus cannot be fitted conveniently into any single socio-cultural mold.

Historians have also been guilty of using the term "Taoist" as an ill-defined label for people imagined to have been involved in certain social activities. For instance, such labels have often been tagged to periodic popular rebellions, which sometimes laid claim to a religious idea or symbol – which may or may not ever have been specifically Taoist – for purposes of enhancing internal solidarity and/or recruiting new participants. In regard to some of those movements, such labels seem at least partly justified; in regard to others, they do not.[5] Yet, various twentieth-century caricatures of "Taoism" often casually, and quite fallaciously, presented the supposed "Taoist" elements of such movements as having been linked to certain antinomian sentiments found in the *Chuang-tzu*. What resulted was a generalized abstraction of "the Taoists" as "those people who oppose government." Naturally, such thinking has clear roots in the efforts of second-millennium Confucians to claim political importance for themselves while denying any to Taoists. The effectiveness of such propaganda was astonishing, and only in the present generation have a few scholars even begun to dissect and expose such depictions as the tendentious cultural constructs that they are.[6]

Another such effort involves the popularity in late twentieth-century minds of fuzzy ideas about Taoism in relation to women and gender.[7] Rarely were such discussions informed by a knowledge of the actual facts pertaining to women in Taoism, much less by consideration of how Chinese women over the ages, Taoist or non-Taoist, might have responded to questions about such matters. In fact, serious efforts by informed specialists to lay out all the pertinent data have only just begun.[8] In what follows, I will briefly introduce some of that data to give some indication of what we can currently say about the gender realities of Taoists over the ages.

Another issue involves the question of whether "Taoists" can truly be aligned with any *social class* that existed in China over the centuries. Most twentieth-century minds accepted the tendentious falsehood that Chinese civilization featured a thoroughgoing socio-cultural dichotomy: there were "the Confucians," who constituted "the elite" – educated, moral, and responsibly engaged in public life – and then there were "the Taoists," frequently rebels, charlatans, or fanatics – disreputable, superstitious, and "gross."[9] According to that long-lived misapprehension, some "Taoists" did manage to delude a few gullible emperors; but in China all "high-class men" knew to avoid them, and to pursue instead the noble Confucian goals of scholarship, moral cultivation, and government service – all supposedly alien to the activities and values of "the Taoists."

Of course, such stereotypes not only require that one not give honest attention to the facts of history. They also define "the high-class" person in terms that exclude women from the category altogether.[10] According to such ideas, it is simply unthinkable that there could have been, for instance, a thousand years ago, a cultured, highly educated Taoist woman who was honored at the court of an illustrious emperor. Yet, Ts'ao Wen-i, "the Perfected One of Literary Reclusion," was just such a person. And the fact of her existence – and of the honor in which she was held – demonstrates the need for us to be much more careful, and much more precise, in our generalizations about the social identity of "Taoists."

Fully to redress such misrepresentations of Taoism, even just regarding the underlying social issues, would require volumes. But I shall at least attempt here to articulate the fundamental questions, and to adduce some of the data currently known to us, in a preliminary effort to determine the true socio-cultural dynamics of the Taoist tradition over the centuries.

The fundamental question may be phrased thus: "What kinds of persons practiced Taoism in premodern China?" Was Taoism, as long alleged, simply a religion of "the ignorant masses" and of occasional "eccentrics" – as one leading scholar of the twentieth century belittled the Ch'üan-chen founder, Wang Che?[11] Or was it perhaps a religion that was cherished and practiced by centuries of thoughtful, respectable men and women – including men and women who were educated, well-born, and active in serving state and society – albeit possibly on terms that differed from those of later Confucians? Since the former representations seem now to have run their course, I shall essay to restore some balance to our picture of Taoism by examining some of the data of all periods with eyes open to the actual social realities.

"Literati Taoism"

According to the interpretive templates that governed most twentieth-century depictions of Taoism, there would seem to have been little place for discussion of Taoist "literati." By setting aside that template, however, we can now see that Chinese history abounded with Taoist scholars, historians, poets, and littérateurs of many sorts, as well as with government officials, imperial academics, and other well-connected members of "the political elite." A complete history of such matters remains to be written. But enough is now known to allow us to be quite clear that "the elite" of imperial China as a whole did *not* regard Taoism as "gross" or "grotesque," at least not before the nineteenth century.

In fact, one could nearly say that the *only* Taoists, throughout history, of whom we can claim to speak with much certainty were Taoists who belonged either (1) to the hereditary *aristocracy* that endured into T'ang times, or (2) to the later "*gentry*" class. Historians debate the precise terminology appropriate for describing such social realities. But the term "gentry" is most often used to designate people of social standing who were generally educated and well-to-do, but could not claim power or privilege on the basis of "noble" bloodlines. Such people formed an important element of Chinese society from Sung times onward. They provided centuries of government functionaries, and, from Mongol times on, it was only through demonstrating proficiency in a narrowly Confucian literary examination that a man could be assured access to such a government position. (Though gentry women were often educated, the exam route was closed to them.) Merchants and landowners often sent their sons to Confucian "academies" (*shu-yüan*) so that they could gain eventual access to government office and thereby secure their family's social and economic status. Yet, a person's membership in "the gentry class" did not, of itself, equate to a high educational level, much less to an interest in any particular value-system. In fact, the rise of the gentry coincided with the cultural consensus that "the Three Teachings are one."

Britain's leading scholar of Taoism, Timothy Barrett, has observed that "references in Sung times to [Ssu-ma Cheng-chen's *Tso-wang lun*] and to other writings by T'ang authors suggest that the Taoists of this period did in the long term achieve some success in creating a spiritualized 'gentry Taoism'."[12] Historians might dispute the application of the term "gentry" to men such as Ssu-ma – who were usually members of the old aristocracy. But by the term "gentry Taoism," Barrett seems to mean something akin to what I am here terming "literati Taoism."

Examples of "literati Taoism" from T'ang times are particularly abundant. For instance, Barrett has shown that the fourth-century Ling-pao "Scripture for Human Salvation" (*Tu-jen ching*)

> was not . . . simply read by (Taoist) adherents . . . An exemplar of seventh-century calligraphy has been preserved which would appear to represent a summary of the text designed to accompany pictorial representations of its contents. . . . Since neither the calligrapher nor the artist were clerics (they were in fact prominent officials of T'ai-tsung's court) it may be presumed that the *Tu-jen ching* had a substantial lay readership.[13]

Further evidence in support of Barrett's conclusion is the fact that a scholar of that period, Ch'eng Hsüan-ying, composed commentaries to the *Tu-jen ching* as well as to the *Lao-tzu* and *Chuang-tzu*.[14]

Meanwhile, Taoist court intellectuals, such as Ssu-ma Ch'eng-chen and the poet Wu Yün, clearly worked to enhance literati involvement with Taoism by composing a variety of works designed to render elements of the Taoist heritage more comprehensible, and more attractive, to other literati. Those works were well known among the political and cultural leaders of T'ang times. In addition, some of the "secular" poets of T'ang times, such as Li Po, show intimate familiarity with detailed elements of the Taoist heritage of the Six Dynasties period, and their works are replete with technical terms and allusions understandable only by those who were familiar with Taoist sacred texts.[15] Moreover, by the early ninth century, a Shang-ch'ing text on meditation, the "Scripture of the Yellow Court" (*Huang-t'ing ching*), was so well known among literati that references to it appear in the examination answers of civil service candidates.[16]

It should therefore come as no surprise that Taoist literati actually held government offices. For instance, according to the high official Ch'üan Te-yü, the Taoist priest Wu Yün was "a scholar (*ju*) of Lu," who held a position in the imperial Han-lin Academy. Ch'üan reports that "such works as [Wu's] *Principles of the Arcana* (*Hsüan-kang*) . . . and his *Discourse on the Possibility of Studying Divine Immortality* (*Shen-hsien k'o-hsüeh lun*) were highly esteemed by scholars of advanced learning."[17] Meanwhile, other T'ang officials, such as Ho Chih-chang, themselves entered the priestly ranks.[18]

Consequently, many Taoist texts of T'ang times were directed at an audience of literati, officials, and would-be officials. Some were reference works intended to give Taoists and non-Taoists alike a sense of the history and heritage of *Tao chiao*. One example is a seventh-century Taoist "encyclopedia" called "The Jewelled Satchel of the Three Caverns" (*San-tung chu-nang*).[19] That work and its compiler, Wang Hsüan-ho, remain virtually unknown even to most scholars of Taoism today.

The same is true of a number of T'ang texts that were intended to introduce officials, and members of the ruling house, to basic Taoist ideas. One was the "Scriptures and Formulae of Taoism" (*Tao-men ching-fa*), which is framed as a colloquy between the Taoist priest P'an Shih-cheng and the T'ang emperor Kao-tsung.[20] A slightly later example was the poet Wu Yün's work *On the Principles of the Arcana* (*Hsüan-kang lun*), as mentioned in Ch'üan Te-yü's report. That "handbook of very elementary Taoism" was submitted to the emperor Hsüan-tsung in the year 754.[21] By that time, the "secrets" of the Taoist "arcana" were actually quite open secrets, which employed "esoteric" terms mostly to intrigue the literati audience. Ssu-ma Ch'eng-chen, for instance, produced a manual on Taoist practice, now-lost, entitled "Esoteric Instructions for Cultivating Reality" (*Hsiu-chen mi-chih*), which was not only widely known among T'ang literati but remained "current in the world" even after the fall of the T'ang.[22] Such publications cannot meaningfully be called "esoteric."

Another intriguing element of T'ang efforts to promulgate Taoism among literati was a short-lived effort to incorporate the contemporary Buddhist doctrine of "Buddha-nature" into Taoist teachings. For instance, the seventh-century "Pivotal Meaning of the Taoist Teaching" (*Tao-chiao i-shu*) states: "The pure, empty and spontaneous Tao-nature is embodied in all conscious beings, and even all animals, plants, trees and rocks possess this Tao-nature."[23] Similar teachings appear in some of Ssu-ma Ch'eng-chen's writings, and in another little-known text that was very widely known in T'ang times: the "Scripture of the Genesis Point" (*Pen-chi ching*).[24] The prominence of that text owed largely to the fact that it was promulgated by imperial decree: in the year 741, the emperor Hsüan-tsung ordered it to be incorporated into *chai* liturgies performed by Taoist priests across the empire, and, since printing was still not developed, he ordered that Taoists at temples across the land should produce copies of it.

The *Pen-chi ching*, like the *Tao-chiao i-shu*, teaches that the true reality of all sentient beings is "*tao*-nature." Echoes of that concept do recur in later ages, but it did not become a central doctrine of Taoism in the way that the concept of "Buddha-nature" did for Ch'an/Zen Buddhists. Scholars have yet to explore the pertinent texts in much depth, so we are not yet sure why Taoists did not see as much value in the idea as their Buddhist contemporaries did. Of course, one simple explanation is that Taoists already had a wide array of other successful models by which literati could practice self-cultivation on terms that were comfortable for them.

On some levels, the "literati Taoism" of T'ang times can be seen as a continuation of elements of the "aristocratic Taoism" that had evolved during the Six Dynasties. Even Ko Hung, who is generally remembered as an advocate of the pursuit of immortality and a devotee of the practice of alchemy, had struggled to make the argument that a Confucian gentleman and respectable government official could profitably add such pursuits to his life. To Ko, there was nothing incongruous in the idea that a respectable gentleman could uphold Confucian values and engage in political acts while also laboring to achieve a status that would transcend life and death. Yet, one wonders how many readers he managed to persuade to accept his particular vision of the Taoist life.

One is tempted to think of "literati Taoism" as something rooted not in Ko's arguments, but rather in the values and practices of less colorful, and less well-known, practitioners of the early medieval period. Texts of the Lou-kuan tradition, for instance, do not seem to share Ko Hung's concern to make an explicit appeal to office-holding literati. They certainly do not share his provocative advocacy of alchemical practices. Yet, writings such as the "Scripture of Western Ascension" (*Hsi-sheng ching*) certainly do seem to offer a model of self-cultivation that would sound comfortable to literati of all ages. The fact that even Ts'ao Wen-i, a famed woman Taoist of the twelfth century, composed a commentary on the "Scripture of Western Ascension" suggests that models of self-cultivation couched in terms of "refinement" or "cultivation" of one's heart/mind – and subtle realities such as "spirit," "vital energy," and *tao* – held enduring appeal for literati of all descriptions, century after century.

To a large extent, such age-old Taoist models were preserved for later ages by the Ch'üan-chen tradition, which endures today. In his "Fifteen Articles on Establishing the Teaching," Wang Che (or someone writing in his name) argued that the Taoist life consists above all in individual self-cultivation, preferably by stepping outside of common society. Wang's followers eventually modified his eremitical ideals to justify a monastic lifestyle, one that already had centuries of Taoist precedents. By maintaining and reintegrating various T'ang and pre-T'ang teachings pertaining to self-cultivation practices, Wang's followers developed a monastic tradition that could successfully compete with that of the Buddhists. Yet in Ch'üan-chen monasties, Taoist practice retained its focus on self-cultivation in age-old Taoist terms, not following Buddhist-inspired models. Unlike Ch'an practitioners, for instance, monastic Taoists do not seem ever to have spent much time discussing, much less trying to "awaken" to, "Tao-nature." As we shall see in the following chapter, people attracted to that model usually found themselves practicing in a Buddist setting, while those drawn to Taoist settings were generally those who were attracted to specifically Taoist terms of personal practice.

Meanwhile, the evidence demonstrates that, even down through the Ch'ing dynasty, many members of what we might call "the literati class" actively studied, practiced, and promoted "Inner Alchemy" and other elements of the Taoist heritage. Those individuals, some of whom will be further discussed in the following chapter, were constantly reworking earlier traditions to create models of personal practice that would be comfortable, and effective, for literati and members of the gentry class who were not attracted to a monastic life.

As we shall see in the following chapter, the emperors of the Yüan, Ming, and Ch'ing periods often took little interest in such forms of Taoism, for they faced far different conditions than did rulers before 1126. Late imperial rulers saw little reason to turn to Taoist *monastic* traditions in pursuit of imperial legitimation. And the demise of the earlier aristocracy, which had provided centuries of emperors with venerable Taoist leaders, led to a loss of Taoist leaders who could provide legitimation on those terms. Scholars of the twenty-first century have much work to do to provide clear and sound explanations of the intertwining social and religious changes that altered the forms that Taoism would take from the conquest period to the present day.

A good step toward a properly nuanced understanding of Taoism would be the recognition of the *diverse social backgrounds* of the various historical leaders and shapers of the various streams that formed the tradition. Some streams, such as the early "Heavenly Master" organization, seem to have had origins among the peasantry. Hence that particular tradition struggled to gain the respect and recognition of members of the upper classes. But many other streams that contributed to Taoism's enduring tradition had origins among members of the medieval aristocracy and the later gentry. At present, the evidence suggests that T'ang Taoists – building upon the universalistic framework devised by fifth-century leaders such as Lu Hsiu-ching – strove in varied ways to develop a comprehensive, ecumenical "religion" which could attract and maintain the interest of people of *all* classes of society, including the "literati" with whom modern minds generally associate the term "Confucian." After the conquest period, Taoism seems to have flourished mostly by developing new models that were more specifically adapted to the particular needs of different elements of society. Yet, important elements of "literati Taoism" survived, and were reintegrated in new ways into the Taoism of modern times.

Women in Taoism: data, interpretation, and issues

The roles that women have played in Taoist life will vary according to one's notion of what "Taoism" is. If by "Taoism" one means the living Cheng-i traditions of Taiwan and coastal China, then women have little or no meaningful role, and have not had for centuries. But, as we have seen, there have actually been many other forms of Taoism. Some we have just begun to recognize, as scholars continue to explore the rich diversity of texts in the *Tao-tsang* and later Taoist collections.

In the living Lung-men tradition, as in its Ch'üan-chen antecedents and in several earlier Taoist traditions, women have played quite meaningful roles indeed. At times, such individuals were clearly exceptions to the rule. But, at other times, Taoists clearly made sincere, and sometimes successful, efforts to provide relatively equal opportunities to any person willing to participate, regardless of gender or class. In addition, women Taoists of various periods even held positions of influence and authority, sometimes in a formally institutionalized setting.

Over the course of history, virtually all Taoist practices – from self-cultivation practices to "thunder rites" – have been fully accessible to women, and we even know of women who have practiced them.[25] The idea that Taoist self-cultivation practices could, or should, be conceived in gender-specific terms would not arise until the nineteenth century.

The sparse records of classical times have very little to tell us about women practitioners. Neither the *Chuang-tzu* nor the *Nei-yeh* can reasonably be read as having anything really to say about gender issues, or about the gender of the person who follows its teachings. The contributors to the *Nei-yeh* do teach that there are attitudes and behaviors that one should forego in favor of others, but associate no gender imagery with any of them.

The *Chuang-tzu* does mention a few female characters. But, like all its characters – even Chuang Chou himself – they are all really literary characters, not historical persons; and even the historical characters that do appear, such as Confucius, are highly fictionalized. For that and other reasons, we can draw no sound historical conclusions from the *Chuang-tzu* about what women were or were not doing or thinking in classical times, or about how they may have contributed to what would later evolve into Taoism.

Neither the *Nei-yeh* nor the *Tao te ching* mention any female practitioners, though of course they never mention any *male* practitioners either, except as vague idealizations. It is traditional to assume that "the sage" in all such contexts necessarily refers to a man. Some scholars even automatically, and quite gratuitously, assume that the term "sage" must denote "the ruler." But those scholars have themselves uniformly been men, who have learned to study Chinese texts from men, and often from men whose mindset, interests, and values were not just Confucian, but specifically Ch'eng/Chu. Within that mindset, women are, at best, a marginal subject for discussion, and few women have ever been invited to do any of the discussing.[26] In the last decades of the twentieth century, a few tried to read the *Tao te ching* as an expression of a long-lost "matriarchal culture," but they generally did so by projecting late twentieth-century ideas onto selected lines without regard for the rest of the text. A truly "gender-neutral" reading of the *Tao te ching* – a reading devoid of the ideological assumptions and contentions of late modern times – has yet to focus upon what the various composers of the *text itself* were, or were not, telling readers about gender issues. And no one has yet attempted to bring the *Tao te ching*'s cognate text, the *Nei-yeh*, into such discussions. In the case of the *Nei-yeh*, it is virtually impossible to find anything that could reasonably be interpreted as gender-specific. To read "the sage" in its opening lines as necessarily male – much less as a ruler – would clearly be unfounded.

With regard to the *Tao te ching*, matters are more complex. There are several passages in it that commend what the text characterizes as "feminine" attitudes or behaviors, such as humility or yielding. Other passages, meanwhile, liken one who lives wisely to a child who values its mother's selfless benevolence. But, as we have seen in Chapter 2, the only pre-imperial manuscripts now extant – the recently discovered Kuo-tien (Guodian) bamboo slips – contain few of the modern text's famous lines about "the mother" or "the feminine." We have little data permitting us to reach firm conclusions about when, within the *Tao te ching*'s pre-history, those lines may have entered the text. The redactors of the "full text" of the *Tao te ching* – such as Huan Yüan or others at the Chi-hsia academy – clearly politicized, and thereby "masculinized," those lines' messages about "the female." As we now have them, the passages in question seem to imply that what is wrong with our normal attitudes and behavior is their excessive "masculinity." Yet, when inspected closely, these teachings do not truly essentialize women *or* men, for they are addressed to all readers, and apply to how *anyone's* life can be shown to be following a good or bad course. In fact, such teachings can be, and have been, interpreted as undercutting "standard" gender categories, for the *Tao te ching* clearly warns that males who follow the attitudes and behaviors that it characterizes as "masculine" will bring disaster to themselves and those around them. The *Tao te ching*, in its full form, even advocates "feminine" behaviors for *rulers*, though the historical rulers of the day were never women. Clearly, the redactors of the *Tao te ching* were using gender terms as potent *metaphors* for certain kinds of *behavior*, not as theoretical definitions of actual gender characteristics.

More important for understanding the classical heritage of Taoism is the fact that virtually all such ideas appear only in a single text, albeit one that has long been fetishized as "the basic text of Taoism." That fact is of particular importance in regard to gender issues, because the *Tao te ching*'s idealizations of "female" behaviors *never* actually became a key feature of "Taoism," either in classical times or in later ages. In classical times, gender metaphors were rare in the *Chuang-tzu*, and in passages of a "Taoistic" flavor in such "eclectic" compilations as the *Kuan-tzu* or *Lü-shih ch'un-ch'iu*. Moreover, those metaphors were seldom embraced by later Taoists, except when a given writer wanted to show continuities of certain later elements – e.g., "Inner Alchemy" – with terms found in old and honored texts. Even when Taoists of later centuries – such as the T'ai-i founder Hsiao Pao-chen, or the unknown author of the *Kao-tao chuan*'s second story about Ho Chih-chang – commend such ideals as "yielding restraint," they seldom added any gender imagery to them.[27] Therefore, far from being "basic" to "Taoism," the *Tao te ching*'s lines about idealized "female" behaviors deserve far less attention than they have hitherto received, and they should *not* be taken as "Taoist" statements about gender realities or gender ideals.

Another key question involves these texts' intended audience. Were *any* of the classical texts *intended* exclusively, or even primarily, to guide the lives of men *rather* than women, or the lives of members of any specific social class? Careful textual and historical research shows that the answer to both questions is unequivocally "no." Yet both Asian and Western scholars have, for generations, amused themselves – and sometimes deluded themselves and the public – with baseless assertions about such matters, generally based on few facts and little critical thought. Generally, those discussions were no more than elements of modern/postmodern discourse – debates about what people today *should* think – not impartial analytical expositions of actual social or historical data. Their underlying narrative was generally one intended either (1) to implicate Taoists with the same (or worse) faults alleged to exist in other cultures and traditions, or (2) to exonerate Taoists of such charges, thereby demonstrating Taoists' superiority to other cultures and traditions – especially our own. In other words, "Taoism" has frequently been read in such a way that it is not actually an element of any traditional Chinese discourse, but rather a part of modern arguments about the merits of ideas and values that moderns have a tradition of arguing about.[28]

If we set aside all such arguments, and simply seek factual answers to rational questions about elements of Taoism or its classical precedents, we can sometimes find answers that, while at times unexpected, are clearly quite sound, and sometimes highly illuminating. For instance, when we read an ancient Chinese text that gives advice presumed useful for achieving governmental goals, we may reasonably infer that its composer presumed the reader to be male, since, in ancient China, political participation by women was not an option: except perhaps for a spouse or close relative of a man who held a public position, no *woman* needed to be persuaded to think or act in a new way in order to have a desired effect on government policy or performance. As mentioned above, some interpreters have simply presumed that the *Nei-yeh* was intended specifically for rulers, *not* because there is any real political advice found anywhere in the text, but simply because those interpreters accept the outdated – and deeply Confucian – idea that all classical Chinese writings were fundamentally political in nature. All sinologists are aware that "Chinese tradition" is replete with commentaries that explain, for instance, each line of ancient poetic works such as the *Shih-ching* and *Ch'u-tz'u* as though they were political tracts that were simply *disguised* as poetry. But, in fact, the reader of the *Nei-yeh*, like that of most sections of the *Chuang-tzu*, is *not* assumed to be someone attempting to engage in or affect political acts, and is therefore someone whose gender cannot be inferred on such a basis.

It is also true that in ancient China women seldom achieved literacy. Hence one could argue that these texts, like any written text, must have been intended only for men. But then, very few *men* in that day and age achieved literacy either. Moreover, such reasoning presumes certain elitist models of "writing" and "reading," which were certainly typical of those who handled texts in imperial times, or at least of those who handled the texts that Chinese scholars and Western sinologists traditionally bothered to read. However, the model of "the lone writer" writing for "the lone reader" ignores other real possibilities regarding how a given text may have come into being.

When we read the *Nei-yeh* (or, for that matter, the *Shih-ching*), it is actually easy to understand it as a text that may have been shared by a family or group, which could very easily have included both men and women. That group would have needed only *one* person who knew how to read. As long as any given family or community had at least one reader, the contents of every kind of text would be fully accessible to *all* its members – readers and non-readers alike. In reality, anyone in any of the "middle kingdoms," or neighboring lands such as Ch'u, may have been interested in learning how to live from a text like the *Nei-yeh*, despite the fact that few individuals, male *or* female, could themselves actually read it.

One should also note that the *Nei-yeh* and the *Tao te ching* are both composed largely in verse. Scholars have suggested that certain sections of the *Nei-yeh* "may have been borrowed from some early Taoist hymn."[29] While that suggestion is wholly conjectural (and does some violence to the term "Taoist") it is certainly true that both of those texts are replete with mnemonic devices. That fact allows us to draw important conclusions about their intended audiences.

Following the "lone writer"/"lone reader" model, rhymes and other literary devices are little more than rhetorical niceties, which can only get in the way when a profound idea is being communicated. For that reason, most of the *Chuang-tzu* – which no one has ever alleged to have emerged from any "oral" setting – is in prose, with few discernible mnemonic elements. For literary purposes, rhymes and parallelism may be pleasant from some aesthetic perspective. But the presence of rhymes and parallelism in the *Nei-yeh* and *Lao-tzu* is of profound *social* significance: such devices were intended to facilitate oral transmission, and remembrance, of teachings designed to be learned by someone who has no interest or ability in examining a written text to be sure that he, or she, has not forgotten anything.

When sinologists assume – as they have nearly always done – that texts such as the *Tao te ching* were produced *by* literate intellectuals *for* literate intellectuals, they are making assumptions that do not seriously take into account the *literary form* of the text. A question that, to the best of my knowledge, has never been asked in this regard is that of *why* an intellectual composing *political* advice for a *ruler* would present those political ideas *in verse*? Did the rulers of fourth-century Ch'i or Wei, or their more hard-nosed neighbors in Ch'in, respond more enthusiastically to political advice that was carefully *rhymed*?

In order to make sense of the teachings found in the *Nei-yeh* and *Tao te ching*, we must recalibrate our thinking to the basic fact that their values and modes of thought emerged from a social setting in which most people, male or female, did not read, had no convenient way to learn to read, and generally had little reason to try to do so. Even rulers had little real reason to learn to read, so long as they had trustworthy aides who read well, or garrulous visitors such as Mencius, who could articulate political theory quite effectively without handing the ruler a written transcript. In fact, the very reason that men such as Confucius and Mencius did so much travelling – in one case, even endangering the Master's life – must have been that their intended audience was not someone who could get the message from any written text. We must bear in mind that, though "the middle kingdoms" and their neighbors like Ch'u did produce a few score written texts, they were all still by and large *oral* societies, wherein most people of *either* gender – even rulers –

acquired and dispensed most information and advice primarily, if not exclusively, by word of mouth.

The form of the *Nei-yeh* and the *Tao te ching* clearly show that they are both texts that originated within an oral tradition. And there is little in their teachings that can reasonably be held to be more or less practiceable by members of one specific gender.

Here we come to the issue of whether "Taoism" may have been open to participation by women *only* in terms of *theoretical possibilities*. In *theory*, the physical activities involved in playing on a nation's World Cup soccer team – running, kicking, etc. – are just as possible for any woman as for any man; yet, the abilities required are in fact abilities that men, being physically larger and stronger, tend to have more in abundance than do women. Religious practices, on the other hand, virtually never require abilities that women cannot develop to the same degree as men.

A key issue for modern minds is whether or not *anyone* and *everyone* can follow a given tradition's ideal path and achieve its highest goals. This issue is different from the question of how many people of any particular description actually undertake such a path. Even Mencius's model of self-cultivation does not logically assume masculine identity for a participant. Yet, within Chinese society, the effects for which a practitioner of his model could hope – as, for instance, in redirecting government policies – were certainly limited by social gender realities. Other Confucian models also tended to be defined on terms that were, in effect if not in intention, gender-specific.

In historical terms, of course, women do show up as participants in numerous forms of Taoism. But to what extent was their participation a result of the fact that the Taoist understanding of life was imagined in such a way that gender identity could *not* function as an *exclusionary* factor?

On certain levels, that question remains difficult to answer. It is fairly easy to show that Taoism – like Confucianism, and certain Buddhist traditions – answered such questions in a way that modern minds often struggle to accept. Modern beliefs insist that "everyone is equal," and that "the path to success" *should* therefore be "open to everyone." Many Asian traditions, however, begin from quite *different* assumptions about life, which, they might argue, are much more realistic. No Asian society ever advanced any notion of universal equality. Indeed, before contact with the modern West, few Asian thinkers of any stripe would have even entertained any such notions. In China, both Confucians and Taoists began with the observation that, in real life, individual people are quite different, and some individuals simply do not succeed at undertakings at which others succeed. In one sense, the imperial examination system, which recruited government officials, was highly elitist: it was designed to separate the sheep from the goats, to certify for government appointment *only* those of the greatest talent and ability. And yet, in another sense, that system was actually *anti*-elitist: it was intentionally designed in such a way that *any* individual could enter the system and meet its challenges successfully – regardless of parentage, wealth, or other social factors, much less any physical factors. Of course, no one gave any thought to our modern notion that such a system could, or should, have been open to women and men alike.

The spiritual life, for both Confucianism and Taoism, was generally understood in similar terms: in both traditions, moral and spiritual *perfectibility* was generally assumed of *everyone*. Moreover, the undertaking of the process of self-perfection was theoretically open to anyone. But, as Hsün-tzu explained, in real life most people will simply never attempt such things, and few who do so will persevere long enough or diligently enough to achieve the goal. Both Confucians and Taoists assumed that *some* individuals will, if given the opportunity, demonstrate a moral/spiritual talent or propensity that others will never demonstrate. Both traditions, therefore, sometimes display an assumption not unlike that of the examination system: our true concern should be to identify those individuals who possess the appropriate talents, and to facilitate their development. Taoists of all ages seem to have assumed that such individuals would be self-selecting: in any setting, certain individuals will tend to distinguish themselves by their alacrity in understanding and pursuing the pertinent moral and spiritual goals.

However, the institutions of Taoism – particularly the fully articulated institutions that began to develop in the fifth century – did what the institutions of Confucianism never attempted to do: they included women in such pursuits, on a basis that clearly suggested that any talented, dedicated woman had the same chance to achieve the Taoist goal as any *man* might. In Chinese culture, tales and stories abound – from early times to the present day – wherein men and women of exceptional perception and dedication succeed where others fail. Sometimes, in literature as in real life, such individuals pass tests of their character and determination without even realizing that they are being tested: they prove their personal worth not only by forgoing worldly fulfillments, but more importantly by shedding self-centeredness, and misconceptions about the spiritual life. Some texts stress that, since each person is intrinsically different, a mentor must mold both the content and the form of any individual's guidance to that person's particular needs and tendencies. Hence, no *uniform* pedagogical system could produce the desired results. In fact, in contrast to Ch'an/Zen Buddhism – which Taoism otherwise deeply influenced – Taoism never formalized any master–student relationship, or even insisted upon the necessity for a practitioner to apprentice him- or herself to any personal instructor. For those who needed it, Taoists developed monastic institutions. But in theory, they assumed that aspirants of sufficient talent might need little more than occasional gentle nudges, and texts of many periods show transcendent beings (*hsien*) providing worthy aspirants with such subtle assistance, often without anyone even knowing it. And the worthy aspirants in such cases included women and men alike.

Moreover, Taoism left its doors open to participation by women through its receptivity to diverse idealizations of the Taoist life itself. In this regard, Taoism was quite different from Buddhism, for, even in the most "liberal" forms of Buddhism, there were still certain old and cherished assumptions about the nature of the goal – the achievement of a condition that was as close as possible to the condition that the Buddha himself achieved. In Taoism, on the other hand, the terms on which one could be said to have reached the goal of life have historically remained open to different definitional assumptions. In Taoism, for instance, a woman who fulfills life's highest ideals by feeding rats and pigeons could find that those compassionate acts resulting in public ascent to Heaven as a transcendent being, as the case of Pien Tung-hsüan clearly shows.[30] Hence in Taoism, characteristics of spiritual accomplishment were not restricted to pursuits that were possible only for males. And in T'ang times, at least, people of both genders, and of all social classes, seem to have had very high regard for Taoist women such as Huang Ling-wei, whose life appears to show not only illiteracy, but total disinterest in models of the spiritual life that could reasonably be construed as gender-specific.

It would be foolish to try to fit Taoism into any polarizational characterizations such as "oppressive" or "liberating." What can be said is that Taoist values were holistic and inclusive, though Taoists lived in Chinese society, where women were generally subjected to gender-specific roles and expectations that were very limiting. Yet the religious life – whether on Buddhist or Taoist terms – was generally not governed by those expectations, and women's secular roles did not simply carry over into religious settings. "Whatever her position within the society in general might have been, as soon as a woman assumed a religious role she obviously not only could act autonomously but was even an accepted 'partner' of the authorities."[31] And even in late imperial China, when some members of Chinese society were binding their little girls' feet, Taoism was a tradition that, to some degree, put its holistic ideals into practice on an *institutional* basis. The degree and manner of their inclusiveness varied according to social and historical factors, which scholars have only recently begun to ponder.

Because our knowledge of Taoist history remains quite limited, it is presently not possible to undertake a thorough analysis of how gender was involved in Taoists' actual lives from age to age. What follows is therefore, again, merely a summary of what is currently known.

Women in Taoist history

Twentieth-century scholars of Taoism, from Maspero onward, often privileged the "Heavenly Masters" (T'ien-shih) tradition, which supposedly endured from the time of Chang Tao-ling to the Cheng-i priests of today. Consequently, more of that tradition's textual data have been studied than those of other Taoist traditions. We have therefore known for decades that the early T'ien-shih tradition – unlike the living Cheng-i tradition – constructed its model of "priesthood" on a basis that was explicitly open to women and men on equal terms. Its primary office, that of the "libationer" (*chi-chiu*), was open to women and men alike, though scholars today have begun to question whether that office was actually clerical or simply a term for lay leaders.[32] We do have some historical data on a few women libationers, most famously "Lady Wei," Wei Hua-ts'un (251–344).[33] On that basis, scholars have been able to determine that "Women and men alike were allowed to perform ritual functions," such as submitting petitions (*chang*) to the unseen powers, or creating talismans.[34] We also know that lay participants were given titles that indicated gradations of achievement, which were parallel for men and women: beginners were styled *tao-nan* or *tao-nü* ("Taoist men" and "Taoist women"), those of intermediate level were styled *nan-kuan* or *nü-kuan* ("capped men" and "capped women"); and advanced participants were called *tao-fu* or *tao-mu* ("Taoist father" and "Taoist mother").[35]

A fifth-century T'ien-shih text outlined the religious roles and responsibilities considered appropriate for laywomen in five specific life-situations:

1 unmarried daughters who live at home;
2 unmarried daughters who leave home (i.e., young women who wish to enter the religious life rather than marry);
3 married women;
4 single women; and
5 daughters who return to live at home.

Categories 4 and 5 both included widows and estranged wives. In each situation, the Taoist woman vows to be conscientious and to take a religious teacher, who could be either male or female, though male masters who lived alone were not permitted to accept female disciples. Under some circumstances, a married woman could take a different teacher than her husband did, but each was to assume a religious surname, i.e., relinquishing his or her family surname.[36]

Data of this kind are very suggestive, though it is not always easy to determine the degree to which such expectations were obligations or merely ideals, or indeed whether they represented community expectations or merely fond ideals of the text's composer and/or his/her immediate circle. Moreover, information such as that presented in that text remains so limited that it would seem excessive to proclaim, as one leading scholar has done, that "the liturgical tradition of the Heavenly Masters grants women a status identical in every respect to that of men."[37] It seems more correct to say that at least the organization's formulators did their best to give women relatively equal roles, though they did not fully escape the pressures of the surrounding society.

Our data do not seem to allow us to determine precisely how much leadership women may actually have provided in the early T'ien-shih organization. One such leader, Wei Hua-ts'un, gained *posthumous* fame within the fourth-century revelations of Shang-ch'ing Taoism. Revelations from "Lady Wei," and other male and female "Perfected Ones," told of the heavenly realm known as Shang-ch'ing. They taught mortals how to purify themselves through visualizational meditation, including the projection of one's own life-energy (*ch'i*) into a visualized feminine being, such as the Mysterious Woman of the Nine Heavens.[38] The ideal underlying such meditational models is holistic, in that the goal is for one to merge one's mortal life with the immortal realities of the higher realms, and to unify one's personal self with a higher personal reality, in terms that suggest the (re)unification of what currently exists as complementary pairs. On that level, the Shang-ch'ing model is compatible with the models found in later "Inner Alchemy" practices, few of which assumed practitioners of a specific gender. The Shang-ch'ing model, however, clearly does seem to assume a masculine identity on the part of the practitioner, and Shang-ch'ing texts do not appear to offer other models that might fit more comfortably into women's lives.

On the other hand, the "Perfected Ones" included a variety of female beings as ideal teachers and co-participants in the most exalted processes of self-cultivation. And they were not simply "goddesses," whose sphere of reality is ontologically unattainable by mortal beings. Since some of them, like Lady Wei, were mortal women who had ascended, their role was *not* simply to serve as lures to male participants presumed to need help sublimating their sexual drive.[39] Rather, the female "Perfected Ones" represented a proof to those men, and to potential *women* aspirants, that women can achieve the highest goals not only in theory, but also in actuality – a fact that allows them to extend their blessings to mortals, of either sex, who would like to follow in their footsteps. The texts of Taoism, and Chinese literature more generally, are replete with accounts of both male and female transcendents who demonstrated to men and women alike that the goal of the religious life can be achieved by dedicated aspirants of either gender.

It is unclear whether or how women took part in the activities of those who produced the early Ling-pao texts. The prescribed practices were accessible to both genders. The recipient of the Ling-pao revelations was a male aristocrat, but the social realities of the tradition's participants remain poorly known, in terms of class, gender, or even numbers. The extant texts of that period have not yet been thoroughly studied, and even those which have been – both in the *Tao-tsang* and outside it – were not compiled with our questions in mind.

The same can be said for the early alchemical tradition known as T'ai-ch'ing. Some twentieth-century writers once argued that the actual practice of *wai-tan* presumed affluence, since presumably there were materials to buy, and only aristocrats could afford them. Once again, such simplistic reasoning ignores some quite logical possibilities, such as persons of means sharing equipment or materials with deserving neighbors, friends, or family members. And the equally simplistic notion that for instance, a farmer could not have taken part in such processes because he *had* to labor in the fields all day would also logically lead to such conclusions as that farmers "had no spare time" to get married or to engage in conjugal relations.

All that can be said of the T'ai-ch'ing tradition is that – like Shang-ch'ing and Ling-pao – it seems to have arisen among the upper classes. Yet, there is no evidence that the men who produced or followed T'ai-ch'ing texts considered their practices unsuitable for their sisters, wives, or daughters. Meanwhile, the self-cultivation models taught in the Lou-kuan tradition – for instance, in the *Hsi-sheng ching* – clearly do not privilege male gender. But in all such settings, the writers simply did not see reason to make mention of whether women and men alike were taking part in their traditions, as was apparently the case in the T'ien-shih tradition. What *can* be said is that the early T'ien-shih tradition made extensive efforts to be socially inclusive, even to the point of making sure to provide activities that anyone – of any age, gender, or ethnic group – could perform. But there are no data that indicate that the new traditions of the Six Dynasties periods did likewise: the Shang-ch'ing, Ling-pao, T'ai-ch'ing, and Lou-kuan traditions seem to have followed the model whereby self-selecting aspirants of strong dedication – regardless of gender – would go beyond what most people ever would.

Once Taoism began developing a sense of common unity around the sixth and seventh centuries, we begin to find information about women participants on *several* levels. First, we begin finding a limited amount of generalized "sociological" data, such as the number of religious establishments specifically dedicated to women practitioners. For instance, in the year 739, during the reign of T'ang Hsüan-tsung, we find mention of 550 abbeys for Taoist women, compared to 1,137 for men. We do *not* know, of course, how many individuals practiced in either setting, but the evidence generally seems to suggest that there were usually more male participants than female. By that period, women clerics officially held the same title as men – *tao-shih*, "priest/priestess" – but there are relatively few priestesses known by name.

In only a few cases, such as that of the once-famous "Flower Maid," Huang Ling-wei (*ca.* 640–721), do we have enough data to make guarded conclusions about the realities of Taoist women's lives. Huang Ling-wei was one of the notable women Taoists of T'ang times.[40] In many regards, her life, like in fact those of most male Taoists throughout history, remains poorly known. Like most Taoists of either gender, Huang evidently wrote nothing, so it is impossible to know her own ideals, her reasons for her life-decisions, the nature of her own religious practices, or her precise relationship to her male or female contemporaries. Like even her contemporary, the politically prominent male leader Li Han-kuang – successor to Ssu-ma Ch'eng-chen, and himself oft sought by emperors – Huang received no notice at all in "the standard histories." Yet, her deeds drew enough attention among her contemporaries that an official named Yen Chen-ch'ing composed two inscription texts commemorating her life. As is typical with most biographies of that period (and, indeed, most early accounts of Jesus, the Buddha, and other celebrated figures), Yen's accounts tell us little of Huang's early life. She was, like other males and females of her day, reportedly ordained as a priestess (*tao-shih*) at the age of twelve. But there are no other data, in any source, pertaining to any aspect of her life until she was about fifty. At that time, for reasons never explained, Huang began a dogged quest to discover the location of a long-lost shrine to Lady Wei. Eventually, she located Lady Wei's shrine and excavated some artifacts, which were promptly confiscated by the empress Wu (to be discussed more fully below), though the empress showed little interest in Huang herself. Huang also discovered another nearby shrine, restored them both, and began regular observances at both sites. By that time, she had attracted a number of disciples – apparently all female – who continued the *chai* rites at this now flourishing religious center for nearly thirty years. Around 721, Huang ascended by means of "mortuary liberation" (*shih-chieh*).[41] A disciple named Li Ch'iung-hsien apparently led the others in maintaining the shrines for a while, and the great *chiao* and *chai* liturgies were periodically performed by priests. (It is unclear whether any of the priestesses ever officiated at such rites when male priests participated.) Yen Chen-ch'ing, our source for nearly all our data on "the Flower Maid," clearly admired her greatly, and wrote of her in terms that make clear that he, and his intended readers, saw nothing problematic about a woman whose life was patently outside the "norms" that we have traditionally assumed to have been standard for all women in premodern China.

It would be dangerous to draw sweeping generalizations about Taoist women from such limited data, tantalizing though it may be. It does seem reasonable to imagine that women may have tended to enter the religious life in smaller numbers than men because of ambient social expectations that women should devote themselves to domestic roles. However, in medieval times, when Taoism flourished, the acceptance of *exceptional* women in Chinese society was apparently far greater than in later times. None of the male "elite" who wrote about women like Huang raised any eyebrows at the idea of such people going unmarried or taking public actions independent of the authority of contemporary males. To all appearances, such gender dynamics – now often proclaimed to have been the governing force in women's lives in all ages, and in fact in all cultures – simply did not apply to women such as Huang or her disciples.

The acclaim that such women gained for their religious activities was unalloyed and long-lasting. For instance, in 882, a provincial governor addressed the imperial throne lauding the holy life of a literate Taoist woman named Hsüeh Hsüan-t'ung. In response, the emperor Hsi-tsung (r. 873–88) issued a rescript, saying:

> [Hers] is indeed the Tao of the heavenly formulae, as expressed in the classics of transcendence . . . Like [Lady]

> Wei's ascent to transcendence, or the Flower Maid's descent into this world, she adds luster to the local district, and illumines our nation and dynasty. It is fitting to commit [such facts] to the officials in the [imperial] history bureau, so that they may inscribe them in the official records. Thus shall her very Tao be exalted. Money shall be donated to the place where she dwelt, and the Taoist altar with its golden registers shall be renovated, in order to extend our reverent feelings in harmony with the highest mystery.[42]

This material is preserved in the most important surviving text regarding women in early and medieval Taoism, the *Yung-ch'eng chi-hsien lu* ["Records of the Assembled Transcendents of the Fortified Walled City"], by the court chronicler Tu Kuang-t'ing. The *Yung-ch'eng chi-hsien lu* was apparently the first comprehensive collection of accounts of female Taoist divinities and exemplary women. And despite a degree of idealization – such as also typified standard biographies of male figures, even in secular historiography – the *Yung-ch'eng chi-hsien lu* preserves useful historical data which help us reconstruct certain aspects of the lives of actual Taoist women. Regrettably, few scholars, even specialists in Taoism, have ever looked at Tu's great text or made any effort to use it to help us understand the social realities of those who practiced Taoism in past ages.[43]

Throughout the late Six Dynasties, T'ang, and early Sung periods, some female priests were apparently ordained around puberty, just as male priests often were. And they lived the spiritual life through self-cultivation and other religious activities, which were typically not gender-specific. Some pursued – and reportedly achieved – the supreme goal of "transcendence" (*hsien*), and they did so through a variety of practices, from visualizational meditation to the ingestion of supernal essences or the performance of altruistic deeds. And female *tao-shih* seem to have shared some of the same *public* roles as their male counterparts: for instance, there is evidence that the great liturgies called the *chiao* and *chai* may have been performed by female officiants.[44] Moreover, texts from the eighth century down to Ming times show that the ordination procedures for female *tao-shih* differed only in that certain ritual actions proceeded from right to left, while for men they proceeded from left to right.[45]

In the entire history of China, only once did a woman rule the empire in her own right. In 690, the empress Wu, commonly known as Wu Tse-t'ien, officially extinguished the T'ang dynasty and founded a new dynasty, named Chou. Until 705, she not only ruled the land *de facto* – as did various other empresses through history, both before and after her – but also *reigned* as "the Son of Heaven." Later historians were so repulsed by that fact that they denied the very existence of her Chou empire and pretended that the T'ang throne had merely been briefly commandeered by a "usurper," whose deeds warranted little attention. But, in reality, empress Wu ruled China in her own name for fifteen years, as she had done *de facto* for some years theretofore. These facts are pertinent not only because the empress continued to patronize Taoists, as her husband, the T'ang emperor Kao-tsung, had frequently done.[46] But, in addition, empress Wu's only daughter, known in history only as "the T'ai-p'ing princess," was ordained as a Taoist priestess in 670. Though that ordination may have been a ruse, scholars of the late twentieth century found that "no less than twelve other princesses are recorded as having followed her precedent and entered Taoist communities during the next two centuries."[47] Yet, even in the best-known case, "we know little of the lady's private life."[48]

Such is also true of another Taoist woman at the very end of the T'ang: the Ch'ing-wei founder Tsu Shu (fl. 889–904). Ch'ing-wei Taoism, known for its therapeutic "thunder rites," spread widely in the Sung period, but of Tsu herself virtually nothing is known.[49] Later Ch'ing-wei traditions report that her teachings were transmitted through a line of female practitioners down to the twelfth century.[50] Earlier, accounts of Huang Ling-wei, from the hand of male officials, report that she had also had female disciples, of whom, of course, very little is known. But the paucity of historiographical data regarding the actual lives of such Taoist women is to be ascribed not to any reluctance to honor female people, but rather to an overwhelming emphasis on data that would seem likely to be regarded as *politically* significant. Even *male* Taoists of great achievements and high social and political standing were sometimes shunned by historians, if their lives could not readily be portrayed as examples of certain specific political paradigms.[51] Even in the case of male Taoists whose lives were written up by writers of every description for centuries – such as Huang's well-known contemporary

Ssu-ma Ch'eng-chen – one could also say, "we know little of the gentleman's private life."

Certain kinds of data seem to indicate that, from the Sung dynasty onward, political and social changes led to a diminution of women's roles in Taoism. For instance, in the year 1077, there were reportedly only some 700 ordained Taoist women, compared to 18,500 men. And by the year 1677, there were no women recognized as priests at all. But, to a large degree, those facts simply indicate that the nature of Taoist institutions was continuing to change, and formal ordination as a *tao-shih* was no longer regarded as a requirement for fulfilling the most important expectations for a Taoist practitioner. With increasing literacy, both men and women could become "lay practitioners" of Taoism, as of Ch'an Buddhism, simply by reading printed texts available at local bookshops and endeavoring to practice the texts' teachings.

A fine example of how laywomen could participate in "gentry Taoism" was a woman of Sung times – Ts'ao Hsi-yün, better known as Ts'ao Wen-i (fl. 1119–1125). Ts'ao won fame as a poet, though she also wrote commentaries on both the *Tao te ching* and the *Hsi-sheng ching*.[52] The emperor Hui-tsung heard of her, summoned her to court – just as emperors had, for centuries, summoned eminent male Taoists – and honored her as "the Perfected One of Literary Reclusion."[53] Her writings, such as the *Ta-tao ke* ["Song of the Great Tao"], have not survived, so we cannot determine her actual beliefs or practices. But in later traditions, such as Ch'üan-chen, Ts'ao was honored as an early practitioner of "Inner Alchemy."[54]

It is noteworthy that the Ch'üan-chen tradition – one of whose founders was Wang Che's woman disciple Sun Pu-erh – was extremely popular among women in its early days: surviving data indicate that somewhere between 20 to 40 percent of the early Ch'üan-chen clergy were female. Still, inscription data concerning early male clerics outnumber those concerning female clerics by thirty to one. And not a single Ch'üan-chen text of the Chin or Yüan periods was authored by a woman – surely an indication of lesser degrees of literacy.[55] Moreover:

> In the late Yuan and early Ming, women Daoists are scarcely mentioned in the sources. Rare exceptions are some wives and mothers of Celestial Masters, who had newly risen to

> national importance and received imperial support. No longer do we find women leaders of temples or convents of the Quanzhen [Ch'üan-chen] or Longmen [Lung-men] schools.[56]

In general, the evidence suggests that the reason for the diminishing roles of women in Taoist public life had to do *not* with any fundamental attitudinal changes among Taoists, but rather with broader social changes taking place in late imperial and modern China. After the Mongol conquest, the government became more authoritarian. It utilized Ch'eng/Chu Confucian ideology to indoctrinate society with an ethos of obedience to authority. Women throughout Chinese society were subjected to increasing restrictions. Eventually, those changes seem to have reduced the opportunities that Taoism had provided for women of earlier ages to play public roles comparable to those of men. Yet, even today, women continue to participate in the liturgical activities at Taoist abbeys. And the laicization of traditions such as "Inner Alchemy" in modern China allowed women as well as men to learn and practice self-cultivation on Taoist terms without having to take formal orders.[57] Much further research will be needed before we can understand the ways in which women contributed to all the undulating currents of Taoist history.

Taoists and dynasts

Throughout the twentieth century, Taoism was often perceived as being outside the mainstream of Chinese society. In fact, it was frequently alleged that Taoism was the refuge of those who rejected the very *notion* of taking part in the socio-political order. In reality, however, the representatives of Taoism were *never* antipathetic to the government of their day and age, much less to the idea of government itself. But some leading sinologists continue to give the opposite impression, i.e., they perpetuate a thousand-year-old Confucian falsehood – that Taoists never cared about playing a constructive role in social and political affairs.[58]

Once again, to see Taoism correctly we must look at historical *facts*, and at the centuries of Taoist texts that propounded the importance of bringing the *socio-political order* into accord with life's deeper realities. For a Taoist to engage in political activity so conceived was not only fully accepted by Taoists throughout imperial times; it was actually an activity in which Taoists actively engaged. Up to Manchu times, China's rulers generally *valued* the Taoist tradition – and its living representatives – as an important resource for legitimizing the imperial government and maintaining a harmonious order within the state. And until Manchu times, Taoism – and its living representatives – was also valued and respected by the "Confucians" who worked in government positions and wrote the "official" histories.

For hundreds of years, Taoist leaders served China's rulers as legitimatory aides, in a variety of distinct roles. A generation of scholars has now demonstrated that Taoism's leading representatives often took a keen interest in the prestige and power of the Chinese emperors, and that the emperors took an equally keen interest in them. As Anna Seidel observed:

> Awe for the Heaven-appointed monarch was at the foundation of Taoism – a religion which might even be characterized as a projection into the unseen world of the old imperial mythology. . . . By exalting the God Emperor, the Taoist priests were nurturing a potent myth – and this was nothing less than the force which held the vast Chinese empire together.[59]

The facts of history thus show that emperors' interest in Taoists over the centuries was not, as Confucian falsehoods have always told us, simply idiosyncrasy on the part of certain befuddled or gullible rulers. Rather, Taoism served a profound and deeply functional role within the political order, by providing generations of rulers with appropriate ceremonial and religious paradigms.

As Anna Seidel showed, Six Dynasties rulers often utilized Taoist ordination rituals as the model for their own enthronement ceremonies. In T'ang times, not only the T'ang ruling house – which sought legitimation in the idea that they were descendents of "Lao-tzu" – but even the "usurper" empress Wu filled their courts with Taoists of every description, performed Taoist rituals (such as *t'ou-lung*, "tossing the dragons"), took lay ordination in Taoist orders, ordained their daughters as Taoist priestesses, and even made Taoist texts such as the *Huang-t'ing ching* – a meditation text of the Shang-ch'ing tradition – the basis of imperial examinations that qualified scholars for government service. Taoist leaders were not only summoned to render religious advice, but were even viewed as protectors of the realm, whose engagement with superhuman forces enabled them to thwart nefarious plots and avert all manner of disasters. In addition, emperors viewed eminent Taoists in terms of a different and quite ancient cultural paradigm – that of the sagely counsellor, whose supportive presence elevates the sovereign to near-mythical heights of glory. The confluence of those paradigms, especially in T'ang times, demonstrates the variety and fluidity of Taoism's relationship with government over the course of Chinese civilization.

In Chinese tradition – within Taoism, Confucianism, and the ritual and ideological traditions of the state itself – earthly authority and spiritual authority were regarded as, in essence, wholly identical. Modern Confucians seldom acknowledged that fact, and modern sinologues sometimes forgot that, into late imperial times, China's rulers and their subjects all shared the belief that all legitimate authority derives directly from *heavenly sources*. For centuries, Taoists and dynasts alike considered it to be Taoist masters' responsibility to assist the sovereign in managing his heavenly mandate. In medieval times, the emperor, the Taoist master, and the divine realities of Heaven were all seen as co-participants in the same process: unifying the world – "all under Heaven" – in a state of "Great Tranquillity" (*t'ai-p'ing*).

To most who study China, the term *t'ai-p'ing* remains known only as a label for various rebel movements, such as the so-called Yellow Turbans of the second century, or the followers of Hung Hsiu-ch'üan in the nineteenth century. Because Hung's "T'ai-p'ing Rebellion" threatened to undo lucrative treaty rights which Western powers like England had wrested from the feeble Manchu rulers, those powers not only suppressed his movement, but cooperated with the Manchus in painting it as a rebirth of old, subversive superstitions – rather than as a Christian-based reform movement that acted, for instance, to give women full equality with men.

In earlier times, the term *t'ai-p'ing* had actually denoted a peaceful and well-ordered society:

> It was a state in which all the concentric spheres of the organic Chinese universe, which contained nature as well

> as society, were perfectly attuned, communicated with each other in a balanced rhythm of timeliness, and brought maximum fulfillment to each living being.[60]

From Han times to the present, Taoist priests (*tao-shih*) assumed a special responsibility to tend to the spiritual dimensions of upholding *t'ai-p'ing*, complementing the real and symbolic activities of the emperor, and those of the local magistrate.[61] In this context, the *tao-shih* was ultimately perceived as an embodiment of the same spiritual efficacy that the virtuous and sagely emperor was theoretically assumed to possess. Taoist spirituality and imperial spirituality were in this respect inseparable: the *tao-shih* was perceived as an incarnation of the spiritual powers of the universe, and it was his responsibility to ensure that the holder of Heaven's mandate received the spiritual guidance and protection necessary for its orderly execution.[62]

Because these facts do not fit into the paradigms by which twentieth-century minds understood what "Taoism" is, it is necessary to trace some of the pertinent political elements of Taoist tradition. It hardly seems necessary to reiterate the political teachings of the texts of classical Taoism, particularly those presented in the *Tao te ching*. One passage of that classic explains principles by which the ruler should "govern the people and serve Heaven (*chih-jen shih-t'ien*)."[63] That phrase could easily have served as a permanent motto of the Chinese imperial state. After all, the official rites of the Chinese state itself – e.g., the *feng* and *shan* rites – were designed to demonstrate the religious correlation between the act of governing the people and the act of serving Heaven. It was in the context of those ritual and ideological underpinnings of the imperial state itself that occupants of the throne turned to *Taoists* to make sure that the emperor performed the *feng* and *shan* rites properly.[64]

By the late twentieth century, even mainstream sinology had accepted the notion the *Tao te ching* was "a handbook for rulers." As we saw in Chapter 2, such ideas are quite simplistic. Yet it is certainly true that by the third century BCE the entire political discourse of China – even under the Legalist regime of the state, and later dynasty, called Ch'in – had become filled with ideas that resonated with those of "the classical Taoists." The fact that the earliest commentary on the *Tao te ching* is found in the writings of the "Legalist" Han Fei suffices to show that no one in that age considered "Taoist ideas" to be "escapist," much less politically "subversive." And by the following century, the composers of the *Huai-nan-tzu* had developed a sophisticated model of government based on the then well-accepted idea that the only good ruler is a ruler who integrates his government with the forces of the cosmos.[65]

It was within just this context – not among "revolting peasants" – that the enduring streams of "later Taoism" actually began to take shape. During the late Han and Six Dynasties periods (first to sixth centuries CE), virtually every segment of the Taoist tradition displayed a *strong* interest in government, based squarely upon Han political thought. In what may be the earliest Taoist "scripture," the *T'ai-p'ing ching*, Heaven (*T'ien*) charged a divine emissary with revealing its salvific message to a worthy ruler. That message was not the product of revolting peasants, but rather an outgrowth of the presentation of comparable texts to emperors at the Han court in the late first century BCE.[66] Likewise, the "divinization" of "Lao-tzu" originated not within the "primitive Taoism" of superstitious masses unable to grasp the importance of "the Confucian state."[67] Rather, it arose *within the Han court*, to serve the needs of the Han emperors. The Han emperor Huan (r. 147–167) instituted imperial sacrifices to "Lord Lao" (*Lao-chün*), an event commemorated in an inscription text composed by a local magistrate in 165 CE. According to that text, the *Lao-tzu ming*, Lao-chün is a cosmic being who descends to earth in each generation to serve as counsellor to a worthy ruler.[68] That understanding of the true nature and significance of "Lao-chün" was not some passing oddity, but rather an influential and enduring belief, as demonstrated in centuries of comparable imperial acts, and comparable inscriptions.

As Taoist religious movements arose in the second and third centuries, they struggled with the principal problem that had occupied Tung Chung-shu and later generations of Han-dynasty thinkers: What happens when historical events seem to show that current rulers are not in accord with the unseen forces of the cosmos? That problem was at the very heart of the *T'ai-p'ing ching*, and of Chang Tao-ling's T'ien-shih movement, just as it had been at the heart of the *Confucian* theories of Tung Chung-shu. For a while, at least, the T'ien-shih leadership appears to have lost hope that the Han ruling house still possessed the spiritual authority to govern the land. Confucians since the time of Mencius had insisted that only a worthy ruler can hold on to "Heaven's mandate" (*T'ien-ming*), and that an unworthy ruler, having lost that mandate, may not only legitimately be toppled, but truly deserves to be replaced. Such ideas, which Tung Chung-shu elaborated in great detail, were certainly not the ideas of anarchists, any more than they were ideas that arose among revolting peasants. And it was precisely from within that well-established framework of Confucian political thought – that the government *must* operate in accord with life's deeper realities – that "the Celestial Masters" arose.

Like everyone else in those days, the leaders of that movement held firmly to the belief that the ideal world-order required a wise and able monarch. But if the monarchy should falter – as it seemed to be faltering in the second century CE – the Celestial Masters, following the same principles that Mencius and Tung Chung-shu had enunciated, should seek to bring about a new political order, which would, unlike the faltering regime, show itself to be in full possession of Heaven's spiritual mandate. It is true that, in the absence of any worthy and capable leader, the T'ien-shih movement's leaders were willing to provide social leadership. But as Michel Strickmann noted, the Celestial Masters preferred to lend their support to a worthy temporal authority:

> Under a worthy dynasty, which governed by virtue of the Tao, the role of the celestial masters was that of acting as intermediaries for celestial confirmation and support. Only when a responsible ruler was lacking were the celestial masters to take over the temporal guidance of the people and hold the supreme power in trust for a new incumbent.[69]

Though students of modern China often associate Taoism with popular revolts, history shows that connections between Taoism and popular rebellion generally developed only when the reigning regime was demonstrably oppressive or ineffective. Whenever there seemed to be a worthy ruler, or even a plausible candidate for worthy ruler, Taoists of virtually every description seemed quite content to acknowledge the legitimacy of his authority. For instance, during the third century, one early leader of the Celestial Master organization bound it to a newly established dynasty through a formal religious endorsement, in the following words:

> Conforming to the Celestial order and profiting from the propitious times, I have, in my function as Master of the State, given the order to Emperor Wu [Ts'ao Ts'ao] to launch the Empire. . . . Now that I will hide from the world, I entrust you to the pure administration and the Taoist government of the Wei [dynasty].[70]

Meanwhile, one of Ts'ao Ts'ao's rivals in south China reportedly courted the semi-legendary Taoist master Ko Hsüan, in order "to enhance the splendour of his throne."[71]

Most later Taoist leaders of every stripe aligned themselves with the government in power in their region at that time. During the fifth century, for instance, the pivotal master Lu Hsiu-ching built up a religious establishment that carried out ceremonies and provided auspicious portents in favor of the Liu-Sung dynasty (420–479). In the rulers of that dynasty, Taoists such as Lu complacently agreed to recognize not only the fulfillment of old messianic prophesies, but also the legitimate continuation of the great Han dynasty.[72] It was, in fact, very simple for those fifth-century Taoists to confirm the Sung rulers as heirs to the great Han emperors, for both ruling houses shared the surname of Liu. One Taoist manifesto of the period declared that "the descendents of the house of Liu, in possession of the Tao, have revived the tradition, and Heaven has bestowed the Chart [a token of political legitimacy] in response."[73]

In the late twentieth century, the best-known example of a Taoist figure who lent legitimatory aid to a Chinese government was a fifth-century figure named K'ou Ch'ien-chih. K'ou reportedly received revelations from divine beings such as Lord Lao and Chang Tao-ling, and in 424 he brought the revealed texts to the imperial court of the Toba Wei dynasty. The Wei emperor, T'ai-wu, saw this event as a sign of heavenly blessing upon his state, and installed K'ou in a formal court office. Like earlier Taoist leaders, K'ou longed for an ideal society of peace and harmony, in which a worthy ruler ruled with Heaven's mandate. He saw the Wei emperor as just such a ruler, and in 442 K'ou performed a formal ceremony for T'ai-wu, bestowing numinous texts upon him and hailing him as "the Perfected Lord of Grand Tranquillity" (*T'ai-p'ing chen-chün*). Through that ceremony, Heaven formally conveyed its blessings on T'ai-wu's reign, and the emperor took *T'ai-p'ing chen-chün* as his official reign title.[74]

Another great Taoist tradition, the Shang-ch'ing tradition, came to political prominence during the Liang dynasty (502–556). At that time, the renowned master T'ao Hung-ching (456–536), a court academician under the preceding two dynasties, engineered the investiture of the Liang's founding emperor, and received official patronage for many years.[75] It is true that in those troubled days, as also in the ninth century, emperors who were insecure in their rule would at times proscribe any religion that he perceived, rightly or wrongly, to constitute a threat. Both Buddhism and Taoism were often the target of such proscriptions. But it should also be noted that such proscriptions were sometimes just pronouncements, which were not effectively carried out. Even those that *were* carried out were frequently reversed a few years later by a subsequent occupant of the throne. It should, moreover, be noted that Taoists such as T'ao Hung-ching were certainly not peasant leaders, but well-placed aristocrats of great learning, who fully accepted the legitimacy and worth of the imperial government.

After the four-century "period of disunion" called the Six Dynasties, north and south China were reunited under a brief native regime called the Sui (589–618). The Sui is generally known for its support of Buddhism. But its founding emperor refurbished the temple at "Lao-tzu's birthplace," and ordered a great literary figure, the official Hsüeh Tao-heng, to compose an inscription text for the restored site. That little-known text, dated 591, closely parallels the *Lao-tzu ming*, wherein the Han emperor Huan first hailed the "divinized Lao-tzu" in 159. In the Sui inscription, the Tao is said to embody itself in Lord Lao, who periodically comes into the world of men in order to provide "continued support for rulers" and "active protection of the people and promotion of Great Peace."[76]

The fact that Chinese emperors of Han and Sui times – native emperors of "legitimate" dynasties several centuries apart – honored Lord Lao as a major protector of the state and the people was *ignored* by virtually all twentieth-century historians of China. Their basic beliefs included the Confucian falsehood that Taoists never played, never sought to play, and never could play, any constructive role in the Chinese political order, wherefore all good and wise rulers relied upon Confucians. Even today, it is still not widely known that centuries of Taoists provided religious support to Chinese rulers and, even more crucially, to rulers who had not been born Chinese, and were therefore working to be accepted as true and worthy rulers by their Chinese subjects.

The Toba were one such regime, but they never achieved their goal of unifying China. A few generations later, however, another group of leaders whose ancestry was partly Chinese and partly non-Chinese found Taoism crucial to their efforts to become China's rulers. So successful were they that they established an enduring imperial government across the whole of China for the first time in centuries, and became leaders of a dynasty whose name is embraced even today by people of Chinese descent across the globe: the T'ang dynasty.

It was under the T'ang (618–907) that Taoism achieved its most extensive official patronage. Taoist leaders were extensively patronized by T'ang rulers in an effort to enhance imperial prestige. The T'ang rulers clearly hoped to perpetuate the legitimatory alliance that earlier dynasties had forged with leaders of the Taoist tradition.[77]

The first key figure in the T'ang dynasts' association with Taoism had actually played related roles in earlier dynasties: Wang Yüan-chih (528–635).[78] Both of Wang's parents had belonged to the political elite of south China, so it is not surprising that he studied under a disciple of T'ao Hung-ching, the most eminent – and politically prominent – Taoist master of the sixth century. In time, Wang was summoned to the court of the brief Ch'en dynasty, then that of the Sui. The Sui emperor Yang-ti "personally performed the ceremonies of a disciple" to Wang, thus invoking the centuries-old paradigm of the Taoist master as the "instructor of emperors and kings" (*ti-wang shih*). Yet, when he ignored Wang's advice against moving the capital, Wang could no longer recognize him as the legitimate Son of Heaven.

One rival force was that of a man named Li Yüan, and Wang "secretly transmitted to him the registers [Taoist emblems of spiritual standing] and the mandate (*fu-ming*)." Li was thereby acknowledged as the founding emperor of the T'ang dynasty. Later, Wang recognized the second T'ang dynast, T'ai-tsung, as "the Son of Heaven of Great Tranquillity (*T'ai-p'ing t'ien-tzu*). Stephen Bokenkamp's statement that "there was nothing in the Taoist conception of history that contradicted in any profound way the Confucian views" about the rulers' "heavenly mandate" is confirmed by the fact that these events are commemorated not only in the official "standard histories," but also in an imperial rescript issued by T'ai-tsung in 635.[79] And the depth of interest in Taoism at T'ai-tsung's court is revealed by the little-known fact that the Ling-pao *Scripture of Human Salvation*, the *Tu-jen ching*, was epitomized in calligraphic works by prominent T'ang officials.[80]

Wang's confirmation that the mandate of Heaven had passed from the Sui to the T'ang engendered a potent alliance between the T'ang ruling house and the leaders of the Taoist tradition. Wang's successor, P'an Shih-cheng (585–682), was "highly honored and respected" by T'ai-tsung's successor Kao-tsung and by his wife, the redoubtable empress Wu (Wu Tse-t'ien). That couple summoned P'an to their court, and the *Tao-tsang* contains what purports to be a colloquy between Kao-tsung and P'an on the essentials of the Taoist religion, the *Tao-men ching-fa* ["Scriptures and Formulae of Taoism"].[81] More importantly, Kao-tsung issued the very first imperial order for the compilation of a Taoist "canon" (675), establishing a tradition that would eventually result in our present *Tao-tsang*.[82]

Traditional sinology succumbed to the Confucian propaganda that "serious scholarship" can only be based on "official" sources, and should never pay any attention to Taoist source materials.[83] But in reality, the *Tao-tsang*, like its predecessors back to T'ang times, *were* "official sources," compiled by some of the nation's most expert scholars, who had been assembled to fulfill an imperial commission. Recent research has shown that data preserved in Taoist texts not only help fill out our picture of past events, but often correct errors committed by the "official historians."[84] But the fact that centuries of emperors – from T'ang times to the Ming – regarded Taoism as important enough to warrant a national effort to compile and preserve all its writings has been ignored by nearly all sinologists.

Most presentations of T'ang history do report that the T'ang rulers, surnamed Li, claimed to be the lineal descendants of Lao-tzu, but most seem to imply that they did so on the basis of a happy coincidence, i.e., that Ssu-ma Ch'ien's first "biography" reported that Li was "Lao-tzu's" surname. In fact, however, the Li clan did not institutionalize their descent myth until after T'ai-tsung had been reminded of the fact that Wang Yüan-chih had legitimized both him and his father as the true holders of Heaven's mandate.[85]

Also little noticed is the fact that the Lou-kuan abbey, near the capital, was the principal center for living traditions about the primacy of "Lord Lao" as teacher/embodier of Tao.[86] Around 620, after having claimed the throne, Li Yüan asked the Taoist leaders at Lou-kuan to make offerings to seek blessings for him, and resultant omens convinced him to honor "Lao-tzu" as his ancestor.[87] The T'ang imperial descent myth was, therefore, not a historical oddity, but a result of the confluence of (1) living Taoist traditions about "Lao-tzu," embodied in such Lou-kuan texts as the *Hsi-sheng ching*; (2) active involvement by Taoists such as Wang Yüan-chih, who apparently shifted some people's perception that Heaven now supported the T'ang, rather than the Sui; and (3) skilled political leaders such as Li Yüan, who understood how to effect a practical and effective legitimation scheme.

In addition, it is seldom noted in connection with the T'ang rulers' pedigree that, from the Han through the Sui, emperors had venerated "Lord Lao" not only as a famous philosopher of ancient times, but also, and more importantly, as a heavenly being who acts, from age to age, to ensure that the human world is under the authority of a wise and worthy ruler. Hence the T'ang rulers' claim that they were Lord Lao's descendants was not merely an assertion of an ancient and uncommon lineage. Rather – exactly like the royal myths of descent from heavenly beings among contemporary ruling houses in Korea and Japan – the T'ang descent myth represented an unprecedented claim of spiritual authority: while earlier rulers had obtained formal blessings from Taoist leaders – thereby receiving confirmation of their status as legitimate stewards of the mandate of Heaven – the T'ang dynasts could even claim such divine blessings as their unique and inalienable birthright.

It was during "the high T'ang" – 705 to 756 – that the symbiotic interplay between Taoist and dynast reached its zenith. Most twentieth-century historians – following their Confucian paradigms – never mentioned this fact at all, or represented it in terms of rulers' personal propensities, particularly those of "the Brilliant Emperor," Hsüan-tsung (r. 712–756). Yet, it would be a mistake to trivialize either the motives or the acumen of such rulers. Hsüan-tsung's patronage of Taoism was in truth part of a multifaceted legitimatory program that was crafted with great precision. Many aspects of that program have now been thoroughly analyzed.[88] But we need to be aware that Hsüan-tsung was, on one level, merely extending and intensifying an interactive legitimatory system that went back for centuries, and had included such disparate sponsors as Sui Yang-ti, the Toba dynasts of the earlier Northern Wei, and the empress Wu, who had briefly extinguished the T'ang dynasty itself yet had continued patronage of Taoism. The impetus for that ongoing legitimatory interplay was not only those rulers' keenness to receive legitimation from Taoist leaders, but such leaders' proactive efforts to demonstrate their tradition's political relevancy. From Wang Yüan-chih at the dawn of the T'ang to Tu Kuang-t'ing in its twilight, Taoist leaders actively, and successfully, showed emperors how useful Taoism could be as an element of the imperial polity.

The prime exemplar in that regard was Ssu-ma Ch'eng-chen (646–735). Not only had Ssu-ma's father and grandfather both held government posts, but all three possessed an imperial bloodline: they were nobles, who belonged to a collateral branch of the clan that had ruled China as the emperors of the Chin dynasty (266–420). Yet, until the 1980s, Ssu-ma's name was virtually unknown among scholars of Chinese history, religion, and culture. Today, specialists know him best as the author of important – if still seldom studied – texts on biospiritual cultivation and developmental self-perfection, such as the *Tso-wang lun* and the *Fu-ch'i ching-i lun*. From the year 1423 – when Taoists at Mao-shan compiled the *Mao-shan chih* ["Records of Mount Mao"] to prove that their connection to the Shang-ch'ing founders was every bit as "unbroken" as that claimed by their T'ien-shih rivals at Lung-hu shan – Ssu-ma was identified as "the Grand Master (*tsung-shih*) in the twelfth generation."[89]

Up to that time, Ssu-ma had generally been celebrated as one of history's greatest calligraphers, though records from the mid-ninth century also hailed him as a painter, who had been "expressive and brilliant in all the arts" and had even "fashioned an elegant lute with an inscription inlaid with beautiful stones."[90] But during his own lifetime Ssu-ma had been most famous in political circles, for fulfilling the ancient and powerful paradigm of the sagely advisor to a ruler who duly upholds Heaven's mandate. One of the oldest themes in Chinese culture was that of the wise and principled advisor (characteristically male) who guides the ruler in the proper exercise of power. In Chinese tradition, the first person to play that role was the Duke of Chou, who reportedly counselled the founders of the Chou dynasty, *ca.* 1100 BCE. Centuries later, Confucius celebrated the Chou founders as paramount political exemplars, largely because of their willingness to rely upon the guidance of their noble advisor. By Han times, accurate memories of such archaic events had been lost, and the formulators of the empire's "restored" traditions told of even more ancient sagely rulers. From that time down to the present, those sage-kings (whether real or legendary) represented the prototype of the illustrious ruler. Conscientious and worthy emperors, and those who wished to be perceived as such, endeavored to imbue their reigns with the aura of sublimity that surrounded the figures of the sage-kings of old. T'ang emperors such as Hsüan-tsung, eager to be perceived as equals of the ancient sage-kings, revived the imperial paradigm of the enlightened ruler who relied upon sagely counsellors for wise and moral guidance. But the individuals whom they employed to play the role of the sagely counsellor were the Taoist leaders of the day.

For instance, in the year 711, the T'ang emperor Jui-tsung summoned Ssu-ma Ch'eng-chen to court in a most extraordinary manner. Rather than issue a standard summons – itself quite an elevated honor – the emperor displayed exceptional respect by having an imperial kinsman personally invite him. The text of that summons is replete with allusions to the legendary Chinese sage-kings of highest antiquity, revealing that the emperor was anxious to have Ssu-ma attend his court just as a legendary worthy had attended the quasi-divine Yellow Emperor. In an inscription text of 742, composed by a high official in the Ministry of Sacrifices, one reads that Ssu-ma had "revived the Virtue (*te*) of Kuang-ch'eng," another worthy whose counsel the legendary Yellow Emperor had reportedly solicited in highest antiquity.[91] From Han times on, the Yellow Emperor had been held up as the ideal exemplar for emperors: a ruler who followed in his footsteps would, it was believed, ascend in both political power and spiritual sanctity. And the same text reports, no doubt hyperbolically, that Jui-tsung "was going to entrust the governance of the realm [to Ssu-ma] with confidence, but he could not obtain and motivate him [for such a responsibility]." Here Ssu-ma is presented as the prototypical sagely counsellor, whose wisdom is so great that the greatest of all emperors would entrust to him the care of the whole empire.

Jui-tsung's successor, the emperor Hsüan-tsung, also summoned Ssu-ma to his court. There, on imperial command, Ssu-ma conferred upon the emperor sacred texts and ritual formulae of Taoism in a lay ordination ceremony. Modern minds – shaped by the anti-Catholic thrust of "the Enlightenment" as well as by modern secularism – tend to dismiss the significance of *all* ceremonial acts. But in pre-modern China, as in all traditional societies, such acts were never "*merely* ceremonial": they were (as even wedding ceremonies traditionally were) acts that called pertinent members of the community to witness the *public acknowledgement* of what is *truly important and real* for the participants.

To understand the real social and political significance of Taoism in Chinese history, we must reverse Confucian bias and modern partiality, and give proper weight to records of imperial events such as the following:

> The Brilliant Emperor (i.e., Hsüan-tsung) summoned [Ssu-ma] to Mt. Wang-wu, and set up an altar and rectory [there] to house him. . . . [He also] commanded Wei T'ao, the President of the Court of Imperial Banquets, to go to [Ssu-ma's] residence, institute sacrificial observances according to the Golden Register (*chin-lu*), and generously reward him.[92]

The *chin-lu* rite was the foremost of the Taoist rituals known as *chai*, and it was of great *political* significance. It "was the most powerful Daoist rite in medieval times," and it was performed to balance *yin* and *yang* (thereby averting natural disasters), to prolong the life of the emperor, and to ensure overall stability in the empire.[93] Anna Seidel noted that "[the] performance of *chai* rituals and the recitation of scriptures for the benefit of the chief of State is recommended in the *Ling-pao Book of Salvation*," i.e., the *Tu-jen ching*.[94] Since the *chin-lu chai* focused on the security of the throne and the welfare of the state, it is hardly surprising that the empress Wu as well as the T'ang emperors Chung-tsung, Jui-tsung, and Hsüan-tsung all sponsored such liturgies.[95] All of them viewed Taoist liturgical procedures as fulfilling both governmental needs and the rulers' own political interests.

A slightly better-known example, from 731, shows how Ssu-ma Ch'eng-chen convinced the emperor to revise old liturgical procedures of the imperial state to bring them into conformance with Taoist views of the world:

> Subsequently, the Master sent up an address, saying, "Currently the sacred sacrifices to the five marchmounts are all [dedicated to] deities of hills and forests, not to deities of Correctness and Perfection (*cheng-chen*). All of the marchmounts have cryptic archives (*tung-fu*), to each of which Perfected Ones (*chen-jen*) of the Supreme Heavens (Shang-ch'ing) have descended to assume their duties. I entreat you to institute separate ritual observances (*chai-ssu*) [to those Perfected Ones]." The emperor acceded to his behest, and accordingly established sacrifices to the Perfected Lords (*chen-chün*). As for both their appearance and their organization, [the emperor] requested the Master to create them in accordance with the Taoist scriptures.

The authenticity of this event is unquestionable, for the text of Ssu-ma's memorial is preserved in T'ang court records.[96] The fact that Hsüan-tsung followed Ssu-ma's advice regarding the mountain deities demonstrates that one of the most renowned rulers in Chinese history considered the traditions of Shang-ch'ing Taoism not merely as legitimate adjuncts to the established state cult that dated back to earliest imperial times, but actually as valuable *correctives* to the imperial tradition itself.[97]

Another case of a Taoist serving the throne in a manner that twentieth-century minds, like Confucian minds, could not even theoretically credit is that of Yeh Fa-shan (631–720).[98] Yeh was the scion of a noble house, with a lineage traceable back to the seventh century BCE. In 713, T'ang Jui-tsung granted Yeh's father a posthumous official appointment, and four years later Hsüan-tsung had a prominent official compose epitaphs for both Yeh's father and his grandfather. Yeh himself interacted with no fewer than five dynasts. And, as odd as it seems to modern minds, Yeh was honored by those rulers, and by generations of Chinese scholars and historians, largely as a wonder-worker.

Many accounts of Yeh's exploits survive, commencing with an inscription text prepared in the name of T'ang Hsüan-tsung himself in 739. In that text, Yeh appears as a loftier, more otherworldly figure than any of his contemporaries. Even Ssu-ma Ch'eng-chen was never painted in such rare colors. Yet Yeh shared with Ssu-ma certain key *political* features: each was seen as having provided signal aid and support to his sovereign, on terms comparable to the worthies of highest antiquity. Hsüan-tsung says that, when he first came to the throne, the court had long been troubled by coups and intrigues, so he had turned to Yeh Fa-shan, not only for reliable advice, but also for aid and protection: "[When] disloyal ministers entertain schemes, evil and rebellion have never failed to ensue. [When] this matter was made clear, [Yeh Fa-shan] surged forth to extend subtle assistance. . . . He can be called ample in virtue and fulfilling the Tao, venerable and luminous." He hails Yeh as having integrated the premier Taoist ideals with the ideal of service to sovereign, state, and society, and expresses gratitude for Yeh's invaluable protection: "It seems that in aiding the state and assisting the ruler, he is exerting himself to make it clear." And, in an epitaph, the emperor evinces a conviction that Yeh's benevolent aid had not ceased even after he had departed the mortal pale:

> Using byways and subtle assistance,
> He transforms spiritually and creates supernaturally . . .
> Subduing rebellions and assisting with pacification,
> He succors completion and seconds the seasons.

All accounts of Yeh Fa-shan concur on one point: his career included, as a principal focus, a protective and supportive role vis-à-vis the throne. And, in the historical annals, he was considered a notable Taoist based not upon any ecclesiastical position, nor upon scholarship or literary achievement, as many others were, but rather upon his fulfillment of the role of champion of the T'ang *state*. Like Ssu-ma Ch'eng-chen, Yeh had played the role of the "worthy advisor" who lent luster to the reigning Son of Heaven, and in so doing had upheld the social and political order. For fulfilling that role, each man was honored by his sovereign as an aide to his reactualization of the utopia of halcyon antiquity, a utopia that the Taoists called *T'ai-p'ing*.

After the rebellion of An Lu-shan in the mid-eighth century, the political centrality of Taoism began to wane. Emperors were forced to focus more intensely upon military and economic challenges, and imperial patronage of Taoism diminished. Fewer Taoist leaders were summoned to court, and fewer Taoist texts circulated among the elite. Imperial officials did collect Taoist writings from around the countryside, to restore losses caused by the burning of libraries during the rebellion. One ninth-century emperor restored an abbey in the capital and donated to it nine cartloads of images and texts from the palace collection. But later wars wrought further havoc on such perishable materials, and a key theme of Taoist activity in those days was the restoration and preservation of such precious remnants from earlier times. Foremost in that endeavor was the court official Tu Kuang-t'ing, perhaps the greatest of all historians who wrote from within the Taoist tradition. His *Li-tai ch'ung-tao chi* ["Records of Reverence for Taoism over the Ages"] – an account of how rulers had patronized Taoism over the centuries – remains untranslated and largely unstudied.

The Taoist underpinnings of the following Sung dynasty (960–1279) remain even less well recognized. Sung sovereignty was proclaimed in 960, but the nation's unification was actually completed around 979, during the reign of the emperor T'ai-tsung. His first reign title, *T'ai-p'ing hsing-kuo* – "The Flourishing State of Grand Tranquillity" – shows that T'ai-tsung saw his restoration of the nation in terms of the Taoist utopian vision. A Taoist text of the early eleventh century – the *I-sheng pao-te chuan* (HY 1275) – again reports decades of revelations at the Lou-kuan abbey, confirming that "the Lord of Grand Tranquillity" possessed Heaven's mandate: "there will be enlightened rulers one after the other."[99]

Even before the land had been reunified, T'ai-tsung had ordered the compilation of several encyclopedic anthologies, including the *T'ai-p'ing kuang-chi* ["Extended Accounts of the Reign of Grand Tranquillity"; completed 978]. The fact that both it and a companion work, the *T'ai-p'ing yü-lan*, bear within their titles T'ai-tsung's *Taoist* reign title is no coincidence: the structure and contents of the *T'ai-p'ing kuang-chi* disclose a vision of an empire understood in terms of *T'ai-p'ing* – a universal harmony in which all things find their proper place and work together, creating a holistic unity in harmony with the higher forces of the cosmos. The fact that such ideas were indeed Taoist is confirmed by the fact that the *T'ai-p'ing kuang-chi*'s first seventy chapters are devoted to lives of male and female "transcendents" (*hsien*). Yet, the following thirty-five chapters focus on Buddhist themes, and later sections dwell on such mundane "Confucian" concerns as provincial and capital examinations. The *T'ai-p'ing kuang-chi* can thus be interpreted as an attempt to reverse the cultural dichotomization that had occurred during Han times, when those who specialized in scholarship and administration (the *ju*) were first distinguished from those who specialized in seeing, and working with, the subtler realities of life, the *fang-shih* (to whom five chapters of the *T'ai-p'ing kuang-chi* are devoted). Hence, the *T'ai-p'ing kuang-chi* can be interpreted as an attempt by Sung T'ai-tsung to revivify the holistic vision embodied in the ancient *T'ai-p'ing ching,* and to reunite it with the *ju* tradition of "scholars" and "officials." The *T'ai-p'ing kuang-chi* can be seen as the emperor's attempt to return to the cultural unity of the early Han, when historians were "Taoistic" men such as Ssu-ma T'an and *ju* "scholars" were men such as Tung Chung-shu, who, while establishing an imperial academy with a Confucian curriculum, worked to explain the subtle interworkings of heaven, earth, and man.[100]

Systematic research on Sung Taoism is even more recent, and even less well developed, than that on T'ang Taoism, and scholars are only now beginning to sort out the nature of the changes that took place. On one level, the "dissolution of the Tang [T'ang] Daoist liturgical system and the demise of communities organized by Daoist rules, ordinations and practices gave rise to a wider class of literate practitioners seeking support for their more inclusive practices and pantheons from emerging gentry communities."[101] So the forms and institutions within which people conceived and practiced Taoism changed significantly after T'ang times. Yet, "Like their Tang predecessors, [Sung rulers] continued to turn to Daoism for state legitimization, cosmic theology and self-cultivation."[102]

At the end of the twentieth century, most scholars believed that "Taoism once again became the official religion in the early eleventh century, but it was not until the twelfth century during the reign of Hui-tsung that a veritable renaissance took place."[103] Such beliefs are quite understandable, for, as we have seen, Hui-tsung (r. 1100–1125) honored the leaders of two emerging sites of Taoist tradition: the Mao-shan center, which claimed to maintain an old Shang-ch'ing "lineage"; and the Lung-hu-shan center, which claimed to maintain an old T'ien-shih "lineage." In 1114, Hui-tsung also summoned Taoists from across the empire to compile a new collection of all Taoist texts, partly to demonstrate his empire's spiritual superiority over the "barbarian" states to the north. On another level, verses that Hui-tsung himself composed to be sung during the "ritual dance" called the *Pu-hsü* ("Pacing the Void") are still sung today by Taoist liturgists in Taiwan.[104]

But, most notoriously, it was to Hui-tsung's court that Lin Ling-su came with his new liturgical tradition called Shen-hsiao ("Divine Empyrean"). The sources for our study of that event are, like those concerning much of T'ang Taoism, quite *biased*. Since Hui-tsung was on the throne when north China was conquered by the Jurchen, later historians projected back onto him – as onto many of the later T'ang emperors – the image of a self-indulgent man deluded by charlatans.[105] They therefore suggest that Hui-tsung's interest in Taoism was motivated largely by the fact that Lin identified the emperor, as well as others at court, with divine beings.

A careful reading of the event, however, shows that Sung Hui-tsung was no more "narcissitic" or "deluded" than T'ang Hsüan-tsung had been: each was an active and capable ruler who made extensive use of Taoism for legitimatory purposes, a fact that outraged Confucian historians. It is now clear that Hui-tsung's main interest was in securing "spiritual defenses against attack by human enemies of the state," particularly the powerful northern regime of the Jurchen.[106] In 1108 – years before he summoned Taoists such as Lin Ling-su to court – Hui-tsung had promulgated "the Rules of the Ling-pao Ritual of the Golden Register."[107] As we have seen, the *chin-lu chai* had been sponsored by a series of T'ang emperors, and with good reason: "The purpose of the Rite of the Golden Register (*Chin-lu chai*, later *chiao*) ever since its inception in the fifth century had been to guarantee the welfare of the imperial house."[108] And with portions of China already lost to the Khitan, and the Jurchen looming across the border, Hui-tsung had more reason than any emperor before him to order the performance of the *chin-lu chai*, and of *any* cognate rites that his loyal subjects could provide – such as those of Lin's "Divine Empyrean."

The Jurchen conquest of the north in 1126 had a profound effect upon *how* the Sung rulers exploited the legitimatory resources of Taoism. From the year 1012, Sung dynasts had affiliated their house "not just with Laozi (whom the Tang regarded as their ancestor) but with their newly discovered ultimate ancestor, the Yellow Lord (Huangdi)."[109] But increasingly more important was the protection they received from divine beings such as Chen-wu, "the Perfected Warrior."[110]

Chen-wu was a "Perfected Lord" (*chen-chün*) associated with the Chung-nan mountains near Ch'ang-an. As seen above, K'ou Ch'ien-chih conferred the title "Perfected Lord of Grand Tranquillity" upon his imperial sponsor in the early fifth century. And Ssu-ma Ch'eng-chen easily persuaded T'ang Hsüan-tsung to establish imperial rites to honor the "Perfected Lords" of the sacred "march-mounts" that marked the comprehensive expanses of imperial sovereignty. Since it was in the Chung-nan mountains that the oldest Taoist monastic center, Lou-kuan, had flourished in earlier times, it is clear that the Sung emperors were diligently drawing all that they could from older Taoist traditions in an effort to protect their nation and solidify their imperium. Their willingness to readjust some of the terms and images found in those traditions shows that their interest in Taoism was highly pragmatic.

Another example of the flexibility that Sung emperors found in Taoism is that they increasingly focused on localized sources of authority. For instance, recent research has shown that, during the Southern Sung (i.e., after 1127), the emperors continued to summon Taoists to court, though they increasingly summoned representatives of the two regional centers that claimed continuity with specific traditions of old: Mao-shan and Lung-hu-shan.[111] Taoists from those centers were "invited to court to perform specific rituals on the government's behalf," but they all "returned to the provinces immediately after the ritual was done."[112] Such changes have not yet been well studied. But with the threat of powerful rival states to the north, the Southern Sung rulers were no longer well positioned to use Taoism to present themselves as sage-rulers of "all-under-Heaven," as T'ang rulers had done. Moreover, their focus on the Taoists of Mao-shan and Lung-hu-shan suggests increasing willingness – now that the aristocracy, with its ties to noble antiquity, was gone – to privilege those Taoists who had been successful in constructing new claims to be living links to Taoism's own "noble antiquity."

Meanwhile, the non-Chinese dynasts in the north had another reason to be uninterested in Taoism as a matter of state: Taoism belonged to the culture of their Chinese subjects, not to their own cultural heritage. The Khitan rulers of the Liao dynasty (907–1125) had tolerated Taoism among their subjects, but were fierce defenders of their own cultural identity, and made no effort to employ Taoism governmentally or politically.[113] Quite different were the Jurchen (a Tungusic people from what we know as Manchuria), who extinguished the Liao and took the whole of the north. The Jurchen were very eager to assimilate themselves into Chinese culture, and members of their ruling house, surnamed Wan-yen, became as deeply involved in Taoism as any Chinese ruler of earlier times had ever been:

> The Taoist priests associated themselves with Chinese and Jurchen scholars and officials. [The Ch'üan-chen Taoist luminary] Ch'iu Ch'u-chi wrote poems and *tz'u* [lyrics] for such Jurchen dignitaries as [the emperor] Shih-tsung, the wife of a prince, the prefect of the Western Capital, the sister of a prime minister, [and] a general . . . There was a Jurchen master who was in charge of the Ch'üan-chen church at Ch'ien-yang . . . T'ai-i Taoism may have been very popular among the Jurchen, for a Jurchen priest named Wan-yen Chih-ning was almost selected as the third high priest of the sect. . . . [and] a Jurchen, Wan-yen Te-ming, did become the Ch'üan-chen high priest in the Yüan [i.e., under the Mongols].[114]

In 1187, the Jurchen emperor Shih-tsung (r. 1161–1189) summoned one of Wang Che's seven famous disciples – Wang Ch'u-i (1142–1217) – to court, because the ruler desired "to receive instructions on 'methods of preserving life'."[115] And the following year, the more famous Ch'iu Ch'u-chi was summoned to the Jurchen capital to oversee an imperial *chiao* ceremony.

Jurchen rule was extinguished by the Mongols, who are usually remembered for the debates they staged between Buddhists and Taoists in 1258 and their subsequent order that all Taoist texts except the *Tao te ching* be burned.[116] But, as always, an astute ruler who wished to secure his imperium could find much of value in Taoism. Even Khubilai was no exception:

> Khubilai's involvement in the Buddhist-Taoist debates . . . had, of course, not endeared him to the Taoist hierarchy. Yet both Khubilai and the Taoists needed each other. . . . Khubilai offered inducements to the various Taoist sects in

> return for their support. He supplied funds for the construction of temples, in particular to those belonging to the Ch'üan-chen sect, the Taoist order favored by the Mongols since Chingghis Khan's time. . . . The Taoists responded to these favors by providing ideological justification for Khubilai and by helping him to perform certain duties expected of a Chinese emperor. One of these tasks was the worship of T'ai-shan, one of the sacred mountains of China, which was a vital responsibility for a Chinese emperor. . . . Khubilai annually would dispatch Taoist leaders to perform the T'ai-shan ceremonies. . . . Their willingness to conduct these ceremonies signaled a kind of support that was transmitted to ordinary believers of Taoism.[117]

Of course, it is never possible to determine the extent to which such signals may have had the intended effect. It is also commonly mentioned that Khubilai "appointed" a Cheng-i leader from Lung-hu shan as "the supervisor of Taoist affairs in South China."[118] But the fact that the Mongols continued their predecessors' active support of Ch'üan-chen Taoism shows that their "recognition" of the leaders at Lung-hu-shan was never an endorsement of specific Cheng-i "lineage" claims, but rather an effort "to keep on good terms with" *any* Taoist leader who had a social following and a willingness to conduct liturgies on behalf of the empire.[119]

When the Mongols were supplanted by the Ming dynasty in 1368, imperial attitudes toward Taoism became more ambivalent. Its founding emperor, T'ai-tsu, "established a Taoist Affairs Academy (*Hsüan-chiao yüan*) to oversee Taoist organizations and temples," and it "supervised a registry of ordained Taoists called the Central Taoist Registry (*Tao-lu ssu*), which was to contol the numbers and conditions of ordination."[120] Of course, even the T'ang emperor Hsüan-tsung had sought to manage Taoist institutions, even as he was promoting them. And it may also be true that, "Although most [Ming] emperors reiterated their commitment to the first emperor's restrictive policies, . . . in fact these policies were not enforced, in part because the emperors themselves believed in Taoism, trusting it to aid in their personal lives and in state affairs."[121]

Just like the T'ang emperor Hsüan-tsung and the Sung emperor Hui-tsung, Ming emperors from the time of T'ai-tsu himself summoned Taoists to their court, "especially those who avoided honors like Chang San-feng [who] could be symbols of legitimacy. These holy hermits would grace only the court of a sage ruler, [so] their presence bore witness to the irresistible virtue of the sovereign."[122] Moreover, since Taoist liturgies "promised to strengthen the power of the throne," Ming emperors – like their predecessors over the ages – "believed that they were enhancing their ability to maintain order in the realm and to be strong and effective monarchs through their practice of Taoism."[123] We should therefore not be surprised that Ming emperors designated official temples throughout the empire, where *chiao* and *chai* liturgies were performed "in support of the state."[124] More particularly, Ming T'ai-tsu "demanded that his sons sacrifice to Xuanwu" (Hsüan-wu, i.e., Chen-wu, "the Perfect Warrior"), and the Yung-lo emperor (r. 1403–1424) credited that deity with bringing him to power during a succession dispute.[125] The Yung-lo emperor established a sanctuary to Hsüan-wu "at the holiest and most northern place of Beijing's forbidden city when he moved the capital there in 1421," and thus the "Perfect Warrior served the Ming as a dynastic protector, just as Laozi had served the Tang, [and] Huangdi the Song."[126] Another son of the dynasty's founder became a Taoist himself.[127] Later Ming emperors continued to summon Taoists to court, and the Chia-ch'ing emperor (r. 1522–1566) appointed one such priest "to conduct Taoist rituals in a number of temples in the vicinity of the court."[128] But the later Ming emperors, like those late in other dynasties, are often portrayed in the same old prejudicial stereotypes: instead of appearing as great and majestic leaders like T'ai-tsu, later emperors are depicted as obsessive and delusional in their Taoist interests.[129]

> Adjusting for these biases, however, a somewhat different picture can be seen. . . . Although Taoism was often maligned in Confucian sources as anti-establishment, in fact, much of Taoist ritual expertise was designed to meet the principal concerns of the government: maintaining the health and the prosperity of the people. Secondly, there was the political value to the performance of Taoist rituals for they served as symbols of the court's concern for the welfare of the people. By ordering regular rites of purification and renewal (*chiao*) and retreat (*chai*) ceremonies at state

> endowed temples, the government was manifesting, through a widely recognized and trusted symbolic form, its wishes for the peace and prosperity of the realm. The population, in other words, responded to the significance of these rituals.[130]

In addition, "local officials also turned to Taoists for help in times of natural disaster or emergency": because "there was often no bureaucratic solution to such problems," public rituals performed at the request of local magistrates provided them with an opportunity to demonstrate their concern.[131] Yet, sometimes such local rituals partook of elements of folk religion, and were not "Taoist" in any definable sense.

The blurring of boundaries between what was Taoist and what was not was actually accelerated by official policy in Ming times. The founder, T'ai-tsu, promulgated an essay on the mutuality of "the Three Teachings" – Taoism, Confucianism, and Buddhism – arguing that the three of them together "constituted the Way of Heaven."[132]

The best example of how Taoists adapted to governmental emphasis on such *mutuality* was the largely unstudied tradition called Ching-ming ("Pure Illumination"). To such traditional Taoist ideals as "purity" (*ching*) and "illumination" (*ming*) it added the Confucian virtues of loyalty (*chung*) and filiality (*hsiao*), and "encouraged practical activity in support of the dynasty." According to Judith Berling, the Ching-ming tradition "seems to have addressed itself to the educated classes (and was) self-consciously designed to appeal to the intellectual elite."[133]

Perhaps the best example of how Ching-ming ideals were fulfilled by Taoists of the era was Lin Chao-en (1517–1598). Born into a family of scholar-officials, Lin initially followed the family tradition of scholarship, then "abandoned examination studies and took up the Way of sages and worthies, determined to seek the means to realize it in myself, obtain it in my mind, and manifest it in my actions."[134] Later, Lin established a school patterned after that of Confucius and, when his coastal district was invaded by Japanese pirates, led community relief efforts. For the next twenty-five years, he worked to propagate an accurate understanding of "the Three Teachings."[135]

Though influenced by Ch'üan-chen models of personal self-cultivation, Lin Chao-en rejected that tradition's monastic focus, along with Cheng-i liturgical traditions. He accepted elements of Buddhism, Taoism, and Confucianism for their usefulness in self-cultivation, and his "nine stages of mind cultivation" resonate with those of Yin Chen-jen's *Hsing-ming kuei-chih* ["Balanced Instructions about Inner Nature and Life-Realities"], an illustrated "Inner Alchemy" text published in 1615. Yet, Lin eschewed traditional "Inner Alchemy" symbology, and constructed a program of "mind-cultivation" designed to feel comfortable to men of his own social, political, and economic class. He thus revived the "gentry Taoism" of T'ang leaders such as Ssu-ma Ch'eng-chen, while stretching into new social directions, demonstrating the Ching-ming ideal of "practical activity in support of the dynasty."

The Manchu rulers who established the Ch'ing dynasty in 1644 had limited interest in Taoism. Their own religion had become overlaid with the Buddhist traditions of Tibet, and they were quite content to continue the Ming dynasty's adoption of Ch'eng/Chu "Neo-Confucianism" for control of their Chinese subjects. In Ch'ing times, Taoists "were progressively marginalized."[136] The degraded status of Taoist clerics "deterred many intellectuals from taking the vow, depriving institutional religion of a supply of educated leadership."[137] Even imperial "believers" in Taoism, such as the Yung-cheng emperor (r. 1723–1736), "promoted a lay religious life," further undermining Taoist institutions that had flourished for the past millennium.

The Manchus continued "recognition" of the Cheng-i Taoists at Mount Lung-hu, and the K'ang-hsi emperor (1662–1722) summoned the reigning "Celestial Master" to perform rites at the Ch'ing court.[138] The Yung-cheng emperor patronized one Lung-hu priest, Lou Chin-yüan (1689–1776), even naming him "grand minister": "Lou retained a high position at court even after the emperor's death."[139] But the Ch'ien-lung emperor (1736–1796) banished from court not only the Lung-hu "Celestial Masters" but also "practitioners of Inner Alchemy that had been established previously at court." Thereafter, "the influence of Daoism continued to decline until, in the Daoguang [Tao-kuang] period (1821–1850), the title 'Perfected of Orthodox Unity' disappeared altogether and the relationship between the court and the Celestial Masters came to an end."[140]

Meanwhile, the Ch'üan-chen tradition "enjoyed a renaissance" in Ch'ing times, which went generally unnoticed by scholars of the twentieth century.[141] Geographically, Ch'üan-chen was centered in the northeast, an area in the imperial backyard that held great promise for gaining political recognition. Conversely, since Ch'üan-chen Taoists were nearby, hence easily visible to imperial authorities, their position was also hazardous, for everything about them was readily observed. If their activities included anything that could be considered subversive, that fact could hardly go unnoticed. Meanwhile, the activities of Taoists centered far away in the south were not so easily subjected to scrutiny.

Moreover, the social realities of Taoism had been deeply affected by the historical changes that had engendered increasing regionalism since the waning days of the T'ang. For centuries, Taoism had flourished among aristocrats in south China. By Ch'ing times, there were no longer any such people, and a noble bloodline no longer propelled a person to political importance or provided political safety. The Manchus were, like the Mongols, in a position that required them to be alert to possible uprisings from a conquered population. But they were not horsemen from the steppe like the Mongols. Rather, they were heirs to the Jurchen, and, like their Jurchen forebears, the Manchus became assimilated to Chinese culture. They did try to maintain their own traditions, but over time they lost that struggle, for it was ultimately not conducive to maintaining effective rule over China.

What *was* conducive to that effort was achieving a rapprochement with the Chinese literati. And Taoists in the north had something more than a long history of literati participants: they lived where the Ch'üan-chen movement had always been based. Ch'üan-chen Taoism had originated among the propertied gentry of the northeast. Its first leaders were literati who had shown success at accommodating themselves to the needs and interests of non-Chinese rulers – not only the Jurchen, but the Mongols as well. And Ch'üan-chen ideals and practices focused on individual self-perfection through self-discipline and meditation – practices quite unlikely to inspire either rebellion or nationalistic fervor.[142]

Hence, literati of Taoist inclinations were well positioned to achieve a politically acceptable expression of Taoism, simply by drawing upon the Ch'üan-chen tradition and the Ching-ming tradition of Ming times. Both of those traditions displayed willingness to accept social and political realities, and to accept the fact that Taoism – if it was to have continued success – would have to highlight certain elements of its heritage while leaving others behind.

Already in T'ang times, Taoist self-cultivation practices had been marketed to literati, even with the addition of such Buddhist ideas as "karma" and an "enlightenment" experience. Writers on "Inner Alchemy" had already been reducing their tradition's use of technical symbology in favor of clarity and simplicity. And, with the advent of printing, Taoists had opportunities to express their ideas in terms that were far from the esotericism of the Six Dynasties, when Taoist texts – all, of course, hand-written – were relatively rare, and were transmitted in a small circle whose members could readily imagine themselves as a privileged elite.

That model of Taoism was passé in an age when aristocratic privilege was gone, replaced by a landed gentry and a merchant class, which took advantage of printing and publishing to teach even their daughters to read and write. Ching-ming Taoism was a far cry from the T'ai-ch'ing Taoism that Ko Hung had loved, simply because times had changed: Taoist models designed for a privileged few made no sense in a world of widespread literacy. And since the Manchus did not live in fear of external threats, forms of Taoism designed to offer protective imperial liturgies – like the Shen-hsiao model of Lin Ling-su – had little market.

It was with awareness of all these realities that Ch'ing Taoists recast the useful elements of their heritage to form "the Dragon Gate," Lung-men. Even today's scholars of Taoism often know nothing about Wang Ch'ang-yüeh, who in 1656 brought what had once been a southeastern literati tradition of "Inner Alchemy" to the Manchu capital, Beijing, in the far northeast. Beijing's White Cloud Abbey (*Po-yün kuan*) was actually founded in the time of T'ang Hsüan-tsung, in the eighth century. In 1421 the Ming emperors had moved their capital from Nanjing in the south to Beijing, and later restored the White Cloud Abbey, where they held ceremonies honoring the Ch'üan-chen luminary Ch'iu Ch'u-chi. Yet it was not until Wang Ch'ang-yüeh that the White Cloud Abbey became the home of a distinctive form of Taoism, which proved successful in Ch'ing times and remains the dominant Taoist tradition in China today.

Wang's Lung-men synthesis integrated the self-cultivation tradition of "Inner Alchemy" with the monastic setting that had emerged in early Ch'üan-chen, while simultaneously gaining imperial sanction to maintain priestly activities. It accomplished those things in two ways. First, it couched Taoist practice in terms of the Ching-ming teaching that "loyalty" and "morality" were basic for individual self-cultivation and self-perfection. Second, it fabricated a historical lineage linking itself back to the Ch'üan-chen founders, who had been not only respectable literati from the landed gentry, but also northerners who had won the support of rulers in every dynasty back to the Manchus' Jurchen ancestors: "The court approved of this concept because it encouraged Confucian morality and also because it drew on Chan Buddhist doctrines that were supported by the early Qing [Ch'ing] emperors as well as by many officials and men of culture."[143] So successful was the Lung-men synthesis that, when Wang Ch'ang-yüeh died, the K'ang-hsi emperor entitled him "Eminent Master who Embraces the One" (*Pao-i kao-shih*), "and ordered a sacrifice hall built with his portrait and a dispatch of officers to be present at a ceremony in his honor."[144]

Recent research by scholars such as Monica Esposito and Mori Yuria have shown that the Ching-ming and Lung-men traditions not only flourished in late imperial China, but flourished in diverse forms, with healthy debates over issues of models of self-cultivation.[145] Moreover, the participants in that discourse were men of social standing and political prominence. Min I-te (1758–1836), for instance, carried on his family's scholar-official tradition by serving in a provincial government position.[146] And Chiang Yü-p'u (1756–1819) was a high official in the imperial government, holding such offices as vice-director of the Ministry of Works.[147] But those facts were not known to scholars – even most specialists in the study of Taoism – until the opening of the twenty-first century. Even today's most knowledgeable scholars of Taoism have much work to do before the Taoism of late imperial China is properly understood, and before the political importance of Taoism throughout imperial history is properly appreciated.

5

THE CULTIVATED LIFE

Life, death, and "transcendence"

One of the most difficult issues in the effort to understand Taoism involves how we understand the final goal of the Taoist life, and the relationship of that goal to the conclusion of natural life processes, i.e., death. Part of the difficulty, of course, owes to the fact that the full range of pertinent data has not yet been uncovered: many Taoist voices – on this as on other matters – remain unheard, while others remain, at present, inaudible whispers. An integration of those hitherto neglected voices into our analysis of how Taoists have looked upon death may help us perceive, and understand, key nuances. A second difficulty owes to the diversity of perspectives on death that Taoists of different periods, traditions, and temperaments seem to have held. Speaking simply, Taoist attitudes toward death have never been reducible to any clear, unequivocal proposition. Consequently, the answer to the question of how Taoists understand death varies according to the interpreter's decisions in selecting his or her primary data.

On another level, of course, the issue of how Taoists have understood the nature and significance of death has been obfuscated *not* by insufficient research, nor by the murkiness or disparity of the data, but rather by the interpretive lenses through which both specialists and non-specialists have viewed the issue. For generations, most writers – both Asian and Western – maintained, often quite dogmatically, that the so-called philosophical Taoists of antiquity were – and logically must be – distinguished from the so-called religious Taoists of later times on the basis of the alleged fact that the latter were devoted to achieving "physical immortality." That illusionary dichotomization derives from a cultural narrative intended to discredit the Taoists of imperial times, to show them as foolish, deluded, and simply the inverse of the real or imagined Taoist philosophers of antiquity. Indeed, for some writers, the only reason to examine Taoist ideas about death has simply been to show that the Taoists of imperial times were really not the "legitimate heirs" of the classical Taoists, but rather a motley gang of charlatans and fools.

Throughout the twentieth century, Western specialists sometimes perpetuated an array of interpretive errors that derived from the work of their primary forerunner, Henri Maspero. Since Maspero was the Western academy's first defender and explicator of Taoism – at least, of Taoism as it evolved through the Six Dynasties – his writings carried the force of holy scripture for later generations of scholars who wished to redeem Taoism from the calumnies and distortions that plagued most pertinent discourse. Maspero bravely defended Taoists of all periods against such calumnies, and adduced texts from the *Tao-tsang* that had never theretofore been adduced in such debates.[1] Because of those achievements, scholars of Taoism in the last quarter of the twentieth century tended to accept Maspero's priorities as correct. His pronouncements about Taoism seem to have echoed in their minds whenever they thought about any issue. Happy to have something erudite to use against the anti-Taoist narrative that still flourished in their own day, such scholars often overlooked the fact that Maspero was sometimes guilty of such things as anachronistic reasoning or taking the part to be the whole.

With a somewhat fuller picture of the full range of Taoist data, it is possible for today's interpreters to correct certain errors contained in Maspero's depictions. It is particularly important to examine what Maspero, and those who followed him, proclaimed about Taoist positions on the nature and significance of death. It is quite evident, of course, that the reader of the *Tao te ching* or *Chuang-tzu* is not urged to compound an efficacious substance and ingest it in hopes of effecting a spiritual goal. But it is quite another thing to contend, as did many in the twentieth century, that the Taoists of imperial times were *essentially* struggling to *avert* death, whereas the Taoists of antiquity had merely espoused a more "enlightened" *acceptance* of death as the natural conclusion to life's cycle.

The key to bear in mind is that *all* such writers were unconsciously struggling with their own unexamined Enlightenment biases. To the Enlightenment mind, there is no basis on which any sane, reasonable person could believe that death is in any way avertable: anyone making any such argument is either a fool, or is "really" saying something *else*, something that "enlightened" minds can regard as plausible – on our own, post-Enlightenment terms. The result was that many who found value in Taoism – including those who studied or wrote about it – felt compelled to defend the axiomatic assumptions of that Enlightenment narrative by somehow *redefining* Taoism in such a way as to demonstrate that "true Taoists" never really believed anything that we today do not believe.

In reaction, other interpreters sought to uphold the inherent "otherness" of Taoism by accentuating, and sometimes exaggerating, some of the points where Taoist discourse clearly diverges from modern discourse. In so doing, some of those defenders inadvertently contributed to the exoticization of Taoism by insisting that certain positions – e.g., regarding death – are of prime importance for understanding Taoism, when in reality the Taoists of past and present had generally not maintained those positions in such ways.

We could thus say that certain scholarly interpreters worked to "demythologize" Taoism in order to make their modern audience more comfortable with the proposition that Taoism is worthy of our respect (and, often, of our appropriation). Others, meanwhile, were happy to discomfort their modern audience by "remythologizing" Taoism in ways that emphasized – and sometimes over-emphasized – elements that modern minds find incredible or distasteful. In both cases, the nuances of the pertinent cultural realities were sometimes compromised by the real or perceived need to address the unconscious biases of modern audiences. In other words, the discourse of Taoism's scholarly defenders was framed primarily to answer its modern critics, rather than to present the full range of Taoist perspectives in a balanced manner, on terms consistent with how Taoists *themselves* had presented them.

When we actually look at the full range of the Taoist data pertaining to the issue of death and its meaning, we can see that Taoists accepted *virtually any* conceivable perspective as a valid perspective. The fact that Taoists gave widely varying answers to the question of what death means was *not* – as twentieth-century interpreters, in Asia and the West alike, often maintained with emotional vehemence – the logical and inevitable result of the "basic fact" that "there are really two kinds of Taoism." Once that false belief has been abandoned, we can begin to see that the divergences among Taoist voices regarding death were very persistent, across every period of history and across every kind of Taoist text, from people of every social category.

It is quite true that certain parts of the *Tao te ching* – and many of the later parts of the *Chuang-tzu* – suggest an insouciant acceptance of death. That position is clearly expressed in the story of Lao Tan's death at the end of *Chuang-tzu* 3, and more colorfully elaborated in the provocative story of Chuang's acceptance of his wife's death in *Chuang-tzu* 18. But though the first story is found within "the inner chapters," we should remember that our *Chuang-tzu* actually dates only to the early fourth century CE, and even those chapters are the result of the chopping and cutting that Kuo Hsiang inflicted upon the much larger work that had been current in Han times. So however much "classical" material Kuo decided to preserve for us within "the writings of Chuang-tzu," the belief that certain chapters were composed by "Chuang Chou himself" ultimately remains an article of faith, comparable to scholars' acceptance or rejection of certain bodies of gospel material as "authentic teachings" of Jesus.[2] Moreover, Kuo Hsiang's preface to his fourth-century packaging of "what Chuang-tzu taught" was long thought lost, so scholars – premodern and modern, Chinese and Western – never fully contemplated how deeply Kuo's acts may have determined all our "knowledge" about Chuang's ideas.

Then, in the twentieth century, Japanese scholars discovered Kuo's preface, preserved at a temple in Kyoto.[3] Regrettably, few scholars have attempted to determine its implications for our efforts to understand the history of Taoist ideas about things such as "life and death." In his preface, Kuo Hsiang confesses that his own interpretive abilities were so unbearably taxed by the content and expression of what appeared in the fifty-two chapters that constituted "*Chuang-tzu*" in his day that "some passages have to be stretched to appear somewhat reasonable, [while] others are so distorted that one can only call them absurd." Since the writings that had come down to Kuo were "really full of daring terms and lofty expressions," large parts of them made no sense to him; he confessed that he "does not think very highly of his [own] talent to study strange doctrines."[4] So what modern interpreters have so long, and so happily, understood to be "the philosophy of *Chuang-tzu*" – with its presumptive discrepancy from the views of later Taoists, especially in regard to death – is, to some important extent, a bowdlerized vision which emerged in the mind of Kuo Hsiang, who confessed that he "sees his virtue as lying in the ability to deal with what is easy to understand."[5]

The problem is that – in the experience of most human beings, in China and everywhere else – the ultimate nature of life and death has *never* fallen into the category of "what is easy to understand." Recent scholarship by Robert Ford Campany has suggested that Ko Hung, who wrote about the same time as Kuo Hsiang, lived in a culture that had for centuries believed that "Heaven, watching over the people below, keeps a record of their righteousness, accordingly bestowing on them many years or few."[6] That concept of an "allotted life-span" (*ming*) indeed appears within many streams of Chinese culture, throughout history. To put Ko Hung's views into perspective, Campany says:

> Rooted in the common religion of late Warring States and Han times (and perhaps earlier), and passed down in funerary practices and in the Han weft texts [often known as "apocrypha"] and the scriptures of Grand Purity [*T'ai-ch'ing*], was a basic assumption about the spirit world and living humans' relationship to it with massive implications for religious practice. Most generally, that assumption was that the world of spirits was organized after the fashion of an imperial bureaucracy. . . . This system was directly responsible for determining and enforcing each person's life span, preallotted at birth. [However, texts] on transcendence revealed various methods for surpassing this allotted life span. . . . [Hence, just] as dying was construed as a bureaucratic process, so the very terms of that construal afforded means of avoiding dying.[7]

Such is clearly the case, and it is quite true that many Chinese writers throughout imperial times, including some practitioners of Taoist "methods," did understand life and death on such terms.

However, one writer who appears *not* to have understood life and death on those terms was the compiler of one of the "Taoist classics" – i.e., one of the texts that circulated among the non-Taoist elite in imperial China, and was thus of at least some interest to sinologues of the nineteenth and twentieth centuries. That text was known to Taoists as "The Perfectional Scripture of Soaring into Emptiness and Accomplishing 'Virtue'," *Ch'ung-hsü chih-te chen-ching*.[8] It appears in the *Tao-tsang* in several settings, including one boasting an imperial commentary by the Sung emperor Hui-tsung.[9] The importance of this work for our understanding of Taoist perspectives on life and death can be seen from the fact that its ideas on the origins of the universe are echoed in Ssu-ma Ch'eng-chen's *Fu-ch'i ching-i lun* ("On the Essential Meaning of the Absorption of *Ch'i*"). Ssu-ma cannot, of course, simply be characterized as "a religious Taoist" whose main concern was to obviate the death-event. In fact, when one takes seriously what Ssu-ma wrote there, and in other surviving texts, as well as the role of Ssu-ma in the history of Taoism, it becomes quite clear that to try to understand him in terms of some "pursuit of physical immortality" – which supposedly differentiated such "religious Taoists" from the ancient "philosophical Taoists" – makes little sense. It is also of historical importance that, back in the fifth century, when Taoist identity was being formulated, Lu Hsiu-ching apparently planned the *Ch'ung-hsü chih-te chen-ching* to be a part of his "Catalogue of the Three Caverns," that is, as part of what is now sometimes called the first "Taoist canon."[10] Be that as it may, many expositions of Taoism give this particular text little mention, and one respected specialist of the late twentieth century went so far as to claim that this text "includes nothing that bears on the development of Taoism."[11] Yet, it is clear that centuries of Taoists, and even important emperors, thought otherwise. So perhaps our twenty-first-century picture of Taoism should incorporate some assessment of "The Perfectional Scripture of Soaring into Emptiness and Accomplishing 'Virtue'," better known by its non-canonical title – the *Lieh-tzu*.

The *Lieh-tzu* was compiled – probably by the author of its first commentary, Chang Chan – in the early fourth century CE. That was precisely the same time that Ko Hung – long falsely asserted by non-Taoists to have been the prime architect of the beliefs of "religious Taoists" – was trying to convince readers that humans truly *could* extend their lifespans indefinitely or otherwise escape real death. And it was also precisely the same time that Kuo Hsiang was, quite conversely, telling later ages that the *Chuang-tzu* had never said anything so "absurd." Each of those contemporary writers was the creator of a text that would eventually become a valued part of the heritage of Taoism – as defined by the decisions of Taoists themselves over the centuries. What each presents must thus be considered a meaningful and valid "Taoist voice." And what each says about death, and what one should do about it, is quite different.

Chang Chan – the apparent compiler of the *Lieh-tzu* – was one of the aristocrats who fled southward when the Chin rulers were displaced from their northern capital in 312. He was also an imperial official, who once held the post of imperial secretary under a ruler of the new "Eastern Chin" dynasty.[12] It is quite ironic that, by the middle of the T'ang dynasty, Chang Chan had become identified – along with such equally implausible fourth-century figures as the Buddhist Chih Tun (Chih Tao-lin) – as an enthusiastic writer on "longevity techniques."[13] Such appropriation of historical figures as messengers for ideas or practices belonging to a later age – which those figures themselves quite likely never imagined – had been common in China since the days when Confucius and Mo-tzu attributed their conflicting doctrines to the legendary sage-kings. As we have seen, Shang-ch'ing works such as the "Declarations of the Perfected" appropriated Mo-tzu himself as an example of those "who declared their end was nigh when they had taken the Gold Elixir (*chin-tan*)."[14] And even the T'ang poet and imperial librarian Ho Chih-chang was, in later centuries, transformed from a staid literatus into a purveyor of life-prolonging pharmika – i.e., a proponent of "immortality" in the most literal sense.[15] Just as the historical data concerning Ho clearly disprove any such interests on the part of the man himself, the later representation of Chang Chan as such a proponent was an astonishingly bold act, on the order of the appropriation of "Confucius" as a spokesman for "Taoist" ideas in sections of the *Chuang-tzu*.

The same is doubtless true, to some extent, of the hagiographical accounts of the immortality-monger Ko Hung. The historical Ko Hung may have enjoyed reading texts describing the alchemical rituals of the T'ai-ch'ing tradition. But he was a scholar of aristocratic heritage, and the "outer folios" (*wai-p'ien*) of his famous

Pao-p'u-tzu express so much "rational humanism" – along Confucian and Legalist lines – that their translator calls him "a conservative defender of common sense."[16] Ko lived at the margins of the imperial elite, claiming the mantle of "the recluse" while holding minor military and clerical posts until he retired to Mount Luo-fu near the south coast in 331.[17] Only the Confucian/Enlightenment struggle against the paradigm-threatening implications of such a figure could mislead scholars such as Holmes Welch into saying of Ko Hung, "It is a sad comment on the state of Confucianism in the Six Dynasties that [the fact that Ko was 'famed for his Confucian learning'] was said of a man who believed that almost anything could be accomplished by taking a pill."[18] Such facile misreadings of basic elements of *wai-tan* resulted from late imperial Confucians' disdain for what they presumed to be revealed by the colorful imagery of Chinese hagiography: to ridicule and caricature everyone involved in such traditions was, for such Confucians, a disingenuous but effective move to immunize *themselves* from criticism, especially from the more suspicious of the Manchu emperors.

To compare Ko Hung's texts on "immortality" with Chang Chan's *Lieh-tzu* is instructive for those seeking to pin down a single, overriding Taoist perspective on death and on its meaning for how we should live life. That is because the *Lieh-tzu* consists largely of passages borrowed from the *Chuang-tzu*, yet seems to end up insisting upon the finality of death, with little indication that a person can – by any means whatsoever – escape it. In fact, it seems quite conceivable that further research may reveal that the scholar-official Chang Chan was well aware of the writings of Ko Hung, and that he composed the *Lieh-tzu*, at least in part, specifically to refute Ko's contention that immortality is a feasible goal for a worthy gentlemen.

Yet, it must be remembered that during the early fourth century CE there was still no such thing as "Taoism" in any coherent sense: neither Chang Chan, nor Ko Hung, nor Kuo Hsiang were members of any social organization that corresponded to the cultural category "Taoism" that we embrace today. They all lived in a time of cultural change, when the religious traditions of the aristocrats of south China were being challenged, and stimulated, by the organizational realities and political patronage enjoyed by the "Heavenly Master" leaders who had burst into their land after the fall of the north in 312. As a consequence, members of the fourth-century aristocracy in the south had begun to examine, re-examine, debate, defend, emend, merge, or reject many differing religious ideas and practices, in various and sundry ways.

We should remember that it was from just this setting that both the revelations of the Shang-ch'ing corpus and the counter-revelations of the Ling-pao corpus erupted during the second half of the century. By the end of the century, the ideas and practices expounded in all those divergent materials presented minds such as that of Lu Hsiu-ching with an incredible diversity of religious models. To people such as Lu, certain textual traditions certainly seemed to be of greater interest and value than others. Yet, they saw the task of creating a new religious identity – that of an adherent of *Tao-chiao*, "the teachings of Tao" – which required a general preservation of *all* such diverse – even competing – religious models.

Ko Hung's contention that the gentleman may learn techniques for prolonging his life without limit, and the *Lieh-tzu*'s *Rubaiyat*-esque admonition to enjoy life while one can, for "tomorrow we die," both represent perspectives on the ultimate issues of life and death that were accepted and preserved as "Taoist" perspectives by countless generations of self-identified/socially-acknowledged "Taoists," down to modern times. Hence, both texts can, and should, be understood as presenting authentic fourth-century Taoist positions on such issues. And they can both be understood as presenting authentic fourth-century Taoist positions that emerged from the same "social class," for both were produced by, and for, members of "the elite," i.e., literati and aristocrats, who were active in government circles and/or associated with men who were.

Comparable diversity is also found among the revelatory traditions of the following century or so, which became so famous among late twentieth-century scholars of Taoism that those traditions – Shang-ch'ing and Ling-pao – often seem to have been presented as the *principal* forms of premodern "Taoism." The Shang-ch'ing revelations clearly did offer aspirants the possibility of a felicitous post-mortem life. The Ling-pao revelations, meanwhile, struggled to integrate Buddhist beliefs about rebirth with indigenous beliefs about death, and are less clear about exactly what "survives" death, and on what terms. Some Ling-pao texts contain images of "transit through extinction" (*mieh-tu*) that suggest a "post-mortem immortality" on various terms, some of which appear fairly beatific.[19] However, as Bokenkamp shows, "the message of the *Scripture of Salvation* . . . is not that death can be eradicated, but that it can be understood and, once understood, smoothly traversed (*du*)."[20] The Shang-ch'ing and Ling-pao revelations occurred not only in the same region and among members of the same "class," but even within clans (the Hsüs and Kos) that had been related by marriage for generations. And the "recipient" of the Ling-pao revelations, Ko Ch'ao-fu, was reportedly the grandnephew of the arch-immortalist Ko Hung. Hence, even among closely related aristocratic Taoists of late fourth-century south China, there was neither a common position on the issues of death and "immortality" nor much concerted effort by proponents of any one given position to suppress, deny, or disprove other positions.

Meanwhile, anyone who turns back to the pages of the *Lao-tzu* and *Chuang-tzu* will find many passages in each text that suggest that a person's goal should be to live a spiritualized life *until* death occurs, scattered among others (e.g., *Lao-tzu* 50) which clearly commend learning how to *prevent* or *evade* death. Such ambiguity – indeed, "inconsistency" – regarding a matter that seems to modern minds so clearly in need of unambiguity has caused many such minds deep consternation.[21] But at least by T'ang times, if not indeed from the fourth century, such ambiguities hardly seem to have been a source of consternation to many Taoists.

It thus cannot reasonably be argued that there is a universal Taoist position regarding life and death, or even a "central" or "primary" Taoist position regarding life and death.[22] The reality is that Taoism is a tradition defined (or perhaps, more correctly, *not* defined) by people who never saw reason to struggle to achieve agreement about most of life's deepest ambiguities. Taoists were never laboring to remain true to some "original message," the way that Christians, Jews, Confucians, and, to some degree, even Buddhists often tried to do. There was no single scripture to which all Taoists through the centuries felt it necessary to tag their beliefs or actions. There was never – at least not past the third century – any Taoist hierarchy that sought to determine doctrine for all Taoists. And there was certainly no effort to achieve or maintain any "philosophical" precision, consistency, or sophistication.

Rather, those who were drawn to understand life, and to express their lives and thoughts, on Taoist terms were a range of people who did not work very hard to find ways to agree with each other. It is not that Taoists of each age "agreed to disagree," as for instance modern Unitarians profess themselves quite happy to do. Rather, it is that the people who self-identified as Taoists in each age understood and accepted the fact that others might, with some justification, understand life on somewhat different terms. On one level, "Taoism" was, like "Hinduism," a catch-all category for a wide range of ideas, practices, and models of and for life, which were acknowledged to belong to this loosely defined category mostly, if not exclusively, by the fact that they clearly did not belong to any of the other available categories.

Such being the case, it is not at all surprising that some Taoists over the centuries argued the possibility of obviating death, and the desirability of attaining a deathless state, and even suggested practical methods for attaining some such state. But, while none can dispute the commonness of texts describing or alluding to such ideas, it is true that Taoists *also* produced and preserved texts that wholly *ignored* such ideas, others whose perspective on life would seem to *preclude* such ideas and practices altogether, and even some that *ridiculed* them, as we shall see. And because those who self-identified as members of "the *Tao-chiao*" were, at the very least, content to identify *all* such texts, ideas, and practices as belonging to their "*Tao-chiao*," all of them must be accepted as *representative* of the "authentic" voices of Taoism.

The "transcendents" and the spiritual aspirations of living mortals

Confusion regarding Taoist views on life and death has been aggravated by a sometimes uncritical use of the term *hsien* as the common referent to the supposed goal of life in "religious Taoism." A fundamental element of that problem is that the term *hsien* has been usually, and quite incorrectly, rendered as "immortal." Both in China and beyond, the term *hsien* was long regarded as a key feature – if not, indeed, as *the* key feature – of "Taoism" as it evolved in imperial times.

The influential H. G. Creel, for instance, proclaimed, "This kind of Taoism, in its varying manifestations, is marked by one constant aim: the achievement of immortality. . . . The immortality in question was a perpetuation of the physical body."[23] Sinologists such as Creel vehemently insisted that the very notion of *hsien*-hood was *ipso facto* contrary to the "essential truths" presented in the classical texts that, in Creel's mind, represented "pure Taoism."

Of course, any impartial observer today has reason to dismiss all Creel's arguments, since the interpretive errors resulting from his unacknowledged biases are now quite evident. Creel came from the traditional sinological framework which had been fathered, as it were, by Confucians, and within that framework it was absurd to suggest that *any* element of post-Han Taoism deserved serious scholary attention. But during Creel's day, the work of Henri Maspero – a respected sinologist who took post-Han Taoism quite seriously indeed – posed a threat to the dogmatic Confucian assumptions of mainstream sinology. So in 1956 Creel published a widely read diatribe calculated (1) to discredit what he caricatured as Maspero's "preoccupation" with post-Han Taoism, and (2) to prove once and for all that "the immortality cult" which stole the noble title of "Taoism" from "Taoist philosophy" is foolish nonsense richly deserving of scholarly contempt.[24]

Of course, Creel never bothered to examine any of the original Chinese sources from the *Tao-tsang* on which Maspero's work was based, or indeed any other texts from the *Tao-tsang* or other pertinent collection of Taoist materials. Rather – following the definitional biases of the Confucian scholar Fung Yu-lan, Creel declared – quite unjustifiably – not only that Ko Hung was "perhaps the ablest theoretician of Hsien Taoism," but also that "philosophic Taoism" was continued in imperial China *not* by anyone who *professed* to practice Taoism, but rather within "the philosophy of Ch'an (or Zen) Buddhism."[25] Such ideas were standard fare in the 1950s, when Holmes Welch wrote in nearly identical terms in his *Taoism: The Parting of the Way*. And in some quarters, those ideas remain uncritically, and sometimes quite emotionally, maintained as a sacred orthodoxy.[26]

Of course, it is now clear to most scholars of Chinese studies that Ko Hung was not the definitive figure of post-Han Taoism. And it is now agreed, at least in principle, that the whole range of texts in the *Tao-tsang* should at least be taken into account when we discuss Taoism in imperial China. It has also been demonstrated by Nathan

Sivin and Michel Strickmann that much of what was long imagined as "Taoism" among the non-Taoists of modern China – including the concept of *hsien* – may have been simply a part of Chinese popular tradition, not something specifically tied to practitioners of Taoism. More specifically, it is now quite clear that a serious reading of Taoist texts over the ages demonstrates that the term *hsien* was not, as Creel insisted, central or fundamental to all the "varying manifestations" of Taoism; and that Creel was utterly wrong in his claim that all post-Han forms of Taoism were "marked by one constant aim: the achievement of immortality [defined as] a perpetuation of the physical body." It is also now clear that Creel – along with Welch and most other sinologists of the mid-twentieth century – was incorrect in his claim that in post-Han Taoism "there is one element that we might expect to find which is completely absent . . . That is the central insight of philosophical Taoism," which Creel does not seem to identify.[27]

Despite such misrepresentations, the idea of the *hsien* is actually rooted in the "classics" of Taoism, where it is used to denote an exemplar of spiritual qualities on a level sufficient to allow a transcendence of human mortality. It is true that the term occurs in neither the *Lao-tzu* nor the *Nei-yeh*, and that in the *Chuang-tzu* it does not appear among his many terms for the idealized person (*chen-jen*, *sheng-jen*, etc.). But in *Chuang-tzu* 12, a wise border guard reportedly tells the sage-king Yao that the "sage" (*sheng-jen*) "after a thousand years departs and ascends as a *hsien*." And in *Chuang-tzu* 1, a character is ridiculed for doubting the reality of the invulnerable "spiritual person" (*shen-jen*) of Mount Ku-sheh, who ascends on dragons and extends protection and blessings to people. Both of those passages are quite consistent with virtually *all* later Chinese images of the *hsien* – Taoist and literary. And they clearly suggest that such a state is both theoretically possible and a worthy goal for a practitioner of "Chuang-tzu's" teachings.

The proposition that a "sage" (*sheng-jen*) can live a thousand years then ascend "as a *hsien*" is quite significant, and is not at all inconsistent with what the *Chuang-tzu* otherwise says about the *sheng-jen*. Though one typically thinks of Chuang's human ideal in such terms as "the true person" (*chen-jen*) or the "spiritual person" (*shen-jen*), the term "sage" is by far the most common term in the *Chuang-tzu* (as, indeed, in the *Nei-yeh* and *Tao te ching*) for a person who fulfills the highest ideals.[28] In *Chuang-tzu* 2 – perhaps the most well-studied of the "philosophical" inner chapters – the "sage" is explained as someone who "wanders beyond the dust and grime": he "leans on the sun and moon, tucks the universe under his arm, merges himself with things, . . . takes part in ten thousand ages and achieves simplicity in oneness."[29] Such imagery accords quite well with the image of the *hsien* in later Chinese culture, both within Taoism and beyond.

That imagery also accounts for its appropriation by Taoist thinkers such as the Ch'üan-chen founder Wang Che. Wang used the term *hsien* as a descriptor of someone who has achieved "purity and tranquillity" (*ch'ing-ching*) by integrating his or her "inner nature" (*hsing*) with his or her "worldly reality" (*ming*). Where Wang's usage differs from what appears in *Chuang-tzu*'s inner chapters is that Wang's "Fifteen Articles" make it clear that such a person qualifies for certification as a "spiritual immortal" (*shen hsien*) while still living his or her ordinary life.[30] And that understanding of the Taoist goal – as a spiritual achievement *within* one's human life – is typical of the entire tradition of Taoist teachings on "self-cultivation." The facts thus show that *later* Taoists' ideal of "becoming a *hsien*" did not, as a rule, deny, or do violence to, the realities of human life and death.

The colorful image of the *hsien* as a being with superhuman abilities was actually a common element of Chinese culture, beginning in Han times. Writings of that period generally mention *hsien* as denizens of distant realms, often winged beings who can fly between earth and higher worlds.[31] But the historian Ssu-ma Ch'ien, writing around 100 BCE, also mentions men from the northerly land of Yen who "practiced the Way of expansive *hsien*-hood (*fang-hsien tao*): they shed their mortal forms and melted away, relying upon matters involving spiritual beings (*kuei-shen*)."[32] Though these images are extremely vague, they provided fuel for centuries of both religious and literary elaboration, among both Taoists and non-Taoists. For instance, in literature from Han to T'ang times, the goddess Hsi Wang Mu was revered, both within and without Taoist circles, as the authority who "controlled access to transcendence." Yet, while poets wove bittersweet images of "transcendence" as an unattainable beatitude, most of the Taoist writers firmly believed that one can indeed transcend "the human condition" – if, as the

Lao-tzu and *Chuang-tzu* taught – one can only learn the subtle secrets and practice them diligently enough.[33]

For instance, the famed T'ang poet/*tao-shih* Wu Yün (d. 778) is credited with a text "On Attaining Spiritual Transcendence through Study" (*Shen-hsien k'e-hsüeh lun*).[34] Because of the youthfulness of the field of Taoist studies, and the preoccupations of twentieth-century scholars, Wu's work has never been translated. And, of course, it was never even glanced at by those like Creel, who preferred to pretend that somehow the "core text" of "religious Taoism" was the idiosyncratic "inner folios" of Ko Hung's *Pao-p'u-tzu*. As we have seen, Ko Hung's ideas cannot reasonably be characterized as representative of Taoism, even among the literate and aristocratic "Taoists" of his own time, his class, and his region. Even if the Ling-pao founder Ko Ch'ao-fu was not in fact a grandnephew of Ko Hung, he was certainly the initiator of a major stream of medieval Taoism. And in that stream there was no hint that "being Taoist" was primarily an effort to achieve "a perpetuation of the physical body."

Ko Hung's ideal of pursuing "immortality" through alchemy did reappear among some leading Shang-ch'ing practitioners, such as T'ao Hung-ching (456–536). But to T'ao, alchemy was a pursuit of spiritual elevation that was assumed to require *the loss of bodily life*.[35] Strickmann's famous report that "Taoist alchemy," thus conceived, actually *required* the practitioner to commit "ritual suicide" should have silenced, once and for all, those who have continued to misinterpret the Taoist life as just an effort to achieve "a perpetuation of the physical body." But, as Strickmann also observed, Taoist understandings of what exactly *does* happen when a successful practitioner reaches the death-event were never very clear, and were certainly never consistent:

> [We] can hardly claim even to know what was supposed to have happened, let alone what Taoists actually did to prepare for this event. In hagiography it is usually suggested that the successful immortal somehow managed to bypass death entirely. He would either ascend under his own power or be conveyed heavenward by an airborne equipage. There are some hagiographic accounts, however, that make willingness to follow a master in apparent suicide the

> crucial test of a disciple's resolution. . . . It is possible that the imprecision of the sources is no accident, and that the secret of ultimate transformation was a mystery in the religious sense. . . . Still, we have not yet studied all of the relevant texts, even on the limited subject of Taoist attitudes toward death.[36]

Anna Seidel, for her part, cautioned that, though many accounts of such events may depict leading practitioners as having "ascended to immortality," most Taoist texts actually suggest a "post-mortem immortality."[37] And other leading specialists today, such as Bokenkamp, make the same point.

On balance, it would seem accurate to say that Taoists of nearly every stripe – from those who penned lines now found in the *Lao-tzu* and *Chuang-tzu*, to practitioners of the many later forms of Taoism – believed that *death cannot be avoided*, and yet *death can certainly be transcended*. To the modern mind, as to "the Confucian mind," such a thought is simply not thinkable. But the people of China who practiced Taoism and composed its various texts clearly included many who found such thoughts quite thinkable indeed.

In this connection, we should remember that many of the world's religious traditions insist that bodily death does not necessarily entail death of the spirit, especially for the most saintly. Of course, Confucianism was not among those traditions, so, whenever Confucian writers looked at Taoists' references to the possibility of enduring beyond death, they saw only nonsense. Christians, meanwhile, have no reason to look askance at suggestions that a person who fulfills the proper spiritual requirements can look forward to "eternal life." Nor do they balk at the idea that such "eternal life" involves *physical death* along with *spiritual immortality*. To those of us familiar with such beliefs, it should be no surprise to read of Taoists who ascended to Heaven and left behind a body. If Christians of all social backgrounds and all educational levels – including centuries of intellectual, social, and cultural leaders – can conceive of an "eternal life" that begins within one's earthly life and endures beyond one's earthly death, do we have any legitimate reason to raise our eyebrows at Taoist beliefs that are in those key ways quite parallel? Certainly, Wang Che's understanding of becoming a *hsien* fits that description quite neatly. As he said:

> Leaving the world does not mean that the body departs. . . . When you realize the Tao, your body will be in the sphere of the ordinary, but your mind [*hsin*] will be in the realm of the sages. Nowadays, people want to avoid death forever and at the same time leave the ordinary world. They are very foolish, indeed, and have not even glimpsed the true principle of the Tao.[38]

It is true, of course, that, when Chinese writers – Taoist and non-Taoist alike – composed accounts of precisely what happened when certain ideal figures left their earthly life, they often stated or implied that the person involved did not really die. Some great figures, such as the Yellow Emperor, are said to have simply ascended to Heaven, in plain view of ordinary observers.[39] Others, however, ascended under less clear circumstances, and were commonly said to have undergone *shih-chieh*, "mortuary liberation."[40] But many accounts of *shih-chieh* are quite famous for denying that the person had really left behind a corpse at all. One example is the T'ang wonder-worker Yeh Fa-shan. One account of his non-death reports that, at the age of 106, Yeh "secretly ingested a divine elixir." Then:

> On the third day of the sixth month, at the hour of noon, the Perfected One (*chen-jen*) [i.e., Yeh] transformed his corpse into a sword. A nebulous chariot called at his door. . . . All the people of the city saw a column of azure smoke rising . . . directly up to touch the heavens. . . . A year after the funeral, the inner and outer coffins opened by themselves. But when the clothing, cap, sword and shoes were seen, it was only then realized that [Yeh] had not died, but had really only "arisen lightly."[41]

Such accounts are deliberately unclear about what, precisely, had occurred, for its various elements cannot be intelligibly reconciled. Meanwhile, in the coffin of Yeh's contemporary Huang Ling-wei, "the Flower Maid," only a shroud and a screed are said to have been found, while in that of Ssu-ma Ch'eng-chen, a staff and pair of shoes were found. Such reports suggest that the person in question had ascended to Heaven at the time of apparent death, and that the body had either been transformed into the objects in question or had somehow been translated away, except for a few of its accouterments. In all such cases, there was a set of events that corresponded outwardly to a conventional human death and burial; but the true details of the matter revealed that the subject had *not* died a *real* death at all.

The concept of "mortuary liberation" was thus a product of the religious imagination, designed to suggest a method of transcending mortality that could not otherwise be described. To make sense of such reports is like trying to make sense of what the *Chuang-tzu* says about the "sage" who "ascends as a *hsien*." What all such depictions reveal is an understanding of the nature of death that is alien to all pertinent elements of the *modern* mentality, within which "death is death," and only a fool would imagine otherwise. To attempt to understand Taoist perspectives on such matters without first setting aside such unexamined beliefs in our own minds inevitably results in incomprehension, or in a reduction of Taoist beliefs and practices to ridiculous caricatures.

When, today, we try to understand how Taoists approached the topic of death and its "transcendence," we must carefully consider the full historical array of Taoist phenomena, and the many varying models for explaining such matters that arose within the minds and lives of Taoists of different periods and different traditions. We must also distinguish those ideas that were expressed by practicing Taoists of every sort, from the highly *romanticized* notions of "the immortals" that abounded more generally in Chinese literature, art, and culture well into modern times.

The ultimate distinction may be that, among practicing Taoists, the goal was *never* simply to find a means of preventing the death-event. Rather, the Taoist goal – from the *Lao-tzu* and *Chuang-tzu* throughout most later forms of Taoism – was to *attain an exalted state of existence through diligent cultivation of the world's deeper realities*. Such attainments were generally predicated upon a process of personal purification and an enhanced awareness of reality – i.e., a process of moral, spiritual, and cognitive growth.[42] Once one has fully completed that process, one is believed to have somehow reached a state that will not be extinguished, even when the physical body ceases to be one's form.

That having been said, however, Taoists of most periods were often happy to leave such matters surrounded by what strikes some modern minds as intolerable ambiguity. As, for instance, Lord Lao himself says in his *180 Precepts*:

> Unless the precepts and regulations are held to, even if a human life lasts 10,000 years, how is it different from an old tree or an ancient rock? It is better to hold to the precepts for a single day and to die as a virtuous man, living without committing evil. If you hold to the precepts, you will serve as a heavenly official, ascending to immortality through corpse-liberation.[43]

"Cultivating reality"

As is so often the case, the issue of death and its transcendence reveals that the Taoist tradition did not typically formulate or promulgate specific positions, nor demand adherence to common positions as a criterion of "membership" in "Taoism." Those who were attracted to Taoism seem to have been those who were not interested in laboring to determine better or worse, much less "correct," ways of conceptualizing the Taoist life. Rather, they seem to have been those who would gladly draw upon any combination of traditional and contemporary cultural elements to facilitate their effort to live the Taoist life as fully as possible.

Such was the case in regard to practice as well as belief. What the tradition did, from the fifth century onward, was to collect and preserve all the models of and for the spiritual life that anyone had ever suggested. Practitioners would then follow the model that held the most appeal to them, with of course whatever modifications or enhancements seemed appropriate in light of current realities.

Yet, it would be wrong to surmise that all those many models of and for the spiritual life had no underlying commonalities, or that they shared no fundamental perspectives regarding what life is and how one should live it. It is possible to identify, on very broad terms, elements of a common "Taoist worldview," as well as a concomitant "Taoist ethos," which informed and stimulated Taoist practice in all its many forms, as well as Taoist modes of engagement with other elements of Chinese culture and society.

At the most basic level, one assumption common to Taoists of most periods is that most people live fundamentally unaware of the true nature of the reality within which their lives take place. As a consequence, most people live their lives on terms that are not in accord with the true nature of their own reality. Their lives are therefore inherently flawed and ultimately fruitless. And, for such people, there is no hope for anything good to ensue when their biological existence ends. Their lives are essentially wasted.

However, in this view, the "true nature" of people's reality is not something ontologically alien to them – not something "out there" that is somehow other than their own nature. Hence, the starting point for making our lives into what they *should* be is learning to discriminate between a fruitless existence – mere survival, then pointless death – on the one hand, and a form of *true* living on the other hand – living in accord with what really is, and engaging in a fruitful process of spiritural development. That learning process was never simply a matter of thinking certain thoughts about life and trying to put them into action. That approach would be as fruitless as living without regard for life's realities. Rather, the Taoist life consists in a process that is focused on a change in experiential awareness.

Elements of other Asian traditions, particularly Hinduism and Buddhism, begin with very similar assumptions. In time, China's Taoists encountered forms of Buddhism in which they found interesting parallels. And, during certain periods, certain Taoists adapted certain Buddhist ideas, further enriching the diversity of Taoist models of and for the spiritual life. Yet, they often found that some Buddhist assumptions did not fully accord with their own. For instance, Taoists generally did *not* accept the idea – common in some forms of Ch'an/Zen – that the desired transformation in experiential awareness was typically a matter of *a sudden event*. Some interpreters lightly assume that Taoists and Buddhists have always been thinking and doing the same thing. But by the time of Ssu-ma Ch'eng-chen, at least, Taoists had pondered the full range of spiritual models long enough to decide that ideals such as "suddenness" made little sense on Taoist terms. As we will see more fully below, an exemplary elder reportedly taught Ho Chih-chang, "One cannot advance swiftly, but must take yielding restraint as the prime concern. . . . [This] is like refusing [to accept] a horse for racing away."[44] Though Taoists in later ages did sometimes appropriate terms such as *wu*, "achieving new experiential awareness" (a term most familiar to students of Zen in its Japanese pronunciation, *satori*) Taoists always integrated such terms into a Taoist perspective on life.

Likewise, Taoists did not find value in the Buddhist assumption that spiritual transformation could take place *merely* as a change in one's consciousness, without any real reference to one's *physical life* or to the subtle processes at work in *the world around us*. Taoists typically believed that personal transformation must be a *holistic* transformation, a transformation of *all* their being – including what other traditions have often distinguished as mind, body, and spirit – in accord with the most subtle and sublime processes at work in the world within which we live.

In the year 2000, a scholar of Chinese religion, Donald Harper, said that Taoism is about personal transformation within a universe that is set up for such transformation.[45] It might be fair to say that the core of Taoist practice – from classical times down to the present – has involved *a practice of self-cultivation within a cosmos comprised of subtly linked forces*.

We must beware of misinterpreting Taoist practices on terms of modern individualism. Taoist theory did *not* accept any dichotomization of "self" from "other." Contrary to the charges of its critics – both among China's Confucians and among modern Westerners – Taoist "self-cultivation" has never been grounded in a belief that each human being has any separate, enclosed, individualized "self" that is more worthy of value and attention than what is outside such enclosures. Rather, Taoists generally assume that one's "self" cannot be understood or fulfilled without reference to other persons, and to *the broader set of realities in which all persons are naturally and properly embedded*. It is this fundamentally *holistic perspective* that sets Taoist ideas and practices apart from most of what is taught in other traditions of China or those of other lands, in Asia or elsewhere.

One problem with many modern presentations of Taoism is that they ignore the importance of the *practices* that Taoists of all ages considered essential to fulfilling the goal of the Taoist life. Those presentations often proceeded from *modern assumptions*, which privilege the holding of certain *ideas* while devaluing our *everyday life*. Hence it was only in recent years that scholars began truly trying to understand and explain Taoist *meditative practices* and *ritual activity* – elements of practice that are alien to the "Enlightenment" beliefs and values embedded within modern academic traditions. A number of recent scholars have produced worthwhile studies of Taoist ritual traditions, shedding light not only on their relevance to Chinese social life but also on their inherent structure and meaning.[46] But those ritual traditions are actually a part of a much broader Taoist concern with self-transformation: the priest who performs a Taoist liturgy can do so only once he (or, in some Taoist contexts, she) has first *reached a proper state of experiential awareness* by means of *specific self-cultivational practices*. The liturgical traditions of Taoism, therefore, cannot truly be understood except within the broader context of Taoist ideas and practices as a whole.

In Taoist tradition, from classical times to the present, certain specific practices were found to have the capacity to give a practitioner an experiential awareness of dimensions of his or her own reality to which he or she had theretofore remained incompletely aware. More specifically, these are practices designed to effect or facilitate a meaningful personal transformation within a universe that is constituted so as to expedite such transformation. The nature of those practices, and the nature of that transformation, is rooted in the act of learning to experience and work with the true structures and energies that subtly link our personal experience to the rest of our living world.

It is true that, to some degree, even some Confucian elements fit that overall model. But the "cultivation of sagehood" pursued by late imperial and modern Confucians diverges from the paradigms of Taoism at certain significant points. For instance, with the apparent exception of Mencius – whose call for a cultivation of "a flood-like *ch'i*" might seem to qualify him as a Taoist – Confucians have seldom been very interested in exploring the transformative implications of *the body's own energies*, or the *connectedness* of those energies with the life-field in which our lives are intrinsically embedded. It may have been for that reason that one young Confucian aspirant, Wang Yang-ming, was frustrated in his attempt to gain experiential awareness of the continuities between the subtle informing structure of his own being and that of a stand of bamboo. An enduring tradition for *most* Confucians has been an assumption that any such subtle informing structures fall within the range of things that "the Master did not speak about," things that the living practitioners should perhaps "respect, but keep at a distance." In other words, because of the overriding socio-political emphases that evolved within Confucianism, an individual's efforts to engage in more holistic transformational practices was usually considered superfluous, if not indeed suspect.

Among Taoists, by contrast, the practices designed to facilitate or effect a meaningful personal transformation have almost always been perceived to link directly with "the subtle informing structure of own's own being," and even, to a large extent, with what might be called "the practitioner's own bodily energies." In Taoism, the fundamental activity in which one ideally engages is a *cultivation of reality*, which takes place through a newly experiential engagement with a specific set of subtle forces, structures, and energies, which are inherent to one's personal reality. In part, one learns – as the unfortunate young Wang Yang-ming was unsuccessful in learning – that *all* those structures and energies stretch throughout *all* that is real, both within one's own personal existence and throughout what unperceptive minds regard as the external universe.

It is here, in what might be called the affirmation of the body and the affirmation of the natural world, that we see something Taoism does not fully share with many other traditions. In Taoism, *both* one's body (or, more properly, one's body/heart/mind/energy/spirit) *and* the social, political, and physical matrices within which one's personal life take place – i.e., realities that Taoists often called one's *ming*, "facts that cannot be changed" – are deemed not only to be real and important, but, in certain key ways, fundamental to one's practice of personal transformation.

Our study of these matters must begin with the earliest known model of cultivational practices – the model suggested in the classical text called the *Nei-yeh* ["Inner Cultivation"], and more fully particularized in the early-Han *Huai-nan-tzu*. In the *Nei-yeh*, to which many elements of Taoist imagery and practice can ultimately be traced, the term *tao* is used as a vague and imprecise synonym for such terms as *ch'i*, which refer, themselves imprecisely, to the salubrious life-forces that the practitioner must work to cultivate. In terms of that theory – if the word "theory" may even be applied to such a nebulous set of ideas – the term *tao* was an indistinct marker for something that we might articulate as "the realities that one ought to cultivate." In the *Nei-yeh*, *tao* was used almost synonymously with such terms as *shen*, which corresponds quite nicely to most meanings of the English word "spirit." I have styled such practices forms of "biospiritual cultivation," for the *Nei-yeh* – like many later Taoist writings – teaches that they begin with the proper regulation of one's physical life.

Many elements of the *Nei-yeh*'s model of biospiritual cultivation resonated in other classical texts, including some seldom noticed by students of "Taoism." For instance, as mentioned in Chapter 2, the *Lü-shih ch'un-ch'iu* (*ca.* 240 BCE) says:

> The foundation of all things is that one must first put one's self (*shen*) into order. . . . If one daily renews one's vital essence (*ching*) and life-energy (*ch'i*) and gets rid of nasty *ch'i* completely, one will return to [the course leading to fulfillment of] one's natural lifespan. [One who does] this is called a Perfected Person (*chen-jen*).[47]

These ideas resonate with *much* of later Taoism, for *chen-jen* is an enduring Taoist term for the human ideal: it stretches from the *Chuang-tzu*, through the *T'ai-p'ing ching* of late Han times, to the Shang-ch'ing revelations of fourth-century China and on to the human examplars of modern Ch'üan-chen Taoism. And the idea of daily renewal of one's vital essence (*ching*) and life-energy (*ch'i*) connects directly with centuries of later Taoists, as well as linking them back to the *Nei-yeh* and to practices outlined in another text from *ca.* 240 BCE, Han Fei's *Chieh-Lao* ["Explaining 'Lao-tzu'"]. As noted in Chapter 2, it says, "Therefore the Sage (*sheng-jen*) saves his essence (*ching*) and spirit (*shen*), and esteems resting in quietness. . . . If the Sage treasures his spirit, then his essence will flourish."[48]

In later centuries, those who self-identified as Taoists developed a wide range both of conceptual frameworks for cultivating "spirit," and of individual and group practices. Yet, as those new frameworks evolved over time, they never fully displaced the classical traditions of biospiritual cultivation. The redactors of what we now call the *Tao te ching* may have urged extending our practices, and the underlying values, into moral, political, and even military spheres. And those ideals persisted and spread in Han times and beyond, from the think-tank setting that produced the *Huai-nan-tzu* to the more wide-ranging setting that produced the *T'ai-p'ing ching*. After the efflorescence of the new social, ritual, and meditative emphases produced by "the Heavenly Masters," the Shang-ch'ing revelations, and the Ling-pao revelations, the Taoist leaders of T'ang times envisioned their tradition as a comprehensive synthesis that included *all* such potent religious traditions. Yet, the formulators of that synthesis never relinquished ideas of "biospiritual cultivation," though they often articulated it in new terms, many of which had very old roots.

The terms in which Taoists expressed their basic understandings of self-transformation shifted and evolved, but certain ideas remained quite constant over the centuries. For instance, a succinct text from T'ang times, the *Ch'ing-ching ching* ["Scripture of Purity and Tranquillity"], eventually "became a central scripture of Complete Perfection [Ch'üan-chen Taoism], whose followers still recite it in their daily services."[49] In terms quite close to those used in the *Nei-yeh* and *Tao te ching*, the *Ch'ing-ching ching* says, "When no desires arise, You have found true tranquillity. . . . In purity and tranquillity, Gradually enter the true Tao."[50] Another eighth-century text, the *Nei-kuan ching* ["Scripture on Inner Observation"] is even closer to the specific, yet vague, terminology of the *Nei-yeh*: "The Venerable Lord said: . . . One must empty one's mind, calm the spirit, and the Tao will come to stay naturally."[51] Elsewhere the *Nei-kuan ching* says:

> Spirit . . . goes on changing and transforming without measure, merges with yin and yang, greatly encompasses heaven and earth, subtly enters the tiniest blade of grass. . . . Purity and tranquillity make it live, defilements and nervousness cause it to perish. . . . You need only keep it empty and still, then life and the Tao will spontaneously be permanent.[52]

Some have called the *Nei-yeh*'s model – in which the practitioner clears the clutter out of his/her heart/mind to allow spiritual forces to enter – an "apophatic" model, and such emphases were indeed reflected in other texts of T'ang and later times. Yet, the broader concept of purifying oneself by keeping still and restraining thoughts and desires is also basic to the teachings of the *Tao te ching* and other Taoist texts and teachings, down to the present.

Within Taoism, different conceptualizations of the process of self-transformation were often accepted by the composer of a single text as equally valid and valuable expressions of the process. One common Taoist model, for instance, expresses the process in terms of "guarding" or "preserving" life's key forces. Such ideas are found from the *T'ai-p'ing ching* and Ko Hung's *Pao-p'u-tzu* through T'ang texts such as the *Chung-chieh wen* ["On All the Precepts"] and later works of "Inner Alchemy."[53]

Another model that endured throughout the history of the tradition was the model of "cultivation" (*hsiu*), a model shared with Confucians from the days of Mencius down to the twentieth century. By T'ang times, the idea that self-transformation meant "cultivation" – both of oneself and of the subtle realities of the universe – had become fundamental for much of Taoist thought. For instance, the ninth-century commentary to the *Hsüan-chu hsin ching* ["Mysterious Pearly Mirror of the Mind"] says:

> The way the Venerable Lord [Lao-chün, "Lord Lao"] taught people to cultivate the Tao is the cultivation of the mind [*hsin*, "mind/heart"]. To cultivate the mind is to cultivate the Tao. Now, the mind is the residence of spirit [*shen*] within the human body. When the mind remains empty and in non-action, then it will, after some time, begin to radiate with the Tao. . . . Guard emptiness, non-being, and the spontaneous flow of life, let your body and spirit become one with the Tao, and you can live forever as an immortal [*hsien*].[54]

Here, as in other T'ang texts, such as the *T'ien-yin-tzu* and writings of Ssu-ma Ch'eng-chen (discussed more fully below), we see that, for Taoists, from T'ang times to the present, "to cultivate the heart/mind is to cultivate the Tao." Yet, we also see continuities with many of the teachings of more ancient texts, including the *Lü-shih ch'un-ch'iu* and *Chieh-Lao* as well as the *Tao te ching*, *Chuang-tzu*, and *Nei-yeh*.

The only element of these passages that one would recognize as unprecedented in those classical texts is the fact that the pertinent instructions are given new weight by being represented as instructions from "Lord Lao." As we have seen, however, "Lord Lao" was a creation of the Chinese imperial court, and by T'ang times he was a very old and venerable feature of Taoist tradition. By then, many Taoist teachings of every description had been accepted as the teachings of Lord Lao.

One example is *Hsi-sheng ching* ["The Scripture of Western Ascension"], from the Taoist masters of the Lou-kuan abbey in the fourth or fifth century CE. The *Hsi-sheng ching* – replete with restatements of many *Tao te ching* passages – presents itself as the final dispensation of the human "Lao-tzu" before he left the present world. After explaning how "Tao" became "manifested in life," "Lord Lao" teaches the development of "spiritual transcendence" (*shen-hsien*) through "putting Reality (*chen*) into effect" in one's personal life. Like the classical *Nei-yeh* and the *Nei-kuan ching* of later T'ang times, the *Hsi-sheng ching* says that, when one is tranquil, "spirit" (*shen*) will abide, but that it will depart if one becomes agitated. By turning away from external vanities, reducing desires and practicing "non-action" (*wu-wei*), one can establish oneself in "emptiness and non-being (*wu*)" through meditation. The result, however, is not some personal immortality, but rather a state of union with Tao, and a long life.[55] Most modern minds familiar with the *Tao te ching* will find the teachings of the *Hsi-sheng ching* to have a slightly different flavor. But all will have no trouble seeing that the Lou-kuan Taoists of the Six Dynasties period understood and practiced Taoism in terms that were continuous with what we know as "the teachings of Lao-tzu."

In T'ang times, Taoists were neither esoteric nor sectarian, but supremely ecumenical: they felt free to articulate their models of practice on any terms that might make sense to any given practitioner. And they were happy to explain their tradition's ancient practices in any way that facilitated the understanding and acceptance of those practices among the audience of their day, including the learned and the socially prominent. Those two factors worked together to produce not merely a true diversity of thought and practice, but what seems to have been an implicit enthusiasm for formulating all manner of new hybrids. The late imperial "synthesis" of "the Three Teachings" – Buddhism, Taoism, and Confucianism – actually got underway in T'ang times, and Taoists remained second to none in their happiness to show that *this* model and *these* practices are, when properly understood, really not incompatible with *those* models and practices.

In regard to personal practice, two of the best-studied examples of T'ang ecumenism were the Taoist physician Sun Ssu-mo (d. 682) and his younger contemporary, Ssu-ma Ch'eng-chen. Both were aristocratic literati, whose activities involved them deeply in the elite society of their day. And both endeavored to make their Taoist ideas and practices fully comprehensible to associates more familiar with other models of self-cultivation. For instance, Sun once advised the poet Lu Chao-lin about "the importance of cultivating the 'inner nature' (*yang-hsing*)." He explained that human fulfillment can take place only if there is balance and order within oneself, and that such order depends upon proper movement of the *ch'i* (life-energy) and *ching* (vital essence).[56] Confucians had conceived self-perfection in terms of cultivating one's "inner nature" (*hsing*) since the days of Mencius. A bit later, the Confucian Li Ao (*ca.* 772–836) would play a key role in stimulating the rise of "Neo-Confucianism" by writing an important, though long-neglected, work entitled the *Fu-hsing shu* ("Book on Returning to One's Inner Nature").[57] Meanwhile, "inner nature" was also fundamental to the thought and practice of T'ang Buddhists, particularly within Ch'an: the later Rinzai Zen model of "seeing (your) nature" (Chinese, *chien-hsing*; Japanese, *kenshō*) goes back to Buddhist appropriations of such indigenous Confucian/Taoist ideas.

To Confucians and Buddhists, however, the term "inner nature" connoted a non-personalized essence, which had no inherent relationship to the realities of one's actual *bodily* experience. To Taoists, on the other hand, the facts of our physical existence were always relevant. Writings by Sun Ssu-mo and Ssu-ma Ch'eng-chen make that point clear, though only a few specialists have ever looked at them.

Among Sun's authentic writings are two therapeutic treatises still current today, the *Ch'ien-chin fang* ["Recipes Worth a Thousand (Pieces of) Gold"] and *Ch'ien-chin i-fang* ["Unusual Recipes Worth a Thousand (Pieces of) Gold"]. In the former, Sun acknowledges the mutual validity of Buddhist medical theory and traditional Chinese principles.[58] But within a Taoist context, Sun is also the assumed author of two influential texts on self-cultivation: the *Chen-chung chi* ["The Pillowbook Records"] and its appendix – apparently once a separate work – the *Ts'un-shen lien-ch'i ming* ["Inscription on Visualization of Spirit and Refinement of *Ch'i*"].[59] Sun's "Pillowbook" explains the practice of self-cultivation as consisting of (1) "prudence," i.e., self-control and moderation in consumption and sensual pleasures; (2) "prohibitions" regarding improper activities in those regards; (3) self-massage; (4) guiding the *ch'i* by visualizational meditation; and (5) "guarding the One" to attain apotropaic powers.[60] Here one sees the integration of diverse elements of centuries of Taoist thought and practice. Intriguingly, however, Sun posits that spiritual success depends upon "an awakened heart/mind" (*chüeh-hsin*).[61] The notion of "awakening" is atypical of ancient or medieval Taoist rhetoric: it seems to reflect Buddhist influence, though Ch'üan-chen Taoists would later embrace such ideas.

Meanwhile, Sun's "Inscription on Visualization of Spirit and Refinement of *Ch'i*" presents a more comprehensive program of self-perfection, involving a five-stage cultivation of the heart/mind along with a seven-stage cultivation of the whole person.[62] In the first stage, one diminishes "the diseases inherited from former lives" by bringing the heart/mind (*hsin*), spirit (*shen*), and vital energy (*ch'i*) into tranquillity. One then ascends through the idealized stages of transcendent person (*hsien-jen*), realized person (*chen-jen*), spiritual person (*shen-jen*), and perfect person (*chih-jen*), until one reaches the ultimate goal, "the source of Tao." Despite the Buddhist concept of rebirth in the first stage, this "path" employs the *Chuang-tzu*'s terms for ideal persons, and is consistent with many other images of Taoist practice, from ancient times to the late imperial period.

Though the historical connections have not yet been fully explored, Sun Ssu-mo's model of the Taoist path is taken up in a text that appears to date from the early eighth century. It is commonly called the *Ting-kuan ching* ["Scripture on Concentration and Observation"].[63] The *Ting-kuan ching* seems to have influenced another exponent of self-cultivation, the illustrious Ssu-ma Ch'eng-chen. Among Ssu-ma's writings is the *Fu-ch'i ch'ing-i lun* ["On the Essential Meaning of the Absorption of *Ch'i*-Energy"], part of which is also known by the title *Hsiu-chen ch'ing-i tsa-lun* ["Miscellaneous Discourses on the Essential Meaning of Cultivating

Perfection"].[64] Instead of a simple outline of useful physiological practices, the *Fu-ch'i ch'ing-i lun* is an organized explication of the nature of biospiritual reality, with guidelines for avoiding negative phenomena, sublimating deficiencies, and establishing a healthy, *ch'i*-filled body.

In other writings by Ssu-ma, the seven-stage cultivation process outlined in Sun's "Inscription on Visualization of Spirit and Refinement of *Ch'i*" reappears, though in even more simplified form. For instance, Ssu-ma's *Tso-wang lun* ["On Sitting in Forgetfulness"] is a very generalized guide for engaging in gradual progression toward union with Tao and attaining "spiritual transcendence."[65]

Ssu-ma also edited, and may well have secretly authored, a brief work called the *T'ien-yin-tzu* ["The Master of Heavenly Seclusion"].[66] The *T'ien-yin-tzu* outlines a "path to spiritual transcendence (*shen-hsien*)" that consists of "five progressive gateways." The "path" begins with a balanced diet and moderation in physical activity; proceeds in the fourth stage to "sitting in forgetfulness" (i.e., forgetting ordinary distinctions between "self" and "other"); and culminates in attainment of "spiritual transcendence." It is instructive that the *T'ien-yin-tzu*'s final stage is characterized both as "entering into Suchness" (a concept borrowed from the *Prajñā-pāramitā* texts of Mahāyāna Buddhism) *and* as "returning to *wu-wei*," language familiar to readers of the *Tao te ching*. And it is also noteworthy that "the Master of Heavenly Seclusion" says quite clearly that, "even in spiritual transcendence, one is still human." This reminder that Taoist practice is aimed at spiritual goals to be achieved *during* one's life – not just averting the death-event, as critics long charged – recurs in centuries of Taoist texts, most of which remain unread by most who have written about Taoism.

Another little-known fact is that Taoists of Ssu-ma's day flirted with Zen-like models. For one thing, some began to find a use for Confucian/Buddhist terms such as "awakening" (*chüeh*) and "realization" (*wu*; in Japanese, *satori*), which would linger in some modern Ch'üan-chen models.[67] But in time, most Taoists preferred to set their models apart from those of Ch'an Buddhists, as, for instance, by denying much value to "sudden" experiences. As the *T'ien-yin-tzu* says, "in cultivating reality (*hsiu-chen*) and developing one's inner nature (*ta-hsing*), no sudden realization (*wu*) is possible: one must necessarily advance by progressing gradually and practicing tranquilly."[68] So later, when Wang Che taught that "to enter the sagely Tao one must first strengthen one's determination for many years," he was simply following a common Taoist model from T'ang and Sung times.[69] As noted above, for instance, an eleventh-century biography of the T'ang imperial librarian Ho Chih-chang says that he retired from office and became a *tao-shih* after a mysterious elder taught him in terms based on teachings from the *Tao te ching* and *Nei-yeh*:

> One cannot advance swiftly, but must take yielding restraint as the prime concern. When one is yielding and restrained, one's desires are few. When one's desires are few, one's spirit is at ease. When one's spirit is at ease, then one does nothing and nothing is left undone.[70]

In Taoism, achieving the spiritual goal has never been something that happens "spontaneously": rather, it emerges out of a demanding personal process, which requires work, dedication, and a sacrifice of self-centeredness.

In the twentieth-century West, Taoist practice was deeply misunderstood by narcissistic pseudo-Taoists, who falsely imagined that "following the Tao" requires no more than "going with the flow" or "just being spontaneous." To the contrary, Taoist practice traditionally rested upon self-discipline as "the foundation that sets up the basic framework of mind and body in which alone the hard work of the path can be accomplished."[71]

Such is one reason that T'ang Taoists tried out Buddhist models and often decided against them. Taoists were *never* "escapists" who desired to flee from "the real world," but rather men and women who valued the deeper, more spiritual dimensions of the world in which our lives are imbedded. In general, those who believed that spiritual transformation required careful attention to one's *bio-physical* life were the people who embraced and refined Taoist methods of cultivation, rather than those typical of Ch'an/Zen or of more intellectualized Buddhist traditions (such as T'ien-t'ai or Hua-yen). The same can be said, broadly speaking, for those whose idea of "developing one's inner nature" involved the idea of a *path* that leads, in successive stages, from "here" – ordinary life – to "there" – the ultimate goal.

It is true that, for some decades at least, T'ang Taoists tried to domesticate the Ch'an/Zen concept of "Buddha-nature." The evidence of this little-known fact is found in major texts of T'ang times, which only a handful of specialists have yet examined. As noted above, one was the *Pen-chi ching* ["Scripture of the Genesis Point"], a text disseminated by imperial order in 741.[72] A basic teaching of the *Pen-chi ching* – and of several contemporary texts, even some attributed to Ssu-ma Ch'eng-chen – is that all sentient beings have a "Tao-nature" (*tao-hsing*), which constitutes our true reality. "Tao-nature" is the subject of an entire section of a still-unexplored seventh-century text of great significance, the *Tao-chiao i-shu* ["Pivotal Meaning of the Taoist Teaching"].[73] These ideas were clearly inspired by Mahāyāna theories of the "Buddha-nature," and were apparently designed to stimulate interest in Taoism among those members of the educated elite who were not drawn to other forms of Taoist self-cultivation. Yet, such ideas are rarely found in Taoist materials of later ages.

What we do see in later Taoism – both in "Inner Alchemy" and within the broader Ch'üan-chen tradition – is an interest in the idea of a *hsing* ("inner nature") that a practitioner can actually *do* something with. That is, those who self-identified as Taoists usually wanted to understand spiritual practice in a way that explains how the individual person can integrate his or her personal reality with something that transcends individual identity. Taoist spiritual practices assume that one must somehow *transform* something *less* "*real*" into something *more* "*real.*" The Rinzai Zen idea that one can attain beatitude simply by "seeing one's nature" – by simply *perceiving* some true "reality" – made little sense to those of Taoist sensibilities.

Taoism and East Asian tantrism

New research has begun to show that the interaction between Buddhists and Taoists was not one-way, as was long supposed. Through the twentieth century, the misconception that the *Lao-tzu* and *Chuang-tzu* constituted "the essence of Taoism" misled many to interpret most later Taoist institutions as mere imitations of Buddhist institutions and practices. But, while there were indeed points at which Taoists clearly did find something worth appropriating from their Buddhist colleagues' heritage, such appropriations went in the other direction as well.

This is particularly true in the role that Taoism played in shaping the "tantric" traditions of East Asia. For example, a specific fourth-century practice of Shang-ch'ing visualizational meditation later reappeared, with slight remodification, in one of the northern "conquest states" as a practice for interacting with a tantric goddess.[74] In fact, whenever there is clear evidence of borrowing between tantrism and Taoism, it is usually clear that the Taoist usage was much earlier.

An important example involves the Taoist expression "cultivating reality" (*hsiu-chen*), a common T'ang term for self-cultivation, seen for instance in the title of one of Ssu-ma Ch'eng-chen's major works. The *Tao-tsang*, in fact, lists some twenty works bearing titles that begin with the term *hsiu-chen*. We have seen each of those terms in earlier connections, as when the *Hsi-sheng ching* advises that one should "put Reality (*chen*) into effect." And much earlier, even before there was any such thing as "Taoism," a contributor to the *Lü-shih ch'un-ch'iu* wrote that, if one "daily renews one's vital essence (*ching*) and life-energy (*ch'i*) . . . [one] will return to [the course leading to fulfillment of] one's natural lifespan" and may be "a Realized *or* Perfected Person" (*chen-jen*).

As noted earlier, *chen-jen* was an enduring Taoist term for a fully perfected being, which was passed down through the *Chuang-tzu,* the *T'ai-p'ing ching*, and the Shang-ch'ing revelations.[75] Down through Sung and Yüan times, Taoist masters of earlier days were often commemorated with the honorific title *chen-jen*, as seen for instance in the title of the *T'ang Yeh chen-jen chuan*, a major collection of materials concerning the thaumaturge Yeh Fa-shan.[76]

Be that as it may, the word *chen* was more than an ancient and enduring Taoist term for a person who had achieved the final goal of Taoist practice: it was also a term that denoted the "goal" itself. Down through modern times, the word *chen* has been a favorite Taoist device for pointing to *life's deepest and most rarefied realities*, to the realities at which Taoist practice is constantly aimed. Often found in pre-T'ang Taoist traditions, the idea of "Reality" (*chen*) became even more central after T'ang times.

For instance, one of the earliest classics of "Inner Alchemy" theory was Chang Po-tuan's eleventh-century work *Wu-chen p'ien*

["Folios on Awakening to Reality"]. And we may not think of Wang Che, the founder of the Ch'üan-chen tradition, as an authority on "Inner Alchemy." But while some texts attributed to Wang may well have been by early followers, one of those works was entitled the "Song of Awakening to Reality" (*Wu-chen ko*). The importance of the term *chen* as an expression of the Taoist spiritual goal is perhaps most fully evidenced by its integration into the very name of the Ch'üan-chen tradition, which means something like "the Completion of Reality."

In the early eighth century, a new form of Buddhism appeared in China, a result of the translational activities of two foreign *ācāryas* ("teachers") who took residence in the T'ang capital, Ch'ang-an. There, of course, T'ang emperors were fully invested in exploiting and patronizing the dominant religion among that era's upper classes – Taoism. The emperor Hsüan-tsung, in particular, knew and loved Taoism, so he welcomed those new Buddhist translators, and eagerly patronized their first Chinese convert, I-hsing – evidently a master of Taoist learning before his conversion.[77] Those Buddhists focused on texts that would later – especially in Japan – become famed as the central texts of "esoteric Buddhism" (Chinese *mi-chiao*; Japanese *mikkyō*); later, those traditions would come to be called Chen-yen (Japanese *Shingon*).[78] It seems that it was largely at the T'ang imperial court that "Chen-yen and Taoism influenced each other."[79] For instance, in 756 the emperor Hsüan-tsung underwent "a high-level Esoteric consecration (*kuan-ting*; *abhiseka*)" at the hands of the famous *ācārya* Amoghavajra.[80] Yet, as researchers have shown, "During the Six Dynasties, Tantric rituals such as 'consecration' (*abhiseka*) . . . and pseudo-Sanskrit *mantras* were already in use in Taoist circles."[81] Though such forms of "esoteric Buddhism" are now commonly called "tantric," it is clear that these particular traditions – indeed, like Ch'an/Zen – were born within T'ang China, as new translations of Buddhist texts were grasped to give new depth and meaning to ritual traditions that were actually rooted as deeply in Taoism as in earlier Buddhist traditions.

A prime example is the very term "Chen-yen," by which "tantric Buddhism" in East Asia has usually been known. Standard wisdom says that the Chinese term *chen-yen* simply originated as a translation of the hoary old Indian term *mantra*. But that Chinese term has often misleadingly been explained as denoting "true words." In reality, such a literal translation obfuscates the term's meaning, for it suggests little more than that the "esoteric Buddhists" of East Asia considered their tradition's teachings to be "words that are correct in their meaning." In actuality, no thoughtful person can find much real meaning in such ideas, for we all know that everyone regards his/her own beliefs to be "true." Such literal translations of the term *chen-yen* obscure not only the nature of the beliefs and practices of "esoteric Buddhism," but also the fact that they were developed under Taoist influence.

Even in India and Tibet, the term *mantra* never simply denoted "words that are correct in their meaning." Rather, it always pertained to *a set of personal practices by which a practitioner transforms his or her fundamental reality through a specific, efficacious vocalization.* Such transformational vocalizations are, not coincidentally, quite comparable to the vocalizations of the primordial salvific "Word" advocated by the early Ling-pao Taoists of the late fourth century. Just as certain Shang-ch'ing visualizational meditations were recast as "tantric" practices centuries later, as noted above, so also certain fundamental Ling-pao vocalizational rituals were absorbed into the practices of certain Six Dynasty Buddhists. And, since the Taoist liturgies practiced in the days of T'ang Hsüan-tsung – when the first "tantric" *ācāryas* began teaching Chinese disciples – were inherited from earlier Ling-pao traditions, it is quite noteworthy that "[by] the fifth century, in rituals of the Ling-pao school, living Taoist priests themselves are called "real men," *chen-jen*.[82] That is, when T'ang "esoteric Buddhists," such as I-hsing, were forming what the later Shingon Buddhists of Japan would regard as their "school," the *name* that they gave their new tradition employed the same highly resonant term that Taoists have embraced from the time of *Chuang-tzu* to the men and women of today's Ch'üan-chen Taoism – the term *chen*.

These profound links between Taoism and the "tantric" traditions of East Asia are not coincidental, and they are not merely of historical interest. Rather, they demonstrate a profound and ongoing interaction between the two traditions, by which characteristic practices and teachings of each were enriched. Both in Taoist practices of self-transformation, and in those found in tantric traditions, the spiritual life is envisioned primarily as a transformation of one's personal experiential existence through practices that involve (re)unification with the subtle forces, structures, and energies that lie beyond the more familiar range of shared personal experience. In both traditions, those practices are necessarily activities that only the individual can undertake, though in doing so he or she is intrisically working to engage him- or herself more fully with a set of invisible realities that connect the individual with all of reality. In both, any person may engage in such practices, and appropriate teachings are offered for anyone who is willing and able to learn them. Yet, each tradition holds that not all such practices are proper for *all* people, since many individuals simply do not have the proper awareness, or the proper self-discipline, to undertake such practices in safety. Hence, in both traditions, the process of self-transformation is offered for any and all persons who have a seriousness of purpose; a trust in the teachings of those who have real knowledge of all the factors involved; and enough respect for others – and for the realities of life, seen and unseen – to guard those who are not properly attuned from the possible perils of improper ritual action.

In part for these reasons, the Taoist tradition, from its earliest periods, has held a special place for men and women who have mastered such processes, people who can attune their own being to what some today call "transcendent" dimensions of reality. In Taoism, those transcendent dimensions of reality are frequently designated *chen*, "Reality"; individuals who have fully integrated their own being with "Reality" are called *chen-jen*, "Realized Persons"; and the process by which such integration is effected is called *hsiu-chen*, "cultivating Reality."

In medieval times, both China's Taoists and the "esoteric" Buddhists of China and Japan taught something that modern minds – ingrained with secularistic assumptions going back to the "Enlightenment" – have agreed to deem unworthy of serious consideration. That is, they taught (1) that individuals who have fully "realized" themselves customarily develop powers and abilities that ordinary people do not have, and (2) that those powers can be turned to public benefit, most often through ritual action. In both China and Japan, from the sixth century onward, such "masters" were frequently brought to the imperial court to perform ritual acts that were widely believed to bring benefits to the whole empire.[83]

In Taoism, such rites were called *chai*, some of which were powerful enough to bring even the dead into a newly sanctified condition.[84] Of much greater important to rulers, however, was "the Ceremony of the Golden Register" (*chin-lu chai*), designed – among other things – to engender stability and prosperity in the empire. All Chinese rulers from the empress Wu to T'ang Hsüan-tsung sponsored the performance of *chin-lu chai*, which were structured in accordance with the "Writs of Reality" (*chen-wen*) of the Ling-pao tradition.[85] In fact, "performance of *chai* rituals and the recitation of scriptures for the benefit of the chief of state is recommended in the *Ling-pao Book of Salvation*," i.e., the *Tu-jen ching*, the primary Ling-pao scripture.[86]

Here we see another example of the altruistic values that have been an unnoticed part of the holistic Taoist worldview from the *Tao te ching* to T'ang times, when emperors even established wildlife refuges at the behest of Taoist leaders.[87] In the traditions of Taoism, the "cultivation of reality" was *never* a selfish pursuit. Rather, it was focused in *a specialized set of practices* by which certain *dedicated practitioners* would endeavor *to effect a full engagement with life's most sublime unseen forces*, in such a way as *to extend the resulting benefits to others around them*.

Yet, as we have seen above, as Taoism came increasingly "under siege" following the conquest of the north in 1126, its practitioners slowly became socially, politically, and ideologically marginalized, and they readjusted their terminology and institutions to come to terms with that marginalization. Some, of course, continued to embrace the hitherto noble and honored ideal of serving society by fulfilling priestly functions, even if they now had to sacrifice their honor in the eyes of members of an increasingly condescending elite. They increasingly turned outward to the general populace to secure their social and economic base, rather than upward to the social and cultural elite, as they had done for centuries. In so doing, the representatives of Taoism maintained their ideals and their traditions, albeit at the cost of accommodating themselves to a political monopoly of religious authority. Just as many Confucians came to terms with such changes by speaking and writing only in terms of the state-imposed Ch'eng/Chu orthodoxy, many Taoists reshaped their rich heritage into the only allowable institutional molds. Especially in the south, Taoist ideals and traditions were maintained by Cheng-i *tao-shih*, who maintained the traditional role of the

Taoist priest, i.e., of bridging the gap between practitioners who have mastered life's invisible forces and those who do not themselves engage in such practices.

In the north, however, Taoists survived mainly by *relinquishing* efforts to fulfill their traditions' ideals by means of *priestly* institutions, and began developing *new* institutions – most often, *monastic* institutions. To maintain their government's endorsement as the "leaders" of Taoism under the suspicious Mongols and authoritarian Ming emperors, the Cheng-i Taoists, who were never monastic, distanced themselves from models of the Taoist life that tended to appeal to the upper classes of Chinese society – to officials, literati, and the gentry class more broadly. By marginalizing themselves from the literati classes, Cheng-i Taoists also marginalized themselves from many of the cultivational models of personal practice that Taoists of earlier periods had cherished, as well as from the Ch'üan-chen monasteries where men and women continued to keep those models of personal practice alive.

In addition, some of the earlier Taoist models of self-cultivation were simply appropriated by members of the "Neo-Confucian establishment" and tweaked to pass muster as "Confucian." Because of the intolerant rhetoric of Chu Hsi and his followers, late imperial Confucians often felt compelled to denounce meditational practices as heretical. Hence, Confucians who found value in such practices often relabelled their own practices in terms that made them appear to be quite distinguishable from Buddhist or Taoist practices. For instance, Neo-Confucian meditation was generally styled "quiet-sitting" (*ching-tso*), to hide the fact that it was little more than a variation on the "sitting Zen" (*tso-ch'an*, Japanese *zazen*) fundamental to Ch'an/Zen Buddhism.[88] Nonetheless, it is notable here that the eleventh-century Confucian theorist Chou Tun-i advocated "quiet-sitting" as an aid to centering the self: his goal was to quiet the mind and re-establish a condition of "sincerity" by controlling the thoughts, emotions, and intentions which impede the pure functioning of the "original mind." Here we see a re-expression of what we might call a generic Chinese model of self-cultivation, which blends a few Buddhist and Confucian ideas with a Taoist model of self-cultivation that had roots going back to the *Nei-yeh* itself. Intellectuals of Ming times further continued the "Confucianization" of Taoist models of personal transformation.[89]

By accentuating terms that would resonate as Confucian – such as *hsing*, "inner nature," to which Mencius, like the T'ang Confucian Li Ao, had said one should "return" – instead of terms that were more clearly identifiable as Taoist, late imperial Confucians sometimes managed to be quite Taoist indeed without being *perceived* to be Taoist.[90]

Meanwhile, as we saw in Chapter 3, such Taoist models of self-cultivation remained central to the Ching-ming ("Pure Illumination") and Lung-men ("Dragon Gate") traditions in late imperial China, both of which were ignored in nearly all twentieth-century scholarship. In their Lung-men reincarnation, Taoist traditions of self-cultivation endure today, a living vestige of the more ecumenical Taoism of medieval times. The living Lung-men tradition preserves elements of a model for practicing self-cultivation that flourished among Taoist literati of earlier centuries, a model that traces back ultimately to classical times. Scholars still have much research to do before we will have a clear understanding of the nature and significance of how today's Taoists understand their personal practices, and the relationship of those practices to their liturgical activities, which remain largely unexplored.

What can be said here in conclusion is that vestiges of nearly every Taoist idea and practice ever attested in China endure in the minds and lives of someone in East Asia today. Many such people, of course, continue to self-identify as Taoist, both in China and throughout the diaspora. Others, meanwhile, are people who identify themselves as Confucians, or as Buddhists, or even as followers of Shintō.[91]

CONCLUSION

At the juncture in history when Taoism came within range of the Western gaze, the gazers' own interpretive dynamics were constituted in such a way that recognizing Taoism's teachings on *Taoist terms* was virtually precluded. Many twentieth-century presentations, and critiques, of Taoism (as indeed of many other traditions) colonialistically ignored the realities indigenous to the tradition, and imposed on it interpretive schemas that devalued it by exalting the assumptions and values of the alien interpreter, confirming the interpreter's moral superiority and thus his right, and moral duty, to conclude that "they are wrong" and "we are right," or "they are stupid" and "we are wise." For example, on the basis of simplistic modernist dichotomies – abetted by centuries of disdain from Ch'eng/Chu Confucians – any Taoist who engaged in or advocated "self-cultivation" was often explained as an egocentric "escapist" who failed to embrace "our" noble principles affirming morality, society, and government.

For instance, at the peak of the "modern" era, in 1948, an influential historian, Etienne Balazs, authored a widely read article of a deeply tendentious nature entitled "Nihilistic Revolt or Mystical Escapism." It concerned certain third-century intellectuals whom Balazs, like some other twentieth-century sinologues, chose to label "Taoist" – though there is no reason to think that the men themselves, or their contemporaries, or later centuries of Taoists ever regarded them as such. Such niceties were of little concern to Balazs, who wrote as follows about those "Taoist" nihilists:

> The Taoist intellectuals were inclined to oscillate between the two extremes of affirming man's value as an individual

> and denying his value as a member of society; but they came to reject utterly the Confucian doctrine of family with all that it implied of social duties, ethical beliefs, and decorous behavior, and by this rejection brought upon themselves the hatred of all right-minded people and persecution at the hands of the authorities.[1]

But hardly a single word of Balazs's characterization of Taoists, or their place in the socio-political matrix of Chinese civilization, truly corresponds to any social or historical reality. In reality, the Taoists of China, premodern and modern, suffered little "hatred" from anyone at all, much less "persecution at the hands of the authorities" – at least not before the excesses of the Maoist "Cultural Revoution." And even the "Neo-Confucian" ideologue Chu Hsi – whose values and principles shaped "Confucian doctrine" throughout modern times – himself composed a commentary to the Taoist alchemical text called the *Ts'an-t'ung ch'i*.[2] Like the many self-affirmed Taoists who valued just such texts over the centuries – and *practiced* in accord with them – Chu Hsi did not thereby "reject utterly" the affirmation of "social duties, ethical beliefs, and decorous behavior."

A clear look at the true facts of history reveals that the Taoists of the third century were actually, like Taoists of every other period, *not* people who denied "man's value as a member of society." To the contrary, the Taoists of that period were busy composing texts – such as the *180 Precepts of Lord Lao* – that explained why unethical behaviors were contrary to the Tao; specified those behaviors in painstaking detail; and articulated very particular ethical injunctions which, if followed, would raise the standards for practicing Taoists well *above* those of the surrounding society. For instance, the *T'ai-p'ing ching*'s explicit injunction against common social practices such as female infanticide make it quite clear that, if anyone in third-century China *did* "reject utterly the Confucian doctrine of family with all that it implied of social duties, ethical beliefs, and decorous behavior," it was certainly *not* "the Taoists."[3]

Even setting aside the unconscionable excesses of Balazs's diatribe – not to mention his ignorance of what *Taoists* over the centuries actually did with their lives, or what the "authorities" of premodern

China thought or did in regard to them – one can see that his position was based on some very simplistic, though still very common, assumptions. For instance, he assumed that "what the Taoists taught" was – as though by definition – simply a wholesale contradiction of whatever the *Confucians* taught. Since, from the earliest days of "sinology," Westerners learned from our Confucian friends that it is the Confucians, *not* followers of any other Chinese value-system of past or present, who authentically champion "man's value as a member of human society," it logically seemed to follow that "the Taoists" can only be explained as people who *deny* man's value as a member of human society – a position that would of course be execrable in the eyes of "all right-minded people."

The fallacy of such beliefs is clear even from a fair-minded assessment of the facts of Confucianism itself. From the earliest days, Confucians generally insisted that fulfilling one's role in society was necessarily grounded in a *moral cultivation* of *oneself*. In the late twentieth century, some scholars – including leading Confucian spokesmen such as Tu Weiming – began insisting that the Confucian program of "self-cultivation" was as much a "religious" or "spiritual" endeavor as it was a moral one. And if that reassessment of how we understand the nature of the Confucian life is justified, we are also justified in asking whether "self-cultivation" – whether in Confucian *or* Taoist terms – ever truly constituted a derogation from – much less a "rejection" of – people's necessary and appropriate "social duties."

Based on the facts, one must conclude that the cultivation of a "flood-like *ch'i*" advocated by contributors to the *Nei-yeh* was in fact *quite* compatible with "social duties" and "ethical beliefs," for *that very practice* was commended by the Confucian "ethical philosopher" Mencius – one of the prime holy saints within Chu Hsi's "transmission of the Tao." In addition, Mencius maintained that doing what is right is ultimately something of which we gain knowledge *not* simply from what "society" teaches us, but ultimately from within our own heart/mind (*hsin*) – the original condition of which was grounded in what "Heaven" has "ordained" (*ming*) for every person. If such is true of a *Confucian* who cultivates his "heart/mind" and "vital energy," then it must logically also be equally true of the *Taoist* who does so. In other words, the notion that Taoists "came to reject utterly the Confucian doctrine . . . with all that it implied of social duties, ethical beliefs, and decorous behavior" is utterly false, and even hinders our appreciation of the full dimensions of Confucianism.

What Taoists rejected was *not* the value of society, *nor* the idea that a person indeed has "social duties." They simply rejected the value of beliefs and practices that are not truly in accord with *the ultimate nature* of reality. In other words, Taoists rejected social beliefs and practices that were based upon non-holistic premises. For instance, though many Confucians, throughout history, did focus on personal self-transformation, others believed that the Confucian life is more properly aimed at a rectification of government, on the assumption that a good society cannot flourish unless those in power act on the basis of proper values. Yet, as we have seen, Taoists of all periods not only *shared* those assumptions, but actually rendered assistance and advice to rulers from age to age, and were hailed for doing so not only by those rulers, but also by centuries of scholars and public officials. Indeed, until the changes that overtook Chinese society after the Mongol conquest, Confucians and Taoists typically *agreed* that Confucians and Taoists were generally of the same mind on basic issues: the need for personal self-cultivation, the need for living a moral life, and the need for government and society to be transformed by the effects of people who fulfill the ideals of moral/spiritual self-cultivation.

As we have seen, the teachings on self-cultivation embedded in the *Nei-yeh* and *Tao te ching* did not, as long assumed, die out over time, nor were they replaced by "grotesque superstitions." Rather, classical ideals continued to shape and define the ideals and practices of later Taoists, even as those Taoists reconceived and re-expressed those ideals in accord with their changing social, cultural, and political conditions.

In Taoism, the ideals of self-transformation in accord with life's deeper realities became a basis not simply for political programs or educational systems, but also for priests (and at times priestesses) who could, by means of ritual action, simultaneously correct the problems of the local community, bolster the efficacy of the government, and point everyone toward a deeper understanding of the realities that truly inform our lives. Confucians *also* had *their* priests, who conducted *their* liturgies at *their* temples. But, unlike Taoists, few Confucians seem to have believed that the proper moral and social ideals could be implemented through liturgical activity, despite Confucius's own deep love for ritual, and his expressed belief that a person who properly conducts certain liturgies can easily bring order to the world.

Despite common misconceptions, Taoism was never in any real sense the opposite of Confucianism. Rather, it was a different set of models for pursuing values that were, to a large extent, common to both. Taoists seldom sought to articulate their models, or their underlying values, by constructing systematic conceptual structures. Yet most segments of the tradition, from classical times to the present, do seem to share certain perceptible concerns and assumptions. On the basis of our ability to perceive those perspectives in the data available to us today, one might characterize the Taoist approach to life as consisting of *a holistic worldview* and an ethos centered upon *holistic transformation* of self, society, and "all the concentric spheres of the organic Chinese universe, which contained nature as well as society," through a variety of interrelated *moral activities and religious practices*.[4]

A good example of those holistic perspectives is found in the *Huai-nan-tzu*, composed under the leadership of Liu An, prince/king of Huai-nan. The *Huai-nan-tzu* is "Taoist," in several strict senses. For instance, like the *Tao te ching* and the *Chuang-tzu*, it is preserved in the *Tao-tsang*, alongside all manner of other texts in which Taoists found inspiration. But the importance of the *Huai-nan-tzu* for understanding Taoism has seldom been appreciated, because the classicist leanings of the early Western sinologues led them to identify "the Taoist classics" on terms that excluded the *Huai-nan-tzu*, despite both its antiquity and its coherence with many elements of *Lao-tzu* – not to mention its incorporation, and further development, of the entire self-cultivational program of the *Nei-yeh*. When, for instance, James Legge translated "the Taoist classics" – thereby teaching "the West" how to identify the Taoist volumes that deserve recognition among "the Great Books of the East" – he did *not* translate, or even really mention, the *Huai-nan-tzu*. The importance of these facts for how "the West" came to understand "Taoism" is immense, for several reasons:

1 the *Huai-nan-tzu* is, like the *Tao te ching* and *Chuang-tzu*, quite "philosophical" in tone, content, and intent;

2 it was composed by men of high education, social eminence, and direct political involvement at the highest levels; and
3 it showed how *self-cultivation* and *correct perception of cosmic realities* could contribute directly to a healthy redirectioning of *the Chinese political order*.

If Legge's "native informants" had been *Taoist* scholars of social prominence and political sophistication – Taoist literati such as Chiang Yü-p'u (1756–1819) or Min I-te (1758–1836) – they might well have counselled him to include the *Huai-nan-tzu* among "the Taoist classics." Had early Western sinologues been guided by Chinese literati from a Taoist background, or at least knew the real history of Taoism, nearly everything said about "Taoism" in the twentieth century would have been very different.

The more aristocratic forms of Taoism that emerged in the Six Dynasties – and became the heart and soul of Taoism in T'ang times – were reflections of the fact that *those who liked to understand their lives in "Taoist" terms* liked to believe that *the individual can, through some sort of cultivational practices, integrate his or her life directly and meaningfully into the deeper realities in which all life is grounded.* That belief resonates with underlying assumptions of the *Tao te ching*, the *Huai-nan-tzu*, and even the *T'ai-p'ing ching*. Even the most influential proponent of *liturgical* activity in the history of Taoism – Lu Hsiu-ching – honored the *Huai-nan-tzu* as one of his tradition's classics. Like Lu, the many other aristocrats, and members of the later "gentry," who shaped the evolution of Taoism through the centuries believed that holistic self-cultivation would benefit self and others simultaneously, as the *Tao te ching* clearly taught.[5]

I am arguing here that there is a conspicuous emphasis on that belief within most phases and segments of Taoism. It did not, to the best of our current historical knowledge, originate specifically among aristocrats. It would seem that we can trace *some* of its roots back to Han-dynasty thinkers who based their ideas on premises that royal diviners of Shang and Chou times followed when advising their sovereign patrons. And certainly by the early third century BCE, the *Tao te ching* had been reworked with such ideas to serve as advice for rulers. Yet, such ideas can also be traced back to the anonymous community that produced the *Nei-yeh*, which cannot easily be categorized as representing any particular social class, and certainly had little interest in political thought. Yet, as the *Huai-nan-tzu* demonstrates quite conclusively, some leading members of the social and political leadership of early Han China embraced the concept that *cultivational participation in life's subtle structures and processes* can *solidify the state* and *benefit society as well as the individual practitioner*. That holistic concept remained a basic Taoist principle, from the Han dynasty to late imperial times.

The fact that Chinese *emperors* continued to find inspiration in the holistic vectors of Taoism is underscored by the early Sung emperors' vision of what the Chinese political order is, and must be, about. Their vision was expressed in the ancient term *t'ai-p'ing*, a term that had once encapsulated the holistic perspectives of members of the Han imperial court, where the *T'ai-p'ing ching* first emerged. The political dimensions of Taoism after T'ang times have yet to be fully recognized, in part because modern Confucians tendentiously portrayed the Chinese world from the tenth century onward as the world in which Ch'eng/Chu intellectuals dominated the public realm. For a generation, scholars have noted that the T'ang emperors were interested in Taoism and claimed descent from "Lao-tzu" himself. But the Sung emperors, who claimed no descent from Lao-tzu, of course – utilized the classical idea of *T'ai-p'ing* to express their own beliefs about what the Chinese empire should be about: *a harmonious integration of all dimensions of existence* – seen and unseen, public and private, religious and secular, civilian and military, male and female, humans and transcendent beings (*hsien*) alike.[6] That vision is reflected in various elements of Sung society and literature, and contributed to the success of later Taoists in proving to the authorities of Yüan and Ming times that Taoism was indeed a noble and respectable element of "the Three Teachings."

These facts of Chinese history, too, remained unknown to Western sinology until the 1990s, but they help us correct our picture of "what Taoism is about." To begin explaining Taoism as it truly was, in terms of the social and historical facts of Chinese history and culture, we need to learn to see that the holistic vision of Sung T'ai-tsung goes back through the historical realities of the Taoist literati of T'ang times, through the teachings of Six Dynasites aristocrats, through the cosmic/political/individual integrations of the *Huai-nan-tzu* and the *T'ai-p'ing ching*, and ultimately back to the *Tao te ching*. Such is the enduring heritage of Taoism.

NOTES

FOREWORD

1 Concerning the often contradictory "accomplishments" of the Tao in Western tradition, see especially Clarke (2000) and the critical symposium on Clarke's book in *Religious Studies Review* 28 (2002): 303–38.

PREFACE

1 See for instance Welch and Seidel 1979, 14–15.

1 UNDERSTANDING TAOISM

1 It was necessary for moderns to lie to themselves about Taoism before they could take it seriously. For many, it was necessary to project a dichotomization of "good Taoism" – narcissistically constructed to reflect modern secular individualism – from "bad Taoism" – caricatured in the same terms used to dismiss Catholicism and any other traditional religion. (For a very clear analysis of how "Taoism" was thus perverted in the writings of such twentieth-century writers as Witter Bynner and Stephen Mitchell, see Bradbury 1992.) And to make the good "Taoism" palatable to moderns, it was necessary to say that it had no specific teachings or practices that might be unpalatable to modern tastes: as "a Taoist," all a person has to do to be good is "to be one with Nature," or believe some such comparable tenet of contrarian modernism. In reality, of course, *no Taoist in recorded history* ever contended that being Taoist is – primarily, or even partially – about "being one with Nature." In other words, the reality of Taoism is the inverse of the modern cultural construct masquerading under that name.

2 On the pedagogical issues addressed here, see further Kirkland 1998a and 2004a.

3 Kohn 2001, 5–6.

4 Skar 2000, 414.

5 Goossaert and Katz 2001, 93.
6 The 1500-odd texts in the *Tao-tsang* – the primary collection of Taoist literature – are commonly identified by reference to two modern concordances, though the numbering in the two systems varies. For simplicity, I shall follow the tradition of citing all writings from the *Tao-tsang* according to the "Harvard-Yenching" numbering system, i.e., with the abbreviation HY. Scholars can now find a thorough cross-referencing of the variant numbering systems in Komjathy 2002.
7 See Berling 1979, 1980, 1993.
8 Cf. Kohn 2001, 93–8.
9 See Kohn 1997b.
10 See Kirkland 2002b.
11 See Kirkland 1996a.
12 Faure 1993, 270.
13 As I shall explain below, it is now apparent that certain things that have been said by Lung-men Taoists about their subtradition – e.g., that its "lineage" goes back to the Ch'üan-chen leader Ch'iu Ch'ang-ch'un, who met Jenghiz Khan – are not "facts," any more than are the claims of modern Zen masters to be part of a "lineage" that goes back to Bodhidharma and ultimately to "the historical Buddha." It was in reaction to the point that Chan's lineage is *not* "a fact" that Faure argued that "Chan is not primarily a concrete social reality," but rather a set of "(re)presentations" by which "a Chan adherent" would express a "performative choice, a strategical move that contributed to question or reinforce traditional classifications" (Faure 1993, 270–1). Faure's ideological position leads him to devalue scholars who find substance in Chan "tradition," such as Yanagida Seizan, and to project upon them the same errors that Daisetsu Suzuki allegedly committed, principally a clandestine effort to present faith-positions as though they were factual. But in his effort to discredit Suzuki and de-reify "Chan," Faure seems vulnerable to the reply that the "concrete social reality" of Chan Buddhism or Lung-men Taoism can be quite readily established on *other* terms. The fact that many twentieth-century advocates of Zen (including some scholars, such as Suzuki) sold modern minds a falsely reified notion of Zen "tradition" does *not* logically preclude a correct understanding of Chan, or of Taoism, as "a social reality": our understanding of such traditions need not be framed in terms of any non-factual elements that may lurk evilly inside traditional representations. In other words, even if we dismiss, for instance, the traditional idea that the current pope stands as today's representative of Christ, the fact that such ideas are "ahistorical" does not logically lead to the conclusion that the Catholic Church or its teachings are "ahistorical." On many levels, that church has quite demonstrably been "a concrete social reality," and so has "Taoism," even if our definition of such terms begins with "the classificatory decisions of people who saw themselves as members of the tradition."

14 The contrary contentions of certain twentieth-century scholars will be addressed below.
15 There may also be individuals in Birmingham and Boston who self-identify as Taoists. But very few of them were born to parents who self-identified as Taoists. Very few of them have ever even spoken with someone who had Taoists among their ancestors. Very few of them are capable of communicating with such a person – virtually all of whom speak Chinese as their native tongue. Very few of them are capable of reading what such people, from age to age, have written to express or explain their beliefs and practices – virtually all such texts are written in Chinese, mostly classical. Very few of them have ever made any personal investment in trying to find out what such people have ever said or done in their practice of Taoism, e.g., by going to live in a long-established community where self-identifying Taoists have practiced together for generations, within their traditional social and cultural setting. To the extent that any individual in Boston or Birmingham meets such criteria, he or she might well be considered "a Taoist." And we may also reasonably extend consideration to individuals who meet some, but not all, such criteria: an Englishman who goes to China, enters a traditional Taoist community, and adjusts his own life to their teachings and practices might arguably be included as "a Taoist," as might a person of Chinese ancestry born in the worldwide diaspora, who may not be fluent in Chinese, and may have been inculcated with cultural traditions that have no connection with Taoism, but who makes efforts to learn the traditions of Taoism that flourished in traditional China, some of which are still flourishing in China today.
16 Scholars of Taoism will see that I am here following one of the arguments put forward by the late Michel Strickmann. For an analysis of his arguments, and my reasons for leaving some of them aside, see Kirkland 1997c.
17 See my entry "Ye Fashan," in Pregadio 2004.
18 A properly critical understanding of "Confucianism" is also beginning to be suggested by some scholars today. See for instance Ebrey 2001.
19 See Kirkland 1997c.

2 THE CLASSICAL LEGACY

1 See, e.g., Graham 1989, 33–53; and Lowe 1992.
2 Kaltenmark 1979, 23.
3 Strickmann 1979, 131–2. On the *Chen-kao*, see Bokenkamp 1996.
4 Strickmann 1979, 174.
5 See Kirkland 1991b.
6 See Stein 1979, 75.
7 See Hsiao 1979, 580–1.
8 See Creel 1974.
9 See, e.g., Yates 1997; and Chang and Feng 1998.

10 It is composed mainly of narratives illustrating "lessons" supposedly found in the *Tao te ching*. But it is distinctly Legalist in tone. Unlike the author of the *Chieh-Lao*, this writer had no respect at all for the ideals of either "the Taoists" or the Confucians. His sole concern was to promulgate Legalist doctrines, and his clear aim in composing the chapter was simply to utilize the standing of a well-known text to gain attention for his ideas. Elements of the *Yü-Lao* are quite close to what we find in Han Fei's other writings, and it is conceivable that Han Fei wrote it himself. Yet there are also some differences, which have led some scholars to surmise that the *Yü-Lao* "was probably written first and included in *Han Fei-tzu* by one of his followers who wanted to bring Legalism back into respectability after the fall of the Ch'in" (Landers 1972, 73).

11 Wang 1965, 240; translation mine. Cf. Liao 1939, 180–1.

12 Wang 1965, 241; translation mine. Cf. Liao 1939, 181.

13 Modern scholarship, Asian and Western alike, has affirmed that the *I ching* originated during the early Chou dynasty, i.e., sometime around 1000 BCE. Thinkers of later ages developed the implications of the *I ching* and built that textual oracle into a storehouse of "wisdom." Until around the sixth century BCE, the *I ching* generally remained the province of diviners – people who worked in the service of rulers and noblemen, and used the oracle to answer their patrons' questions, just as the diviners of the Shang dynasty had done with their "oracle bones." (See Smith 1989; Pines 2002, 86–7, 145–6.) During the Eastern Chou period (i.e., eighth to third centuries BCE) anonymous commentaries to the *I ching* began to appear. Though in Han times they were all incorporated into the text as the *I ching's* "wings," research has revealed that the commentaries were the product not of one continuous tradition, but rather of different traditions. The *Shuo-kua* (and possibly the *Wen-yen* – "Wings" 7 and 8), both of which consist of narrow technical interpretations, might be called the product of a "technical school," possibly confined to the official diviners at the Chou court. Those materials date from no later than the fifth century BCE, and might be as early as the seventh century. The *T'uan-chuan* and *Hsiao-hsiang-chuan* ("Wings" 1, 2, and 4) can be interpreted as the product of a "commentatory school"; they date no later than the fifth century BCE. The *Ta-chuan* ("Wing" 6) seems to derive from thinkers of the fifth to third centuries BCE: it combines the moral idealism of Confucianism with the naturalistic idealism of Taoism. Han-dynasty interpreters added other materials, such as the *Tsa-kua*.

14 In the *Daoism Handbook* chapter "Divination as Taoist Practice," Sakade Yoshinobu explores various divinatory practices associated with elements of Taoism over history. However, he takes pains to emphasize that "divination is a practice that informs and supports Taoism but is not essentially Taoist in itself" (Sakade 2000, 562).

15 Few are aware that the *Tao-tsang* also contains writings about the

I ching from such famous Sung-dynasty "Neo-Confucian philosophers" as Chou Tun-i (HY 157) and even Chu Hsi (HY 998). See Kohn 1990; Despeux 2000b. Even twentieth-century Confucians had to admit that their own "Ch'eng/Chu" tradition – which Chu Hsi claimed to have passed from Confucius to Mencius to Chou Tun-i and on to Chu himself – owed a great deal to cosmological diagrams that were originally acquired from a rather shadowy tenth-century Taoist named Ch'en T'uan. Convinced by historical reports in the "standard history" of the Sung dynasty, Fung Yu-lan (1953, 2: 440) says, "it would appear that the early Sung practioners [*sic*] of the so-called 'numerology' [including Chou Tun-i] all traced their origin back to Ch'en T'uan, who himself, as we know, was a famous exponent of Taoist techniques for acquiring immortality."

16 The fundamental concept of *yin* and *yang* is simply that there are two basic aspects of reality within the world of nature and human activity. Originally, the term *yin* referred to the shady side of a natural landscape, and *yang* referred to the sunny side. At some point, someone decided to extend the meaning of those terms so that they became "shorthand" for everything in life that is comprised of natural counterparts. Such counterparts as wetness and dryness, passivity and activity, femininity and masculinity, can be called "complementary opposites"; i.e., they are totally different and yet naturally complete each other: neither could exist by itself, because each gives both existence and meaning to the other. As a line in the *Tao te ching* notes, concepts such as "highness" are meaningless unless they stand in contrast to "lowness" (Chapter 2; the line is already present in the Guodian text). Similarly, shadiness is meaningless except in contrast to sunniness, wetness is meaningless except in contrast to dryness, and femininity is meaningless except in contrast with masculinity. It is essential to understand, however, that the nature of such forces in *yin–yang* thought is not an antagonistic relationship. It is not a "dualism," an assertion that the world is comprised of forces that are intrinsically separate and hostile, like "truth and falsehood," or "good and evil." In ancient and medieval China, *yin* and *yang* were always understood as existing in harmonious balance. Only in late imperial times did it become common for Chinese writers to attach positive assocations to *yang* and negative associations to *yin*.

17 Sometimes the term is translated as the "Five Phases," "Five Agents," or "Five Elements." *Hsing* literally means "to go," so ultimately the term *wu hsing* means something like the five "processes" or "operations." But it is often difficult to understand *wu hsing* with those verbal connotations, because the five forces were always identified by the very concrete terms "fire," "water," "earth," "metal," and "wood." It is best to think of those concrete elements as metaphors: each of the five forces is a natural force that was identified with a common natural substance in order to convey its properties more clearly.

18 Han thinkers eventually developed a system of correspondences in which everything can be correlated to one of the five fundamental forces: five colors, five tastes, five musical notes, five directions, and so on. These ideas provided a system of categorization through which everything in the universe could be shown to be related to everything else in an orderly and comprehensible manner. These ideas have often been associated with the name of the Confucian thinker Tung Chung-shu (*ca.* 195–115 BCE). But recent research has shown that, while Tung did employ the categories of *yin* and *yang*, he probably had little interest in "five forces" theory. The complex system of correspondences that is usually remembered as the truest expression of Han thought actually developed in the first century BCE.

19 Pertinent analyses include Jensen 1998 and Nylan 2001.

20 The "Neo-Confucian" patriarch Chou Tun-i advocated "quiet-sitting" (*ching-tso*, the Confucian version of *zazen*) as an aid to centering the self: his goal was to quiet the mind and re-establish a condition of "authenticity" by controlling the thoughts, emotions, and intentions which impede the pure functioning of the "original mind." In other words, centuries of Confucians were meditating for the same reasons that Taoists and Buddhists meditated. And some famed Confucian intellectuals – from the orthodox Ch'eng/Chu patriarch Chang Tsai (1020–1077) down to K'ang Yu-wei (1858–1927), the only Confucian ever to be granted full political control of the entire nation – professed to have experienced "enlightenment" just like Buddhists reported. Yet the Confucian scholars who taught Westerners "what Confucians believe" relentlessly suppressed such information.

21 Cf. Kirkland 1996d and 2001a.

22 Kirkland 2001a.

23 Ssu-ma says: "Chuang-tzu was a person of Meng, named Chou. He once was a functionary at Ch'i-yüan in Meng, in the same time period as King Hui of Liang [r. 370–319 BCE] and King Hsüan of Ch'i [r. 319–301 BCE]." (The passage appears in *Shih chi* 63; see Ssu-ma Ch'ien, *Shih chi* 7.2143–5. A sound translation of the passage appears in Hsiao 1979, 276–7. A paraphrase masquerading as a translation of the passage appears in Fung 1953, I: 221.) But there is no way to know where Ssu-ma may have found such data, and no way to verify whether *any* of those data are correct. Heretofore, most scholars have generally just accepted such reports at face value. But no one who thinks critically can do so. "Meng," for instance, is not the name of any known state of pre-Ch'in times. Moreover, many scholars simply read "Ch'i-yüan" not as a place-name, but as a reference to a stand of lacquer trees. According to *later* Han writings, "Meng" had been a dependency of the state of Sung, the most southeasterly of the "middle kingdoms" of the Chou world, just south of Lu. On the basis of that later report, some scholars have constructed elaborate theories explaining "Chuang-tzu's thought" as an expression of the supposed culture of the Sung kingdom, which

had reportedly been founded by scions of the preceding Shang dynasty. (See Watson 1968, 1–2.) But there is no external confirmation that "Meng" was really a locality in Sung, or that "Chuang-tzu" had actually been a person from Meng. As we know from analysis of Ssu-ma's varied reports about where "Lao-tzu" was from, sometimes the historian would report as fact what was actually no more than hearsay or conjecture. In the case of "Lao-tzu," late twentieth-century archaeological finds of the Ma-wang-tui and Guodian texts do connect part of the text that eventually went by that name to localities in the ancient kingdom of Ch'u. So, since Ssu-ma's attribution of "Lao-tzu" to Ch'u is thus somewhat plausible, some might jump to the conclusion that his attribution of "Chuang-tzu" to Meng must be equally plausible. But we cannot be sure that Meng was truly in Sung, and there have been no archaeological finds of texts that pertain to the *Chuang-tzu*.

24 Graham was sure that the later strands within the *Chuang-tzu* dated to the first century of the Han dynasty, and that the latest such strand could be dated to about 130 BCE. Liu Xiaogan rejected that dating, and accepted every bit of the *Chuang-tzu* as the product of late pre-Han period. But Liu argued just the same way for the dating of the *Lao-tzu*, and, examined critically, it looks as though Liu's stance was intended to bolster traditional Chinese positions and preserve the luster of antiquity at any cost. Both those scholars' efforts, though diligent and worthwhile, were efforts to reconstruct the strands within a Han or pre-Han text by performing an autopsy on the 33-chapter text that Kuo Hsiang gave us. The problem with any conclusions based on such an autopsy is that we know that the text that Kuo started with consisted of 52 chapters; that Kuo excised lots and lots of what he found in it; that he did so on the basis of his own personal inclinations, not on any grounds that pertain to chapters' "authenticity"; and that he rewove everything that he preserved on the basis of his own personal views about organization and style.

25 *Chuang-tzu* 33; my translation follows Watson 1968, 373; cf. Graham 1981, 282–3.

26 See especially Yearley 1983; and Kirkland 2001a.

27 Very little has been written on the *Nei-yeh*, in any language. For an overview, see my entry "Neiye" in Pregadio 2004. To date, there are only three complete English translations. Two are by W. Allyn Rickett: Rickett 1965, 151–79; and Rickett 1998, 15–55. While Rickett's scholarship is impeccable, his renderings are sometimes infelicitous. The only other English translations are the extracts in Roth 1996; and the full translation in Roth 1999. See my extensive review of Roth 1999 in Kirkland 2001c.

28 On the nation of Ch'u, see Cook and Major 1999.

29 The scholarly discussions of the provenance of the *Nei-yeh* are summarized in Roth 1999, 23–5. There has not yet been much in the way of textual analysis that suggests clear "layers" in the *Nei-yeh*.

30 Rickett dates the *Nei-yeh* to the late fourth or early third century; Graham to the fourth; and Roth to the mid-fourth. There are reasons to suspect that the Confucian thinker Mencius (d. *ca.* 308 BCE) was acquainted with certain key ideas found in the *Nei-yeh*. Since those ideas seem more integral to the *Nei-yeh*'s universe of discourse than to that of Mencius, it seems more plausible to imagine that Mencius drew upon the *Nei-yeh*'s ideas than to imagine the inverse. If Mencius did indeed know the *Nei-yeh*, its date would certainly be well before the end of the fourth century. In the next section I discuss the textual prehistory of the *Tao te ching*. In sum, the evidence suggests that "the full text" now found in the received text and the Ma-wang-tui text was not yet "set" until sometime during the course of the third century.

31 The *Nei-yeh* is found in chapter 49 of the *Kuan-tzu*; two later, apparently derivative texts – *Hsin-shu* ["The Arts of the Mind/Heart"] *shang* and *hsia* – are found in *Kuan-tzu*, chapters 36–7.

32 One section, entitled "Water and Earth" (*Shui Ti*), maintains for instance that "Man is water," and that "the sages' transformation of the world lay in understanding water" (Rickett 1998, 103, 107). Such perspectives cannot be correlated with any of the supposed "schools" of "classical thought" that the Han taxonomists saw fit to invent. Yet, appended to the Guodian bamboo slips that are at present the oldest known evidence for the *Tao te ching* are slips that scholars now know by their opening line, "The Great One gave birth to Water" (*T'ai-i sheng shui*). (See Henricks 2000, 122–9.) Notably, however, the four chapters of our received text of the *Tao te ching* in which water appears as a primary symbol for the characteristics of Tao, and thus of a sage, are all missing from the Guodian slips. They are chapters 8, 23, 43, and 78. (Cf. Henricks 2000, 18.) So might not the taxonomists of Han times have considered grouping together texts on such themes, and labelling them "the School of Water" (*shui-chia*)? And if they had done so, could not the *Tao te ching* have been placed in that category, especially since it was not entitled "*Tao te ching*" until later times? If they made their taxonomic decisions differently, what would our inherited concept of "classical Taoism" now be?

33 See Knoblock and Riegel 2001; and Sellmann 2002.

34 See Sellmann 2002, 199–205.

35 See the section "Cultivating Reality" in Chapter 5.

36 The enduring importance of *ching*, *ch'i*, and *shen* in the Chinese medical tradition may be seen, for instance, in their inclusion as "basic principles" in Fan 1996, 29–30. Fan's explanations of *ching*, *ch'i*, and *shen* are in close harmony with the explanations seen in the *Nei-yeh* and the derivative sections of the *Huai-nan-tzu*.

37 Roth says, "This inner cultivation practice and the cosmology that surrounds it seems to have been carried over into the mystical practices of the later Taoist religion, although the historical details by which this transmission occurred are so obscure that perhaps they will never be

known for certain" (Roth 1999, 8). In fact, the details of that transmission remain obscure only until one opens the *Tao-tsang* and reads the self-cultivation texts that Taoists composed over the centuries – something that twentieth-century scholars of "classical Taoism" virtually never did. I shall summarize some of the evidence for Taoists' ongoing "transmission" of such ideas and practices below.

38 On the numbering of sections of the *Nei-yeh*, see note 41 below.

39 David Nivison still maintains that "Mencius is not hinting at a mysterious, otherwise unarticulated part of his philosophy here, but seems merely to be drawing on popular medical notions impressionistically to describe what moral vigor feels like" (Nivison 1999, 776). One wonders, however, *how* we can be *sure* that some part of Mencius's philosophy might not have gone "unarticulated," or might have been articulated but remained unrecorded, or may have been recorded but lost as redactors worked with their text. And why should such possible elements of Mencius's thought be dismissed as "mysterious," or reduced to "impressionistic" metaphors? The answer, of course, is that late imperial and modern Confucians are uncomfortable with the idea that Mencius really cultivated his *ch'i* and wanted his disciples to do likewise: to the Confucians whose worldview crystallized around the values of Chu Hsi, all such ideas are revoltingly non-Confucian. Yet, even Nivison now has to admit that the "philosophers" at the Chi-hsia academy included "those who urged a form of quietist self-cultivation philosophy involving 'nourishing *qi*,' and a poetic chapter in the *Guanzi* ('Nei ye' . . .) preserves some of this thinking. Mencius must have been familiar with it" (ibid.). It is just that we "know" that Mencius cannot really have meant what he says in this passage, and we must therefore explain it away.

40 Waley 1934, 49.

41 The text itself has no internal subdivisions, and some scholars have divided it into fifteen, eighteen, or twenty-two sections. Roth divides it into twenty-six, and my citations will follow his numbering system.

42 Roth 1996, 126. It should be clearly noted that there is no trace in the *Nei-yeh* of the much later Chinese idea that *ching* ought to be identified with some sexual force or substance. It should also be noted that such later ideas are fundamentally non-Taoist, as explained in Kirkland 1994a.

43 Translation mine; cf. Rickett 1965, 158; Rickett 1998, 39; Roth 1999, 46. The last lines are clearly parallel in structure, forcing us to think carefully about its referents.

44 One thinks most readily of chapters 1 and 25 of the *Tao te ching*, and of the opening chapter of the *Huai-nan-tzu*. The cosmogonic chapters of the *Tao te ching* are examined in Girardot 1977.

45 Chad Hansen has argued persuasively that the common belief that the more familiar Taoist texts present "the Tao" as a Parmenidean "unchanging, abstract one behind the many" is deeply mistaken, and

explains the mistake as having originated among the Neo-Confucians. See Hansen 1992, 27.

46 E.g., Graham 1989, 104. Such assertions are rooted in the nineteenth-century assumption that "religion" is primitive, "philosophy" is sophisticated, and in the "progress" of history Man gradually learned that unseen beings do not really exist. Such problems are found in the writings not only of Western heirs of "the Enlightenment" but also in those of its Chinese heirs; particularly from the time of Mao on, Chinese scholars have blended Marx's dismissal of religion with that which Confucians have falsely attributed to Confucius himself, and have struggled to invalidate "idealistic" teachings. A specific problem here is a widespread misuse of the term "shamanism" for any kind of "popular" religious activity in which humans interact directly with unseen personal beings; see Davis 2001, 1–3. Taoists of later periods certainly did, at times, interact with unseen personal beings, but by that token Krishna in his chariot or Moses on his mountaintop would have to be explained as having "shamanic origin." In reality, true shamanism is a specialized system whereby a highly trained person establishes a relationship with (but is never "possessed" by) an other-than-human personal being (who has will and agency, if not indeed consciousness) in order to resolve a trauma; Apache culture preserves elements of shamanism, though that of their Navajo cousins does not. In the opening section of the *Nei-yeh*, the structure of the final lines excludes any idea that the "spiritual beings" themselves "enter" the person who comes to be characterizable as "sagely." Rather, theirs is a universal force that is not personal – it has no will, consciousness, or agency – and yet is the source of "life," including the life of grain (which our worldview can easily enough comprehend) and the life of stars (which our worldview cannot). I contend that we must do our best to eke out the worldview of those who composed such texts, guided by the strict principles of exegesis, using philology to tell us what each line intends to say; and I assume that what we learn in that manner will be different from what we think ourselves, as well as different from what we learn when we read *Chuang-tzu* or the *Tao te ching*.

47 That is, they have sought and "found" in such texts references to a universal transcendent, which is, they claim, necessarily the same for all writers from all ages and cultures: it is a transcendent "Reality" to which one gains access by meditating in a seated posture until one develops a "mystical gnosis" qualitatively distinct from normal experience. Such is the thrust of Roth 1999, as of various twentieth-century interpreters of the *Tao te ching*. One wonders whether Mencius was practicing yoga *strictu sensu*, or whether he perhaps failed to attain a "pure consciousness event" because he was foolishly trying to "cultivate his flood-like *ch'i*" while standing erect or lying recumbent. Cf. Kirkland 2001c.

48 See, e.g., Munro 1969, 185–93.

49 Scholars who read classical texts often find that, when a line contains the word *te* ("virtue"), the commentator says, *te te yeh*, *te* (virtue) is *te* (acquisitional)." Since most scholars have been trained to read Chinese texts on Confucian terms, that frequent refrain is utterly nonsensical, and is generally explained away as an illustration of how the word *te* ("virtue") is to be pronounced. The problem with that explanation is that any man, woman, or child of any era who has any basic reading ability already knows how to pronounce the word *te*. There are no other pronunciations of the character, and there is no context in which a mispronunciation could therefore happen, much less cause the reader to fail to grasp the writer's meaning. Rather, the comment *te te yeh* really *says* something about the *meaning* of the term *te* ("virtue"), but says it within a universe of discourse that was nearly extinct in the twentieth-century. That universe of discourse cannot be reconstructed by a scholar today simply on the basis of passages in standard Chinese dictionaries, for those dictionaries were compiled by lexicographers whose corpus of textual knowledge was primarily Confucian, or at least "non-Taoist literati materials" – poetry, histories, etc. No such dictionary explains the meaning of any term by citing the various senses in which it is used throughout the range of important *Taoist* texts, so twentieth-century scholars neither understood Taoist uses of such terms, nor were even taught to consider looking in the *T'ai-p'ing ching*, the *Hsi-sheng ching*, or the *Wu-chen p'ien* to find out what a given term meant to various kinds of Taoists in different periods. Here is a point at which we see the hitherto unacknowledged anti-Taoist bias of twentieth-century sinology in general, and one method of eliminating it: read *Taoist* texts, and use *them* – *not* what we all learned from traditional Chinese scholars of the late imperial and modern periods – to guide us in our efforts to understand and explain the data of Taoism.

50 Though I use both pronouns here, it is important to beware of assuming that any text or thinker of ancient China taught ideas that would, at that time, have necessarily been considered applicable to women's lives as well as to men's. In the case of Confucius, for instance, that assumption would be highly unwarranted. In the case of Taoist texts, however, the situation is much more ambiguous. Since there is little evidence as to the intended audience of the *Nei-yeh*, and since it is difficult to see anything in its teachings that could readily be construed as gender-specific, I shall write as though the practitioner of its teachings could theoretically be either male or female. One should bear in mind, however, that there is little evidence that anyone in ancient China ever gave thought to these issues.

51 The term *hsin* occurs some twenty-five times in the brief text, compared to seventeen uses of the term *ch'i* and twelve uses of the term *ching*.

52 Some scholars, like Roth, believe that they see here a reference to meditational practices very similar to Indian yoga, just as scholars of earlier generations, like Arthur Waley, claimed to find them in the *Tao te*

ching. I, however, find no evidence in the text that one is supposed to sit down in a certain way, at certain times, and engage in yogic meditation. Rather, it seems to suggest a constant process of self-control that is, I believe, something that one is supposed to be doing *while* one otherwise engages in one's regular life-activities. As far as I can see, the *Nei-yeh*'s model is more comparable to the early Buddhist model of constant "mindfulness," and to Dōgen's model of Zen meditation: it is not that one must learn to "practice meditation" *instead of* working, but rather that one should learn to practice meditation *while* one is working. The Zen mind *cannot* be said to be a state of consciousness that one can attain *only* during specific moments, when one is sitting in a certain position. If that were true, getting up to sweep, to peel vegetables, or to engage in any other actions would seem to require *cessation* of one's essential spiritual "practice." The spiritual ideal in such traditions is to engage oneself in the practice of proper "mindfulness," "prayerfulness," or "meditation" all *throughout* one's day, not in moments that one *takes out of* one's day. If the composers of the *Nei-yeh* believed that the practitioner actually needs to go and sit down in order to breathe correctly, they somehow utterly failed to say so, in any passage of the text.

53 Translation mine. Cf. Rickett 1965, 159; Rickett 1998, 41; Roth 1999, 52.

54 The terms *ching* and *shen* are both used in the *Tao te ching*, but never together, and never clearly referring to spiritual forces or to processes within a person. *Ching* appears only in *Tao te ching* 21. *Shen* is used in chapter 39 to refer to spiritual beings; in chapter 29 as a modifier of *t'ien-hsia* ("the world"); and in chapters 6 and 60 – where it is usually understood as referring to spiritual beings, but might conceivably refer to spiritual forces within a person. In the "inner chapters" of the *Chuang-tzu*, the term *ching* appears but twice. It appears much more frequently (thirty times) in the "outer" and "mixed" chapters, where the compound term *ching-shen* appears eight times.

55 Harold Roth (private communication) has noted that the "Syncretist" fifteenth chapter of the *Chuang-tzu* contains ideas akin to those found in the *Nei-yeh*.

56 A religious comparison may be in order here. In many religious contexts (e.g., in Shintō), people engage in ritual worship in the devout expectation that a certain divinity will approach the place of worship and stay for the period of worship. In other contexts (e.g., in Christianity and Judaism), believers generally assume that God is always present in some meaningful sense. In a Christian cathedral, God is never truly absent: worship does not cause God to come hither from some other place, and the conclusion of worship is not experienced as God leaving to go elsewhere. The former scenario is reminiscent of the spiritual practices described in the *Nei-yeh*, while the latter is more reminiscent of the worldview envisaged in the *Tao te ching* and the *Chuang-tzu*.

57 Rickett 1965, 155.

58 *Pace* Graham, who issues the unsubstantiated assertion that the *Nei-yeh* is "as usual addressed primarily to the ruler" (Graham 1989, 104). There is only a single passage in the entire text of the *Nei-yeh* that even marginally suggests a political framework:

> To transform without altering the *ch'i*,
> To change without altering the awareness,
> Only the gentleman (*chün-tzu*) who clings to oneness is able to do this!
> If one can cling to oneness and not lose it, one can master (*chün*) the myriad things.
> The gentleman acts on things; he is not acted on by things.
> From the orderliness of having attained oneness
> He has a well-governed heart/mind within himself.
> (Consequently,) well-governed words issue from his mouth,
> And well-governed activity is extended to others.
> In this way, he governs the world.
> When a single word is obtained, the world submits;
> When a single word is fixed, the world heeds.
> This is what is called "public rightness" (*kung*).

(Translation mine; cf. Rickett 1965, 161; Rickett 1998, 44; Roth 1999, 62.) Note, however, that this passage does *not* assume that the reader is already a ruler. Rather than assuming that the reader has been born into the position of ruler, or has somehow maneuvered himself into political power, it teaches that a highly adept practitioner can, through meditation, achieve the ability to exert influence over the world. There seems to be no other passage in the text that assumes any political interest on the part of the reader at all, and one has to stretch the meaning even of this one passage to understand it as "political."

59 On the commonalities in the use of the term *ch'i* in the two texts, see Rickett 1965, 155–6.

60 Translation from Rickett 1998, 40. Cf. Rickett 1965, 159; Roth 1999, 50.

61 See, e.g., Graham 1989, 306–11.

62 Oddly, the Rousseau-ian misreadings of the *Tao te ching* that misled some in the late twentieth century to take it as providing an antidote to imagined poisons of "civilization" are not fully explored in Clarke 1997 or Clarke 2000.

63 In addition to Clarke's analyses, see Kirkland 2001a. One version of that reading can be seen in certain analyses by the learned philosopher Chad Hansen. Hansen perpetuates the notion that Taoism is essentially an attempt to undermine acceptance of "convention" (Hansen 1992, 223–4). But most of his so-called "Daoist theory of knowledge" is woven from selected passages of the *Chuang-tzu*. It is at least true that such issues seem to be addressed in the *Chuang-tzu*. But in the *Nei-yeh*,

there is no trace of any critique of the interrelationships between culture and knowledge or desire that Hansen presents as the keystone of the "Daoist theory of knowledge."

64 See *Tao te ching* 47, 73, 77, 79, 81.

65 The character *T'ien* appears in a number of passages of the *Nei-yeh*, but usually as part of the compound *T'ien-Ti* ("Heaven and Earth"). There is one passage stating that, if one practices properly, one's will or intention will proceed in a heavenly fashion (cf. Rickett 1965, 167). So if the compilers believed in Heaven as an active agency that makes choices about life's events and intervenes to guide those events in a certain direction, there is little indication of it in the text.

66 See Kirkland 2002a.

67 The most likely possibility would seem to be a line that, in Rickett's translation, says that, when one has brought the *ch'i* to rest by means of one's *te*, "all things obtain their fulfilment" (Rickett 1965, 158). But the original text is actually far less clear. It reads *wan-wu pi te*, which Roth translates more literally as, "the myriad things will to the last one be grasped" (Roth 1999, 129). Rickett's reading feels more comfortable in light of the overall tenor of classical Chinese thought, but Roth's seems more in line with the tenor of the *Nei-yeh*. The commentator clearly shares Rickett's interpretation, for he says concerning this line, "if one uses one's awareness to bring peace to things, things all obtain benefit." But there is no reason a priori to assume that the commentator understood the original sense of the line. Most other passages that might seem to suggest moral teachings are equally debatable.

68 An up-to-date introduction to these matters is Chan 2000.

69 See Henricks 2000, 205 n. 2.

70 Early analyses of the now well-studied Ma-wang-tui texts include Loewe 1977 and Jan 1977. Among good translations of the Ma-wang-tui *Lao-tzu* are Henricks 1989 and Mair 1990.

71 Since most scholars of the 1990s had begun using the pinyin romanization system, the spelling "Guodian" is now virtually universal. For the first assessment of the archeological reports, see Bumbacher 1998. Specialists may locate the published text, and findings of Chinese scholars, in *Guodian Chumu zhujian* and in Cui 1998. Discussions among Chinese and Western scholars appear in Allan and Williams 2000. The only translation to date is in Henricks 2000.

72 It is noteworthy that none of the extant Guodian slips contain any passage that corresponds to any part of chapters 67 to 81 of the received text. Some scholars assume that the tomb originally contained slips covering "the whole 81 chapters," and that the grave-robbers who got to it before the archaeologists simply happened to reach in and pull out all of the slips that included passages from chapters 67 to 81. Such precision pillaging by robbers who were reaching blindly into an unopened tomb would constitute a remarkable feat. More importantly, the "comments" on "Lao-tzu" in chapters 20 and 21 of the *Han-fei-tzu*

also lack reference to sections 68 to 81 of the extant *Tao te ching*. That fact seems unlikely to be a coincidence, and it suggests that Han Fei, or someone writing in his name, was reading a text of the *Tao te ching* that corresponded to the Guodian version, rather than to the received edition or to either of the Ma-wang-tui texts. The significance of such facts – particularly for narrowing down the date and geographic provenance of each version of the evolving text – awaits further research.

73 Some have tried to read the Guodian texts as an *Ur-text*, i.e., as a base text to which third-century redactors added other materials to fill out the "whole" of the *Tao te ching* that we know from the Ma-wang-tui and Wang Pi editions. Others, however, think that "the Guodian Laozi" may represent fragmentary remnants of a fuller text, which would therefore date back to some point in the fourth century BCE.

74 Chinese scholars who have rearranged sections of the received text so that it "makes better sense" range from Ma Hsü-lun in the 1920s to Yen Ling-feng in the 1970s; Western scholars who have done the same thing range from J. J. L. Duyvendak in the 1940s to Michael Lafargue in the 1980s.

75 See most recently Henricks 2000, 133–6.

76 As Arthur Waley correctly said, "In short, Ssu-ma Ch'ien's 'biography' of Lao Tzu consists simply of a confession that for the writing of such a biography no materials existed at all" (Waley 1934, 108).

77 According to Ssu-ma Ch'ien's first account, "Lao-tzu" had been a man named Lao Tan, an archivist for the Chou ruling house from whom Confucius had once sought advice about propriety (*li*). Other sources indicate that Confucius may indeed have met someone named Lao Tan. But the evidence indicates that that person probably had nothing to do with "Taoist thought," much less with the *Tao te ching* itself. In any event, it most certainly does not look like something written by a person whose opinions on "propriety" Confucius would have valued.

78 See Graham 1990. On the various Chinese cultural constructs concerning "Lao-tzu" through the ages, see Boltz 1987b; and Kohn 1998a, 1998b.

79 This "reconstruction" is, of course, a product of my current analysis of the pertinent available data. I expect it to evolve on the basis of future research and discoveries.

80 For those who regard the *Chuang-tzu* as a principal exposition of "classical Taoism" – equal or superior in importance to the *Tao te ching* – the fact that no trace of it has shown up in ancient tombs has troublesome implications.

81 For an introduction to the issues involved in using the Buddhist materials, see for instance Reynolds and Hallisey 1987; and Williams 2000, 21–34.

82 Biblical scholars have spent generations developing and applying pertinent and effective critical models, with a signficant degree of success. For one window into such research, see Kirkland 1977.

83 Kohn 1991. See my review, Kirkland 1993c. A brief synopsis of the text in question appears in Kohn 2000b, 292 (there, however, the work's title is mistakenly transcribed as "*Jisheng jing*").

84 There are indeed signs that the redactors were including advice for those involved in government, but it is not possible to say that such advice had always been present in the material that they were redacting.

85 William Baxter, a specialist in ancient Chinese linguistics, has astutely observed: "The existence of other texts with similar chacteristics, such as certain chapters of the *Kuan-tzu* [i.e., the *Nei-yeh*], have been recognized for some time; but the canonical status of the *Lao-tzu* may have tended to hide the importance of these similarities. Study of these sometimes obscure texts may clarify the history of the *Lao-tzu* more than comparison with other texts which happen to have been recognized as classics" (Baxter 1998, 249).

86 Here, again, we must be careful not to read alien ideas into our text. While *tzu-jan* is a conspicuous ideal in Wei-Chin thought (e.g., in Kuo Hsiang's commentary to the *Chuang-tzu*), it is a very *minor* element in the *Tao te ching*. The term appears only four times (chapters 17, 23, 25, and 64). And it is by no means clear that it *ever* connotes "spontaneity." For instance, the end of chapter 64 says that the sage can "enhance the *tzu-jan* of the myriad things," and it is hard to understand how a ruler or exemplary person could cause others to become more "spontaneous."

87 It is quite certain that the concept *wu-wei* originated in circles *outside* those from which the *Tao te ching* itself emerged. Not only was the term used by Confucius, but it was a key component of the political philosophy of the "Legalist" Shen Pu-hai. See, e.g., Creel 1974, esp. 176–9.

88 See chapter 43. Chapters 2, 51, and 77 (and chapter 10 in the received text) seem to endorse "acting" in relation to other persons, provided one's actions are not possessive or controlling. The phrase *wei wu-wei* appears in Guodian A, and in two chapters of the received text (3 and 63), but it is absent from the Ma-wang-tui text of chapter 3.

89 The term *li* appears in nine chapters of the received text, and in the opening lines of Guodian A, which are becoming famous for lacking the attack on Confucian values seen in the corresponding lines of the received text (chapter 19). In the received version, the Confucian virtues are excoriated along with "sageliness" (elsewhere the human ideal of the *Tao te ching*), and "benefit" is disparaged, in a context that suggests "selfish struggle for personal profit" (just as Mencius criticized the term). However, other chapters (e.g., 8, 73, and 81) clearly use the term *li* positively. And the Guodian text – which has "benefiting the people" valued positively, and no attack on "sageliness" – now shows that some late redactor mangled the text in an effort to discredit the Confucians of northerly states such as Lu.

90 The general lines of this analysis, first published in 1995, seem now to

accord with those of the ideas of the contemporary scholar Kuo I (Guo Yi): see Henricks 2000, 20–1.

91 The first view is best known as that of Arthur Waley (1934, 46–9); the latter is that of Allyn Rickett.

92 Translation mine. These lines appear both in the received text and in the Ma-wang-tui version; the Guodian text, however, lacks them, though it does have the "opening seven lines" of the full text's "chapter 20."

93 Not only is this voice quite different in tone from what we find elsewhere in the material, but references to "the mother" that are so common in the familar "full text" are conspicuously few in the Guodian slips. Cf. Henricks 2000, 18 n. 5 and 21.

94 It may or may not be coincidental that Ch'i was at the northeastern fringe of the "middle kingdoms": it was well north of Lu – home of Confucius and possibly Mo-tzu – on the way toward Yen, a land where, Ssu-ma Ch'ien says, some people "practiced the Way of expansive transcendence (*fang-hsien tao*): they shed their mortal forms and melted away, relying upon matters involving spiritual beings (*kuei-shen*)": Ssu-ma Ch'ien, *Shih-chi* 28.1368–9.

95 *Shih-chi* 74.2346–7; 46.1895; a partial translation masquerading as a full translation appears in Fung 1953, I: 132–3. See also Roth 1999, 20–2.

96 Ssu-ma Ch'ien, *Shih-chi* 46.1895 n. 5. No title is mentioned for Huan's two-section work.

97 The fact that Ssu-ma was separated from this particular crime by some two hundred years, as well as by the Ch'in cultural holocaust, which had devastated people's knowledge of bygone days by executing men of learning and burning all their books, has been largely ignored in this connection. Also ignored has been the fact that under such circumstances Ssu-ma was under some pressure to demonstrate that "great books" were indeed duly great by pegging their authorship to "great men." Furthermore, the fact that Ssu-ma's own father – the initiator of the *Shih-chi* itself – had been a devotee of "the Taoist school" surely put some additional pressure on the son to concoct "biographies" of "Lao-tzu" and "Chuang-tzu" that were interesting and plausible, from the point of view of the target audience, and upheld each text as the product of a "great man." (On Ssu-ma T'an's "Taoist" sympathies, see for instance Durrant 1995, 5–8.) By Ssu-ma's time, the text in question had come to be known as the greatest classical text of "the Taoist school" – one whose wisdom Han emperors had honored and attempted to follow . . . until the days of the ruthless emperor Wu (r. 140–87). Emperor Wu was Ssu-ma's own patron, and this ruler had found "Taoist" ideas so threatening to his reign that he had gone so far as to condemn his own kinsman Liu An, prince of Huai-nan, to be executed for the offense of having sponsored, and participated in, a "Taoist think-tank" of his own. (Liu An actually committed suicide before his sentence could be carried

out; see Vankeerberghen 2001.) Ssu-ma Ch'ien, already having been castrated for having dared to say something displeasing to Emperor Wu, may have ended up editing his "biographies" so as to leave "the right impression," especially when the historical evidence was inconclusive.

98 See Roth 1999, 24–5, for the opinions of various Asian and Western scholars.

99 Rickett 1998, 24–7, 56–8, 69–70.

100 It is notable that the *Daoism Handbook*, published in 2000, concludes its chapters on the *Tao te ching* (24–5) and *Chuang-tzu* (44–8) with animadversions on those texts' importance for later Taoists. The *Nei-yeh*, meanwhile, receives only one passing mention in the entire volume.

101 For the Ch'ing materials, see Esposito 2000, 633, 636. More on Ssu-ma Ch'eng-chen will be said below.

102 As we will see, there were certainly exceptions: Ko Hung, the famous author of the *Pao-p'u-tzu*, found little of value in those Taoist "classics." But a realistic delineation of the boundaries of "Taoism" might well show Ko as outside the mainstream, indeed perhaps intentionally so.

103 Schipper 1993, 220 n. 33. See Kirkland 1995b.

104 In standard Confucian histories – and in all the Western textbooks based upon them – noble and effective emperors were generally portrayed as having steered clear of "Taoists." To the present day, histories of China present the skewed, and quite false, picture that China's educated "elite" – the bulwarks of the imperial state – were overwhelmingly "Confucian," while the peasant masses who often revolted against the state were "Taoist." All these matters will be more fully analyzed below.

105 Sporadic efforts by rulers such as T'ang Hsüan-tsung to elevate "Chuang-tzu" and "Lieh-tzu" and "Wen-tzu" to the level of imperial importance were quite unsuccessful.

106 See Kohn 1998a and 1998b. Some of the roles of Lao-tzu in Taoism are highlighted in Kohn 1996; but one should note that the account of Lao-tzu that she translates there, from Ko Hung's *Shen-hsien-chuan*, casts him in the role of "a successful practitioner of immortality": Ko "had no interest in stylizing him as the Dao, as the religious followers did" (p. 54).

107 See Kohn 1998c. "The value and sense which the Taoists attribute to their sacred writings" is usefully summarized in Robinet 1993a, 19–28; cf. Thompson 1985; Kirkland 2004b.

108 These central elements of Taoist thought, generally ignored before the present generation of specialists, are outlined in Schipper 1993, 113–19. Another long-ignored facet of these beliefs is that "the mystical vision of the body in Taoism" probably "served as a model of reference in Chinese medicine" (p. 124), which focuses on transformations

of life-energy (*ch'i*), unlike the more materialistic models of Western medicine, which deny the existence or value of such realities.

109 Robinet 1997, 29.

3 THE COURSE OF THE TAOIST TRADITION

1 On these matters, see particularly Barrett 2000a.

2 Chang T'ien-yü, "Historian of K'ou-chü," 1 October 1335, in the preface to his "Register of (Those with) Arcane Qualities" (*Hsüan-p'in lu*, HY 780). See Kirkland 1986a, 213–14.

3 The historical summary presented here is a fuller development of ideas first presented at a 1995 Tokyo conference, subsequently published as Kirkland 1997c. A Japanese translation by Maruyama Hiroshi appears as Kirkland 1998c. Kirkland 2002d is a recent revision and expansion of the historical outline. For other good overviews of the history of Taoism, see Barrett 2000a and Schipper 2000.

4 Of course, further examination of the *Lü-shih ch'un-ch'iu* and other sources from Ch'in times might alter this picture substantially. Ch'in stele inscriptions have recently been brought into focus (Kern 2000). But the brevity of Ch'in rule after the conquest means that there was little time for "Ch'in thought" to develop. And the paucity of reliable data has often made it hard to identify extant writings that may have really emerged from that period. There are reasons to conjecture that the *Kuan-tzu* chapters called "The Arts of the Mind/Heart" (*Hsin-shu, shang*, and *hsia*: *Kuan-tzu*, chapters 36–7) may represent Ch'in-period reworkings of the *Nei-yeh*. But further research on such matters remains to be done.

5 See Kirkland 1995a and Queen 1996.

6 Fuller and somewhat divergent versions of Tung's ideas appear in the *Ch'un-ch'iu fan-lu* ("Luxuriant Dew of the Spring and Autumn Annals"), which scholars have determined to be largely the work of later hands.

7 See DeWoskin 1983.

8 See Wang Ming 1979; Kandel 1979; Kaltenmark 1979; and Hendrischke 2000.

9 See Liu Ts'un-yan 2003.

10 In the twenty-first century, leading specialists have begun debating whether the organization's "libationers" were really clerics, as long imagined, or merely senior lay leaders. See Schipper 2001.

11 Though it is not preserved intact in the *Tao-tsang*, a Tun-huang manuscript preserves part of it. It was sometimes cited in early bibliographies as a work by Chang Tao-ling, but more often attributed to his grandson Chang Lu. See Hendrischke 2000, 145–6. A full translation of the surviving *Hsiang-erh*, with an extensive introduction, appears in Bokenkamp 1997, 29–148. Bokenkamp (pp. 61–2) evidently agrees with Ōfuchi Ninji that the title correctly translates as "Thinking of You," but "the somewhat ridiculous prospect of writing throughout

of the 'Thinking of You' commentary" causes him to leave the title untranslated. I read the character *erh* in terms of its cognate particle *erh*, and see the title as suggesting that "here I am just thinking," i.e., just thinking along with what I read in each line of the *Tao te ching*.

12 See Bokenkamp 1997, 49–50.

13 On these materials, see Yamada 1989.

14 See Pregadio 2000, 172–4. A full study of this tradition by Pregadio is in preparation.

15 See Sailey 1978.

16 See Strickmann 1978b and 1981; and Robinet 1993a and 2000.

17 See Schafer 1978b; Bokenkamp 1996; and Kroll 1996.

18 Cf. Strickmann 1979; and Pregadio 2000, 185–6.

19 See Pregadio 2000, 169–77, 182–6, and Pregadio 1996.

20 See Seidel 1984 and Mollier 1986.

21 Yüan-shih T'ien-tsun seems to have been an abstract figure created by the composer of the *Tu-jen ching*, not the focus of any pre-existing cultus. One should also note that scholarly references to Yüan-shih T'ien-tsun nearly always assign a masculine gender to this figure, though the scripture itself does not seem to specify any gender.

22 The first full translation and study of the *Tu-jen ching* appears in Bokenkamp 1997, 373–438. A recent summation of our knowledge of Ling-pao traditions is Yamada 2000.

23 Cf. Bokenkamp 2001.

24 See Bell 1987b and 1988.

25 See Mather 1979.

26 See Seidel 1983.

27 See Kohn 1998b.

28 See Kohn 1991, and my review in Kirkland 1993c.

29 See Kohn 1995, and my review in Kirkland 1996c.

30 Sharf 1991, 37.

31 See Lagerwey 1981.

32 This observation was made decades ago by the polymath Joseph Needham, whose multi-volume *Science and Civilisation in China*, which commenced in 1954, was continued by colleagues after his death. Though it is now itself rather dated, see for instance Colin Ronan's abridgment of Needham's first two volumes, Needham 1976, 85–113.

33 See Engelhardt 2000. See also Sivin 1968 and 1987.

34 See Engelhardt 2000, 92–3, and Sivin 1968.

35 See Kirkland 1998b, 112–15, and Engelhardt 2000, 93.

36 See Kirkland 1998b, 97–106.

37 For a critical analysis of these views, which Michel Strickmann proposed in the 1970s, see Kirkland 1997c.

38 See Kirkland 1986b.

39 It is true that the very first work in today's *Tao-tsang* is the Ling-pao *Tu-jen ching*. It is also true that it fills more fascicles than any other work in the entire corpus. But the original *Tu-jen ching* was much briefer.

And Strickmann demonstrated convincingly that it was expanded in both size and importance at the end of the Northern Sung, when the emperor Hui-tsung was laboring to build the strength of his nation at a time when foreign threats were looming. See Strickmann 1978a.

40 See Skar 2000; Kirkland 2002e.

41 See Kohn 2003.

42 See Kirkland 1986c.

43 See Schafer 1977; and Kirkland 1991a.

44 See Cahill 2000; cf. Kirkland 2001b.

45 See Kirkland 1998b, 104–6, and Verellen 1989a.

46 A good presentation of these and later historical events can be found in Mote 1999.

47 Typical examples are Seidel 1990 and 1997, and Robinet 1997.

48 The most detailed presentation of the new developments in Sung and Yüan Taoism is Skar 2000. There are now two wide-ranging presentations of Ming Taoism: Berling 1998 and de Bruyn 2000. The only detailed presentation of Taoism in the Ch'ing period is Esposito 2000. After editing the *Daoism Handbook*, Livia Kohn incorporated some of the findings of such scholars into her introductory text, Kohn 2001.

49 See generally Boltz 1987a, 38–41; Reiter 1988; and Skar 2000.

50 Skar 2000, 421. See also Boltz 1987a, 33–8. The first full study devoted to T'ien-hsin Taoism is Hymes 2002.

51 See Strickmann 1978a; Boltz 1987a, 23–30.

52 The prime example is found in a deeply problematic work, Saso 1978, reprinted with minor revisions as Saso 2000. Of "the popular Shen-hsiao order founded by Lin Ling-su," Saso claims, "The Taoists of this sect were at first considered heterodox, proponents of a kind of black magic for harming people. But according to tradition, they were drawn back into orthodoxy by learning of Thunder Magic from the famous thirtieth generation Heavenly Master" (Saso 1978, 12). Saso's uncritical acceptance of such outrageously sectarian calumnies led to a famously stinging review by Michel Strickmann (1980b). The 2000 edition receives a more lenient review by Barbara Hendrischke in *Journal of Chinese Religions* 29 (2001).

53 See Boltz 1987a, 30–3.

54 See Skar 2000, 430–2.

55 A staunch defense of the Cheng-i claim of unbroken continuity with the "Heavenly Masters" of late Han times is found in Barrett 1994. Barrett's scholarship is impeccable, but his argument ultimately seems to be that, since no one has yet presented "a smoking gun" that definitively disproves the Cheng-i claims of continuity, we are therefore justified in accepting them. Other scholars, including Henri Maspero, have read the data quite differently. See my entry "*tianshi*" in Pregadio 2004.

56 Cf. Bielefeldt 1988. Given how widely the story of "the flower sermon" came to be accepted as "sacred history" by twentieth-century Westerners, it is remarkable that Bernard Faure's energetic decon-

struction of Ch'an/Zen "tradition" (Faure 1993) does not even bother to mention it.

57 The construction of the retroactive Shang-ch'ing "lineage" of *tsung-shih* has not yet received the necessary scholarly attention. Even my own research in the 1980s on the biographical materials pertaining to T'ang figures such as Ssu-ma assumed validity in the idea that the *Mao-shan chih* ["Records of Mount Mao"; HY 304] was "actually but the Yüan crystallization of a continuous tradition of record-keeping at Mao-shan" (Kirkland 1986a, 214). The extant *Mao-shan chih* dates to *ca.* 1320, and research by scholars such as Ch'en Kuo-fu found that it went back to a shorter text produced in 1150. (Ibid.; cf. Boltz 1987a, 102–5.) But it is now clear that the notion of "a continuous tradition of record-keeping at Mao-shan" *before* 1150 deserves more discriminating attention. Of the T'ang "prelates" listed in the *Mao-shan chih*'s "lineage" of "patriarchs," Edward Schafer wrote that some are depicted, there and in other sources, on such terms that "we doubt altogether [the person's historical existence], or at best suspect a thoroughly fictionalized biography" (Schafer 1989, 78). Schafer's valuable study lays forth "the anecdotal history of the chief priests of Mao Shan, both mountain and sect, in T'ang times . . . based primarily on the hagiographic accounts given in *Mao Shan chih*." He grants that "it is to be expected that they may be, in some degree, tainted by pious prejudice," but confesses that "I have not attempted to determine or correct any such factor, but have solemnly recorded the views of the faithful" (Schafer 1989, 87). In retrospect, Schafer's contention that "the entire official sequence [of Mao-shan patriarchs was] already established in T'ang times" does not seem to withstand critical analysis: it is true that the title *tsung-shih* does appear in some T'ang accounts of Taoists such as Ssu-ma, but in contexts where it seems actually to have represented just one of a number of common honorifics that were applied quite informally to a wide array of eminent Taoists of the day, as was indeed true of the title *T'ien-shih*, "Heavenly Master." Again, see my entry "*tianshi*" in Pregadio 2004.

58 For instance, Sung Hui-tsung, in Lin's Shen-hsiao cultus, was essentially portrayed as a god, but that did not stop Hui-tsung from simultaneously recognizing one priest as "the twenty-fifth Shang-ch'ing 'Grand Master'" and another as "the thirtieth 'Heavenly Master'." It does not seem that there was really any great dispute among Taoists of that period regarding such identifications, much less any evidence of deep concern about presumed issues of religious "legimacy."

59 de Bruyn 2000, 611.

60 See Liu 1975, 115–16, and de Bruyn 2000, 604–5. The entire political history of Taoism is examined more fully in Chapter 4.

61 See Yao 1980, 27–40. These movements are so obscure that they receive only one line in any part of Kohn 2000a (Yao 2000, 567), and are mentioned nowhere in Boltz 1987a or Franke and Twitchett 1994.

62 Yao 1980, 33–4. On "maternal loving-kindness" in the *Tao te ching*, see Kirkland 2002a.
63 Yao 1980, 35–6.
64 On this term and its meaning, see Chapter 5.
65 See Reiter 1984; another translation appears in Kohn 1993, 86–92. Recent scholarship has suggested that the "Fifteen Articles" may have been produced by early followers rather than by Wang himself.
66 See Boltz 1987a, 155–6.
67 On Ch'iu and the other followers of Wang Che, see Boltz 1987a, 149–67, and Yao 2000.
68 See Liu 1975, 115, and Chapter 4.
69 The monastic traditions of early and medievel Taoism are now thoroughly analyzed in Kohn 2003.
70 See Berling 1979.
71 See Kirkland 1992b, 1993a.
72 See Kirkland 1986b.
73 See Berling 1993.
74 Another example that parallels the Chung-hsiao/Ching-ming tradition is sometimes called "the Tzu-t'ung cult." "The Divine Lord" at the center of that "cult" was a deity better known as Wen-ch'ang, often called "the patron deity of the literary arts." Originally, he was a thunder-deity specific to a mountain in Szechwan. But between 1168 and 1181 he transmitted revelations to a gentleman named Liu An-sheng, the result of which was the *Book of Transformations* (*Hua-shu*), a text preserved in the *Tao-tsang* and elsewhere. As Kleeman has demonstrated, the 1181 revelation "was directed toward scholars," while another in 1194 was intended to attract "a broader selection of worshipers from diverse segments of society" (Kleeman 1994, 71). The *Book of Transformations* constituted "a map revealing how an aspiring immortal could pursue his goal through ethical endeavor, service to the state, and religious praxis" (Kleeman 1994, 41). A near-contemporary text that makes exactly the same points was the *T'ang Yeh chen-jen chuan* (HY 778); see Kirkland 1986a, 135–9, 389–402, 417–30. Like the *Hua-shu*, it uses a colorful figure to show readers that "personal cultivation through appropriate conduct will result in progress toward a transcendent goal" (Kleeman 1994, 41).
75 See Liu 1984; Boltz 1987a, 199–202; and Esposito 2000.
76 See Boltz 1987a, 200.
77 For the earliest Taoist uses of such printing, see Barrett 1997.
78 See Berling 1998, 985; Esposito 2000, 650; and Despeux 1985.
79 See Despeux 2000a.
80 Material from various periods on "sexual yoga" are gathered in an influential but highly problematic work, Wile 1992. Wile casually dismisses the sound analyses of scholars such as Liu Ts'un-yan and Kristofer Schipper who demonstrate that Taoist self-cultivation had no connection with "the arts of the bedchamber" (*fang-chung shu*). He

insists (p. 149) that both phenomena are components of a "sexual school" that has been united "for more than two thousand years" by "the cultivation of *ch'i*." Of course, by that logic, it follows that "the sexual school" was founded by the Confucian moral theorist Mencius, who encouraged the cultivation of *ch'i* (see *Mencius* IIA.2). See the reviews of Wile by Sivin 1994; Robinet 1993b; and Kirkland 1994a. On *fang-chung shu* and its misunderstood relationship with Taoism, see Kirkland, "*Fangzhong shu*," in Pregadio 2004.

81 Yoshioka 1979.

82 Passing mentions of Ch'üan-chen traditions and institutions appear in Dean 1993 and Dean 2000. But Dean's general presentation of Taoist ritual is a presentation of Cheng-i practices, and, though he calls the monastic Ch'üan-chen "school" a "ritual tradition," he does not explain the nature of Ch'üan-chen ritual practices.

83 Outsiders can today visit such Taoist centers, though distance, expense, and lingering political problems often make doing so somewhat difficult. Those who cannot make the journey in person can enjoy a vicarious visit by reading Porter 1993. The Taoist Restoration Society also allows outsiders to provide financial support to Taoist centers in China today.

4 THE SOCIO-POLITICAL MATRIX OF TAOISM

1 See Dean 1993, 1998, 2000.

2 See Little 2000a, 2000b; Takimoto and Liu 2000; and Hahn 2000. An example of the importance of epigraphy for the study of Taoism is Reiter 1998a.

3 Robinet 1997, 20.

4 In premodern Chinese historiography, some "hermits" were casually depicted as having displayed certain characteristics that the historians imagined to be "Taoist." Careful analysis of all pertinent data generally allows us to discern the plausibility of such depictions. See generally Kirkland 1986a. There were also historical individuals whom an emperor sometimes sought to press into the role of "the ornamental hermit," so that his reign would appear more illustrious to contemporaries. Some of those seem to have been people who could reasonably be termed "true hermits," such as the T'ang figure Wang Hsi-i (Kirkland 1986a, 147–59, 444–7). Others were eminent Taoist masters, such as Li Han-kuang, who were "hermits" only in the sense that they apparently abhored being summoned to court (Kirkland 1986c). Others (perhaps including P'an Shih-cheng) may have been in between; see my entry "Pan Shizheng" in Pregadio 2004. Biographical materials were often composed in ways that obsured such distinctions.

5 See, e.g., Lai 1999.

6 An examination of such matters appears in Clarke 2000, 103–11.

7 Cf. Clarke 2000, 111–16.

8 Though scholars such as Schafer and Cahill have done much to illumine

the roles of Taoist women in certain periods, until recently the only comprehensive survey was Despeux 2000a. Despeux and Kohn 2003 has just appeared.

9 Girardot 2002, 316–22, explores the role of the nineteenth-century translator James Legge in persuading Westerners – not to mention Chinese scholars who wished to be respected by Westerners – that the followers of "popular" Taoism were followers of something "gross," "corrupt," and "grotesque."

10 See Kirkland 2002c.

11 Welch 1965, 145. Welch – whose views were the standard in that decade – characterized the Ch'üan-chen religious model as "fanatical," and did not struggle very successfully to disguise his disdain for such "sects": "we just have to get them out of the way before we can proceed."

12 Barrett 1996: 69.

13 Barrett 1996, 81–2.

14 See Kirkland 2002f, and Robinet's entry "Cheng Xuanying" in Pregadio 2004.

15 Among the numerous studies of such matters are Kroll 1986 and Cahill 1993.

16 Barrett 1996, 82–3.

17 Ch'üan Te-yü, "Biography of Venerable Master Wu" (*Wu Tsun-shih chuan*), translated in Kirkland 1986a, 106–7. For more on Wu Yün and his works, see Schafer 1981, 1983; Kirkland 1986a, 96–111, 324–42; and de Meyer 2000. De Meyer is presently preparing a monograph on Wu's life and works.

18 Kirkland 1989.

19 See Reiter 1982, 1990.

20 See Barrett 1996, 38–40, and my entry "Pan Shizheng" in Pregadio 2004.

21 Waley 1950, 106. Cf. Kirkland 1998b, 103. A recent and as yet unpublished translation of the *Hsüan-kang lun* is Cook 2000.

22 See Kirkland 1986a, 275.

23 Sharf 1991, 57. Section 29 of the *Tao-chiao i-shu* is devoted to the idea of "*tao*-nature." For more on that text, see Kirkland 1998b, 110–11.

24 Kirkland 1998b, 109–10. Evidence of the *Pen-chi ching*'s popularity in T'ang times is provided by the fact that no fewer than eighty-one manuscripts of it were discovered in the caches at Tun-huang.

25 Some moderns have become obsessed with the notion that the *Nei-yeh*'s model of cultivating *ch'i* – which reappears in Taoist texts throughout imperial and modern times – involved sexuality, because in late imperial and modern China the notion of preserving "vital essence" was appropriated by numerous non-Taoist writers concerned with enhancing healthy sexuality: they simplistically identified "vital essence" (*ching*) with male semen. If such had indeed been at the core of Taoist self-cultivation practices, they would quite logically have been inaccessible to women. But in fact, all Taoist practices actually involve the refinement

of biospiritual energies and the elevation of personal awareness, not merely bodily fluids.
26 Cf. Kirkland 2002c.
27 For the *Kao-tao chuan* passage, see Kirkland 1991b, 219–22.
28 See Bradbury 1992; Kirkland 1992a, 2001a.
29 Rickett 1965, 154.
30 Cahill 2000.
31 Bumbacher 2000, 510.
32 See Schipper 2001, 91.
33 See particularly Schafer 1977; and Despeux 2000a, 387–8. Hendrischke says "there is no hint of women libationers in the second-century movements" (Hendrischke 2000, 157), but our extant sources are incomplete. We do know that a text presenting moral precepts specifically for women – the *T'ai-yin ch'ing-chieh* ("Pure Precepts of Grand Yin") – once existed, but exists no more. See Schipper 2001, 93 n. 2.
34 Bumbacher 2000, 515.
35 See further ibid., 514–15.
36 See Overmyer 1991.
37 Schipper 1993, 58.
38 See Schafer 1978b; Kroll 1996.
39 A fascinating analysis of how Tu Kuang-t'ing later sanitized the image of the Mysterious Woman of the Nine Heavens to render it more comfortable for a Taoist "gentleman" is Cahill 1992b. Of course, earlier T'ang leaders of Tu's tradition, such as Ssu-ma Ch'eng-chen, had also worked to package Taoism for literati tastes, as indeed one could say that Lu Hsiu-ching himself did.
40 See Schafer 1977; Cahill 1990, 33–4; Kirkland 1991a; Kirkland 1993b.
41 See my entry "*shijie*" in Pregadio 2004.
42 *Yung-ch'eng chi-hsien lu* 116.17b–18a; see further Kirkland 1991a, 71–2.
43 See further Cahill 1984, 1986a, 1986b, 1990, 1993. Cahill is preparing a complete translation of the *Yung-ch'eng chi-hsien lu*.
44 For instance, the texts analyzed in Kirkland 1991a seem to suggest that women officiants carried on observances at the shrines that Huang Ling-wei renovated.
45 Despeux 2000a, 389.
46 Ironically, empress Wu was on the throne when the priestess Huang Ling-wei found the long-lost shrine of "Lady Wei," but showed limited interest in Huang's achievements. See Kirkland 1991a, 51–3. For more on the reign of the empress Wu, see Guisso 1978.
47 Barrett 1996, 35–6. On the ordination of the T'ai-p'ing princess, see Benn 1991, 10–11. Benn argues convincingly that her ordination was spurious, but the ordination of two of emperor Jui-tsung's daughters in 711 (the subject of Benn 1991) was very real.
48 Schafer 1985b, 10.

49 See Boltz 1987a, 38–9, 68–70.
50 Reiter 1988, 38–51.
51 See Kirkland 1991a, 70–3, and 1986c.
52 See van der Loon 1984, 104, 106.
53 See Despeux 2000a, 391–2.
54 Despeux 2000a, 392, notes that Ts'ao is mentioned in an inscription in Beijing's White Cloud Abbey, today's center of Chinese Taoism.
55 Goossaert 2001, 118.
56 Despeux 2000a, 393.
57 Some of the realities of women who practiced "Inner Alchemy" in early twentieth-century China are seen in Liu 1997.
58 See Kirkland 2002c.
59 Seidel 1983, 370, 368.
60 Seidel, 1987a, 251. Cf. Eichhorn 1957; and Pokora 1961.
61 See Schipper 1993, 55–60.
62 Though there were women *tao-shih* in many periods, they seem never to have been pressed into imperial service in this, or any other, capacity.
63 *Tao te ching* 59 in the received text; the passage is already found in the Guodian text (B.1).
64 In 725 T'ang Hsüan-tsung turned to Ho Chih-chang for help in arranging the ritual procedures, and summoned a Taoistic recluse named Wang Hsi-i to accompany the emperor to the mountaintop where he announced to Heaven that the mandate was secure. See Kirkland 1993b.
65 Cf. Vankeerberghen 2001.
66 Kandel 1979; Hendrischke 2000.
67 The term "primitive Taoism" was so used in Mather 1979, 105–8.
68 See Seidel 1969a; and Kohn 1998a, 39–41.
69 Strickmann 1980a, 1047.
70 *Cheng-i fa-wen T'ien-shih chiao chieh k'o ching* (HY 788), 17b–18a, as translated in Seidel 1983, 348.
71 Seidel 1983, 350 n. 224.
72 See Seidel 1984.
73 The *(T'ai-shang) San-t'ien nei-chieh ching* (HY 1196), 1: 9a, as translated in Seidel 1983, 349.
74 See generally Mather 1979, and Kohn 2000b, 284–5.
75 See Bell 1987c; Strickmann 1978b, 1979.
76 Kohn 1998a, 43; cf. Wright 1978, 137. Wright, a historian who wrote before Taoist studies seriously began, presents all the pertinent facts, though his interpretive comments still reveal Confucian assumptions. For instance, he says, "The earliest Taoist religion had perhaps been that of the Yellow Turbans, who rose in massive rebellion in the second century A.D." (p. 136); yet, on the following page, he argues from the relative "paucity" of Taoist inscriptions from Sui times that "one is driven to conclude that religious Taoism had not yet developed the

influence among the common people that it was to attain in later centuries." How Taoism could have arisen as a "massive rebellion" is unclear, if it had little influence "among the common people." It should also be noted that today's leading historian of Taoist art, Stephen Little, has begun finding Taoist artifacts in museums around the world that have never appeared in earlier catalogues because they were simply never recognized as Taoist.

77 See generally Barrett 1996; Benn 1977, 1987; and Kirkland 1986b.

78 The "official" histories suggest that Wang lived some 126 years, but the Taoist histories establish that he died on 1 November 635, at the age of 107. See Barrett 1996, 28; Benn 1977, 31–43; Wechsler 1985, 69–73; and my entry "Wang Yuanzhi" in Pregadio 2004.

79 For Bokenkamp's view, see Bokenkamp 1994. See also Seidel 1969b and 1984.

80 See Barrett 1996, 81–2.

81 HY 1120. See Kirkland 1998b, 103.

82 The order for the compilation of a complete corpus of Taoist writings seems not to have been made until the reign of T'ang Hsüan-tsung in the 740s. See Liu 1975, 111, and Reiter 1998a.

83 See Kirkland 2004c.

84 The dates of Wang Yüan-chih, as mentioned in note 78 above, are one example. Others are given in Kirkland 1986a.

85 See Kirkland 1998b, 86–8. The importance of ancestry for rulers in that era is also seen in the Japanese case. See Kirkland 1997d.

86 Kohn 1998a, 1997a.

87 Benn 1977, 24–5.

88 See especially Benn 1977.

89 See Kirkland 1986a, 260–1, 276.

90 Kirkland 1986a, 241. Ssu-ma continued to be hailed as a painter and calligrapher for hundreds of years; see ibid., 257, 262.

91 See Kirkland 1997a.

92 See Kirkland 1986a, 54–5, 274.

93 Benn 2000, 320. See further Kirkland 1986a, 11–12.

94 Seidel 1983, 351 n. 226.

95 See Benn 1977, 103. A report by Tu Kuang-t'ing states that emperor Jui-tsung's daughter, the Taoist priestess known as the Yü-chen princess, was fond of Ssu-ma, and the standard histories report that in 735 she was ordered to perform the *chin-lu chai* with him at his abbey. See Benn 1991, 14–15.

96 See Kirkland 1986a, 55.

97 It seems slightly hyperbolic, however, to assert that the event shows that "Taoist domination of this important area of state ceremonial became complete" (Barrett 1996, 55).

98 See further Kirkland 1992b.

99 See Lagerwey 1987a, 257–8.

100 See further Kirkland 1993a.
101 Skar 2000, 413. Cf. Schipper 2000, 48–50.
102 Skar 2000, 419.
103 Ebrey and Gregory 1993, 26–7.
104 See Ebrey 2000, 95.
105 On the problem of piercing such "historiographical prejudices," See Kirkland 1997b. A preliminary probe of the sources on Lin Ling-su is Strickmann 1978a.
106 Skar 2000, 422.
107 Strickmann 1978a, 341.
108 Ibid., 341–2.
109 Skar 2000, 419.
110 See Little 2000a, 291–311.
111 Hymes 2002, 175–81. It should be noted that the kind of data that Hymes assembled regarding Sung Taoists have not yet been collected regarding Taoists of other periods, so it is unclear how greatly the dynamics of Sung times may have differed from those of other periods. But we *can* say that, because the north was now under foreign control, Taoists from *northern* centers such as Lou-kuan could no longer be included.
112 Ibid., 176. Hymes suggests various possibilities as to why Southern Sung Taoists did not stay at court.
113 See Wittfolgel and Feng 1949, 213–29, 298–307.
114 Tao 1976, 107.
115 Yao 2000, 571.
116 See Liu 1975, 115; and Rossabi 1988, 203–4. The tone of the sources here suggests the likelihood that the Buddhists fomented imperial antagonism to Taoism, and those sources must, as ways, be treated with suspicion.
117 Rossabi 1988, 146. See also ten Broek and Yiu 1950.
118 Rossabi 1988, 204.
119 Ibid.
120 Berling 1998, 960.
121 Ibid., 962.
122 Ibid., 964.
123 Ibid.
124 Ibid.
125 de Bruyn 2000, 599.
126 Ibid.
127 Berling 1998, 958.
128 Ibid., 966–7.
129 Beginning with the successor of the Yung-lo emperor, de Bruyn's accounts (2000, 600–4) are replete with exactly the same reports of Taoist fanaticism among Ming emperors that one finds in the standard accounts of the later T'ang emperors. All accounts of "bad last emperors" – who finally bring down their dynasty after generations of

"excessive fervor" in pursuing Taoism – should be read with great scepticism. As Berling (1998, 967) says, "The official historical sources deplore [Taoists'] influence on the emperor and tend to highlight the esoteric and lurid aspects" of their real or supposed activities.

130 Berling 1998, 967–8.
131 Ibid., 971.
132 Ibid., 978.
133 Ibid., 980.
134 Berling 1980, 64.
135 See Liu 1967; Franke 1973; Fang 1976; Berling 1980; Berling 1998, 984–96.
136 Esposito 2000, 623.
137 C. K. Yang, quoted in Esposito 2000, 624.
138 Esposito 2000, 625.
139 Ibid., 626.
140 Ibid., 627.
141 Yang 1961 – a splendid analysis of religion in late Ch'ing society – is devoid of most of the Confucian stereotypes that afflicted twentieth-century sinology. Yet, Yang mentions Ch'üan-chen Taoism only once, suggesting that it was involved in "sporadic nationalist resistance . . . against the Chin and Yüan rulers" of the thirteenth to fourteenth centuries (p. 218). Nowhere does Yang mention that Ch'üan-chen Taoism even survived into Ming or Ch'ing times, even in its Lung-men incarnation.
142 In the twentieth century, the only scholars who ever studied Wang Che and his movement were Chinese, Japanese, and German. It was common in the writings of the first two groups to find Wang's movement explained either as an analogue of the Protestant Reformation or as a nationalistic resistance movement. Such ideas stretch the historical evidence.
143 Esposito 2000, 629.
144 Ibid., 629–30.
145 Aside from her chapter in Kohn 2000a, little of Esposito's important research has been published in English; and Mori's only publication in a Western language (2002) is quite recent.
146 Esposito 2000, 630.
147 Mori 2002, 172.

5 THE CULTIVATED LIFE

1 See Barrett 1981.
2 In Kirkland 1977, I used textual data to make the argument that one understanding of Jesus's use of parables was the earliest, and proposed that it was Jesus's own understanding. However, the second position does not rest firmly upon the first, and the reasonability of leaping from the first to the second remains up to the interpreter's sensibilities.

3 See Knaul 1982.
4 Ibid., 54.
5 Ibid.
6 This passage from the "Book of Documents" (*Shang shu*) is translated and discussed in Campany 2002, 47–8 n. 110.
7 Ibid., 47.
8 HY 668.
9 HY 731.
10 See Kohn 1995, 153. For more on the Tun-huang manuscripts that list the contents of Lu's planned "canon," cf. Bokenkamp 2001, 182.
11 Robinet 1997, 25. The *Daoism Handbook* (Kohn 2000a), like many other studies of the Taoist traditions, mentions the text only in passing.
12 See Despeux 1989, 228–9.
13 Ibid.
14 Strickmann 1979, 131–2. On the *Chen-kao*, see Bokenkamp 1996.
15 See Kirkland 1991b.
16 Sailey 1978, xv.
17 On the life and career of Ko Hung, see ibid., xiv–xxii, 277–98, and Campany 2002, 13–17. Campany generally accepts the position that Ko had completed his major writings (including the *Pao-p'u-tzu*) by about 318, though he may have "augmented or revised" them during his retirement at Mount Luo-fu.
18 Welch 1965, 129.
19 Bokenkamp 1989.
20 Bokenkamp 1997, 392.
21 For instance, Stephen Eskildsen says: "The latent tension between longevity and transcendence, along with an uneasy sense of doubt toward the possibility of physical immortality, certainly must have existed through the period covered in this study" (Eskildsen 1998, 156). While one can indeed hear an array of different voices in the period, it is hard to find expressions of "uneasiness" or "doubt" in the texts. It may thus be only in modern minds that such texts' different perspectives on life and death produce any "latent tension," comparable, perhaps, to what a Catholic might imagine to exist among Unitarians.
22 Cf. Bokenkamp 1989, 17.
23 Creel 1970, 7.
24 The article "What is Taoism?" (Creel 1970, 1–24) was first published in 1956.
25 Creel 1970, 22–3.
26 A representative example is Billington 1997, 97–106.
27 Creel 1970, 24.
28 The term *sheng-jen* actually appears in the received text of the *Chuang-tzu* some 114 times, more often than all of those other terms combined.
29 Translation from Watson 1968, 46–7.
30 *Ch'ung-yang li-chiao shih-wu lun* (HY 1223), article 12. See Reiter 1984, 52; Kohn 1993, 91–2.

31 See Kaltenmark 1953.
32 *Shih-chi* 28.1368–9.
33 See Cahill 1993.
34 In HY 1045.
35 See Strickmann 1979.
36 Ibid., 130–1.
37 See Seidel 1987b.
38 Article 15, translated in Kohn 1993, 92.
39 See ibid., 351–2.
40 See Robinet 1979, and my entry "*shijie*" in Pregadio 2004.
41 This report is from the thirteenth-century *T'ang Yeh chen-jen chuan*. See the translation in Kirkland 1986a, 427–8.
42 Cf. Kirkland 1991b.
43 Translated in Hendrischke and Penny 1996, 21.
44 This passage from the eleventh-century *Kao-tao chuan* is translated and fully explored in Kirkland 1991b, 219–22.
45 Oral remarks at the 2000 annual meeting of the Association for Asian Studies, San Diego.
46 See most notably Lagerwey 1987a and Schipper 1993.
47 *Lü-shih ch'un-ch'iu* 13; translation mine. See Yin 1958, 186; cf. Knoblock and Riegel 2001, 102. Writing of the later *Hsi-sheng ching*, Kohn aptly notes: "Here it becomes clear that for Taoists the term 'body' (*shen*) means the various emotional and psychological values attached to oneself, not simply the body as a physical entity" (Kohn 1989c, 197).
48 See Wang 1965, 251–2; translation mine. Cf. Liao 1939, I: 196, 199–200.
49 Kohn and Kirkland 2000, 363.
50 Translation from Kohn 1993, 27–8. A somewhat inaccurate translation of the *Ch'ing-ching ching* appears in Wong 1992; see Pregadio 1994 and Kirkland 1994b. An expert exposition of this highly influential text has yet to be produced.
51 Translation from Kohn 1989c, 220.
52 Ibid., 207–8.
53 See Kohn 1989b.
54 Translation from Kohn 1993, 219.
55 My reading of certain passages of the *Hsi-sheng ching* differs from that of Livia Kohn in her translation, Kohn 1991, as explained in Kirkland 1993c. Here I would note only that, whenever the text uses the term *ch'ang-chiu*, "long enduring" (long familiar to readers of *Tao te ching* 59), Kohn renders it as "immortal"; I cannot find justification in the text itself for such a reading.
56 This conversation is found recorded in one of the T'ang "standard histories," *Hsin Tangshu*, 196.5597; this material is analyzed in Sivin 1968, 106–19. Sun was posthumously elevated to godhood and credited with the authorship of numerous texts on alchemy. Sivin also presents

evidence that Sun was a Taoist with a T'ien-shih pedigree; see Sivin 1978, 312 n. 18.

57 See Barrett 1992. Barrett shows that Li's work must be understood in terms of the syncretic culture of T'ang China, and that it was misunderstood by later Neo-Confucians, who exaggerated Li's debt to Buddhism. So misunderstood was his work among the narrow-minded ideologues of Chu Hsi's tradition that even today's dominant Western paradigms for understanding Confucianism often make no mention of Li's contribution. See Kirkland 2002c.

58 Engelhardt 2000, 92–3. Another text attributed to Sun is the *Hui san-chiao lun* ["On the Reconciliation of the Three Teachings"], which has not yet received scholarly attention. It would seem worthwhile to learn whether Sun played a significant role in stimulating the *san-chiao* principles of later Taoist schools such as Ch'üan-chen.

59 HY 833. The *Chen-chung chi* appears in the *Tao-tsang* without attribution (HY 836); an abbreviated edition, entitled *She-yang chen-chung fang* ["Pillowbook of Methods for Nourishing Life"], is preserved in the *Yün-chi ch'i-ch'ien* (HY1026), chapter 33. See Engelhardt 1989, 288–90.

60 See ibid., 279–88.

61 Ibid., 291.

62 The text is reproduced and translated in Kohn 1987a, 119–23, 177–80.

63 The full title of this text is *Tung-hsüan ling-pao ting-kuan ching-chu* (HY 400). It also appears in *Yün-chi ch'i-ch'ien* 17.6b–13b, and as an appendix to Ssu-ma Cheng-chen's *Tso-wang lun*. The text is reproduced (pp. 181–6) and translated (pp. 125–44) in Kohn 1987a.

64 The most complete version of this text, in nine sections, is preserved in *Yün-chi ch'i-ch'ien* 57. The first two sections appear independently in the *Tao-tsang* under the title *Fu-ch'i ch'ing-i lun* (HY 829); the remaining sections appear under the title *Hsiu-chen ch'ing-i tsa-lun* (HY 277). The text is summarized in Engelhardt 1989, 269–77, and analyzed more fully in Engelhardt 1987.

65 HY 1030; it has now been translated in Kohn 1987a; 1989c; 1993, 235–41.

66 HY 1026; the text is reproduced in Kohn 1987a, 188–90. See Kohn 1987a, 145–55; 1987b; 1993, 80–6; 1989b.

67 Again, modern Confucians have struggled fiercely to deny the relevance of the fact that Mencius (5A.7, 5B.1) underwent "awakening" (*chüeh*), though perhaps not quite in the sense of later Confucians whose ideas had been affected by Buddhism.

68 Translation mine. See Kohn 1987a, 188, and her translation, Kohn 1987a, 128.

69 The quotation is from the twelfth of the "Fifteen Articles."

70 On the gradual elevation of Ho to "immortality," as this pericope from the *Kao-tao chuan* was embellished in later texts, see Kirkland 1991b, 220.

71 Kohn 1993, 95.
72 See Chapter 4, and Bokenkamp 1986, 142–3; Kirkland 1998b, 109–10.
73 HY 1121. See Sharf 1991, 40, 56–60; and Kirkland 1998b, 110–11.
74 Gimello 2002.
75 Cf. Lagerwey 1987b.
76 See Kirkland 1986a, 135–9, 389–402, 417–30; and my entry "Ye Fashan" in Pregadio 2004.
77 See Weinstein 1987, 54–7. Weinstein (p. 57) notes that I-hsing's Taoist training is "a fact not mentioned in Buddhist sources."
78 Of course, most think of Japanese "esoteric Buddhism" only in terms of the Shingon "school" founded by Kūkai in the early ninth century. But, in fact, "esoteric" ideas and practices had by that time been known in Japan for generations. And "the esoteric tradition" (*mikkyō*) was also an element of the "Tendai school" founded by his contemporary Saichō. The name of that school – in Chinese, *T'ien-t'ai* – was simply the name of a mountain in China where Buddhists and Taoists had practiced in close proximity to each other since early T'ang times. Ssu-ma Ch'eng-chen himself lived at Mount T'ien-t'ai, and the Buddhist elements in some of his teachings likely owe much more to his personal interaction with Buddhists there than to a reading of Buddhist texts. These historical interactions deserve much more study.
79 Orzech 1987, 237.
80 See Weinstein 1987, 57.
81 Orzech 1987, 237.
82 Lagerwey 1987b, 233.
83 Of course, Chinese rulers – and reportedly leaders of steppe peoples who conquered parts of north China in the early fourth century – had valued such ritual masters for generations.
84 See Boltz 1983; and Lagerwey 1987a, 168–237.
85 See Kirkland 1986a, 11–12, 54–5; and Benn 2000, 320–1.
86 Seidel 1983, 351 n. 226.
87 See Kirkland 1986b.
88 Some maintained that "quiet-sitting," unlike Buddhist meditation, was not directed toward achieving "enlightenment," but the same was actually true in contemporary Ch'an/Zen. There, "enlightenment" is already intrinsic to one's true reality, and *zazen* was, like Confucian meditation, merely a device to facilitate the quieting of the mind that would allow one's true reality to be in full fruition. All that ever really distinguished "quiet-sitting" from any form of Buddhist or Taoist meditation was a general absence of specific precepts regarding technique. An intriguing exposition of the practice by a twentieth-century Japanese Confucian is found in Taylor 1988.
89 See Liu 1970a, 1970b; Berling 1979, 1980.
90 Cf. Mabuchi 2002, 139.
91 A question that has, as yet, hardly received any attention is that of

whether elements of medieval Taoist practice might be preserved by practitioners of the little-known Japanese tradition called Shugendō. Shugendō – the origins of which seem to be at least as old as the "esoteric teachings" planted in Japan by Kūkai, *ca.* 800 – is a tradition whose practitioners cultivate the abstruse spiritual properties of life without tagging their practices to any canonized texts, recognized lineages, temple institutions, or conceptualized theories. Rather, they tend to keep their activities to themselves, sometimes living as *yamabushi* in the mountains of Japan and engaging in what their tradition is called: *Shugendō*, a term which translates quite literally as "the Tao of Cultivation and Refinement." The very term *shugen* – in Chinese, *hsiu-lien* – was an enduring term for Taoist practice from the formative period onward, and the possible connections between Shugendō and earlier Taoist traditions deserve fuller attention. The problematic nature of ideas about Taoist influence in early Japan has been noted in Kirkland 1986d and more fully explored in Barrett 2000b.

CONCLUSION

1 Balazs 1964, 234.
2 For a description of Chu Hsi's *Chou-i ts'an-t'ung ch'i chu*, see Liu Ts'un-yan's entry in Hervouet 1978, 369–70.
3 See Kaltenmark 1979, 38.
4 The quotation is from a definition of *t'ai-p'ing*, "Grand Tranquillity," in Seidel 1987a, 251.
5 See Kirkland 1986b and 2002a.
6 See Kirkland 1993a.

REFERENCES AND BIBLIOGRAPHY

Allan, Sarah, and Crispin Williams, eds. 2000. *The Guodian Laozi: Proceedings of the International Conference*. Berkeley: Society for the Study of Early China.

Balazs, Etienne. 1964. *Chinese Civilization and Bureaucracy*. New Haven and London: Yale University Press.

Barnhart, Michael, ed. 2002. *Varieties of Ethical Reflection: New Directions for Ethics in a Global Context*. New York: Lexington Books.

Barrett, Timothy. 1981. "Introduction." In Maspero 1981, vii–xxi.

—— 1987. "Taoism: History of Study." In Eliade 1987, 14: 329–32.

—— 1992. *Li Ao: Buddhist, Taoist, or Neo-Confucian*. Oxford: Oxford University Press.

—— 1994. "The Emergence of the Taoist Papacy in the T'ang Dynasty." *Asia Major*, third series, 7: 89–106.

—— 1996. *Taoism under the T'ang*. London: Wellsweep Press.

—— 1997. "The *Feng-tao k'o* and Printing on Paper in Seventh-Century China." *Bulletin of the School of Oriental and African Studies* 60.3: 538–40.

—— 2000a. "Daoism: A Historical Narrative." In Kohn 2000a, xviii–xxvii.

—— 2000b. "Shintō and Taoism in Early Japan." In Breen and Teeuwen, eds. 2000, 13–31.

Baxter, William. 1998. "Situating the Language of the *Lao-tzu*: The Probable Date of the *Tao-te-ching*." In Kohn and Lafargue 1998, 231–53.

Bell, Catherine. 1987a. "Tu Kuang-t'ing." In Eliade 1987, 15: 80–1.

—— 1987b. "Lu Hsiu-ching." In Eliade 1987, 9: 50–1.

—— 1987c. "T'ao Hung-ching." In Eliade 1987, 14: 287–8.

—— 1988. "Ritualization of Texts and Textualization of Ritual in the Codification of Taoist Liturgy," *History of Religions* 27: 366–92.

Benn, Charles. 1977. "Taoism as Ideology in the Reign of Emperor Hsüan-tsung." Dissertation, University of Michigan.

—— 1987. "Religious Aspects of Emperor Hsüan-tsung's Taoist Ideology." In *Buddhist and Taoist Practice in Medieval Chinese Society*, ed. D. W. Chappell. Honolulu: University of Hawaii Press. 127–46.

—— 1991. *The Cavern-Mystery Transmission: A Taoist Ordination Rite of A.D. 711*. Hololulu: University of Hawaii Press.

—— 2000. "Daoist Ordination and *Zhai* Rituals." In Kohn 2000a, 309–38.

Berling, Judith. 1979. "Paths of Convergence: Interactions of Inner Alchemy Taoism and Neo-Confucianism." *Journal of Chinese Philosophy* 6: 123–48.

—— 1980. *The Syncretic Religion of Lin Chao-en*. New York: Columbia University Press.

—— 1993. "Channels of Connection in Sung Religion: The Case of Pai Yü-chan." In *Religion and Society in T'ang and Sung China*, ed. Patricia Ebrey and Peter Gregory. Honolulu: University of Hawaii Press, 307–33.

—— 1998. "Taoism in Ming Culture." In *The Cambridge History of China*, vol. 8: *The Ming Dynasty*, Part 2. Cambridge: Cambridge University Press, 953–86.

Bielefeldt, Carl. 1988. "Rethinking Zen Studies: The Case of Sacred History." MS.

Billington, Ray. 1997. *Understanding Eastern Philosophy*. London and New York: Routledge.

Bokenkamp, Stephen. 1986. "Taoist Literature, Part I: Through the T'ang Dynasty." In Nienhauser 1986, 138–52.

—— 1989. "Death and Ascent in Ling-pao Taoism." *Taoist Resources* 1.2: 1–20.

—— 1994. "Time After Time: Taoist Apocalyptic History and the Founding of the T'ang Dynasty." *Asia Major*, third series, 7: 59–88.

—— 1996. "Declarations of the Perfected." In Lopez 1996, 166–79.

—— 1997. *Early Daoist Scriptures*. Berkeley: University of California Press.

—— 2001. "Lu Xiujing, Buddhism, and the First Daoist Canon." In *Culture and Power in the Reconstitution of the Chinese Realm, 200–600*, ed. Scott Pearce, Audrey Spiro, and Patricia Ebrey. Cambridge, MA: Harvard University Press, 181–99.

Boltz, Judith Magee. 1983. "Opening the Gates of Purgatory: A Twelfth-Century Taoist Meditation Technique for the Salvation of Lost Souls." In Strickmann 1983, 487–511.

—— 1987a. *A Survey of Taoist Literature: Tenth to Seventeenth Centuries*. Ann Arbor: University of Michigan Center for Chinese Studies.

—— 1987b. "Lao-tzu." In *Encyclopedia of Religion*. New York: Macmillan, 8: 454–9.

Bradbury, Steve. 1992. "The American Conquest of Philosophical Taoism." In *Translation East and West: A Cross-Cultural Approach*, ed. Cornelia N. Moore and Lucy Lower. Honolulu: University of Hawaii College of Languages, Linguistics and Literature and the East-West Center, 29–41.

Breen, John, and Mark Teeuwen, eds. 2000. *Shintō in History: Ways of the Kami*. Honolulu: University of Hawaii Press.

Bumbacher, Stephan Peter. 1998. "The Earliest Manuscripts of the *Laozi* Discovered to Date." *Asiatische Studien* 52: 1175–84.

—— 2000. *The Fragments of the Daoxue Zhuan*. Frankfurt am Main: Peter Lang.

Cahill, Suzanne. 1984. "Beside the Turquoise Pond: The Shrine of the Queen Mother of the West in Medieval China." *Journal of Chinese Religions* 12: 19–32.

—— 1986a. "Reflections on a Metal Mother: Tu Kuang-t'ing's Biography of Hsi-wang-mu." *Journal of Chinese Religions* 13/14: 127–42.

—— 1986b. "Performers and Female Taoist Adepts: Hsi Wang Mu as Patron Deity of Women in T'ang China." *Journal of the American Oriental Society* 106: 155–68.

—— 1990. "Practice Makes Perfect: Paths to Transcendence for Women in Medieval China." *Taoist Resources* 2.2: 23–42.

—— 1992a. "Marriages Made in Heaven." *T'ang Studies* 10–11: 111–22.

—— 1992b. "Sublimation in Medieval China: The Case of the Mysterious Woman of the Nine Heavens." *Journal of Chinese Religions* 20: 91–102.

—— 1993. *Transcendence and Divine Passion: The Queen Mother of the West in Medieval China*. Stanford: Stanford University Press.

—— 2000. "Pien Tung-hsüan: A Taoist Woman Saint of the T'ang Dynasty." In *Women Saints in World Religions*, ed. Arvind Sharma. Albany: State University of New York Press.

Campany, Robert Ford. 2002. *To Live as Long as Heaven and Earth: A Translation and Study of Ge Hong's Traditions of Divine Transcendents*. Berkeley: University of California Press.

Chan, Alan. 2000. "The *Daode jing* and its Tradition." In Kohn 2000a, 1–29.

Chang, Leo, and Yu Feng. 1998. *The Four Political Treatises of the Yellow Emperor*. Honolulu: University of Hawaii Press.

Cheung, Frederick Hok-ming, and Ming-chiu Lai, eds. 1999. *Politics and Religion in Ancient and Medieval Europe and China.* Hong Kong: Chinese University Press.

Clarke, J. J. 1997. *Oriental Enlightenment: The Encounter Between Asian and Western Thought.* London: Routledge.

—— 2000. *The Tao of the West: Western Transformations of Taoist Thought.* London: Routledge.

Cook, Constance, and John Major, eds. 1999. *Defining Chu: Image and Reality in Ancient China.* Honolulu: University of Hawaii Press.

Cook, Theodore. 2000. "Wu Yun's *Mystic Mainstays*: A Daoist Treatise of the Eighth Century C.E." Thesis, Indiana University.

Creel, H. G. 1970. *What Is Taoism? and Other Studies in Chinese Cultural History.* Chicago: University of Chicago Press.

—— 1974. *Shen Pu-hai: A Chinese Political Philosopher of the Fourth Century B.C.* Chicago: University of Chicago Press.

Cui Renyi. 1998. *Jingmen Guodian Chujian Laozi yanjiu* [Studies in the Bamboo-slip "Laozi" from Guodian in Jingmen]. Beijing: Kexue chubanshe.

Danto, Arthur. 1988. *Mysticism and Morality: Oriental Thought and Moral Philosophy.* New York: Columbia University Press.

Davis, Edward L. 2001. *Society and the Supernatural in Song China.* Honolulu: University of Hawaii Press.

Dean, Kenneth. 1993. *Taoist Ritual and Popular Cults of Southeast China.* Princeton: Princeton University Press.

—— 1998. *Lord of the Three in One: The Spread of a Cult in Southeast China.* Princeton: Princeton University Press.

—— 2000. "Daoist Ritual Today." In Kohn 2000a, 659–82.

deBary, W. T., and Irene Bloom, eds. 1999. *Sources of Chinese Tradition.* 2nd edn, Vol. 1. New York: Columbia University Press.

de Bruyn, Pierre-Henry. 2000. "Daoism in the Ming (1368–1644)." In Kohn 2000a, 594–622.

De Meyer, Jan. 2000. "Linked Verse and Linked Faiths: An Inquiry into the Social Circle of an Eminent T'ang Dynasty Taoist Master." In De Meyer and Engelfriet 2000, 148–83.

De Meyer, Jan, and Peter Engelfriet, eds. 2000. *Linked Faiths: Essays on Chinese Religions and Traditional Culture in Honour of Kristofer Schipper.* Leiden: Brill.

Despeux, Catherine. 1985. "Les lectures alchimiques du *Hsi-yu-chi.*" In Naundorf et al. 1985, 61–76.

—— 1986. "L'ordination des femmes Taoïstes sous les T'ang." *Études Chinoises* 5.1–2: 53–100.

—— 1989. "Gymnastics: The Ancient Tradition." In Kohn 1989a, 225–61.

—— 2000a. "Women in Daoism." In Kohn 2000a, 384–412.

—— 2000b. "Talismans and Diagrams." In Kohn 2000a, 498–540.

Despeux, Catherine, and Livia Kohn. 2003. *Women in Daoism*. Cambridge, MA: Three Pines Press.

DeWoskin, Kenneth. 1983. *Doctors, Diviners, and Magicians of Ancient China: Biographies of Fang-shih*. New York: Columbia University Press.

Durrant, Stephen. 1995. *The Cloudy Mirror: Tension and Conflict in the Writings of Sima Qian*. Albany: State University of New York Press.

Ebrey, Patricia. 2000. "Taoism and Art at the Court of Song Huizong." In Little 2000a, 95–111.

—— 2001. *The Five "Confucian" Classics*. New Haven: Yale University Press.

Ebrey, Patricia, and Peter Gregory. 1993. *Religion and Society in T'ang and Sung China*. Honolulu: University of Hawaii Press.

Eichhorn, Werner. 1957. "T'ai-p'ing und T'ai-p'ing Religion." *Mitteilungen des Instituts für Orientforschung* 2: 113–40.

Eliade, Mircea, ed. 1987. *Encyclopedia of Religion*. New York: Macmillan.

Engelhardt, Ute. 1987. *Die klassische Tradition der Qi-Übungen: eine Darstellung anhand des Tang-zeitlichen Textes Fuqi jingyi lun von Sima Chengzhen*. Wiesbaden: Franz Steiner.

—— 1989. "*Qi* for Life: Longevity in the Tang." In Kohn 1989a, 263–96.

—— 2000. "Longevity Techniques and Chinese Medicine." In Kohn 2000a, 74–110.

Eskildsen, Steve. 1998. *Asceticism in Early Taoist Religion*. Albany: State University of New York Press.

Esposito, Monica. 2000. "Daoism in the Qing (1644–1911)." In Kohn 2000a, 623–58.

Fan, Warner J.-W. 1996. *A Manual of Chinese Herbal Medicine*. Boston and London: Shambhala.

Fang, Lienche Tu. 1976. "Lin Chao-en." In Goodrich 1976.

Faure, Bernard. 1993. *Chan Insights and Oversights: An Epistemological Critique of the Chan Tradition*. Princeton: Princeton University Press.

Franke, Herbert, and Denis Twitchett, eds. 1994. *The Cambridge History of China*, Vol. 6: *Alien Regimes and Border States, 907–1368*. Cambridge: Cambridge University Press.

Franke, Wolfgang. 1973. "Some Remarks on Lin Chao-en." *Oriens Extremus* 20, 161–74.

Fung Yu-lan. 1953. *A History of Chinese Philosophy*, 2 vols, trans. Derk Bodde. Princeton: Princeton University Press.

Gimello, Robert. 2002. "Dhāranī and Deity: The Place of the Occult in Chinese Buddhism." Paper delivered at the conference on Tantra and Daoism, Boston University.

Girardot, Norman J. 1977. "Myth and Meaning in the *Tao te ching*." *History of Religions* 16: 294–328.

—— 2002. *The Victorian Translation of China: James Legge's Oriental Pilgrimage*. Berkeley: University of California Press.

Girardot, Norman J., Liu Xiaogan, and James Miller, eds. 2001. *Taoism and Ecology*. Cambridge, MA: Harvard University Press.

Goodrich, L. Carrington, ed. 1976. *Dictionary of Ming Biography*. New York: Columbia University Press.

Goossaert, Vincent. 2001. "The Invention of an Order: Collective Identity in Thirteenth-Century Quanzhen Taoism." *Journal of Chinese Religions* 29: 111–38.

Goossaert, Vincent, and Paul Katz. 2001. "New Perspectives on Quanzhen Taoism." *Journal of Chinese Religions* 29: 91–4.

Graham, Angus C. 1981. *Chuang-tzu: The Seven Inner Chapters*. London: Allen & Unwin.

—— 1989. *Disputers of the Tao: Philosophical Argument in Ancient China*. Chicago: Open Court.

—— 1990. "The Origins of the Legend of Lao Tan." In *Studies in Chinese Philosophy and Philosophical Literature*. Albany: State University of New York Press, 111–24.

Guisso, Richard. 1978. *Wu Tse-t'ien and the Politics of Legitimation in T'ang China*. Bellingham: Western Washington University.

Guodian Chumu zhujian [The Bamboo Slips from the Ch'u Tomb at Kuo-tien]. 1998. Beijing: Wenwu chubanshe.

Hahn, Thomas. 2000. "Daoist Sacred Sites." In Kohn 2000a, 683–708.

Hansen, Chad. 1992. *A Daoist Theory of Chinese Thought: A Philosophical Interpretation*. New York: Oxford University Press.

Hendrischke, Barbara. 2000. "Early Daoist Movements." In Kohn 2000a, 134–64.

Hendrischke, Barbara, and Benjamin Penny. 1996. "The 180 Precepts Spoken by Lord Lao." *Taoist Resources* 6.2: 17–29.

Henricks, Robert. 1989. *Lao-tzu Te-Tao Ching*. New York: Ballantine Books.

—— 2000. *Lao Tzu's Tao Te Ching: A Translation of the Startling New Documents Found at Guodian*. New York: Columbia University Press.

Hervouet, Yves, ed. 1978. *A Sung Bibliography*. Hong Kong: Chinese University Press.

Hsiao Kung-chuan. 1979. *A History of Chinese Political Thought*, trans. Frederick Mote. Princeton: Princeton University Press.

Hymes, Robert. 2002. *Way and Byway: Taoism, Local Religion, and Models of Divinity in Sung and Modern China*. Berkeley: University of California Press.

Jan Yun-hua. 1977. "The Silk Manuscripts on Taoism." *T'oung Pao* 63: 65–84.

Jensen, Lionel. 1998. *Manufacturing Confucianism: Chinese Traditions and Universal Civilization*. Durham, NC: Duke University Press.

Kaltenmark, Max. 1953. *Le Lie-sien tchouan: biographies légendaires des Immortel Taoïstes de l'antiquité*. Peking: Centre d'Études Sinologiques.

—— 1979. "The Ideology of the *T'ai-p'ing ching*." In *Facets of Taoism*, ed. Holmes Welch and Anna Seidel. New Haven: Yale University Press, 19–45.

Kandel (Hendrischke), Barbara. 1979. *Taiping Jing: The Origin and Transmission of the "Scripture on General Welfare."* Hamburg: Gesellschaft für Natur- und Völkerkunde Ostasiens.

Kern, Martin. 2000. *The Stele Inscriptions of Ch'in Shih-Huang: Text and Ritual in Early Chinese Imperial Representation*. New Haven: American Oriental Society.

King, Richard. 1999. *Orientalism and Religion: Postcolonial Theory, India and "The Mystic East."* London: Routledge.

Kirkland, Russell. 1977. "The Earliest Understanding of Jesus' Use of Parables: Mark 4: 10–12 in Context." *Novum Testamentum* 19: 1–21.

—— 1982. Review of Maspero 1981. *Journal of Asian Studies* 42: 395–7.

—— 1984. "Chang Kao: Noteworthy T'ang Taoist?" *T'ang Studies* 2: 31–6.

—— 1986a. "Taoists of the High T'ang: An Inquiry into the Perceived Significance of Eminent Taoists in Medieval Chinese Society." Dissertation, Indiana University.

—— 1986b. "The Roots of Altruism in the Taoist Tradition." *Journal of the American Academy of Religion* 54: 59–77.

—— 1986c. "The Last Taoist Grand Master at the T'ang Imperial Court: Li Han-kuang and T'ang Hsüan-tsung." *T'ang Studies* 4: 43–67.

—— 1986d. Review of Felicia Bock, *Classical Learning and Taoist Practices in Early Japan*. *Asian Folklore Studies* 45: 129–31.

—— 1989. "From Imperial Tutor to Taoist Priest: Ho Chih-chang at the T'ang Court." *Journal of Asian History* 23: 101–33.

—— 1991a. "Huang Ling-wei: A Taoist Priestess in T'ang China." *Journal of Chinese Religions* 19: 47–73.

—— 1991b. "The Making of an Immortal: The Exaltation of Ho Chih-chang." *Numen* 38: 201–14.

—— 1992a. "Person and Culture in the Taoist Tradition." *Journal of Chinese Religions* 20: 77–90.

—— 1992b. "Tales of Thaumaturgy: T'ang Accounts of the Wonder-Worker Yeh Fa-shan." *Monumenta Serica* 40: 47–86.

—— 1993a. "A World in Balance: Holistic Synthesis in the *T'ai-p'ing kuang-chi*." *Journal of Sung-Yüan Studies* 23: 43–70.

—— 1993b. "Three Entries for a T'ang Biographical Dictionary: Wang Hsi-i, Huang Ling-wei, Ho Chih-chang." *T'ang Studies* 10–11: 153–65.

—— 1993c. Review of Kohn 1991. *Journal of Chinese Religions* 21: 165–72.

—— 1994a. Review of Wile 1992. *Chinese Literature: Essays, Articles, Reviews* 16: 161–6.

—— 1994b. Review of Wong 1992. *Religious Studies Review* 20: 354–5.

—— 1995a. "Tung Chung-shu." In *Great Thinkers of the Eastern World*, ed. Ian McGreal. New York: HarperCollins, 67–70.

—— 1995b. Review of Schipper 1993. *Religious Studies Review* 21: 63.

—— 1996a. "The Study of Religion and Society in Contemporary Asia: Colonialism and Beyond." *Bulletin of Concerned Asian Scholars* 28.3/4: 59–63.

—— 1996b. Review of Glen Dudbridge, *Religious Experience and Lay Society in T'ang China*. *Journal of Asian Studies* 55: 977–8.

—— 1996c. Review of Kohn 1995. *Journal of Asian Studies* 55: 152–3.

—— 1996d. "Taoism." In *Philosophy of Education: An Encyclopedia*, ed. J. J. Chambliss. New York and London: Garland, 633–6.

—— 1997a. "Ssu-ma Ch'eng-chen and the Role of Taoism in the Medieval Chinese Polity." *Journal of Asian History* 31.2: 105–38.

—— 1997b. Review of Barrett 1996. *Taoist Resources* 7.1: 61–8.

—— 1997c. "The Historical Contours of Taoism in China: Thoughts on Issues of Classification and Terminology." *Journal of Chinese Religions* 25: 57–82.

—— 1997d. "The Sun and the Throne: The Origins of the Royal Descent Myth in Ancient Japan." *Numen* 44: 109–52.

—— 1998a. "Teaching Taoism in the 1990s." *Teaching Theology and Religion* 1.2: 121–9.

—— 1998b. "Dimensions of Tang Taoism: The State of the Field at the End of the Millennium." *T'ang Studies* 15–16: 79–123.

—— 1998c. "Chūgoku ni okeru Dōkyō no Rekishi-teki Gaikan," trans. Maruyama Hiroshi. In *Dōkyō no rekishi to bunka* [Taoist History and Culture], ed. Yamada Toshiaki and Tanaka Fumio. Tokyo: Hirakawa shuppansha, 1–29.

—— 2000. "Explaining Daoism: Realities, Cultural Constructs, and Emerging Perspectives." In Kohn 2000a, xi–xviii.

—— 2001a. "Responsible Non-Action in a Natural World." In Girardot et al. 2001, 283–304.

—— 2001b. Review of Sharma 2000 and Cheung and Lai 1999. *Journal of Chinese Religions* 29: 349–52.

—— 2001c. "A Quest for 'The Foundations of Taoist Mysticism'." Review of Roth 1999. *Studies in Central and East Asian Religions* 12/13: 203–29.

—— 2002a. "Self-Fulfillment through Selflessness: The Moral Teachings of the *Daode jing*." In Barnhart 2002, 21–48.

—— 2002b. "On Coveting thy Neighbor's Tao: Reflections on J. J. Clarke's *The Tao of the West*." *Religious Studies Review* 28.4: 309–12.

—— 2002c. Review of deBary and Bloom 1999. *Education About Asia* 7.1: 62–6.

—— 2002d. "The History of Taoism: A New Outline." *Journal of Chinese Religions* 30: 177–93.

—— 2002e. "Paradigms for Transforming Reality: Continuities and Contacts Between Tantric and Taoist Traditions." Paper presented at the Tantra and Daoism Conference, Boston University.

—— 2002f. Review of Yu 2000. *Journal of the American Oriental Society* 122.3: 629–33.

—— 2004a. "Hermeneutics and Pedagogy: Methodological Issues in Teaching the *Tao te ching*." In *Essays in Teaching the Tao te ching*, ed. Warren Frisina and Gary DeAngelis. Oxford and New York: Oxford University Press.

—— 2004b. "Taoism." In *Worldmark Encyclopedia of Religious Practice*. New York: Gale.

—— 2004c. "Historiography and the Tao: Ssu-ma Ch'eng-chen in the *Chen-hsi chuan* and the *Chiu T'ang shu*." *Journal of Asian History*, in press.

Kleeman, Terry. 1994. *A God's Own Tale: The "Book of Transformations" of Wenchang, the Divine Lord of Zitong*. Albany: State University of New York Press.

Knaul (Kohn), Livia. 1982. "Lost *Chuang Tzu* Passages." *Journal of Chinese Religions* 10: 53–79.

Knoblock, John, and Jeffrey Riegel, trans. 2001. *The Annals of Lü Buwei*. Stanford: Stanford University Press.

Kohn, Livia. 1987a. *Seven Steps to the Tao: Sima Chengzhen's "Zuowang Lun."* Nettetal: Steyler Verlag.

—— 1987b. "The Teaching of T'ien-yin-tzu." *Journal of Chinese Religions* 15: 1–28.

—— ed. 1989a. *Taoist Meditation and Longevity Techniques*. Ann Arbor: University of Michigan Center for Chinese Studies,1989.

—— 1989b. "Guarding the One: Concentrative Meditation in Taoism." In Kohn 1989a, 125–58.

—— 1989c. "Taoist Insight Meditation: The Tang Practice of *Neiguan*." In Kohn 1989a, 193–224.

—— 1990. "Chen Tuan in History and Legend." *Taoist Resources* 2.1: 8–31.

—— 1991. *Taoist Mystical Philosophy: The Scripture of Western Ascension*. Albany: State University of New York Press.

—— 1993. *The Taoist Experience: An Anthology*. Albany: State University of New York Press.

—— 1995. *Laughing at the Tao: Debates among Buddhists and Taoists in Medieval China*. Princeton: Princeton University Press.

—— 1996. "Laozi: Ancient Philosopher, Master of Immortality, and God." In Lopez 1996, 52–63.

—— 1997a. "Yin Xi: The Master at the Beginning of the Scripture." *Journal of Chinese Religions* 25: 83–139.

—— 1997b. Review of Michael Saso, *The Gold Pavilion*. *Taoist Resources* 7.1: 69–73.

—— 1997c. "The Date and Compilation of the *Fengdao Kejie*, The First Handbook of Monastic Daoism." *East Asian History* 13/14: 91–118.

—— 1998a. *God of the Dao: Laozi in History and Myth*. Ann Arbor: University of Michigan Center for Chinese Studies.

—— 1998b. "The Lao-tzu Myth." In Kohn and LaFargue 1998, 41–62.

—— 1998c. "The *Tao-te-ching* in Ritual." In Kohn and LaFargue 1998, 143–61.

—— ed. 2000a. *Daoism Handbook*. Leiden: Brill, 2000.

—— 2000b. "The Northern Celestial Masters." In Kohn 2000a, 282–308.

—— 2001. *Daoism and Chinese Culture*. Cambridge, MA: Three Pines Press.

—— 2003. *Monastic Life in Medieval Daoism*. Honolulu: University of Hawaii Press.

Kohn, Livia, and Russell Kirkland. 2000. "Daoism in the Tang (618–907)." In Kohn 2000a, 339–83.

Kohn, Livia, and Michael LaFargue, eds. 1998. *Lao-tzu and The Tao-te-ching*. Albany: State University if New York Press.

Kohn, Livia, and Harold Roth, eds. 2002. *Daoist Identity: History, Lineage and Ritual*. Honolulu: University of Hawaii Press.

Komjathy, Louis. 2002. *Title Index to Daoist Collections*. Cambridge, MA: Three Pines Press.

Kroll, Paul. 1978. "Szu-ma Ch'eng-chen in T'ang Verse." *Society for the Study of Chinese Religions Bulletin* 6: 16–30.

—— 1986. "Li Po's Transcendent Diction." *Journal of the American Oriental Society* 106: 99–117.

—— 1996. "Seduction Songs of One of the Perfected." In Lopez 1996, 180–7.

Lagerwey, John. 1981. *Wu-shang pi-yao: somme taoïste du vie siècle.* Paris: École Française d'Extrême-Orient.

—— 1987a. *Taoist Ritual in Chinese Society and History.* New York: Macmillan.

—— 1987b. "Chen-jen." In Eliade 1987, 3: 231–3.

Lai, Chi-tim. 1999. "Daoism and Political Rebellion during the Eastern Jin Dynasty." In Cheung and Lai 1999, 77–100.

Landers, James Russel. 1972. "The Political Thought of Han Fei." Dissertation, Indiana University.

Leslie, Donald, Colin Mackerras, and Wang Gungwu, eds. 1975. *Essays on the Sources for Chinese History.* Canberra: Australian National University Press, 1973; Columbia: University of South Carolina Press, 1975.

Liao, Wen-kuei. 1939. *Complete Works of Han Fei Tzu*, 2 vols. London: Probsthain.

Little, Stephen, ed. 2000a. *Taoism and the Arts of China.* Berkeley: University of California Press.

—— 2000b. "Daoist Art." In Kohn 2000a, 709–46.

Liu, Xun. 1997. "In Search of Immortality: A Study of Travel in Early Twentieth Century *Neidan* Poems." *Taoist Resources* 7.1: 23–41.

Liu Ts'un-yan. 1967. "Lin Chao-en: Master of the Three Teachings." *T'oung-pao* 53: 253–78.

—— 1970a. "The Penetration of Taoism in the Ming Confucian Elite," *T'oung-pao* 52: 31–103.

—— 1970b. "Taoist Self-Cultivation in Ming Thought." In *Self and Society in Ming Thought*, ed. W. T. deBary. New York: Columbia University Press, 291–331.

—— 1975. "The Compilation and Historical Value of the *Tao-tsang.*" In Leslie et al. 1975, 104–19.

—— 1984. "Wu Shou-yang: The Return to the Pure Essence." In *New Excursions from the Hall of Harmonious Wind.* Leiden: Brill.

—— 2003. "Was Celestial Master Zhang a Historical Figure?" MS.

Loewe, Michael. 1977. "Manuscripts Found Recently in China." *T'oung Pao* 63: 99–136.

Loewe, Michael, and Edward Shaughnessy, eds. 1999. *The Cambridge History of Ancient China: From the Origins of Civilization to 221 B.C.* Cambridge: Cambridge University Press.

Lopez, Donald S. Jr., ed. 1996. *Religions of China in Practice.* Princeton: Princeton University Press.

Lowe, Scott. 1992. *Mo Tzu's Religious Blueprint for a Chinese Utopia.* Lewiston, NY: Edwin Mellen Press.

Lynn, Richard John. 1999. *The Classic of the Way and Virtue: A New*

Translation of the Tao-te ching of Laozi as Interpreted by Wang Bi. New York: Columbia University Press.

Mabuchi Masaya. 2002. "A Mid-Ming Reappraisal of the *Laozi*: The Case of Wang Dao." In Kohn and Roth 2002, 127–46.

Mair, Victor. 1990. *Tao Te Ching*. New York: Bantam Books.

Maspero, Henri. 1981. *Taoism and Chinese Religion*, trans. Frank A. Kierman, Jr. Amherst, University of Massachusetts Press.

Masuo Shin'ichirō. 2000. "Daoism in Japan." In Kohn 2000a, 821–42.

Mather, Richard. 1979. "K'ou Ch'ien-chih and the Taoist Theocracy at the Northern Wei Court, 425–51." In Welch and Seidel 1979, 103–22.

Mollier, Christine. 1986. "Messianisme taoïste de la Chine médiévale." Dissertation, Université de Paris.

Mori, Yuria. 2002. "Identity and Lineage: The *Taiyi jinhua zongzhi* and the Spirit-Writing Cult to Patriarch Lü in Qing China." In Kohn and Roth 2002, 165–84.

Mote, Frederick. 1999. *Imperial China: 900–1800*. Cambridge, MA: Harvard University Press.

Munro, Donald. 1969. *The Concept of Man in Early China*. Stanford: Stanford University Press.

Naundorf, G., K. H. Pohl, and H. H. Schmidt, eds. 1985. *Religion und Philosophie in Ostasien*. Würzburg: Königshausen & Neumann.

Needham, Joseph. 1976. *The Shorter Science and Civilisation in China*, abridged, Colin A. Ronan. Cambridge: Cambridge University Press.

Nickerson, Peter. 2000. "The Southern Celestial Masters." In Kohn 2000a, 256–82.

Nienhauser, William, ed. 1986. *The Indiana Companion to Traditional Chinese Literature*. Bloomington: Indiana University Press.

Nivison, David. 1999. "The Classical Philosophical Writings." In Loewe and Shaughnessy 1999, 745–812.

Nylan, Michael. 2001. *The Five "Confucian" Classics*. New Haven: Yale University Press.

Orzech, Charles. 1987. "Chen-yen." In Eliade 1987, 3: 233–8.

Overmyer, Daniel. 1991. "Women in Chinese Religion: Submission, Struggle, Transcendence." In *From Benares to Beijing: Essays on Buddhism and Chinese Religion in Honour of Prof. Jan Yün-hua*, ed. Koichi Shinohara and Gregory Schopen. Oakville, Ontario: Mosaic Press.

Penny, Benjamin. 1996. "Buddhism and Daoism in *The 180 Precepts Spoken by Lord Lao*." *Taoist Resources* 6.2: 1–16.

—— 1998. "The Celestial Master, Pope Pius IX, and Italy's 1848 Revolution." Paper presented at the biennial meeting of the Asian Studies Association of Australia, Sydney.

—— 2000. "Immortality and Transcendence." In Kohn 2000a, 109–33.

Pines, Yuri. 2002. *Foundations of Confucian Thought: Intellectual Life in the Chunqiu Period, 722–453 B.C.E.* Honolulu: University of Hawaii Press.

Pokora, Timoteus. 1961. "On the Origin of the Notions T'ai-p'ing and Ta-t'ung in Chinese Philosophy." *Archiv Orientalni* 29: 448–54.

Porter, Bill. 1993. *Road to Heaven: Encounters with Chinese Hermits*. San Francisco: Mercury House.

Pregadio, Fabrizio. 1994. Review of Wong 1992. *Journal of Chinese Religions* 22: 191–3.

—— 1996. *Zhouyi Cantong Qi: dal libro dei mutamenta all'elixir d'oro.* Venice: Cafoscarina.

—— 2000. "Elixirs and Alchemy." In Kohn 2000a, 165–95.

—— ed. 2004. *Encyclopedia of Taoism*. London: RoutledgeCurzon. In press.

Queen, Sarah. 1996. *From Chronicle to Canon: The Hermeneutics of the Spring and Autumn, According to Tung Chung-shu*. New York and Cambridge: Cambridge University Press.

Reiter, Florian. 1982. "Das Selbstverständnis des Taoismus zur frühen T'ang-zeit in der Darstellung Wang Hsüan-ho's." *Saeculum* 33: 240–57.

—— 1984. "Ch'ung-yang Sets Forth his Teachings in Fifteen Discourses: A Concise Introduction to the Taoist Way of Life of Wang Che." *Monumenta Serica* 36: 33–54.

—— 1988. *Grundelemente und Tendenzen des religiösen Taoismus: das Spannungsverhältnis von Integration und Individualität in seiner Geschichte zur Chin-, Yüan-, und frühen Ming-Zeit*. Stuttgart: Franz Steiner Verlag.

—— 1990. *Der Perlenbeutel aus den Drei Höhlen: Arbeitsmaterialen zum Taoismus der frühen T'ang-Zeit*. Wiesbaden: Otto Harrassowitz.

—— 1998a. "The Taoist Canon of 749 A.D. at the 'Southern Indian Belvedere' in Jen-shou District, Szechwan Province." *Zeitschrift der Deutschen Morgenländischen Gesellschaft* 146: 111–24.

—— 1998b. *The Aspirations and Standards of Taoist Priests in the Early T'ang Period*. Wiesbaden: Otto Harrassowitz.

Reynolds, Frank, and Charles Hallisey. 1987. "The Buddha." In Eliade 1987, 2: 319–32.

Rickett, W. Allyn. 1965. *Kuanzi: A Repository of Early Chinese Thought*. Hong Kong: Hong Kong University Press.

—— 1998. *Guanzi: Political, Economic, and Philosophical Essays from Early China*. 2 Vols. Princeton: Princeton University Press.

Robinet, Isabelle. 1979. "Metamorphosis and Deliverance from the Corpse in Taoism," *History of Religions* 19: 37–70.

—— 1989. "Original Contributions of *Neidan* to Taoism and Chinese Thought." In Kohn 1989a, 297–330.

—— 1991. *Histoire du Taoïsme des origines au XIVe siècle*. Paris: Editions du Cerf.

—— 1993a. *Taoist Meditation: The Mao-shan Tradition of Great Purity*, trans. Julian Pas and Norman Girardot. Albany: State University of New York Press.

—— 1993b. Review of Wile 1992. *Journal of Chinese Religions* 21: 201–4.

—— 1997. *Taoism: Growth of a Religion*, trans. Phyllis Brooks. Stanford: Stanford University Press.

—— 2000. "Shangqing: The Highest Clarity." In Kohn 2000a, 196–224.

Rossabi, Morris. 1988. *Khubilai Khan: His Life and Times*. Berkeley: University of California Press.

Roth, Harold. 1991. "Psychology and Self-Cultivation in Early Taoistic Thought." *Harvard Journal of Asiatic Studies* 51: 599–650.

—— 1996. "The Inner Cultivation Tradition of Early Daoism." In Lopez 1996, 123–48.

—— 1999. *Original Tao: Inward Training (Nei-yeh) and the Foundations of Taoist Mysticism*. New York: Columbia University Press.

Sailey, Jay. 1978. *The Master Who Embraces Simplicity: A Study of the Philosopher Ko Hung*. San Francisco: Chinese Materials Center.

Sakade Yoshinobu. 2000. "Divination as Daoist Practice." In Kohn 2000a, 541–66.

Saso, Michael. 1978. *The Teachings of Taoist Master Chuang*. New Haven: Yale University Press.

—— 2000. *Daoist Master Chuang*. Eldorado Springs, CO: Sacred Mountain Press.

Schafer, Edward. 1977. "The Restoration of the Shrine of Wei Hua-ts'un at Lin-ch'uan in the Eighth Century." *Journal of Oriental Studies* 15: 124–37.

—— 1978a. "The Capeline Cantos: Verses on the Divine Loves of Taoist Priestesses." *Asiatische Studien* 32: 5–65.

—— 1978b. "The Jade Woman of Greatest Mystery." *History of Religions* 17: 387–98.

—— 1981. "Wu Yün's 'Cantos on Pacing the Void'." *Harvard Journal of Asiatic Studies* 41: 377–415.

—— 1982. "Cantos on 'One Bit of Cloud at Shamanka Mountain'." *Asiatische Studien* 36: 102–24.

—— 1983. "Wu Yün's Stanzas on 'Saunters in Sylphdom'." *Monumenta Serica* 35: 1–37.

—— 1985a. *Mirages on the Sea of Time: The Taoist Poetry of Ts'ao T'ang*. Berkeley: University of California Press.

—— 1985b. "The Princess Realized in Jade." *T'ang Studies* 3: 1–23.

—— 1989. *Mao Shan in T'ang Times*. 2nd edn. Boulder, CO: Society for the Study of Chinese Religions.

Schipper, Kristofer. 1993. *The Taoist Body*, trans. Karen C. Duval. Berkeley: University of California Press.

—— 2000. "Taoism: The Story of the Way." In Little 2000, 33–55.

—— 2001. "Daoist Ecology—The Inner Transformation: A Study of the Precepts of the Early Daoist Ecclesia." In Girardot et al. 2001, 79–93.

Seidel, Anna. 1969a. *La divinisation de Lao tseu dans le taoïsme des Han*. Paris: École Française d'Extrême-Orient.

—— 1969b. "The Image of the Perfect Ruler in Early Taoist Messianism," *History of Religions* 9: 216–47.

—— 1983. "Imperial Treasures and Taoist Sacraments—Taoist Roots in the Apocrypha." In Strickmann 1983, 291–371.

—— 1984. "Taoist Messianism." *Numen* 31: 161–74.

—— 1987a. "T'ai-p'ing." In *The Encyclopedia of Religion*. New York: Macmillan, 14: 251–2.

—— 1987b. "Post-Mortem Immortality, or: The Taoist Resurrection of the Body." In *GILGUL: Essays on Transformation, Revolution and Permanence in the History of Religions*, ed. Shaked D. Shulman and G. G. Strousma. Leiden: Brill, 223–7.

—— 1990. *Taoismus: die inoffizielle Hochreligion Chinas*. Tokyo: Deutsche Gesellschaft für Natur- und Völkerkunde Ostasiens.

—— 1997. "Taoism: The Unofficial High Religion of China." *Taoist Resources* 7.2: 39–72.

Sellmann, James. 2002. *Timing and Rulership in Master Lü's Spring and Autumn Annals*. Albany: State University of New York Press.

Sharf, Robert. 1991. "The 'Treasure Store Treatise' (*Pao-tsang lun*) and the Sinification of Buddhism in Eighth-Century China." Dissertation, University of Michigan.

Sharma, Arvind, ed. 2000. *Women Saints in World Religions*. Albany: State University of New York Press.

Sivin, Nathan. 1968. *Chinese Alchemy: Preliminary Studies*. Cambridge, MA: Harvard University Press.

—— 1978. "On the Word 'Taoist' as a Source of Perplexity." *History of Religions* 17: 303–31.

—— 1987. *Traditional Medicine in Contemporary China*. Ann Arbor: University of Michigan Center for Chinese Studies.

—— 1994. Review of Wile 1992. *Journal of Asian Studies* 53: 184–6.

Skar, Lowell. 2000. "Ritual Movements, Deity Cults, and the Transformation of Daoism in Song and Yuan Times." In Kohn 2000a, 413–63.

Skar, Lowell, and Fabrizio Pregadio. 2000. "Inner Alchemy (*Neidan*)." In Kohn 2000a, 464–97.

Smith, Kidder. 1989. "*Zhouyi* Interpretations from Accounts in the *Zuozhuan*." *Harvard Journal of Asiatic Studies* 49: 421–63.

Stein, R. A. 1979. "Religious Taoism and Popular Religion from the Second to Seventh Centuries." In Welch and Seidel 1979, 53–81.

Strickmann, Michel. 1978a. "The Longest Taoist Scripture." *History of Religions* 17: 331–54.

—— 1978b. "The Mao Shan Revelations: Taoism and the Aristocracy." *T'oung Pao* 63: 1–64.

—— 1979. "On the Alchemy of T'ao Hung-ching." In Welch and Seidel 1979, 123–92.

—— 1980a. "Taoism, History of." In *The New Encyclopedia Brittanica, Macropedia*. Chicago: Encyclopedia Brittanica, 17: 1044–50.

—— 1980b. "History, Anthropology and Chinese Religion." *Harvard Journal of Asian Studies* 40: 201–48.

—— 1981. *Le taoïsme du Mao Chan: chronique d'une révélation*. Paris: Institut des Hautes Études Chinoises.

—— ed., 1983. *Tantric and Taoist Studies*, 2. Brussels: Institut Belge des Hautes Études Chinoises.

Takimoto, Yūzō, and Liu Hong. 2000. "Daoist Ritual Music." In Kohn 2000a, 747–64.

Tao, Jing-shen. 1976. *The Jurchen in Twelfth-Century China*. Seattle: University of Washington Press.

Taylor, Rodney. 1978. *The Cultivation of Sagehood as a Religious Goal in Neo-Confucianism: A Study of Selected Writings of Kao P'an-lung*. Missoula, MT: Scholars Press.

—— 1988. *The Confucian Way of Contemplation: Okada Takehiko and the Tradition of Quiet-Sitting*. Columbia: University of South Carolina Press.

ten Broek, Janet Rinaker, and Yiu Tung. 1950. "A Taoist Inscription of the Yüan Dynasty: The *Tao-chiao pei*." *T'oung Pao* 40: 60–122.

Thompson, Laurence. 1985. "Taoism: Classic and Canon." In *The Holy Book in Comparative Perspective*, ed. Frederick Denny and Rodney Taylor. Columbia: University of South Carolina Press, 204–23.

van der Loon, Piet. 1984. *Taoist Books in the Libraries of the Sung Period*. London: Ithaca Press.

Vankeerberghen, Griet. 2001. *The Huainanzi and Liu An's Claim to Moral Authority*. Albany: State University of New York Press.

Verellen, Franciscus. 1989a. *Du Guangting (850–933): taoïste de cour à la fin de la Chine médiévale*. Paris: Collège de France.

—— 1989b. "Liturgy and Sovereignty: The Role of Taoist Ritual in the Foundation of the Shu Kingdom (907–925)." *Asia Major*, 3rd series, 2: 59–78.

—— 1992. "'Evidential Miracles in Support of Taoism': The Inversion of a Buddhist Apologetic Tradition in Late Tang China." *T'oung Pao* 78: 217–63.

—— 1994. "A Forgotten T'ang Restoration: The Taoist Dispensation after Huang Ch'ao." *Asia Major*, 3rd series, 7: 107–53.

Waley, Arthur. 1934. *The Way and its Power*. London: George Allen & Unwin.

—— 1950. *The Poetry and Career of Li Po*. London: George Allen & Unwin.

Wang Hsiao-po, and Leo Chang. 1986. *The Philosophical Foundations of Han Fei's Political Theory*. Honolulu: University of Hawaii Press.

Wang Huan-piao, ed. 1965. *Han-Fei-tzu hsüan*. Beijing: Zhonghua shujü.

Wang Ming. 1979. *Tai-p'ing ching ho-chiao*. Beijing: Zhonghua shujü.

Watson, Burton. 1968. *The Complete Works of Chuang Tzu*. New York: Columbia University Press.

Wechsler, Howard. 1985. *Offerings of Jade and Silk: Ritual and Symbol in the Legitimation of the T'ang Dynasty*. New Haven: Yale University Press.

Weinstein, Stanley. 1987. *Buddhism Under the T'ang*. Cambridge: Cambridge University Press.

Welch, Holmes. 1965. *Taoism: The Parting of the Way*. 2nd edn. Boston: Beacon Press.

Welch, Holmes, and Anna Seidel, eds. 1979. *Facets of Taoism: Essays in Chinese Religion*. New Haven: Yale University Press.

Wile, Douglas. 1992. *Art of the Bedchamber*. Albany: State University of New York Press.

Williams, Paul. 2000. *Buddhist Thought*. London and New York: Routledge.

Wittfolgel, Karl, and Feng Chia-sheng. 1949. *History of Chinese Society: Liao*. Philadelphia: American Philosophical Society.

Wong, Eva. 1992. *Cultivating Stillness: A Taoist Manual for Transforming Body and Mind*. Boston: Shambhala.

Wright, Arthur. 1978. *The Sui Dynasty*. New York: Knopf.

Yamada, Toshiaki. 1989. "Longevity Techniques and the Compilation of the *Lingbao wufuxu*." In Kohn 1989a, 99–124.

—— 2000. "The Lingbao School." In Kohn 2000a, 225–55.

Yang, C. K. 1961. *Religion in Chinese Society*. Berkeley: University of California Press.

Yao, Tao-chung. 1980. "Ch'üan-chen: A New Taoist Sect in North China during the Twelfth and Thirteenth Centuries." Dissertation, University of Arizona.

Yao, Ted (Tao-chung). 2000. "Quanzhen – Complete Perfection." In Kohn 2000a, 567–93.

Yates, Robin, trans. 1997. *Five Lost Classics: Tao, Huang-Lao, and Yin-Yang in Han China*. New York: Ballantine.

Yearley, Lee. 1983. "The Perfected Person in the Radical Chuang-tzu." In *Experimental Essays on Chuang-tzu*, ed. Victor Mair. Honolulu: University of Hawaii Press, 125–39.

Yin Chung-jung. 1958. *Lü-shih ch'un-ch'iu chiao-shih*. Taipei: Chung-hua ts'ung-shu wei-yüan hui.

Yoshioka, Yoshitoyo. 1979. "Taoist Monastic Life." In Welch and Seidel 1979. 220–52.

Yu, Shiyi. 2000. *Reading the "Chuang-tzu" in the T'ang Dynasty: The Commentary of Ch'eng Hsüan-ying*. New York: Peter Lang.

INDEX

Note: "n." after a page number indicates the number of a note on that page.